For Our Parents

Contents

Preface

A housewife heaves laundry from a washer to a dryer. An auto-parts worker feeds bits of metal into a punch press. A seamstress runs dress material through a sewing machine. A nickel miner attacks a wall of rock with a massive cutting tool. An office clerk types statistics into a computer terminal. An industrial chemist checks a dial on a vat. Six workers on the job. Six moments snatched from six different working days.

These are the fleeting images we usually get of other people's jobs. Conjured up from memories of wash days, gleaned from quick glances at advertisements, news clips, or glossy company publications, or from peeks through factory and office windows, these snapshots offer us an alien, partial, and distorted impression of the world of work. To a large extent, these images seem alien because we have not performed the jobs ourselves, and because working life is normally locked away from the public eye. What little we know from our own jobs and those of our friends and relatives is fragmented and isolated from any larger understanding. The mass media could multiply and weld these images together, but instead present us with little more than dry statistics on production and employment or glittering, fictionalized vignettes of corporate oil barons. What is missing is the understanding that work is a *process* whereby flesh-and-blood human beings actively transform raw materials into finished products or perform vital services within a complex social setting.

Of course, our experience will often tell us that more is going on in these jobs than the incomplete images suggest. Just outside the range of our vision, for example, may perch an office manager or plant foreman pushing the workers to complete their work. We may also know that the state-of-the-art technology that pounds away in the modern mine or that hums quietly in the word-processing room was designed by industrial engineers and adopted by corporate executives without consulting workers or considering their needs and interests. The distortion, then, comes from assuming that comprehending the world of work is simply a matter of watching workers set their tools and machines in motion; in reality, it is about social and economic power and the modes of controlling human behaviour.

This book is an attempt to describe and analyse the work of Canadian men and women – to demonstrate that our six workers and millions of others are part of a labour process, the contours of which are continuously being established, broken down, and re-formed through the dynamic interaction of the participants themselves. In contemporary Canadian society, the principal actors in any labour process – with the important exception of the work of the housewife – are the owners and managers of corporate industry and their workers. For Canadian capitalists, the strategy for survival requires their relentless attention to their workers' time on the job: make them work harder, give them fancier tools, replace them with machines, but, above all, keep up with the competition by keeping the labour costs down ("increasing productivity," as it is euphemistically phrased by modern economists). Canadian workers, on the other hand, enter into an arrangement to turn over their ability to work in return for their wages, without which they could not survive. They may well have, then, a concern with their employer's long-term prosperity, and, in this and other ways, their interests may coincide or converge with those of their bosses. At the same time, however, workers have an interest in maintaining or improving their wages and in preventing themselves from being so overworked that they are incapable of returning to their jobs. They also bring to their work some non-economic, moral concerns about fairness, equity, and human dignity that do not fit on the company balance sheet. Their interests are, therefore, distinct from and antagonistic to those of their employer. Conflict is thus inevitable in the capitalist workplace. It can take the form of great tumultuous confrontations in strikes, and it can extend well beyond the workplace into other social and political spheres. But most often it emerges within the work process as a kind of industrial trench warfare of management initiative and worker resistance. This is especially evident in the current context of technological change. Behind all the hoopla about microtechnology is the reality that these machines are only the latest weapons in the capitalist arsenal to intensify the labour process and cheapen production costs, frequently at the expense of workers.

This book belies the suggestion that there is any kind of independent technological imperative that is responsible for sweeping changes in the world of work. The goals of today's innovators and the predicted impact of the technology on the work process have a familiar ring to those who have studied the development of a nineteenth-century print shop, a turn-of-the-century steel mill, or a twentieth-century office. Skilled labour is subdivided into specialized fragments and parcelled out to less skilled, lower-paid workers, often operating new machinery. Managerial ability to control and intensify the pace of work and to displace workers is consequently strengthened. But even as workers succumb to these processes, they act to challenge them, subvert them, and/or change their meaning in the day-to-day work experience. Since the emergence of wage labour and the factory system, the story has been the same.

The essays in this book address some of the major themes in this evolution of work in Canada. Paul Craven and Tom Traves discuss the unique problems facing the pioneers of industrial capitalism – the railway corporations – and their paternalistic solutions, which foreshadowed by half a century similar managerial strategies in other sectors. Gregory Kealey, David Frank, and Mercedes Steedman consider the experience of skilled workers within three quite different capitalist workplaces – the print shop, the coal mine, and the tailor shop. Steedman, Veronica Strong-Boag, Graham Lowe, and Ester Reiter confront the particular work experience of women, domestic and industrial, unpaid and paid. Lowe also probes the new division of labour between blue and white collars, which produced the new work world of the office. The editors trace the transformation of work within the steel mill, home to one of the new mass-production industries that rose up in the first half of the twentieth century. Ian Radforth and John Foster tell the stories of two major industries, logging and longshoring, whose labour processes changed little before technological and managerial cyclones swept through them in the 1950s and 1960s. Finally, both Ester Reiter and Don Wells bring back reports from the belly of the beast. Reiter spent several months working in a fast-food outlet where she discovered the new workplace dynamics of the service industry; and Wells similarly relates his observations on the archetypal modern work process, the auto assembly line. To introduce these specific studies, the editors present a historical overview and an assessment of the most important issues that animate the current debate on the capitalist labour process.

Together the contributors to this book present a powerful antidote to the boundless enthusiasm about the benefits flowing from the transformation of industry. They underline the need to make ideologically laden abstractions like "progress," "technological change," and "productivity" more concrete in order to lay bare their real meaning. They turn back the claims for "progress" through three successive industrial revolutions and raise the question: "whose progress?" And like so many workers along the way, they suggest that the balance sheet of benefits and losses must include more than simply jobs created or lost, wages cut or raised, and productivity stalled or boosted, to which so much of the current debate on microtechnology is limited. Workers expect dignity, pride, fulfilment, a sense of accomplishment from their jobs. One hundred years ago a popular labour organization calling itself the Holy and Noble Order of the Knights of Labor regularly celebrated the nobility of "honest toil." Until the recent statement of the Canadian Conference of Catholic Bishops, we have heard little of this rhetoric in the twentieth century.

In the uncertain world of the 1980s, it is no longer enough to argue simply for jobs. Canadian workers have a right to demand: what *kind* of jobs?

Do these essays hold out hope for a humane outcome of the technological transformation through which we are passing? They provide no definitive answer because they so plainly indicate that new machines fit into managerial power struggles with workers, and that the final outcome of those battles can never be predicted with any degree of accuracy. In part, our optimism about the future can come from the imagination and determination of working people to reinvest their jobs with power and creativity. But the issues at stake are much larger than the confines of any one workplace. Like the Cape Breton miners of the 1920s, we can only look to social and political solutions of the sort Canadian capitalists have so far been unwilling to stomach. In order to avoid the false options of fatalism and futurism, we must slow the pace of innovation and open up the process to more rigorous, public investigation and to active, informed debate *before* the profoundly disruptive changes are made. Technological change – indeed, all transformations in the workplace – must become a social process that we all control. There is still time.

We are grateful to the Ontario Arts Council and the Labour Studies Programme at McMaster University for financial support in the preparation of this book and to the Social Science Federation of Canada for a grant in aid of publication. We also appreciated the initial enthusiasm and continuing support of David Norton at McGill-Queen's University Press.

Without our good friends in the Labour Studies Research Group, this book might not have been possible. Our lively discussions and debates with them over nearly four years inspired this project and improved the final product immeasurably.

And for patience, support, encouragement, and love, we owe a special debt to Daiva Stasiulis.

C.H.
R.S.

Contributors

PAUL CRAVEN teaches in the Social Science Division at York University and is the author of *"An Impartial Umpire": Industrial Relations and the Canadian State, 1900–1911*, as well as many articles on Canadian political economy.

JOHN BELLAMY FOSTER teaches sociology at the University of Oregon in Eugene, Oregon. His wide range of publications include *The Faltering Economy: The Problem of Accumulation under Monopoly Capitalism*.

DAVID FRANK teaches history at the University of New Brunswick and is the editor of *Acadiensis*. He has written extensively on Cape Breton working-class history.

CRAIG HERON teaches in the Social Science Division and History Department at York University and has published several articles on Canadian working-class history.

GREGORY S. KEALEY teaches history at Memorial University of Newfoundland and is the editor of *Labour/Le Travail*. He has written *Toronto Workers Respond to Industrial Capitalism, 1867–1892* and *Dreaming of What Might Be: The Knights of Labor in Ontario, 1880–1900* (with Bryan D. Palmer), as well as numerous articles on Canadian working-class history.

GRAHAM S. LOWE teaches sociology at the University of Alberta. He has written many articles on a variety of work-related topics and co-edited *Working Canadians: Readings in the Sociology of Work and Industry*.

IAN RADFORTH is a post-doctoral fellow at the University of Toronto and has written widely on the history of workers in northern Ontario.

ESTER REITER teaches sociology at Memorial University.

MERCEDES STEEDMAN taught sociology at Laurentian University for several years and is completing a doctorate at the University of London.

ROBERT STOREY teaches in the Labour Studies Programme and the Sociology Department at McMaster University. The main focus of his published work has been Hamilton's steelworkers.

VERONICA STRONG-BOAG teaches women's studies and history at Simon Fraser University. She has published *The Parliament of Women: The National Council of Women of Canada, 1893–1929* and many articles on Canadian women's history.

TOM TRAVES is dean of arts at York University. His publications include *The State and Enterprise: Canadian Manufacturers and the Federal Government, 1917–1931* and *Essays in Canadian Business History*.

DON WELLS is a labour educator, researcher, and writer. He is the author of *Soft Sell: Quality of Working Life Programmes and the Productivity Race*.

On the Job

CRAIG HERON AND ROBERT STOREY

On the Job in Canada

On any given day, Canadian workers arrive on the job in such a huge variety of workplaces that we might well ask whether all these jobs have anything in common. Is it possible to generalize about such a diversity of human experience? We believe it is. The kaleidoscope of specific occupations should not blind us to some consistent patterns in the world of work in Canada. In the following pages we outline the main themes in the evolution of labour processes in Canada and highlight the central dynamics in the changing nature of work.

At the core of this analysis is the impact of working for wages – selling one's ability to labour to employers who view that labour-power as a factor of production to be used as intensively and cheaply as possible in their process of capital accumulation. All labour processes involve the application of certain instruments to raw materials to produce goods or services that have use value. But in capitalist labour processes, those goods or services also have an exchange value, and in their production a capitalist hopes to generate surplus value. The amount of surplus that can be extracted from the labour process depends ultimately on the degree of control capitalists hold over how their workers apply tools and machines to their tasks. Workers, however, tend to have their own notions about the fairness and equity that should apply to their wages and their experience on the job. Thus, a "frontier of control" results from the ongoing process of initiative and resistance between workers and their bosses. While this set of relationships is rooted in the private realm of capital accumulation, its essential ingredients have been transplanted into apparently non-profit sectors, like schools, hospitals, and other branches of public service. Selling one's labour-power has now become broadly similar in all jobs in the capitalist labour market.

The complex class relationships that emerge when workers and employers confront each other this way – the managerial policies, the strikes, the labour legislation – contain a second crucial dimension, a sex / gender system often called "patriarchy," which predates capitalism but which persists in new forms within capitalist society. Women have always experienced class differently from men. They have lived and worked within confining patriarchal definitions of their primary responsibility for domestic labour, which has left most women in the household and which has shaped their participation in the wage-labour market. Similarly, though on a more limited scale, capitalist social relations have incorporated pre-existing discrimination against racial and ethnic groups, so that Chinese or Italian or Portuguese newcomers have been drawn into the Canadian labour force on different terms from their Anglo-Celtic workmates. To understand the changing nature of work in Canada, then, it is necessary to account for the specific forces of capitalist development that gave most workplaces their essential shape, as well as the differences that gender and race or ethnicity could make.

The general shape of labour processes in Canada has evolved through changes in what has been termed "the social structures of accumulation,"[1] that is, the specific, shifting configurations of economic activity, class formations and conflicts, and state intervention that mark off specific stages of capitalist development. The Canadian economy that provided the jobs has taken its particular texture from two parallel sets of productive activity. First, from the beginning of the European settlement, resource extraction for external markets in France, Britain, and finally the United States has been crucial – initially fish and furs, later agricultural, forest, and mineral products. These industries have had their own erratic pace of growth and decline, special requirements for labour and technology (often quite primitive until well into the twentieth century), and frequently a high degree of seasonality in production. From the mid nineteenth century onward, however, a second, quite different path of development emerged as indigenous capitalists began to industrialize in order to supply the varied needs of a growing domestic population in British North America, especially the expanding numbers of commercial farmers. With help from the Canadian state's tariff policies, the cities and towns of southern Ontario, Quebec, and, for a few decades, the Maritimes created a highly industrialized economy with a wide range of manufacturing industries, technological sophistication, and a steady demand for an occupationally diverse work force. The initial link between these two relatively distinct sectors of resource extraction and manufacturing was the railway, which spread quickly through the countryside in the 1850s and across the barren wastes in subsequent decades as the best means of moving resources to market, but which also continued to stimulate new industrial development. These long ribbons of steel remained the main arteries of the Canadian economy for more than a century, meeting the outside commercial world in the bustling Canadian ports on the Atlantic, the St Lawrence, and the Pacific.

These broad sweeps of development fell into four roughly defined periods

– the first ending around 1850, the second lasting to the 1890s, the third to World War II, and the fourth down to the present. There was no firm dividing line between each of these stages. Each was preceded by a transitional phase precipitated by an economic crisis – in the 1840s, 1890s, 1930s, and 1970s – during which established relationships in the workplace and the marketplace were shaken up and slowly reconstituted on new terms. While each period was distinguished by new structures, institutions, and forms of struggle, there were enough lags and continuities that by the 1980s we still find in Canada a residue of much earlier eras in firm size, technology, labour markets, and organization of workers and employers. We will consider the distinctive characteristics of each of these periods in turn, before raising some of the theoretical implications suggested by Canada's particular development.

INDEPENDENT COMMODITY PRODUCTION TO 1850

In the two centuries before 1850, the most visible economic activities in New France and British North America were the gathering and shipping out of natural resources for European markets – primarily fish, furs, wheat, and timber. Yet for most of that period, the great majority of European settlers in what was to become Canada lived and worked in family units of independent commodity producers on the margins of the commercial capitalist economy. In tiny communities scattered along the Atlantic coast, families co-operated in catching and curing the fish; and throughout the colonies, farm families hacked away at the dense forests to clear space for their simple crops and then to live off the land. Most families provided for their own needs and had only relatively limited contact with the market when they sold or bartered any surplus production or took short-term employment in order to pay off debts or to buy the few necessities they could not produce themselves. Only in the 1840s were many farmers beginning to sow substantially more acres of wheat to be sold as a cash crop for export. In many of these same communities of "producers" were handfuls of self-employed artisans – blacksmiths, stonemasons, shoemakers, tailors, and the like – whose handicraft production serviced small, local markets. Compelled to cope with a harsh natural environment, isolated by poor transportation routes, and facing highly unstable European markets for their staple goods, few of these independent commodity producers could be expected to take the bit of capitalist entrepreneurship; in many respects their mode of living and working resembled that of European peasant-proprietors.[2]

Labour in and around the households of independent commodity producers was varied and demanding. A gender division of labour sent men into the fields, into the artisanal workshops, or out in the boats while the women stayed behind to mind the children, tend the kitchen gardens and livestock, and prepare a wide range of commodities for domestic consumption – food, clothing, soap, candles, medicines, and much more. The survival of independent commodity production units depended on the success of this female labour. Marriages, in fact, were highly practical arrangements before which the women's skills and abilities would be assessed, and widowers wasted little time in finding new wives to perform the crucial domestic tasks. The division of labour was never so rigid as to keep women out of the fields or workshops if their help was needed, and, despite the husband/father's legal status as patriarchal head of household and his right to participate in a wider public life, the hard physical labour demanded of both men and women produced a kind of economic partnership between the sexes. In general, there was a sense of all family members contributing their labour to their mutual support, with the household as the organizing base of the family's communal work. Co-operative, unwaged work might also involve the wider community, as in the celebrated "bees" organized for clearing new land, building a barn, or husking corn.[3]

The primary tensions in a society of independent commodity producers pitted farming and fishing families against merchants who marketed their wheat and fish and held them in the thrall of debt; against speculative, absentee, or seigneurial landowners who restricted easy access to the land or skimmed off some of their meagre surplus; and against the various "family compacts" whose oppressive control of the colonial state and administration of land policies seemed to hamper the producers' independence and material well-being. The rights and grievances of these producers echoed through the insurrections of 1837–8 in Upper and Lower Canada, in the farmers' agitations in Prince Edward Island, and in the Nova Scotia reform movement in the same period.[4]

Wage labour was certainly not unknown in these pre-industrial societies. In the first half of the nineteenth century, the western Canadian fur trade, the logging industry, and canal construction all required hired men, largely drawn from French-Canadian farm families and the growing pool of impoverished Irish immigrants. Domestic servants, farm labourers, seamen, and skilled craftsmen, like shipwrights and iron workers, also worked for wages. Most of these wage-earners had a close, direct relationship with their employers, characterized by a kind of paternalism and typically codified in individual contracts of employment, or indentures, which were made legally enforceable through British statutes or colonial legislation like the 1848 Master and Servant Act in Canada West. By the 1830s and 1840s, however, some of the skilled workers had begun to form local craft unions and to mount bitter strikes, like the journeymen printers' battles with William Lyon Mackenzie and George Brown in Toronto. And, even more dramatically, Irish canal labourers adapted their Old Country secret societies to new purposes and confronted their contractors in violent battles, which for the first time brought the state's military might to bear in support of employers. Yet both on the canals and in the lumber camps, the lines of class identification were normally weaker than ethnic solidarities, as Irishmen spilled the blood of French Canadians or divided against each other in age-old feuds between Cork and Connaught. In any case, much of the wage labour in all these pre-industrial workplaces involved only short-term or seasonal absence from family farms or fishing villages, and few workers expected to remain wage-earners for life. Independent farming, fishing, or craftsmanship remained the ideal as well as the reality for most British North Americans.[5]

The modes and social relations of independent commodity production would change somewhat as more and more farmers turned to commercial agriculture, but the old patterns remained remarkably resilient in Canada. Not only did agriculturalists and rural dwellers, living and working in family units with little hired help, remain numerically predominant until well into the twentieth century, but significant pockets of population continued to survive on the basis of subsistence agriculture and part-time employment, notably in Atlantic Canada, parts of Quebec, eastern and northern Ontario, northern stretches of the Prairies, and the interior of British Columbia. Not until after World War II did Canada see a steep decline in this "semi-proletarianized" rural population.[6]

THE RISE OF INDUSTRIAL CAPITALISM, 1850–1890

By 1850, a transformation was under way which would propel British North America into the industrial capitalist age. The colonial merchants' concerns about an efficient transportation network to compete with American exporters led to the construction of hundreds of miles of railway lines. These in turn opened up wider markets for local producers and stimulated a new demand for railway equipment. At the same time, as wheat farmers became more oriented to cash crops, a larger domestic market opened up for consumer goods like agricultural implements, stoves, and textiles. In this golden age of capitalist entrepreneurship, master artisans expanded their workshops, merchant-industrialists set up new factories, transportation companies erected production facilities of major proportions, and new coal mines opened on the east and west coasts to produce fuel for the new age of steam power. At first this new industrial activity developed in the chill breezes of free trade, but when the American market disappeared behind high tariff walls, Canadian businessmen evolved a development strategy based on a protected manufacturing sector serving a large domestic population of agriculturalists. In 1879, the federal government tied the package together as a "National Policy" of high-tariff protection for industry, railway building across the Prairies, and promotion of immigration. The result was a brief burst of accelerated industrialization in the 1880s, widely dispersed across the Maritimes, Quebec, and Ontario. Throughout the last quarter of the nineteenth century, however, the economy continued to suffer from overproduction, business failures, unemployment, and out-migration of population. Only at the turn of the century did the national-policy formula begin to work.[7]

In order for industrial capitalism to take hold in Canada, the uncertain labour market of the early nineteenth century had to be altered. A rapid increase in immigration helped, especially after the Irish famine of the late 1840s, but equally important was the disappearance of easily accessible land, which would leave new immigrants and farmers' children with little choice but to seek wage labour. By the 1850s, that process was producing a work force of primarily full-time wage-earners. Moreover, many of the new immigrants were experienced industrial workers, especially skilled men, who left Britain or the United States intending to take up similar work in Canada. These workers brought with them a familiarity with existing work practices and a legacy of workplace struggle that were soon incorporated into colonial industry.[8]

The symbol of the new era was the smoke stack belching into the colonial skies from steamships, railway locomotives, and industrial enterprises in the major cities. Yet, however dramatic and eye-catching, the new steam-powered machinery should not overshadow even more important changes in workplace organization and relationships. Jobs were changing, as employers set out to break down skills into more narrowly specialized tasks performed by less skilled, lower-paid workers, like the hundreds of women and children who found their way into textile, footwear, tobacco, and food-processing factories. As often as possible, these new operatives would handle new machinery intended to speed up their tasks; but in the late nineteenth century, technology in most industries remained relatively primitive, and mechanization was quite uneven across the industrial landscape. In some sectors, like clothing, production processes combined some centralization under the manufacturer's roof with outwork in homes or contract shops. In many cases, however, craftsmen's skills could not be diluted much at all, and employers had to hire large numbers of them to run lathes in railway shops, set type in newspaper offices, "puddle" iron at iron works, or extract coal from the ground. The use of subcontractors, the harsh discipline of iron-fisted foremen, and the widespread adoption of piecework to goad workers to higher levels of production suggest the importance of human relationships on the job, rather than machine-paced work rhythms.[9]

At the same time, the growing separation of work and home was arousing a new concern. Many employers joined campaigns to reshape working-class behaviour outside the workplace by stamping out the erratic habits of pre-industrial working life and inculcating new norms of sobriety, industry, punctuality, and self-discipline. These moral reformers took aim at working-class leisure patterns, especially the consumption of the "demon rum" and the desecration of the sabbath. In a similar vein, they created new institutions to implant a stricter industrial discipline in the hearts and minds of the urban poor – "houses of industry" for the desperately poor, penitentiaries and sundry other penal institutions for workers who turned to crime, and most important, public schools to teach future workers "system, order, punctuality, and good conduct." A new work ethic was being forged for the industrial capitalist age.[10]

The emerging working class responded to this new work environment in many diverse ways. Perhaps the most important involved adapting domestic life to a reliance on wages as sole income. As in the pre-industrial past, families continued to operate as tiny collectivities of mutual support, but no longer produced their own subsistence in and around the household. Now sons and daughters would often join their fathers in the paid work force outside the home, and all wages would be pooled. Married women now normally stayed home to care for the young and old and to perform the still labour-intensive tasks of feeding and clothing the family's wage-earners. Only a crisis like death, illness, or injury of the male head of household would send his wife or widow back out to work for wages. The working-class home thus became the mechanism for workers' survival in an economy based on wage labour, as well as the refuelling station for labour-power needed in capitalist industry.[11]

This new separation of work and home, of waged and unwaged labour, had particular implications for women, as the gender division of labour became much more sharply defined. Women participated in the paid labour market only when their primary responsibilities in the home would permit, normally only between school and marriage, and their transiency in that predominantly male work world shaped their treatment by employers and male workers. They were offered only the least skilled jobs, were paid at half the wage rates of men, and seldom found support from male workers for adjusting that inequality. They were also recruited into jobs designated as "women's work" – usually some transference into capitalist production of traditionally female tasks in the household, such as food and clothing production or nurturing and service. The largest number of women wage-earners entered domestic service, while many others worked in textile mills, garment shops, confectionery plants, and the like, or as poorly paid teachers and nurses. In the working-class home, women still performed essentially the same work, but in contrast to the households of independent commodity producers, they were now dependent for their survival on the wages of the family wage-earners, who were most often men. The rise of industrial capitalism had not created the oppressive patriarchal ideology and division of labour, which obviously predated it by centuries, but it had incorporated pre-capitalist gender divisions in such a way as to change the social relations of production by separating the privatized, unpaid, "feminine," domestic sphere from the public, waged, "masculine" sphere. Along with this distinction came a "cult of domesticity" that suffused the life-style of middle-class families and those working-class families struggling for a meagre level of decency and respectability in an insecure environment. Working-class men who supported this ghettoization of women and the ideal of the "family wage" were undoubtedly attempting to shore up working-class living standards against erosion by low wages, but they were also defending an element of male privilege and masculine identity in which the paid work world was steeped. In the class-conscious rhetoric of the times, they were protecting their "manhood."[12]

Inside industry itself, the workers most frequently contesting the emerging work relationships were the skilled men, who retained the shop-floor autonomy, power, and pride to sustain an aggressive craft-union movement, first organized on a local basis and ultimately linked up in continental ("international") organizations. By the turn of the century, many of these groups of workers had consolidated their hard-won workplace customs and routines into detailed union codes of rules and regulations, which they struggled to have accepted in contracts with employers, in the first attempt to establish a "rule of law" within Canadian industry. Yet their job control was never secure from employers' challenges, and industrial conflict flared up repeatedly wherever craftsmen still retained a significant role in the production process.[13]

These late nineteenth-century craftsmen have occupied centre stage in much of the writing on the workplace in this period.[14] Much attention has been focused on the workers' control that these men exercised on the job. Many writers in Canada and elsewhere who have studied them, however, have been struck by their narrow defence of exclusivist craft interests, at the expense of the less skilled.[15] In Britain an extensive literature has grown up concerning whether or not these skilled men composed an "aristocracy of labour,"[16] while in the United States new research has pointed to their roles as subcontractors who hired and supervised subordinate workers for their own profit.[17] Similar work on skilled workers' relations with women workers has revealed their anxiety to return the "working girls" to the domestic sphere where they would pose less threat to their jobs, their craft status, and their masculinity.[18] These workers were even more aggressive in trying to drive out Asian workers, especially in British Columbia.[19]

Yet the story does not end there. Canadian historians in particular have drawn our attention to the larger vision of the craftsman, who criticized the dominant tendencies of the period toward consolidation of industry and degradation of the worker and his or her job. It was these men who provided the compelling rhetoric about the "nobility of labour" in the Nine-Hours movement in the 1870s and even more dramatically in the all-inclusive

Knights of Labor (and the Provincial Workmen's Association in Nova Scotia) in the 1880s. In these movements, craft pride was transformed into working-class consciousness and assertiveness.[20] There was undoubtedly a deep ambivalence in the activities of these craftsmen that produced a craft, race, and gender exclusivism on the one hand, and a wider social criticism and leadership of generalized working-class interests on the other. This dilemma exemplifies the fragmentation that industrial capitalism was creating among workers, constantly forcing them onto the defensive against erosion of their workplace traditions, living standards, and sense of human dignity.

In any case, it was craftsmen's struggles that brought the Canadian state into a new phase in mediating work relations. In the early years of industrialization, the state had assisted capitalist employers by supporting workplace discipline with the force of law and permitting them to drag their workers into court to punish disobedience or insubordination. In the 1870s, however, the state legalized trade unions and their limited rights to picket; and by the 1880s, it was legislating some minimum standards of employment in mines and factories, primarily to protect women and children. The federal government even met the challenge of industrial militancy and radical rhetoric from the Knights of Labor by appointing a large Royal Commission on the Relations of Capital and Labour in 1886. The Commission travelled about the country hearing evidence on the new modes and relations of work, but its report produced nothing more concrete than the establishment of Labour Day as an annual holiday. The heavy hand of state repression in support of employers was never completely lifted, however; rigid legal constraints and ready use of military force to intervene in strikes remained effective curbs on working-class resistance.[21]

In this first phase of industrialization, then, entrepreneurs had begun to assemble the necessary work force, to instil the appropriate work discipline, to attempt to cheapen the costs of production by subdividing labour into lower-paid, less skilled fragments, and to mechanize wherever possible. By the 1890s the results were ambiguous. In some industries, like textiles, complex machinery clattered away with relatively low skill requirements. Many others, however, were only part way along such a path of transformation. The small, unstable Canadian market made economies of scale difficult, and many of the more skilled workers had banded together to resist any degradation of their labour. Industrial capitalism, in fact, seemed so novel and alien that the Knights of Labor, as well as the massive farmers' movements of the period,[22] could still pose alternative visions of a more co-operative, humane future. It was nonetheless clear that half a century of industrial development had thoroughly altered the role and place of women within the workplace, largely excluding them from any control over the shape of the public work world, which was primarily a terrain contested by men.

THE CONSOLIDATION OF
MONOPOLY CAPITALISM,
1890–1940

A whole new industrial age dawned at the close of the nineteenth century. In an unprecedented wave of economic expansion, thousands of new Prairie farmers pushed wheat to the top of the export list, while the forest industries struggled to keep up with the apparently insatiable demands of the United States for newsprint. New mining operations for hitherto neglected minerals – nickel, copper, lead, zinc, gold, silver – dotted the landscape of northern Ontario and Quebec and the interior of British Columbia. Vast new construction projects were launched, notably two more railways to the West Coast. Manufacturing expanded dramatically behind tariff walls, as completely new industries appeared – steel, auto, chemicals, pulp and paper, meatpacking, and electrical goods. A more tight-knit national bourgeoisie (centred in Montreal and Toronto) was pulling together the decentralized regional fragments into a more integrated national economy, which would eventually gut the Maritimes of much of its industrial life and restrict the development of northern and western Canada to a resource hinterland. Yet it was a highly fragile structure, which threatened to collapse on a regular basis. Boom periods in the first decade of the century, the World War I years, and the late 1920s were separated by deep troughs of depression just before the war, in the first half of the 1920s, and, most tragically, through the entire decade of the 1930s. These wild fluctuations in the business cycle would put serious pressure on industrialists to cut costs in order to survive and on workers to cope with their employers' aggression and the disciplining power of unemployment.[23]

Presiding over most sectors of the Canadian economy were huge new corporations, both home-grown giants like Dominion Cottons, Massey-Harris, and the Steel Company of Canada, and new American branch firms like the Ford Motor Company and Canadian Westinghouse.[24] Within their far-flung corporate empires, the pressing need for centralized co-ordination of production and the competitive pressures of much larger markets prompted a new concern for more direct control over operating costs. The development of cost accounting was part of a new movement toward "systematic management" within commerce and industry (introduced much earlier by the railway corporations), which produced a new group of professional managers. Cutting production costs, especially labour, became a central concern.[25]

One result was the deployment of more sophisticated technology, driven by more flexible power sources like electricity and gasoline and reaching a kind of apotheosis in the assembly line in Henry Ford's Canadian and American auto plants. Massive mechanization transformed almost every industry, and by the 1920s a far larger percentage of the work force were machine-operators than in the late nineteenth century. This time technological change had a qualitative difference from the first "industrial revolution": it incorporated much more scientific research (and more scientists) in solving production problems, and, in contrast to the informal experimentation by craftsmen on the shop floor (characteristic of the earlier phase of industrialization), it was carried on in research laboratories directly connected to major corporations, especially in new industries like chemicals and electrical goods.[26]

At the same time, many firms experimented with new, more centralized, more cost-conscious, and more authoritarian managerial systems, in order to move effective control of the labour process from the shop floor to the front office. The most famous hand-servant of these efficiency-conscious employers was Frederick Winslow Taylor, father of so-called scientific management (or Taylorism), whose staff invaded the shop floor armed with stop watches to measure the "scientifically" precise time required to complete a specific task and to gather up workers' shop-floor know-how, which could then be reorganized and parcelled out from the central planning and scheduling office. Incentive-wage payments would then encourage workers to keep up to management's production standards. There were Taylorist experiments in Canada, notably at the CPR's Angus Shops in Montreal, but recent studies have concluded that the actual impact of Taylor's own complex managerial package on North American industry was limited. Quite often, a great deal of latitude was still left with foremen and superintendents who, despite centralized employment offices, managed to control hiring and promotion and built departmental empires based on harsh supervision and favouritism. Workers consequently lived in constant fear of dismissal on a whim or in response to any "trouble-making" (like union organizing). Most employers nonetheless took their cue from Taylor's advice to wrench as much independent decision making about the pace and form of production as possible away from workers on the job and to centralize control over the labour process in managerial hands. Within this loose consensus, they simply adopted whatever managerial devices suited their particular situation.[27]

Owners and managers of Canadian corporations found they had greater flexibility for their workplace experiments as a result of a huge new pool of labour created by the massive immigrant wave of the early twentieth century that arrived in large part because of the promotional work of the federal government. Many of these newcomers had travelled from peasant villages in southern and eastern Europe, China, and Japan, and like their predecessors a century earlier, never intended to remain full-time workers. Some were earning cash in order to establish themselves on Prairie homesteads or in small retail businesses within their ethnic communities in Canada. Many others lived a frugal life in crowded urban boardinghouses or work-camp bunk-houses in order to send their savings back to their families in the old country and then to return home themselves. Canadian employers thus assembled a shifting, heterogeneous, polyglot work force, arranged in a stratified hierarchy with the non-Anglo-Celtic newcomers at the bottom in the dirtiest, heaviest, worst-paid manual jobs. Ethnic tensions had divided English, Irish, and French workers at many points in the nineteenth century, but the problem was magnified enormously by the proliferation of new ethnic and racial groups in a context of capitalist manipulation to undermine wages and erode skills. Even for the immigrants who eventually stayed in Canada as workers, the cultural gulf separating them from their Anglo-Celtic workmates would last at least until World War II.[28]

The great expansion of the managerial function had a further fragmenting effect on the work force. Office staffs swelled to unprecedented proportions to handle the flood of paperwork generated by this transformation of the "means of administration." Small armies of predominantly female clerical workers soon emerged to give the Canadian working class a whole new complexion and to open up another wide rift, this time between blue- and white-collar workers. Within the new offices there were, nevertheless, strong parallels with the organization of work in factories – fragmentation of the well-rounded clerk's job into specialized tasks and mechanization of many of them with typewriters, adding machines, dictaphones, and data-processing equipment.[29]

The reshaping of labour processes in Canada with widespread mechanization, subdivision of labour, and centralization of management spelled the death of craft-dominated modes of production, but the process was more complicated than most popular notions of deskilling have suggested. We should be clear about our point of comparison. The late nineteenth-century workshop was not a static NeverNever Land of custom and tradition. It was an incessant battleground between workers and their employers over workplace control in which many craftsmen had already lost much ground in several industries. The skilled workers who remained, especially in the all-important metal trades, were wage-earners who, for all their continuing craft autonomy, were working in a considerably altered context from the self-employed artisan of old. In the early twentieth century, many more skills were undermined or diluted, though by no means all of them. Some skilled workers simply had the variety of their tasks reduced while retaining high levels of technical competence in their jobs – some iron moulders and most garment cutters, for example. Some new skills appeared, like those of linotype operators and tool and die makers.[30] Perhaps most important, a new, more occupationally homogeneous work force of "semi-skilled" machine-operators emerged with ambiguous skill attributes. Workers filling these jobs required less training than the old craft apprenticeships and lacked the all-round knowledge of the whole production process. But they were given more responsibility at the centre of the production process than the old-time day-labourers (whose usefulness for brute labour was declining with widespread mechanization). The "semi-skilled" jobs could be complex enough to require some care, attention, and familiarity with the work in order to perform quickly and effectively. By the end of World War I, many employers were anxious to reduce the turnover of such workers and to keep them steadily at their jobs. Some of these workers would eventually use their enhanced importance in the production process as the basis for building industrial unions.[31] "Deskilling," it seems, was not as straightforward a process as many capitalists hoped (and as many theorists have assumed).

On the whole, workers greeted the new work world of monopoly capitalism with suspicion and hostility. Many of them kept their distance from the new jobs in mines and mills by quitting frequently and moving on, or, in the case of women and immigrants, returning home. Widespread labour turnover meant that within one year a man might have jobs in a steel mill, a construction camp, a coal mine, and a farmer's wheat field, while in the same period a woman might move from wrapping candy in a confectionery plant, to running a machine in a knitting mill, to folding sheets in a laundry, to cleaning someone else's house. Employers increasingly saw this informal, individualized form of resistance as a problem that required renewed efforts to encourage workers to stay on the job.[32]

Yet at the same time, many workers made a stand to defend familiar workplace routines and to demand living wages. Although under relentless attack, craft unionism hung on and surged up with renewed vigour during World War I. Many of the less skilled were also organizing into all-inclusive industrial unions – radical centres like the Industrial Workers of the World (IWW) and the One Big Union (OBU), as well as one-industry organizations of miners, railway workers, textile workers, steelworkers, meatpackers, and others. Corporate employers had no room for unions in their industrial autocracies and strove to drive out those in existence and to keep out any newcomers. Besides firing and blacklisting union activists and breaking strikes with professional scabs, companies were beginning, by World War I, to provide programs of corporate welfare – recreation programs, insurance and pension plans, profit-sharing schemes, and industrial councils – to promote loyalty and commitment to the firm. Successive explosions of industrial conflict nonetheless rocked the work world of early twentieth-century Canada. Detailed studies of pre-war strikes in southern Ontario and the Maritimes have revealed how often workers were battling over their right to some control within the labour process. The war years intensified these conflicts by giving workers steady employment at high wages. This was a more secure base from which to fight back and unleashed a powerful rhetoric of democracy and public service that workers could turn into a demand for "industrial democracy."[33]

The climax came in 1919 when almost 3.5 million working days were lost through 459 strikes, highlighted by the general strike in Winnipeg. The confrontation between labour and capital was also extending into politics, where vigorous labour parties were chalking up impressive victories in municipal and provincial elections by the end of the war. A central political demand connected the industrial and political struggles: the eight-hour day. During the spring and summer of 1919, a hastily assembled Royal Commission on Industrial Relations observed the intensity of Canadian workers' revolt and their remarkable solidarity in hearings across the country. In some cases, such as the Cape Breton coalfields, the post-war industrial conflict was convincing workers to contest the entire structure of ownership and control in their industry.[34]

All of the momentum of workers' industrial and political challenge, however, was crushed in the early 1920s by the combined impact of a severe depression and an employers' anti-union offensive.[35] Except for construction and a few small pockets like printing, craft unionism would never revive, its basis permanently eroded by the transformation of work processes. The first industrial unions were also largely destroyed, but they would reappear sporadically in the inter-war period – first, in the late 1920s and early 1930s under communist leadership, and then, in the late 1930s, under the inspiration of the American Congress of Industrial Organizations (CIO). By the beginning of World War II, however, these unions had made few inroads into Canadian industry. Generally, employers continued to control their workplaces unbridled by the presence of any formal worker presence.[36] It was an age of authoritarian, repressive management that old-timers still recall with a shudder of fear and resentment.[37]

Women workers played a marginal role in these workplace confrontations,[38] largely because of their short spell in the paid work force between school and marriage, their isolation in female job ghettoes, and the reluctance of their unionized male workmates to devote much energy to helping them organize.[39] Their resistance tended most often to be informal (quitting and moving on) and by the 1920s their intolerance for one form of wage labour – domestic service – had forced middle- and upper-class employers to end their reliance on live-in servants and to begin the mechanization of housework. In their own homes, working-class wives and mothers were still the domestic managers they had been since industrial capitalism had first brought about the separation of work and home. Preparing their families to meet the rhythms of work in the factories, mines, and offices was still an extremely labour-intensive process. Mass marketing of ready-made clothing and processed food like bakery bread and canned goods had slightly reduced some of the domestic labour, as had the installation of running water, gas, and electricity. But the vast majority of Canadian households remained technological backwaters until World War II, and women were still confined to this sphere for most of their lives.[40]

The opening decades of the twentieth century were also a period in which the Canadian state significantly expanded its role in workplace relations. In response to pressure from the labour movement, the federal government and several provincial administrations opened labour departments to monitor workplace relations. They gradually made a few additions to the statute books that required employers to meet some minimal employment standards, most particularly workers' compensation for industrial accidents and minimum wages for women. Typically these measures did no more than stabilize and routinize existing workplace relations. Far more important, however, were the state's efforts to curb workers' militancy. Troops were sent into strike situations even more frequently than in the past and almost invariably provoked violent responses. The courts hammered away at union security and freely granted employers a new weapon, the injunction. The most vigorous use of state repression was probably in Winnipeg in 1919, where the federal government intervened decisively by arresting and deporting strike leaders. The most famous form of state intervention, however, combined the twin goals of meeting enough of workers' demands to encourage legitimation of the industrial system and imposing the iron heel of repression. In 1907, the young William Lyon Mackenzie King drafted a new piece of federal legislation, the Industrial Disputes Investigation Act (IDIA), which prohibited strikes and lockouts in specified industries until a conciliation board had met and reported. Experience soon proved that the so-called cooling-out period did more damage to unions than to employers. Although the act was declared unconstitutional in 1923, its key features would remain a cornerstone of the Canadian state's industrial-relations policies throughout the twentieth century.[41]

Workers' resistance to the terms and conditions of employment and the frequently violent industrial conflict flared up most often when the reserve army of potential strikebreakers was smaller, when the process of industrial transformation was accelerated, and when a dramatic crisis like the war had disrupted normal social relationships. Throughout the period, sporadic industrial trench warfare raged more quietly on the shop floor out of the public eye, as small groups of workers and their bosses confronted each other daily along the "frontier of control" over managerial initiatives to alter or speed up work processes.[42] Yet there was another parallel pattern of worker / management relations that was more evident during periods of severe unemployment or following major defeats on the picket lines or at the ballot box. Many writers have used the term "consent" for a form of working-class consciousness that seemed to reveal a willingness to accept workers' subordination in industry. With thousands of immigrants flooding in to compete for jobs, with blacklists, spies, and company police at work, and with iron-willed magistrates ready to clamp down on troublemakers, it is easy to see how "consent" was actually fear, insecurity, and an unwillingness to rock the boat in the face of economic and political coercion. The corporate paternalism of welfare plans and favouritism in hiring and promotion could help condition workers to accept the coercive framework of their working lives more equably.[43] That consciousness and behaviour could be evoked more indirectly as well. Many workers absorbed appealing ideologies that encouraged quiescence or class collaboration – social Catholicism among Quebec workers, protectionist, jingoist Toryism among southern Ontario factory hands, and Maritime Rights activism in the East, for example.[44] Whatever the source, habits of deference had settled in among many Canadian workers by the 1930s, especially among those who clung to their jobs.

In the forty years before World War II, then, the labour process in Canada had been reshaped in fundamental ways. Large new corporate employers, struggling with an uncertain economic environment, had undertaken to restructure their workplaces with new technology and more centralized, authoritarian managerial systems that would wrest control of the labour process from workers on the job, especially from skilled workers and their unions. In the process they had produced new occupational categories and a new, ethnically stratified work force. But they had also locked horns with many angry, resentful workers. With the help of a sympathetic state, the employers had driven out most craft unions and prevented consolidation of industrial unions; and they believed they had won more solid control over their production processes. By the end of the period, however, the seeds of future conflicts had been sown. During the depression of the 1930s, the work force had stabilized somewhat, as immigration dried up and workers settled into scarce jobs. They had made a greater commitment to the industries in which they worked, but deeply resented the poor wages and the arbitrary tyranny of front-line supervisors. It was a work force, which, although no longer maintaining formal control mechanisms in the workplace, often had substantial informal power and autonomy on the job as a result of the unevenness and ambiguity of the deskilling process and the effective leverage of so many semi-skilled workers. Workers could also draw some strength from the increased interdependence of production units within corporate consolidations, which a determined group of workers in one unit could disrupt. Canadian capitalists, it seems, had not delivered a knock-out blow to the workplace power of the Canadian working class; they had merely changed the battlefield. Primarily it was the overstocked labour market in so many of the inter-war years that prevented workers from mounting any more substantial challenges. Another world war would bring a remarkable transformation in workplace relations.

THE CHALLENGE OF INDUSTRIAL
DEMOCRACY, 1940 TO THE
PRESENT

A fourth period in the evolution of capitalist labour processes in Canada began to take shape during World War II and stretched over the next four decades. In contrast to preceding periods, it was marked by almost unbroken prosperity until the onset of a serious international economic crisis in the 1970s. The prosperity provided the basis for a huge expansion of the service sector, where most of the new jobs were emerging by the end of the period. Within that long phase of high output and relatively full employment, however, some major restructuring of the Canadian economy took place. The protected national market for manufactured goods was slowly dismantled to conform to the new patterns of international free trade, inspired by the post-war General Agreements on Tariffs and Trade (GATT). In the new "international division of labour," many industries like electrical goods and clothing began to wither away in the face of cheaper Third World competition. At the same time, American industry, hungry for natural resources, penetrated Canada more aggressively in search of oil, forest products, and minerals. In both manufacturing and resource extraction, continental economic integration had resulted in a staggering increase in American ownership by the 1960s. In this new economic environment, the state played a much more active role in promoting economic development and attempting to stabilize business cycles with the new fiscal and monetary tools of Keynesianism. The collaboration of capitalists, politicians, and state bureaucrats over which C.D. Howe presided during World War II continued and expanded in post-war decades. Eventually, however, the Ottawa mandarins discovered that the regulatory tools of one nation-state were feeble instruments in a context where industrial development and economic relations were dominated by a new institution – the multinational / transnational corporation, with branches and widely diversified investments around the globe.[45]

A third major technological revolution accompanied this economic expansion. Elaborate new machines replaced old manual techniques in most major resource industries like forestry, mining, fishing, and agriculture in particular.[46] Manufacturing and communications companies similarly introduced sophisticated new technologies, while in the transportation sector, deisel replaced steam power on trains and mechanized loading and unloading devices transformed the country's ports.[47] As in the past, the trend of all this mechanization was to cut costs by replacing workers and speeding up work processes. But what distinguished this period from the two previous "industrial revolutions" was the effort to automate work – to find machines that would run themselves. The key to this transformation became the computer, which was large, bulky, and expensive when first developed during World War II, but which became infinitely more flexible with the insertion of the microchip in the 1970s. Computerized technology has been rapidly replacing human labour in manufacturing, communications, service industries (like banks, supermarkets, gas stations), and, most dramatically, in offices, where clerical workers from accountants to filing clerks have found their traditional jobs disappearing.[48]

As in previous phases of technological change, displacement of workers by computers has been accompanied by deskilling – word-processor pools are a striking example – and some reskilling, although most studies suggest that those learning the new skills in computer application are not the largely female labour being displaced. Even more important, however, is the ability of the new technology to control the work force more effectively, both by setting the pace of production and by monitoring the performance of operators of word processors, cash registers, lathes, and other machines with more precision than F.W. Taylor could ever have dreamed of.[49] The lingering economic recession of the early 1980s has slowed the spread of this "technical control" of the labour process into workplaces,[50] but the wave of the future is clear.

The work force assembled in this technologically more sophisticated economy had some important new dimensions. The traditionally large, flexible pool of underemployed, "semi-proletarianized" Canadian farm dwellers declined drastically after World War II as farmers' children left for the city in unprecedented numbers.[51] Immigrants continued to flow in from southern Europe and the Caribbean to find jobs in sectors where muscle power was still in demand, especially in construction and domestic service; yet immigration also brought many professionals from eastern Europe and Asia.[52] In general, the work force used in this new phase of economic development was much better educated, and a demand grew for technically trained personnel, usually with college or university degrees: engineers, research scientists, computer analysts, and other members of the so-called new working class.[53]

An important shift in employment patterns was the much greater use of female labour, including for the first time rising numbers of married women. Labour shortages during World War II had enabled many women to breach some of the bastions of exclusively male work in various versions of "Rosie the Riveter," but they had been promptly sent home at the end of the war. By the 1960s, however, larger numbers of women, including married women, were working more-or-less full time in the burgeoning female job ghettoes in offices and service-sector enterprises. Working-class families were now keeping their teenagers in school longer, while their mothers took over the role of secondary wage-earners. For most families this transition was made easier by the emergence of consumer services like take-out food and by the accessibility of new gadgets for mechanizing housework, from automatic washers and dryers to electric floor polishers. But for women it created the new burden of the "double day" – a shift in the factory, office, or store, followed by continuing responsibility for most domestic labour in the family home.[54]

No change in the workplace was more striking, however, than the unionization of hundreds of thousands of Canadian workers after 1940. The war provided the catalyst, although the seeds had been sown in the 1930s in the many struggles of unemployed workers and the first efforts at building industrial unions under the umbrella of the CIO. By the outbreak of the war, these unions had established only a tenuous toehold in a few sectors like steel, auto, textiles, clothing, and coal mining, but within two years, full employment and labour shortages had strengthened the organizers' hands. A strike wave, which reached a new peak of militancy in 1943, was propelled by workers' resentments at the wage freeze imposed by the Mackenzie King government, the continuing tyrannies of shop-floor management, and provincial and federal governments' reluctance to force employers to sit down at the bargaining table with recognized unions.[55]

Moreover, as in World War I, workers seized on the wartime rhetoric of combating fascist tyranny and began to demand more democracy in the workplace. Employers fought back with a new flurry of corporate welfare, especially company unions and industrial councils. They also attacked as "totalitarian" the labour movement's connections with Canada's resurgent social-democratic party, the Co-operative Commonwealth Federation (CCF). But in Ottawa, a shrewd prime minister watched with more astuteness the CCF's incredible rise to the top of the public opinion polls in 1943 and the party's near victory in the Ontario provincial election the same year. Frustrations built up at the point of production were once again spilling over into the realm of electoral politics. In an effort to stave off the erosion of its political base, the King government moved sharply to the left. A new commitment to establishing a minimal social-security net for workers brought unemployment insurance, children's allowances, and promises of much more, with the result that for the first time, workers' complete dependence on their employers for income had been partially relieved. At the same time, the Cabinet enacted an order in council, PC 1003, that provided for the recognition of unions, compulsory collective bargaining, and close state supervision of industrial relations, along with the old IDIA compulsory conciliation procedures. This temporary wartime measure became a permanent fixture of the industrial-relations landscape at the federal and provincial levels in the late 1940s, but only after thousands of Canadian workers in virtually every major industrial sector had won their employers' grudging recognition of their unions in the biggest strike wave in Canadian history. Long, bitter disputes tied up auto plants, steel mills, rubber plants, packing houses, railways, and many other workplaces between 1945 and 1947; in most cases workers won the right to have their unions negotiate for them and to have employers deduct union dues from their pay cheques.[56]

The victory that Canadian workers won from their bosses in almost all mass-production, resource-extractive, and transportation industries, and which the state then proceeded to recognize in its post-war labour legislation, was an ambiguous legacy. On the one hand, workers established regular procedures for collectively negotiating their wages and for protecting their organizations' right to exist. They were thus able to achieve higher wages and shorter hours (the forty-hour week finally arrived in the 1950s) and in general to ensure for themselves and their families a vastly better standard of living – indeed, a whole new style of life based on suburban homes, family cars, and sundry consumer goods. On the job, collective agreements now demanded new standards of fairness and equity from front-line supervisors that reduced competition and division between workers. Seniority clauses and grievance procedures prevented foremen and superintendents from promoting favourites or dismissing workers on whim. A "rule of law" had finally arrived inside many workplaces. Post-war bargaining also included efforts to simplify and standardize wage rates across whole industries. Overall, the greatest beneficiaries were probably the minority ethnic and racial groups within the work force who had suffered the worst abuses in the pre-war industrial regime.

On the other hand, limitations on this new collective power of workers were severe. According to the wide-ranging "management rights" clause in most collective agreements, employers still held onto control over the power to run their businesses, organize their production processes, and discipline their workers. Although in practice, four decades of negotiation and grievance arbitration would impinge somewhat on untrammelled employer control, the success of industrial democracy clearly did not mean a return to the workplace control mechanisms of nineteenth-century craftsmen. Moreover, the state imposed strict legal constraints on trade-union activity, forbidding strikes during the conciliation process and during the lifetime of the collective agreement, and broke working-class solidarity by banning sympathy strikes. Union officials were, therefore, cast in the role of policemen over their membership to keep them within legal bounds. Finally, the resolution of conflict on the shop floor was pushed into grievance procedures modelled on the legal system and were thus handled primarily by lawyers or other trained staff rather than by workers themselves. In many instances the procedure was painfully slow, insensitive, expensive, and ineffective in meeting workers' concerns.[57]

This much-discussed post-war "compromise" was not an inevitable outcome of bureaucratization, but a product of a particular period of struggle in which the state intervened decisively to contain and fragment a burgeoning movement of working-class militancy and solidarity. At the same moment, the state joined employers and the media in whipping up a cold-war hysteria, which broke the momentum of all progressive movements and set the stage for the expulsion of many seasoned communist trade-union leaders (and in a few cases, whole unions) from the Canadian labour movement. The potential for widening and deepening the working-class challenge to its subordination within the capitalist workplace was thus never allowed to reach fruition.[58]

For nearly two decades, the post-war institutionalization of industrial relations worked more or less as intended, confining most industrial conflict to relatively safe bureaucratic channels.[59] In the mid 1960s, however, the system began to break down. An explosion of strikes that extended into the mid 1970s shattered the relative calm. Illegal "wildcat" strikes, rejections of negotiated contracts, and internal challenges to union leadership were signs that the tensions arising from employers' freedom to speed up and innovate and from the emerging problem of rapid inflation in an increasingly unstable world economy were boiling over. This new militancy was also inspired by a blossoming youth culture that celebrated personal freedom and self-expression. The same factors were producing more turbulence on the shop floor, particularly increased labour turnover, absenteeism, and sabotage. This continuing ferment testified to the persistent autonomy of informal work groups, both from complete subordination to management and from the union leadership that collaborated in the collective-bargaining process. In some regions, the country's new social-democratic party, the New Democratic Party, gathered some momentum from this industrial unrest.[60]

Some of the same resentments at the bureaucratic insensitivity of a highly centralized management and at deteriorating wages brought a new set of actors into the industrial-relations system: public-sector workers. After a cautious process of turning the old government employees' associations into effective bargaining agents, and eventually into full-fledged unions, these workers convinced provincial and federal governments to enact legislation granting them most of the same rights to organize and bargain collectively that so many blue-collar workers had won in the 1940s, although often with tighter restrictions on their freedom to strike. The state's role in the industrial-relations system thus shifted abruptly from external mediator to central participant. By the mid 1970s, public-sector unions were negotiating for virtually all state employees and included almost 40 per cent of all union membership in Canada.[61] Para-public sectors like schools and hospitals also found the professionals on their staff – nurses, teachers, professors, librarians, technicians – turning into militant unionists. Their employers' attempts to cope with funding crises by more rigid application of private-sector managerial practices and resistance to salary increases threatened these workers' image of their status as professionals.[62] In fact, at the peak of strike activity in the early 1970s, it was workers from government offices, schools, and hospitals whom the media featured most prominently on the picket lines.

Significantly, women workers figured more conspicuously in the struggles of the 1970s – a sign both of the impact of the emerging feminist movement and of women's increasing commitment to full-time employment.[63]

By the beginning of the 1980s, then, union organization in Canada had grown to a level where nearly two non-agricultural workers in every five were union members and almost three in every five were covered by union contracts, in sharp contrast to the United States, where union membership has been steadily declining.[64] Canadian workers had also developed an international reputation for combativeness – second only to Italy in proneness to strike. Yet that militancy has remained fragmented by related problems: the tight strictures of collective-bargaining legislation, which structures negotiations on a factory-by-factory basis and forbids sympathy strikes; and the persistent caution of a top union leadership that is more accustomed to bureaucratic manoeuvring than to mass mobilization and is legitimately concerned about safeguarding the existence of its organizations. Only in Quebec, where francophone nationalism and Marxism have infused the labour movement, have workers connected up their individual workplace battles in a "Common Front," and even there the unity was largely limited to the public sector.[65] The repressive function of the post-war "compromise" has helped to constrain and divide workers.

At the same time, not only have trade unionists been divided from each other, but the much more numerous unorganized workers have been left completely outside this industrial battle zone. These workers continue to find jobs in a "secondary" labour market, where small, more peripheral, or more labour-intensive enterprises demand few skills, pay low wages, guarantee little or no job security, and are run in the no-nonsense, authoritarian style of earlier capitalist management. It is here that we find Canada's many working poor – most particularly women and the new racial and ethnic minorities, who, as in the past, find themselves at the bottom of the occupational hierarchy, and whose vulnerability makes them extremely difficult to organize. More skilled workers in the "primary" sector have often been reluctant to try, but, contrary to the assumptions of some theorists of labour-market segmentation, they have not shown complete indifference: the existing minimum-wage requirements, however inadequate, found their way onto the statute books largely because the labour movement demanded them. The rapid growth of part-time work in the past decade suggests that this work experience in the secondary labour market is not about to disappear.[66]

Whatever the divisions within the Canadian working class, employers, politicians, and state officials have been concerned for nearly twenty years that Canada's bureaucratized system of industrial relations has not succeeded in keeping workers on the job or in curbing their demands, especially for higher wages. By the end of the 1960s, the era of free collective bargaining and the "rule of law" in the workplace was unravelling in the face of renewed worker militancy and economic recession, both of which combined with increasing foreign competition to cut heavily into profit margins. After the federal state failed to win union leaders' voluntary consent to a restricted incomes policy, it imposed compulsory wage controls on all workers between 1975 and 1978 and on public-sector workers in the early 1980s. Most provincial administrations followed suit. Governments also used frequent back-to-work legislation and even jailed labour leaders in a pattern of disrupting legal collective-bargaining procedures that has been accurately called "permanent exceptionalism."[67] Some provincial jurisdictions, more-over, have been enacting legislation to weaken the rights of trade unions to organize and bargain.

Simultaneously, the Canadian state has been aggressively promoting new forms of consultation between workers and their bosses that bypass the collective-bargaining process and encourage non-confrontational negotiation of problems. A new national Labour Market and Productivity Centre appeared early in 1984, with the federal government's blessing. Special committees in the workplace to discuss occupational health and safety and technological change have also been encouraged. "Quality of working life" schemes promoted by federal and provincial agencies ostensibly offer workers more interesting and challenging work through such measures as job rotation, job enrichment, "quality circles" to discuss quality control and productivity, and the formation of semi-autonomous work groups. Yet, like their predecessors – company unionism and industrial councils – these schemes tend, in practice, to be devices for reorganizing the workplace and intensifying work with the consent of the worker. In the context of stiffer international competition and pressures to adopt the latest technologies, a relatively small number of employers have found these schemes effective. Many more are turning to another device promoted by the Canadian state for the same purpose: profit sharing.[68] The goal of state intervention in the past decade has been primarily to help shore up the faltering Canadian capitalist system by restricting or suspending workers' hard-won rights to bargain collectively over the terms of their employment and to convince workers to accept some curtailment of their immediate material interests. Only in the context of the economic crash of the early 1980s, when official unemploy-ment rates passed 12 per cent nationally (or probably closer to 20 per cent if "discouraged" workers were counted), did this strategy seem to work. However, the recent resurgence of strikes and union organizing – which has hit anti-labour bastions like Eaton's – suggests that the long-term outcome is not clear.[69]

The post-war "compromise" has thus come unstuck. The industrial-relations system created in the 1940s to guarantee both stability in the work world and the continued subordination of workers to employers has proved incapable of meeting the seismic shocks of technological change, mass unionization, and international economic crisis. On the job, workers have had to confront the redesigning and intensification of production processes, which their employers have pushed forward relentlessly in an effort to survive in a restructured economy. One result has been one of the highest rates of industrial accident and disease in the Western world.[70] At the same time, workers have found their formal organizations of resistance mired in bureaucracy and legal restraint. They have also found an international inflationary spiral eating away at their real wages and the state moving in to coax them, and if necessary to compel them, to accept less in the name of economic recovery for their employers' firms. By the early 1980s, it was clear that Canadian industrial relations had entered a new phase – probably dating from the imposition of wage and price controls in 1975 – in which workers' power at the point of production was once again under attack.

TOWARD A THEORY OF THE LABOUR PROCESS

In recent years many writers and researchers in Canada and elsewhere have been probing the world of work of the past and present with renewed vigour. Besides the many fruitful empirical studies carried out by social historians, industrial sociologists, labour economists, and feminist writers, serious efforts have been made to develop a satisfactory theoretical framework that takes account of the richness of detail unearthed and the wide variation in experience between industries and between countries.[71] The results have been impressive but inconclusive; no theoretical consensus has emerged. Most of the best of this theorizing has taken place within a framework of Marxism and feminism, but large areas of disagreement remain even among these groups. We do not propose to resolve all these debates, but will suggest some of the key concepts that need to be incorporated into any theory, at least if it is to make sense of the labour processes in Canada.

In the first place, we need to keep at the forefront of any theorizing the simple fact that the working class is made up of both men and women. The gender division of labour was not a new creation of the capitalist era, but it had a new meaning in capitalist society. As we saw, industrial capitalist development shifted most production out of the home and divided the formerly unitary work world into separate spheres of unpaid domestic labour in the household and waged labour in the capitalist labour market, the former a female enclave, the latter overwhelmingly male. Over time, women found their domestic responsibilities reoriented toward the reproduction of labour-power to be expended outside the household – feeding and clothing the wage-earners and nurturing the future workers, the children – and their household tasks eventually focused more on consumption and less on production. Their participation in the paid work force was shaped by patriarchal notions of appropriate female work and by the overarching demands of their domestic responsibilities. Until the middle of the twentieth century, marriage normally ended women's waged employment. Even in the past thirty years, the growing numbers of married women who continue to work through much of their adult lives are those who still bear most of the responsibility for domestic labour.

In general, the rhythms of women's domestic labour have always been quite different from those in capitalist industry. Women's work is spread through most of their waking hours and lacks a clear separation of work time and leisure time. Nevertheless, women's work is structured by the rhythms of capitalist industry, especially by the comings and goings of the wage-earners. Of course, this labour is not performed directly for any capitalist employer. In fact, it is a crucial part of the way in which a working-class family functions as a tiny collectivity of self-help to cope with the impact of market forces on the family household through both wages and retail prices. Working-class women have shown plenty of evidence of commitment to this family and class solidarity. During the many decades when domestic labour remained so labour intensive, they may have maintained some of the sense of a working partnership that had characterized the independent commodity producers' households. Yet recognition of women's active participation in the working-class family's struggles for decency amidst economic insecurity should never blind us to the central reality of their lives – that they lived and worked in a different structural relationship to the capitalist system from their fathers, brothers, husbands, and sons, and were constrained by the persistence of male hegemony in the work world.[72]

Second, if we turn to the world of paid work, we need to recognize that workers and their bosses did not confront each other inside a bell jar. Too often writers have ignored the wider economic context of individual units of production that exerted pressure on any single employer or group of workers. In any industry, the state of markets for products and for labour can play a crucial role in determining the importance and the timing of changes in the labour process, as well as workers' abilities to resist those changes. The intensity of competition and the degree of monopolization (or oligopolization) are particularly important: contrast, for example, the printing or clothing industries with the steel or pulp and paper industries. New technology or a new organization of production might be ignored or delayed if neither could offer a significant edge over competitors. The Steel Company of Canada's reluctance to modernize its sheet-metal mills until the mid 1930s was only one example of a pattern found in many Canadian industries. Similarly, Canadian employers were confronted with a highly variable labour supply that influenced the pace of mechanization and the wages they were compelled to pay. The availability of new pools of labour, especially women and racial or ethnic minorities, often conditioned the willingness and necessity to modernize their operations. Today, the reserve army of labour at the disposal of corporations has become world-wide.

Ultimately market factors, combined with available technology, give each production process its uniqueness and even each national industry its distinctiveness from other nations' parallel industries. This case has been made effectively in a recent comparison between the British and American steel industries.[73] In fact, it is only with this sensitivity to markets that labour processes in a country like Canada can be properly analysed. In the resource-extractive industries, we know how sensitive to international markets industrialists have to be. In the manufacturing sector, which produced primarily for the domestic market, a high-tariff structure protected Canadian factories, but the small market frequency inhibited workplace innovations. And, when American manufacturing corporations leaped the tariff walls and established on Canadian soil branch-plant operations with some of the most sophisticated production processes, Canadian manufacturers had to adapt. At the same time, as we have seen, labour markets from which these industries drew their workers had some characteristics particular to Canada, most notably the steady influx of immigrants (especially those from non-Anglo-Celtic backgrounds) and the continuing existence of a semi-employed subsistence population in rural areas.

Third, we need a much more dynamic theory of the transformation that has gone on within capitalist labour processes over the past century. There is a pervasive tendency, inspired principally by Harry Braverman, to view the process of change as a consolidation of untrammelled capitalist power within a more centralized, bureaucratic management – a once-and-for-all victory over working-class autonomy on the shop floor.[74] There is no question that capitalists made great strides in that direction, and shaped new, more alienating norms of work for many wage-earners. But the path was never as smooth nor the victories as clear-cut as some have suggested. New production processes could take on unintended meanings once workers adjusted and adapted them on the job. Certainly workers were not passively content to let those processes roll over them. Resistance continued in informal work groups and through new unions. Many of these struggles were undoubtedly contained by restrictive legalisms and bureaucracy, but as the re-emergence of militancy in the 1960s indicated, they could not be permanently suppressed. The workplace has remained a "contested terrain" of capitalist initiative and worker response.

A fourth concern arising directly from our insistence on this dynamic view of labour-process transformation is the question of skill. Once again, Braverman's pervasive influence has not been helpful. What has happened to skill in the twentieth century? Certainly the decentralized work world of the nineteenth-century craftsman disappeared, but the new occupational mix was almost invariably more complex than a simple thesis of deskilling and "proletarianization" would indicate. Many skilled workers, like tailors or machinists, undoubtedly faced disintegration of their trades into less skilled fragments, wherein poorly trained workers handled specialized new machinery. Some, however, simply had various auxiliary tasks stripped away so that they could apply their technical competence more intensively. Even within the most thoroughly transformed industries, skills survived among set-up and maintenance men like toolmakers and millwrights (although they had made a significant shift from the core of the production process to the periphery). And some new skills emerged: on the railways, in printing, and much later in logging and mining, for example, the arrival of new technology did not necessarily translate into mindless, unskilled, machine-paced assembly lines, since operating some of the new mechanical devices required a new set of skills different from handicrafts but no less valuable (though often less portable).[75] In some cases, the totally new industries implanted in Canadian soil simply bypassed the old, craft-dominated sectors – the iron puddlers, for example, or the shipwrights and leather workers on horse goods. In others, long-term unemployment could sever craftsmen from their work and force them into poorly paid unskilled labour. Many skilled workers in the Maritimes must have suffered that fate.[76] The picture is clouded still further by the growth of the ambiguous "semi-skilled" work force, whose familiarity with its mechanized jobs proved to be essential for efficient production and beneficial for organizing industrial unions. Clearly a distinction needs to be kept in mind between skills inherent in the job and those attached to an individual after years of on-the-job experience.[77]

maritimes

Skill, however, is normally more than simply technical competence. It can also be socially constructed. Studies have often revealed how little time is actually required to learn some recognized "skills," and how little time in on-the-job apprenticeships is actually spent teaching them (although it is hard to imagine a socially constructed skill surviving long without some technical know-how attached to it).[78] In contrast, the considerable skills of women have been systematically downgraded within the particular ideology of industrial capitalist society.[79] So too have the abilities of less "respectable" workers like loggers.[80] Seeing the social construction of skill as combining ideology and collective action[81] is helpful in understanding what happened to craft skills between the late nineteenth and early twentieth centuries. Skilled workers had struggled to create craft unions, with elaborate rules governing trade practices and apprenticeships. At the same time, however, they had been able to draw on a deep reservoir of popular respect for and celebration of the "dignity of toil" (meaning manual labour, "earning one's bread by the sweat of the brow"), which ran through both farmers' and workers' movements and was regularly acknowledged by community leaders like clergymen or politicians.[82] Such an ideological defence of manual competence even allowed new groups of relatively skilled workers within modernizing industry – locomotive engineers, mule spinners, rolling-mill hands, garment cutters, linotype operators – to don the respectable mantle of craftsmanship and form their own craft unions. In the early twentieth century, however, not only did monopoly capitalists battle skilled workers and their unions into submission, but the populist ideology of craftsmanship and "honest toil" was displaced by one of managerialism, in which the professional manager took the place of the craftsman in popular culture.[83] Without the ideological patina of the past, skill was stripped down to its technical content, and new groups of skilled workers had only pay differentials and a modicum of shop-floor respect to distinguish them from the less skilled. Significantly, few of these reskilled men created their own unions as their counterparts had done in the late nineteenth century. At the same time, however, newer groups of university-trained technical workers were wrapping themselves in the robes of "professionalism," with their own associations, certification procedures, and code of ethics to secure and enhance their status in the workplace.

Skill is best understood in a specific historical context in which definitions are altered to match the changing dimensions of skilled work and the new characteristics of the skilled worker. Over the course of the development of industrial capitalism, especially in the early years of the twentieth century, work was degraded and workers robbed of skills. New skills were also created and workers upgraded or reskilled. At the centre of these related processes of deskilling and reskilling has been the struggle between workers and their employers to define and control skilled work.

Fifth, we need a more satisfactory integration of workers' own consciousness into the process of workplace transformation, in order to understand the dialectic of resistance and consent. It is not satisfactory to characterize workers simply as either passive victims or seething rebels. In Canada they have shown themselves to be both, depending on the material and ideological circumstances, but more regularly they exhibit considerably more complex attitudes. Workers invariably bring to their jobs some notions of fairness and natural justice and often some kind of gut-level class spirit of "them and us," nourished in working-class communities and stimulated by contemporary political developments. These motivate their behaviour as much as the machines or their bosses' carrot-and-stick managerial policies and are expressed with varying intensity over time. But people work and struggle in a coercive context that makes outright resistance extremely difficult because of courts, police, the threat of unemployment and poverty, and the numbing repetitiveness of their jobs. Under these circumstances it should not be surprising that they have participated, apparently consciously, in a relationship that implies their own subordination.

Other factors in the "manufacturing of consent" that emphasize workers' active participation have been the subject of much recent speculation. Prior orientation to work (peasant consciousness, female domesticity), ideological conditioning (Methodism, Catholicism, Toryism, anti-communism, consumerism, patriarchal ideologies), ideological "misleading" (liberalism, social democracy, communism), labour-market segmentation, employer manipulation on the job (welfarism and job ladders), and labour-process mechanisms like game playing on the job mystify or mask real workplace relations.[84] All these play a role in encouraging workers to live with their subordination rather than to challenge it, but no one of these explanations could ever account for the variation in working-class consciousness, especially the sudden shifts to more militancy or radicalism. A number of writers have usefully stressed that workers operate on two levels of normative reference – the "abstract," in which the dominant values of their community or society come to bear on purely abstract judgments, and the "situational," in which practical choices in concrete circumstances produce a "negotiated version" of hegemonic values. Autoworkers in World War II who voted to support their union's no-strike pledge and then proceeded to engage in an unprecedented level of strike activity present one example of this process.[85]

Another persuasive analysis reminds us of the "dual character of labour" within capitalism that can generate both resistance and consent.[86] On the one hand, capitalists want as much work as possible out of the labour-power they purchase from workers; on the other, because the commodity they have bought is not a machine but human labour-power, with all its subjectivity, and can never in any real sense be completely controlled, they must turn over their instruments of production to the workers and rely on their co-operation in order to get the work performed at all. Labour has thus both an exchange value and a use value for employers. So, too, for workers, who need access to the means of production both to earn wages and to expend their labour-power producing use value. They are thus simultaneously interested in maintaining the relationship and the unit of capital in which they work (consent) and in challenging the way that the instruments of production are used, especially as they affect the wages paid and the quality of the work experience (resistance). This complex line of argument highlights the one aspect of the capitalist labour process that is usually completely overlooked: that workers can, and undoubtedly do, make a distinction between the wage nexus and the social utility of their labour (its use value), which arguably sustains them in many otherwise oppressive workplaces.

In Canada, as elsewhere in the advanced capitalist world, there has not been a single, permanent shift in working-class consciousness that resulted in complete submission and deference to capitalist authority (sometimes posed as the move from "formal" to "real" subordination and usually tied to the defeat of the craft worker). Instead a pattern of ebbing and flowing, of surging and receding, is evident: in 1867, the dramatic rise of labour in 1872 and the mid 1880s would have seemed unimaginable; in 1905 no one would have predicted the phenomenal upheaval of 1919; in 1935, the explosion of 1946 militancy would have seemed laughable; and in the serenity of the 1950s, no one was anticipating the turbulence of the late 1960s and early 1970s. Each of these moments of widespread working-class resistance followed periods of profound shifts in the economy and in the structure of the workplace, but most often some major social or political crisis, especially a war, was necessary to disrupt the existing habits of consent, material and ideological. At each of these moments, in fact, a new current of radicalism percolated through the ranks of workers – labourism, socialism, communism, New-Left anti-authoritarianism, Quebec nationalism, feminism. And in each case a battle raged to determine the basis for a new stabilization – a permanent victory for labour (not necessarily a revolution, but at least an entrenchment of gains won into a new social consensus, as appeared after World War II), or a reconsolidation of unbridled capitalist hegemony. The consent following these upheavals was most often a resignation to a defeat experienced through broken strikes, electoral defeats, and/or large-scale unemployment (as in the 1890s, 1920s, and early 1980s). Too loose use of the term "consent," in fact, could be misleading, since it may fail to grasp the reluctant compliance, bitterness, resentment, irony, and fatalism without hopelessness that are still so evident among workers on the job.

Our final concern is to emphasize the importance of the state in this dynamic process. First, it has facilitated employers' innovation and transformation of work processes and their responses to working-class resistance by marshalling a reserve army of recruits for industry, especially through immigration and education programs, and by subsidizing the "modernization" of workplaces through tax write-offs and direct grants. Second, the state's coercive powers through the courts, police, and military have long provided a crucial disciplinary structure buttressing capitalist control of the labour process. But at moments of intense class conflict, the state has been even more important in mediating between capital and labour so as to restore social harmony. At stake are the legitimacy of the capital-accumulation process and of the existing power relations in the workplace and in society generally. In Canada this role has combined the introduction of a truncated welfare state with legally sanctioned collective-bargaining procedures, most dramatically witnessed in the mid 1940s. But in comparison with most European countries, coercion has overshadowed legitimation.[87]

In the final analysis, the problem of constructing a theory of the labour process is that there is no one single labour process within capitalist society. It is certainly not impossible to discern general tendencies in the actions of capitalists and workers that surpass the particularities of individual workplaces. Indeed, the concern of capitalists to cut labour costs and increase productivity seems central to any labour process in a capitalist economy. Similarly, workers' actions against management offensives form distinguishable patterns within and across industries. In building a theory of the labour process, however, it is necessary to keep in mind that the outcome of these struggles can never be predicted. With so much at stake, workers and their employers are simply too stubborn and too resourceful to conform to any overly tidy theory.

NOTES

1 David M. Gordon, Richard Edwards, and Michael Reich, *Segmented Work, Divided Workers: The Historical Transformation of Labor in the United States* (Cambridge 1982), 9.

2 R.C. Harris and John Warkentin, *Canada Before Confederation* (New York 1974); C. Grant Head, *Eighteenth Century Newfoundland: A Geographer's Perspective* (Toronto 1976); Steven Antler, "The Capitalist Underdevelopment of Nineteenth-Century Newfoundland," in Robert J. Brym and R. James Sacouman, eds, *Underdevelopment and Social Movements in Atlantic Canada* (Toronto 1979), 179–202; Gerald Sider, "The Ties That Bind: Culture and Agriculture, Property and Propriety in the Newfoundland Fishery," *Social History* 5 (1980): 1–39; Peter Neary and Patrick O'Flaherty, eds, *By Great Waters: A Newfoundland and Labrador Anthology* (Toronto 1974), 42–60; Andrew Hill Clark, *Three Centuries and the Island: A Historical Geography of Settlement and Agriculture in Prince Edward Island, Canada* (Toronto 1959); Robert Leslie Jones, *History of Agriculture in Ontario, 1613–1880* (Toronto 1946), 1–174; Leo Johnson, *History of the County of Ontario, 1615–1875* (Whitby 1973), 1–171; and "Independent Commodity Production: Mode of Production or Capitalist Class Formation?" *Studies in Political Economy* 6 (Autumn 1981): 93–112; Douglas McCalla, "The Wheat Staple and Upper Canadian Development," Canadian Historical Association, *Historical Papers* (hereafter HP), 1978, 43–6; Allan Greer, "Fur Trade Labour and Lower Canadian Agrarian Structures," ibid., 1981, 197–214, and "Wage Labour and the Transition to Capitalism: A Critique of Pentland," *Labour/Le Travail* (hereafter LLT) (forthcoming), and *Peasant, Lord, and Merchant: Rural Society in Three Quebec Parishes* (Toronto 1985); Graeme Wynn, *Timber Colony: A Historical Geography of Early Nineteenth Century New Brunswick* (Toronto 1981), 11–86; Edwin C. Guillet, *Pioneer Arts and Crafts* (Toronto 1968); Michael S. Cross, ed., *The Workingman in the Nineteenth Century* (Toronto 1973), 17–31.

3 Beth Light and Alison Prentice, eds, *Pioneers and Gentlewomen of British North America, 1713–1867* (Toronto 1980); David Gagan, "'The Prose of Life': Literary Reflections on the Family, Individual Experience and Social Structure in Nineteenth Century Canada," *Journal of Social History* 9 (1976): 367–81; Rosemary R. Ball, "'A Perfect Farmer's Wife': Women in 19th-Century Rural Ontario," *Canada: A Magazine*, 1975, 3–21; Leo Johnson, "The Political Economy of Women in the 19th Century," in Janice Acton et al., eds, *Women at*

Work: Ontario, 1850–1930 (Toronto 1974), 13–32; Louise A. Tilly and Joan W. Scott, *Women, Work, and the Family* (New York 1978); Guillet, *Pioneer Arts and Crafts*.

4 Johnson, *History of the County of Ontario*; Michael S. Cross, "1837: The Necessary Failure," in Cross and Gregory S. Kealey, eds, *Readings in Canadian Social History, Volume 2: Pre-Industrial Canada, 1760–1849* (Toronto 1982), 141–58; Lillian Gates, "The Decided Policy of William Lyon Mackenzie," *Canadian Historical Review* (hereafter CHR) 40 (1959): 185–208; Fernand Oullet, "Les insurrections de 1837–38: un phénomène social," *Histoire sociale/Social History* (hereafter HS/SH) 2 (November 1968): 54–84; Colin Read, *The Rising in Western Upper Canada: The Duncombe Revolt and After* (Toronto 1982); Errol Sharpe, *A People's History of Prince Edward Island* (Toronto 1976), 73–6; J. Murray Beck, *Joseph Howe, Volume 1: Conservative Reformer, 1804–1848* (Kingston and Montreal 1982).

5 H. Clare Pentland, *Labour and Capital in Canada, 1650–1860* (Toronto 1981), 1–60; Donald MacKay, *The Lumberjacks* (Toronto 1978); Wynn, *Timber Colony*, 11–86; Judith Fingard, *Jack in Port: Sailortowns in Eastern Canada* (Toronto 1982); Greer, "Fur Trade Labour"; Peter Russell, "Wage Labour Rates in Upper Canada, 1818–1840," HS/SH 16, no. 3 (May 1983): 61–70; Eugene Forsey, *Trade Unions in Canada, 1812–1902* (Toronto 1982), 9–31; Sally Zerker, *The Rise and Fall of the Toronto Typographical Union, 1832–1972: A Case Study in Foreign Domination* (Toronto 1982), 3–49; G.S. Kealey, "Work Control, the Labour Process, and Nineteenth-Century Canadian Printers," in this volume; Catherine Vance, "Early Trade Unionism in Quebec: The Carpenters and Joiners General Strike of 1833–1834," *Marxist Quarterly* 3 (1962): 26–42; William T. Wylie, "Poverty, Distress, and Disease: Labour and the Construction of the Rideau Canal, 1826–1836," LLT 11 (Spring 1983): 7–30; Ruth Bleasdale, "Class Conflict on the Canals of Upper Canada in the 1840s," ibid., 7 (Spring 1981): 9–40; H.C. Pentland, "The Lachine Strike of 1843," CHR 29 (1948): 255–77; Michael S. Cross, "The Shiners' War: Social Violence in the Ottawa Valley in the 1830s," ibid., 54 (1973): 1–26; Bryan D. Palmer, *Working Class Experience: The Rise and Reconstitution of Canadian Labour, 1800–1980* (Toronto 1983), 1–55.

6 James Sacouman, "Semi-Proletarianization and Rural Underdevelopment in the Maritimes," *Canadian Review of Sociology and Anthropology* (hereafter CRSA) 17 (1980): 232–45; Leo Johnson, "Precapitalist Economic Formations and the Capitalist Labour Market in Canada, 1911–71," in James E. Curtis and William G. Scott, eds, *Social Stratification: Canada* (Scarborough 1979), 89–104.

7 Pentland, *Labour and Capital*, 130–75; John McCallum, *Unequal Beginnings: Agriculture and Economic Development in Quebec and Ontario until 1870* (Toronto 1980); Paul Craven and Tom Traves, "Canadian Railways as Manufacturers, 1850–1880," HP, 1983, 254–81; Gregory S. Kealey, *Toronto Workers Respond to Industrial Capitalism, 1867–1892* (Toronto 1980), 3–34; Thomas William Acheson, "The Social Origins of Canadian Industrialism: A Study of the

Structure of Entrepreneurship" (PH D dissertation, University of Toronto 1971); L.D. McCann, "The Mercantile-Industrial Transition of the Metal Towns of Pictou County, 1860–1931," *Acadiensis* 10 (1981): 29–64; Robert Babcock, "Economic Development in Portland (Me.) and Saint John (N.B.) during the Age of Iron and Steam, 1860–1914," *American Review of Canadian Studies* 9 (1979): 1–37; Ian McKay, "Capital and Labour in the Halifax Baking and Confectionery Industry in the Last Half of the Nineteenth Century," LLT 3 (1978): 63–108; Glenn Williams, *Not For Export: Towards a Political Economy of Canada's Arrested Industrialization* (Toronto 1983).

8 Leo Johnson, "Land Policy, Population Growth, and Social Structure in the Home District, 1793–1851," *Ontario History* 58 (1971): 41–60; Gary Teeple, "Land, Labour, and Capital in Pre-Confederation Canada," in Teeple, ed., *Capitalism and the National Question in Canada* (Toronto 1972), 43–66; H.C. Pentland, "The Development of a Capitalist Labour Market in Canada," *Canadian Journal of Economics and Political Science* 25 (1959): 450–61; Del Muise, "The Making of an Industrial Community: Cape Breton Coal Towns, 1867–1900," in Don Macgillivray and Bryan Tennyson, eds, *Cape Breton Historical Essays* (Sydney 1980), 76–94.

9 Joanne Burgess, "L'industrie de la chaussure à Montréal, 1840–1870: Le passage de l'artisanat à la fabrique," *Revue d'histoire de l'Amérique française* 31 (1977): 187–210; Bettina Bradbury, "Women and Wage Labour in a Period of Transition: Montreal, 1861–1881," HS/SH 17, no. 33 (May 1984): 115–31; Susan Mann Trofimenkoff, "One Hundred and Two Muffled Voices: Canada's Industrial Women in the 1880s," *Atlantis* 3 (1978): 66–82; Kealey, *Toronto Workers*, 37–97; Bryan D. Palmer, *A Culture in Conflict: Skilled Workers and Industrial Capitalism in Hamilton, Ontario, 1860–1914* (Toronto 1979), 71–96; McKay, "Capital and Labour"; Paul Craven and Tom Traves, "Dimensions of Paternalism: Discipline and Culture in Canadian Railway Operations in the 1850s," in this volume; David Russell, "Fines, Piece Work, Factory Morality, and Blackholes: Factory Discipline in Nineteenth Century Montreal," *The Register* 3, no. 1 (March 1982): 83–101; Gregory S. Kealey, ed., *Canada Investigates Industrialism: The Royal Commission on the Relations of Labor and Capital, 1889* (Toronto 1973); Raphael Samuel, "Workshop of the World: Steam Power and Hand Technology in Mid-Victorian Britain," *History Workshop* 3 (Spring 1977): 6–72.

10 Pentland, *Labour and Capital*, 176–99; Stephen A. Speisman, "Munificent Parsons and Municipal Parsimony: Voluntary vs Public Poor Relief in Nineteenth Century Toronto," *Ontario History* 65 (1973): 33–49; Joey Noble, "'Class-ifying the Poor': Toronto Charities, 1850–1880," *Studies in Political Economy* (hereafter SPE) 2 (Autumn 1979): 109–28; Alison Prentice, *The School Promoters: Education and Social Class in Mid-Nineteenth Century Upper Canada* (Toronto 1977); J.M. Beattie, *Attitudes Towards Crime and Punishment in Upper Canada, 1830–1850* (Toronto 1977); Graeme Decarie, "Something Old, Something New ...; Aspects of Prohibitionism in Ontario in the 1890s," in Donald Swainson,

ed., *Oliver Mowat's Ontario* (Toronto 1972), 154–71; E.P. Thompson, "Time, Work Discipline, and Industrial Capitalism," *Past and Present* 38 (1967): 56–97; Daniel T. Rodgers, *The Work Ethic in Industrial America, 1850–1920* (Chicago 1974).

11 Bettina Bradbury, "The Family Economy and Work in an Industrializing City: Montreal in the 1870s," HP, 1979, 71–96; and "Fragmented Family: Family Strategies in the Face of Death, Illness and Poverty, Montreal, 1860–1885," in Joy Parr, ed., *Childhood and Family in Canadian History* (Toronto 1982), 109–28; Jane Humphries, "Class Struggle and the Persistence of the Working Class Family," *Cambridge Journal of Economics* (hereafter CJE) 1 (1978): 241–58; Bruce Curtis, "Capital, the State, and the Origins of the Working-Class Household," in Bonnie Fox, ed., *Hidden in the Household: Women's Domestic Labour Under Capitalism* (Toronto 1980), 101–34. See also Gita Sen, "The Sexual Division of Labour and the Working-Class Family: Towards a Conceptual Synthesis of Class Relations and the Subordination of Women," *Review of Radical Political Economy* (hereafter RRPE) 12 (1980): 76–86.

12 D. Suzanne Cross, "The Neglected Majority: The Changing Role of Women in 19th Century Montreal," in Susan Mann Trofimenkoff and Alison Prentice, eds, *The Neglected Majority: Essays in Canadian Women's History* (Toronto 1977), 66–86; Trofimenkoff, "One Hundred and Two Muffled Voices"; Bradbury, "Family Economy"; Heidi Hartmann, "Capitalism, Patriarchy, and Job Segregation by Sex," *Signs* 1 (1976): 137–69; Michele Barrett, *Women's Oppression Today: Problems in Marxist-Feminist Analysis* (London 1980), 152–86; Barbara Welter, "The Cult of True Womanhood," *American Quarterly* 18 (1966): 151–74. A growing body of literature is beginning to grapple with the connections between work experience and working-class masculinity. See, in particular, Cynthia Cockburn, *Brothers: Male Dominance and Technological Change* (London 1983); Paul Willis, *Learning to Labour: How Working Class Kids Get Working Class Jobs* (London 1977); and "Shop Floor Culture, Masculinity, and the Wage Form," in John Clarke, Chas Critcher, and Richard Johnson, eds, *Working-Class Culture: Studies in History and Theory* (London 1979), 185–98; Andrew Tolson, *The Limits of Masculinity* (London 1977); Paul Hoch, *White Hero, Black Beast: Racism, Sexism and the Mask of Masculinity* (London 1979); Stan Gray, "Sharing the Shop Floor," *Canadian Dimension* 18, no. 2 (June 1984): 17–32.

13 Forsey, *Trade Unions*; Kealey, *Toronto Workers*; Palmer, *Culture in Conflict*, and *Working-Class Experience*, 60–135; Robert Storey, "Industrialization in Canada: The Emergence of the Hamilton Working Class, 1850–1870s" (MA thesis, Dalhousie University 1975).

14 Kealey, *Toronto Workers*, 64–97; Palmer, *Culture in Conflict*, 71–96; Ian McKay, "Workers' Control in Springhill, 1882–1927" (paper presented to the Canadian Historical Association 1981); David Montgomery, *Workers' Control in America: Studies in the History of Work, Technology, and Labor Struggles* (New York 1979), 9–31.

15 McKay, "Capital and Labour"; Craig Heron, "The Crisis of the Craftsman: Hamilton Metal Workers in the Early Twentieth Century," LLT 6 (Autumn 1980): 7–48.

16 For a good review of the debate, see John Field, "British Historians and the Concept of the Labor Aristocracy," *Radical History Review* 19 (Winter 1978–79): 61–85.

17 Dan Clawson, *Bureaucracy and the Labor Process: The Transformation of U.S. Industry, 1860–1920* (New York 1980), 71–125.

18 Ruth Frager, "No Proper Deal: Women and the Canadian Labour Movement, 1870–1940," in Linda Briskin and Linda Yantz, eds, *Union Sisters: Women in the Labour Movement* (Toronto 1983), 44–64; Barbara Taylor, "'The Men Are as Bad as Their Masters ...': Socialism, Feminism and Sexual Antagonism in the London Tailoring Trade in the Early 1830s," *Feminist Studies* 5 (1979): 7–40; Ruth Milkman, "Organizing the Sexual Division of Labor: Historical Perspectives on 'Women's Work' and the American Labor Movement," *Socialist Review* 49 (January–February 1980): 95–150.

19 W. Peter Ward, *White Canada Forever: Popular Attitudes and Public Policy toward Orientals in British Columbia* (Montreal 1978); Paul Phillips, *No Power Greater: A Century of Labour in British Columbia* (Vancouver 1967).

20 Kealey, *Toronto Workers*, 124–290; Palmer, *Culture in Conflict*, 125–98; Gregory S. Kealey and Bryan D. Palmer, *Dreaming of What Might Be: The Knights of Labor in Ontario, 1880–1900* (New York 1983); John Battye, "The Nine-Hour Pioneers: The Genesis of the Canadian-Labour Movement," LLT 4 (1979): 25–56; Steven Langon, *The Emergence of the Canadian Working Class Movement, 1845–1875* (Toronto, 1975); Craig Heron, "Labourism and the Canadian Working Class," LLT 13 (Spring 1984): 45–76.

21 Paul Craven, "The Law of Master and Servant in Mid-Nineteenth-Century Ontario," in David H. Flaherty, ed., *Essays in the History of Canadian Law* (Toronto 1981), I, 175–211, and "Workers' Conspiracies in Toronto, 1854–72: A Re-Examination," LLT 14 (Fall 1984): 49–72; Craven and Traves, "Dimensions of Paternalism"; Fingard, *Jack in Port*, 140–93; Kealey, *Toronto Workers*, 124–53; James C. Cameron and F.J.L. Young, *The Status of Trade Unions in Canada* (Kingston 1960), 24–9, and *Canada Investigates Industrialism*, ix–xxvii; Desmond Morton, "Taking on the Grand Trunk: The Locomotive Engineers Strike of 1876–7," LLT 2 (1977): 5–34, and "Aid to the Civil Power: The Canadian Militia in Support of Social Order, 1867–1914," CHR 51 (1970): 407–25.

22 L.A. Wood, *A History of Farmers' Movements in Canada* (Toronto 1975), 13–155; Russell Hann, *Farmers Confront Industrialism: Some Historical Perspectives on Ontario Agrarian Movements* (Toronto 1975).

23 Williams, *Not For Export*; Kenneth Buckley, *Capital Formation in Canada, 1896–1930* (Toronto 1955); Tom Naylor, *The History of Canadian Business, 1867–1914, Volume II: Industrial Development* (Toronto 1975); Joseph Smucker, *Industrialization in Canada* (Toronto 1980); T.W. Acheson, "The National Policy

and the Industrialization of the Maritimes," *Acadiensis*, 1 (Spring 1972): 3–28;
David Frank, "The Cape Breton Coal Industry and the Rise and Fall of the British
Empire Steel Corporation," *ibid.*, 7 (Autumn 1977): 3–34; James D. Frost, "The
'Nationalization' of the Bank of Nova Scotia, 1880–1910," ibid., 12, no. 1
(Autumn 1982): 3–38; Michael Bliss, *A Canadian Millionaire: The Life and
Business Times of Sir Joseph Flavelle, Bart., 1858–1939* (Toronto 1978); James
R. Struthers, *No Fault of Their Own: Unemployment and the Canadian Welfare
State, 1914–1941* (Toronto 1983).

24 Abram Ernest Epp, "Co-operation among Capitalists: The Canadian Merger
Movement, 1909–1913" (PH D dissertation, Johns Hopkins University 1973);
J.C. Weldon, "Consolidations in Canadian Industry, 1900–1948," in L.A.
Skeoch, ed., *Restrictive Trade Practices in Canada* (Toronto 1966); Tom Traves,
*The State and Enterprise: Canadian Manufacturers and the Federal Government,
1917–1931* (Toronto 1979), 73–100; Mira Wilkins, *The Emergence of Multi-
national Enterprise: American Business Abroad from the Colonial Era to 1914*
(Cambridge, Mass. 1970); Herbert Marshall et al., *Canadian-American Industry:
A Study in International Investment* (Toronto 1976).

25 Graham S. Lowe, "The Rise of Modern Management in Canada," *Canadian
Dimension* 14, no. 3 (December 1979): 32–8; Joseph A. Litterer, "Systematic
Management: The Search for Order and Integration," *Business History Review* 35
(1961): 461–76; Bryan D. Palmer, "Class, Conception, and Conflict: The Thrust
for Efficiency, Managerial Views of Labor, and the Working Class Rebellion,
1903–1922," RRPE 7 (1975): 31–49; Daniel Nelson, *Managers and Workers:
Origins of the New Factory System in the United States, 1880–1920* (Madison
1975); Alfred D. Chandler, Jr, *The Visible Hand: The Managerial Revolution in
American Business* (Cambridge, Mass. 1977).

26 Richard Edwards, *Contested Terrain: The Transformation of the Workplace in the
Twentieth Century* (New York 1979), 111–29; Craig Heron, "Working-Class
Hamilton, 1895–1930" (PH D dissertation, Dalhousie University 1981), 193–287;
Craig Heron and Robert Storey, "Work and Struggle in the Canadian Steel
Industry, 1900–1950," in this volume; Stephen Meyer III, *The Five-Dollar Day:
Labor Management and Social Control in the Ford Motor Company, 1908–1921*
(Albany 1981); David F. Noble, *America By Design: Science, Technology, and
the Rise of Corporate Capitalism* (New York 1977); David Albury and Joseph
Schwartz, *Partial Progress: The Politics of Science and Technology* (London
1982).

27 Palmer, "Class, Conception, and Conflict"; Nelson, *Managers and Workers*,
55–78; Craig Heron and Bryan D. Palmer, "Through the Prism of the Strike:
Industrial Conflict in Southern Ontario, 1901–14," CHR 58 (1977): 430–4; Heron,
"Crisis of the Craftsman"; Heron and Storey, "Work and Struggle."

28 Cross, "Shiners' War"; Bleasdale, "Class Conflict"; J.I. Cooper, "The Quebec
Ship Labourers' Benevolent Society," CHR 30 (1949): 336–43; Donald Avery,
"Dangerous Foreigners": European Immigrant Workers and Labour Radicalism

in Canada, 1896–1932 (Toronto 1979); Jorgen Dahlie and Tissa Fernando, eds, *Ethnicity, Power and Politics in Canada* (Toronto 1981); Edmund Bradwin, *The Bunkhouse Man* (Toronto 1972); Robert F. Harney, "Montreal's King of Italian Labour: A Case Study of Padronism," LLT 4 (1979): 57–84; N.F. Dreisziger et al., *Struggle and Hope: The Hungarian-Canadian Experience* (Toronto 1982); Harry Con et al., *From China to Canada: A History of the Chinese Communities in Canada* (Toronto 1982); Ward, *White Canada Forever.*

29 Graham Lowe, "Class, Job, and Gender in the Canadian Office," LLT 10 (Autumn 1982): 11–38, and "Mechanization, Feminization, and Managerial Control in the Early Twentieth-Century Canadian Office," in this volume; Margery W. Davies, *Woman's Place Is at the Typewriter: Office Work and Office Workers, 1870–1930* (Philadelphia 1982).

30 Heron, "Crisis of the Craftsman"; Kealey, "Work Control"; Wayne Roberts, "Artisans, Aristocrats, and Handymen: Politics and Unionism among Toronto Skilled Building Trades Workers, 1896–1914," LLT 1 (1976): 92–121. See also William Lazonick, "Industrial Relations and Technical Change: The Case of the Self-Acting Mule," CJE 3 (1979): 231–62; Jonathan Zeitlin, "Craft Control and the Division of Labour: Engineers and Compositors in Britain, 1890–1930," ibid., 263–74; Wayne Lewchuk, "The British Motor Vehicle Industry: The Roots of Decline, 1896–1982," in William Lazonick, ed., *The Decline of the British Economy* (forthcoming).

31 See Heron and Storey, "Work and Struggle," for a specific example of this process. Andrew L. Friedman has argued that managers actually encourage what he calls "responsible autonomy" on the job as part of their strategy of control; see *Industry and Labour: Class Struggle at Work and Monopoly Capitalism* (London 1977).

32 Heron and Storey, "Work and Struggle"; Heron, "Working-Class Hamilton"; Meyer, *Five-Dollar Day.*

33 Heron and Palmer, "Prism of the Strike"; Ian McKay, "Strikes in the Maritimes, 1901–1914," *Acadiensis* 13, no. 1 (Autumn 1983): 3–46, and "Workers' Control in Springhill"; Stuart Marshall Jamieson, *Times of Trouble: Labour Unrest and Industrial Conflict in Canada, 1900–66* (Ottawa 1968), 62–157; A. Ross McCormack, *Reformers, Rebels, and Revolutionaries: The Western Canadian Radical Movement, 1899–1919* (Toronto 1977); David J. Bercuson, *Fools and Wise Men: The Rise and Fall of the One Big Union* (Toronto 1978); Larry Peterson, "The One Big Union in International Perspective: Revolutionary Industrial Unionism, 1900–1925," LLT 7 (Spring 1981): 41–66; Paul MacEwan, *Miners and Steelworkers: Labour in Cape Breton* (Toronto 1976), 3–150; David Frank, "The Cape Breton Coal Miners, 1917–1926" (PH D dissertation, Dalhousie University 1979); Jacques Rouillard, *Les travailleurs du coton au Québec, 1900–1915* (Montréal 1974); Phillips, *No Power Greater*; Charles Allen Seager, "A Proletariat in Wild Rose Country: The Alberta Coal Miners, 1905–1945" (PH D dissertation, York University 1981); Heron, "Working-Class Hamilton."

34 Gregory S. Kealey, "1919: The Canadian Labour Revolt," LLT 13 (Spring 1984): 11–44; Heron, "Labourism"; David Jay Bercuson, *Confrontation at Winnipeg: Labour, Industrial Relations, and the General Strike* (Montreal 1974); Norman Penner, ed., *Winnipeg, 1919: The Strikers' Own History of the Winnipeg General Strike* (Toronto 1973); Nolan Reilly, "The General Strike in Amherst, Nova Scotia, 1919," *Acadiensis* 9, no. 2 (Spring 1980): 56–77; Frank, "Cape Breton Miners"; Seager, "Proletariat"; Brian F. Hogan, *Cobalt: Year of the Strike, 1919* (Cobalt, n.d.); Craig Heron and George de Zwaan, "Industrial Unionism in Eastern Ontario: Gananoque, 1918–21," *Ontario History* (forthcoming).

35 Jamieson, *Times of Trouble*, 192–213.

36 Ibid., 214–75; Irving Abella, *Nationalism, Communism, and Canadian Labour: The CIO, the Communist Party, and the Canadian Congress of Labour, 1935–1956* (Toronto 1973); S.D. Hanson, "Estavan 1931," in Irving Abella, ed., *On Strike: Six Key Labour Struggles in Canada, 1919–1949* (Toronto 1974), 33–78; Desmond Morton, "Aid to the Civil Power: The Stratford Strike of 1933," ibid., 79–92; Abella, "Oshawa 1937," ibid., 93–128; Evelyn Dumas, *The Bitter Thirties in Quebec* (Montreal 1975); Terry Copp, ed., *Industrial Unionism in Kitchener, 1937–47* (Elora 1976), and "The Rise of Industrial Unions in Montreal, 1935–45," *Relations industrielles/Industrial Relations* (hereafter RI/IR) 37 (1982): 843–75; Ralph Ellis, "The Unionization of a Mill Town: Cornwall in 1936," *The Register* 2, no. 1 (March 1981): 83–101; Gloria Montero, ed., *We Stood Together: First-Hand Accounts of Dramatic Events in Canada's Labour Past* (Toronto 1979), 1–68; Robert Storey, "Workers, Unions, and Steel: The Shaping of the Hamilton Working Class, 1935–1948" (PH D dissertation, University of Toronto 1981); John Manley, "Organizing the Unorganized: Communists and the Struggle for Industrial Unionism in the Canadian Automobile Industry, 1922–1936" (paper presented to the Canadian Historical Association 1981); Wayne Roberts, ed., *Organizing Westinghouse: Alf Ready's Story* (Hamilton 1980).

37 Storey, "Workers, Unions, and Steel"; Raymond Houlahan, "A History of Collective Bargaining in Local 200, UAW" (MA thesis, University of Windsor 1963); Roberts, *Organizing Westinghouse*, and *Baptism of a Union: Stelco Strike of 1946* (Hamilton 1981).

38 For evidence of sporadic women's militancy, see Frager, "No Proper Deal"; Joan Sangster, "The 1907 Bell Telephone Strike: Organizing Women Workers," LLT 3 (1978): 109–30; Wayne Roberts, *Honest Womanhood: Feminism, Femininity, and Class Consciousness among Toronto Working Woman, 1893 to 1914* (Toronto 1976); Star Rosenthal, "Union Maids: Organized Women Workers in Vancouver, 1900–1915," *BC Studies* 41 (Spring 1979): 36–55; Catherine McLeod, "Women in Production: The Toronto Dressmakers' Strike of 1931," in *Women at Work*, 309–30.

39 Veronica Strong-Boag, "The Girl of the New Day: Canadian Working Women of the 1920s," LLT 4 (1979): 131–64; Frager, "No Proper Deal"; Marie Campbell,

"Sexism in British Columbia Trade Unions, 1900–1920," in Barbara Latham and Cathy Kess, eds, *In Her Own Right: Selected Essays on Women's History in B.C.* (Victoria 1980), 167–86.

40 Veronica Strong-Boag, "Keeping House in God's Country: Canadian Women at Work in the Home," in this volume; Genevieve Leslie, "Domestic Service in Canada, 1880–1920," in *Women at Work*, 71–126; Susan Strasser, *Never Done: A History of American Housework* (New York 1982); Jane Synge, "Young Working Class Women in Early 20th Century Hamilton – Their Work and Family Lives," in A.H. Turritin, ed., *Proceedings of the Workshop Conference on Blue-Collar Workers and Their Communities* ... (Toronto 1976), 137–45; Gail Cuthbert Brandt, "'Weaving It Together': Life Cycle and the Industrial Experience of Female Cotton Workers in Quebec, 1910–1950," LLT 7 (1981): 113–26.

41 Michael J. Piva, "The Workmen's Compensation Movement in Ontario," *Ontario History* 67 (1975): 39–56; Veronica Strong-Boag, "Working Women and the State: The Case of Canada, 1889–1945," *Atlantis* 6, no. 2 (Spring 1981): 1–9; Linda S. Bohnen, "Women Workers in Ontario: A Socio-Legal History," *University of Toronto Faculty of Law Review* 31 (1973): 45–74; Heron and Palmer, "Prism of the Strike"; McKay, "Strikes in the Maritimes"; Don Macgillivray, "Military Aid to the Civil Power: The Cape Breton Experience in the 1920s," *Acadiensis* 3, no. 2 (1974): 45–64; Paul Craven, *"An Impartial Umpire": Industrial Relations and the Canadian State, 1900–1911* (Toronto 1980).

42 The classic American studies are Stanley B. Mathewson, *Restriction of Output among Unorganized Workers* (New York 1931); Donald Roy, "Banana Time: Job Satisfaction and Informal Interaction," *Human Organization* 18 (1958): 158–68, and "Quota Restriction and Goldbricking in a Machine Shop," *American Journal of Sociology* 57 (1952): 427–42.

43 Robert Storey, "Unionization versus Corporate Welfare: The 'Dofasco Way,'" LLT 12 (Autumn 1983): 7–42.

44 Jacques Rouillard, *Les syndicats nationaux au Québec de 1900 à 1930* (Québec 1979); Alfred Charpentier, *Cinquante ans d'action ouvrière* (Québec 1971); Heron, "Working-Class Hamilton," 490–584; Ernest R. Forbes, *The Maritime Rights Movement, 1919–1927: A Study in Canadian Regionalism* (Montreal 1979).

45 Paul Phillips and Stephen Watson, "From Mobilization to Continentalism: The Canadian Economy in the Post-Depression Period," in Cross and Kealey, eds, *Readings in Canadian Social History, Volume 5: Modern Canada, 1930–1980s* (Toronto 1984), 20–45; Wallace Clement, *Continental Corporate Power: Economic Linkages between Canada and the United States* (Toronto 1977); Patricia Marchak, *In Whose Interests: An Essay on Multinational Corporations in a Canadian Context* (Toronto 1979); Robert Bothwell and William Kilbourn, *C.D. Howe: A Biography* (Toronto 1979); Reginald Whitaker, *The Government Party: Organizing and Financing the Liberal Party of Canada, 1930–58* (Toronto 1977), 165–215; David Wolfe, "Economic Growth and Foreign Investment,"

Journal of Canadian Studies 13 (Spring 1978): 3–20; Barry Bluestone and Bennett Harrison, *The Deindustrialization of America: Plant Closings, Community Abandonment, and the Dismantling of Basic Industry* (New York 1982); Folker Frobel, Jurgen Heinrichs, and Otto Kreye, *The New International Division of Labour* (Cambridge, Mass. 1980).

46 Ian Radforth, "Logging Pulpwood in Northern Ontario," in this volume; Patricia Marchak, *Green Gold: The British Columbia Forest Industry* (Vancouver 1983); Wallace Clement, *Hardrock Mining: Industrial Relations and Technological Changes at INCO* (Toronto 1981); Rick Williams, "Inshore Fishermen, Unionization, and the Struggle against Underdevelopment Today," in Brym and Sacouman, *Underdevelopment and Social Movements*, 161–75.

47 David F. Noble, *Forces of Production: A Social History of Industrial Automation* (New York 1984); Sin Tze Ker, "Technological Change in the Canadian Iron and Steel Mills Industry, 1946–1969" (PH D thesis, University of Manitoba 1972); Zerker, *Rise and Fall*, 253–77; Elaine Bernard, *The Long Distance Feeling: A History of the Telecommunications Workers' Union* (Vancouver 1982), 152–72; Joe Davidson and John Deverell, *Joe Davidson* (Toronto 1978), 121–151; Rosemary Speirs, "Technological Change and the Railway Unions, 1945–1972" (PH D dissertation, University of Toronto 1974); John Foster, "On the Waterfront: Longshoring in Canada," in this volume.

48 Heather Menzies, *Computers on the Job: Surviving Canada's Microcomputer Revolution* (Toronto 1982).

49 Ibid., and Menzies, *Women and the Chip: Case Studies of the Effects of Informatics on Employment in Canada* (Toronto 1981); Bernard, *Long Distance Feeling*; Marchak, *Green Gold*; *The New Demeaning of Work* (Winnipeg 1984); Noble, *Forces of Production*; Philip Kraft, "The Industrialization of Computer Programming: From Programming to 'Software Production,'" in Andrew Zimbalist, ed., *Case Studies in the Labour Process* (New York 1979), 18–50; Evelyn Nakano Glenn and Roslyn L. Feldberg, "Proletarianizing Clerical Work: Technology and Organizational Control in the Office," ibid., 51–72.

50 Peter Dungan, "Mass Unemployment and Technological Change in the 1980s – What Are the Prospects?" *Labour Relations News*, September 1983.

51 Johnson, "Precapitalist Economic Formations"; Radforth, "Logging Pulpwood."

52 Freda Hawkins, *Canada and Immigration: Public Policy and Public Concern* (Montreal 1972); Grace M. Anderson and David Higgs, *A Future to Inherit: The Portuguese Communities of Canada* (Toronto 1976); Con et al., *From China to Canada*, 204–67; Makeda Silvera, *Silenced: Talks with Working Class West Indian Women about Their Lives and Struggles as Domestic Workers in Canada* (Toronto 1983).

53 Paul Axelrod, "Higher Education, Utilitarianism, and the Acquisitive Society: Canada, 1930–1980," in Cross and Kealey, *Modern Canada*, 179–205; Serge Mallet, *Essays on the New Working Class* (St Louis 1975); Charles Derber, ed., *Professionals as Workers: Mental Labour in Advanced Capitalism* (Boston 1982).

54 Ruth Roach Pierson, *Canadian Women and the Second World War* (Ottawa 1983);
Pat and Hugh Armstrong, *The Double Ghetto: Canadian Women and Their
Segregated Work* (Toronto 1978), and *A Working Majority: What Women Must Do
for Pay* (Ottawa 1983); Pat Armstrong, *Labour Pains: Women's Work in Crisis*
(Toronto 1984); Patricia Connelly, *Last Hired, First Fired: Women and the
Canadian Work Force* (Toronto 1978); Paul and Erin Phillips, *Women and Work:
Inequality in the Labour Market* (Toronto 1983); Meg Luxton, *More Than a
Labour of Love: Three Generations of Women's Work in the Home* (Toronto 1980);
Julie White, *Women and Part-Time Work* (Ottawa 1983).

55 Jamieson, *Times of Trouble*, 276–94; Storey, "Workers, Unions, and Steel";
Laurel Sefton McDowell, *"Remember Kirkland Lake": The Gold Miners' Strike
of 1941–42* (Toronto 1983), and "The Formation of the Canadian Industrial
Relations System during World War Two," LLT 3 (1978): 175–96, and "The 1943
Steel Strike against Wartime Wage Controls," ibid., 10 (Autumn 1982): 65–85;
Montero, *We Stood Together*, 47–112; Roberts, *Organizing Westinghouse*.

56 J.L. Granatstein, *Canada's War: The Politics of the Mackenzie King Government,
1939–1945* (Toronto 1975), 249–93; Whitaker, *Government Party*, 132–64;
Dennis Guest, *The Emergence of Social Security in Canada* (Vancouver 1980),
101–38; Carl Cuneo, "State, Class, and Reserve Labour: The Case of the 1941
Canadian Unemployment Insurance Act," CRSA 16 (1979): 47–70; McDowell,
"Formation"; David A. Wolfe, "The Rise and Demise of the Keynesian Era in
Canada: Economic Policy, 1930–1982," in Cross and Kealey, *Modern Canada*,
46–78; Jamieson, *Times of Trouble*, 295–342; Storey, "Workers, Unions, and
Steel"; David Moulton, "Windsor 1945," in Abella, *On Strike*, 129–62; Daniel
Coates, "Organized Labour and Politics in Canada: The Development of a
National Labour Code" (PH D thesis, Cornell University 1973).

57 Heron and Storey, "Work and Struggle"; Don Wells, "Autoworkers on the Firing
Line," in this volume; David Brody, *Workers in Industrial America: Essays on the
Twentieth Century Struggle* (New York 1980), 173–214; George Lipsitz, *Class
and Culture in Cold War America: "A Rainbow at Midnight"* (South Hadley,
Mass. 1982); Leo Panitch and Donald Swartz, "Towards Permanent Excep-
tionalism: Coercion and Consent in Canadian Industrial Relations," LLT 13 (Spring
1984): 133–57; Seymour Faber, "Rank and File Insurgency: The State and the
Unions," *Our Generation* 11, no. 4 (Winter 1976): 38–43.

58 Abella, *Nationalism, Communism, and Canadian Labour*, 66–167; Jerry Lembke,
"The International Woodworkers of America in B.C., 1942–1951," LLT 6
(Autumn 1980): 113–48; John Stanton, *Life and Death of the Canadian Seamen's
Union, 1936–1949* (Toronto 1978); Merrily Weisbord, *The Strangest Dream*
(Toronto 1983).

59 Jamieson, *Times of Trouble*, 344–94. There were, nonetheless, some extremely
bitter strikes in the 1950s; see, for example, Guy Bélanger, "La grève de
Murdochville (1957)," LLT 8–9 (Autumn 1981–Spring 1982): 103–36.

60 Jamieson, *Times of Trouble*, 395–451; Myrna Kostash, *Long Way From Home:*

The Story of the Sixties Generation in Canada (Toronto 1980); J.H.G. Crispo and H.W. Arthurs, "Industrial Unrest in Canada: A Diagnosis of Recent Experience," RI/IR 23 (1968): 237–64; Brody, *Workers in Industrial America*, 204–8; Wells, "Autoworkers"; Walter Johnson, ed., *Working in Canada* (Montreal 1975); and *The Trade Unions and the State* (Montreal 1978); J.A. Frank, "The 'Ingredients' in Violent Labour Conflicts: Patterns in Four Case Studies," LLT 12 (Autumn 1983): 87–112; E.G. Fisher, "Strike Activity and Wildcat Strikes in British Columbia, 1945–1975," RI/IR 37 (1982): 284–301; see also the several studies done for the Task Force on Labour Relations, especially Maxwell Flood, *Wildcat Strike in Lake City* (Ottawa 1968). On the NDP, see Desmond Morton, *NDP: The Dream of Power* (Toronto 1974).

61 Allen Ponak, "Public Sector Collective Bargaining," in John Anderson and Morley Gunderson, eds, *Union-Management Relations in Canada* (Don Mills 1982), 343–78; Davidson and Deverell, *Joe Davidson*; Anthony Thompson, "The Nova Scotia Civil Service Association, 1956–1967," *Acadiensis* 12, no. 2 (Spring 1983): 81–105; Montero, *We Stood Together*, 183–204; Bruce McLean, *"A Union amongst Government Employees": A History of the B.C. Government Employees' Union, 1919–1979* (Vancouver 1979); Joe Rose, "Growth Patterns of Public Sector Unions," in Gene Swimmer and Mark Thompson, eds, *Public Sector Labour Relations – Will It Survive the '80s?* (Ottawa 1983).

62 Mark Thompson, "Collective Bargaining by Professionals," in Anderson and Gunderson, *Union-Management Relations*, 379–97; Derber, *Professionals as Workers*.

63 Julie White, *Women and Unions* (Ottawa 1980); Briskin and Yantz, *Union Sisters*; Heather Jon Maroney, "Feminism at Work," *New Left Review* 141 (September–October 1983): 51–71.

64 Bradley Dow, "The Labour Movement and Trade Unionism: Summary Outline," in W.D. Wood and Pradeep Kumar, eds, *The Current Industrial Relations Scene in Canada, 1982* (Kingston 1982), 201–65.

65 Carla Lipsig-Mummé, "Quebec Unions and the State: Conflict and Dependence," *Studies in Political Economy* 3 (Spring 1980): 119–46; Jean Boivin, "Labour Relations in Quebec," in Anderson and Gunderson, *Union-Management Relations*, 422–56.

66 The literature on segmented labour markets is voluminous. For a recent statement, see Gordon et al., *Segmented Work, Divided Workers*. For a critique of this perspective, see Jill Rubery, "Structured Labour Markets, Worker Organization, and Low Pay," CJE 2 (1978): 17–36.

67 Panitch and Swartz, "Towards Permanent Exceptionalism"; John Deverell, "The Ontario Hospital Dispute, 1980–81," SPE 9 (Fall 1982): 179–90; Wolfe, "Rise and Demise"; Allan M. Maslove and Gene Swimmer, *Wage Controls in Canada, 1975–78: A Study in Public Decision Making* (Montreal 1980); Peter Warrian and David Wolfe, *Trade Unions and Inflation* (Ottawa 1982).

68 Vivienne Walters, "Occupational Health and Safety Legislation in Ontario: An

Analysis of Its Origins and Content," CRSA 21 (1984): 413–34; Donald Swartz, "New Forms of Worker Participation: A Critique of Quality of Working Life," SPE 5 (Spring 1981): 55–78; Charles Hechsher, "Worker Participation and Management Control," *Journal of Social Reconstruction* 1, no. 1 (1980): 77–102; Don Wells, *Squeeze Play: Quality of Working Life Programmes and the Attack on Labour* (Ottawa 1984); *Globe and Mail*, 20 October 1983, 32; 10 December 1983, 22; 28 December 1983, 8; 3 January 1984, 37; 27 January 1984, 1; 17 January 1984, 4; 16 February 1984, 10; 6 March 1984, 8; 24 March 1984, 9.

69 On the current industrial situation, see the special issue of SPE 11 (Summer 1983).

70 Charles E. Reasons, Lois L. Ross, and Craig Paterson, *Assault on the Worker: Occupational Health and Safety in Canada* (Toronto 1981).

71 The volume of new theoretical literature on the labour process is overwhelming. Some of the more insightful and influential books include Barrett, *Women's Oppression Today*; Michael Burawoy, *Manufacturing Consent: Changes in the Labor Process under Monopoly Capitalism* (Chicago 1979); Clawson, *Bureaucracy and the Labor Process*; Edwards, *Contested Terrain*; Friedman, *Industry and Labour*; Gordon et al., *Segmented Work, Divided Workers*; Craig R. Littler, *The Development of the Labour Process in Capitalist Societies* (London 1982); Harry Braverman, *Labor and Monopoly Capital: The Degradation of Work in the Twentieth Century* (New York 1974).

72 Luxton, *More Than a Labour of Love*, and "From Ladies Auxiliaries to Wives' Committees," in Briskin and Yantz, *Union Sisters*, 333–47; Sarah Eisenstein, *Give Us Bread but Give Us Roses: Working Women's Consciousness in the United States, 1890 to the First World War* (London 1983).

73 Bernard Elbaum and Frank Wilkinson, "Industrial Relations and Uneven Development: A Comparative Study of the American and British Steel Industries," CJE 3 (1979): 275–303.

74 Braverman, *Labor and Monopoly Capital*.

75 Mercedes Steedman, "Skill and Gender in the Canadian Clothing Industry, 1890–1940," in this volume; Heron, "Crisis of the Craftsman"; Craven and Traves, "Dimensions of Paternalism"; Kealey, "Work Control"; Radforth, "Logging Pulpwood"; Clement, *Hardrock Mining*; Roberts, "Artisans, Aristocrats, and Handymen."

76 See, for example, Ian McKay, "Class Struggle and Mercantile Capitalism: Craftsmen and Labourers on the Halifax Waterfront, 1850–1902," in Rosemary Ommer and Gerald Panting, eds, *Working Men Who Got Wet* (St John's 1980), 289–319.

77 Cockburn, *Brothers*, 112–15; David Lee, "Beyond Deskilling: Skill, Craft and Class," in Stephen Wood, ed., *The Degradation of Work?: Skill, Deskilling and the Labor Process* (London 1982), 146–62.

78 Ken Kusterer, *Know-How on the Job: The Important Working Knowledge of "Unskilled Workers"* (Boulder 1978); Charles More, "Skill and the Survival of Apprenticeship," in Wood, *Degradation of Work?*, 109–21.

79 Barrett, *Women's Oppression Today*, 152–86; Anne Phillips and Barbara Taylor, "Sex and Skill: Notes Towards a Feminist Economics," *Feminist Review* 6 (1980): 79–88; Veronica Beechey, "The Sexual Division of Labour and the Labour Process: A Critical Assessment of Braverman," in Wood, *Degradation of Work?*, 54–73.

80 Radforth, "Logging Pulpwood."

81 Littler, *Development of the Labour Process*, 9; see also H.A. Turner, *Trade Union Growth, Structure and Policy* (London 1962).

82 Palmer, *Culture in Conflict*, 97–122.

83 Reginald Whitaker, "Scientific Management Theory as Political Ideology," SPE 2 (Autumn 1979): 75–108; Samuel Haber, *Efficiency and Uplift; Scientific Management in the Progressive Era, 1890–1920* (Chicago 1964). Richard Sennett and Jonathan Cobb discovered workers' lack of self-esteem as manual labourers in the 1960s; see *The Hidden Injuries of Class* (New York 1973).

84 See, in particular, Burawoy, *Manufacturing Consent*.

85 James Rinehart, "Contradictions of Work-Related Attitudes and Behaviour: An Interpretation," CRSA 15 (1978): 11, Michael Mann, "The Social Cohesion of Liberal Democracy," *American Sociological Review* 35 (1970): 423–39; Martin Glaberman, *Wartime Strikes: The Struggle Against the No-Strike Pledge in the U.A.W.* (Detroit 1980).

86 Peter Cressey and John MacInnes, "Voting for Ford: Industrial Democracy and Control of Labour," *Capital and Class* 11 (1980): 5–33.

87 See Richard Hyman, *Industrial Relations: A Marxist Introduction* (London 1975); Leo Panitch, "The Role and Nature of the Canadian State," in Panitch, ed., *The Canadian State: Political Economy and Political Power* (Toronto 1977), 3–27; Paul Stevenson, "The State in English Canada: The Political Economy of Production and Reproduction," *Socialist Studies/Etudes socialistes* 1 (1983): 88–128; Michael Burawoy, "Between the Labour Process and the State: The Changing Face of Factory Regimes under Advanced Capitalism," *American Sociological Review* 48 (1983): 587–605; Bob Jessop, *The Capitalist State* (Oxford 1982).

PAUL CRAVEN AND TOM TRAVES

Dimensions of Paternalism: Discipline and Culture in Canadian Railway Operations in the 1850s

Canada's economic historians have said a good deal about the rapid expansion of the colony's railway system in the 1850s – the mere 66 miles of track at the beginning of the decade grew to more than 2,000 by its close – but they have virtually ignored the corresponding growth of the railway workforce.[1] Yet this was the decade in which the railways became the country's first large-scale integrated industry and the giants among them became the country's greatest employers of labour. By the middle of the decade, the Grand Trunk, with its 2,600 workers on trains, in yards, shops, offices, warehouses and stations, and along the line of railway, was Canada's largest employer with a monthly payroll of $110,000. In second place was the Great Western (GWR), with a payroll about one-quarter the size of the Grand Trunk's (GTR).[2]

Railway work comprised many types of jobs. Train crews consisted of enginemen, firemen, conductors, and brakemen, with one or more baggage-men as well in the passenger service.[3] Cleaners, pumpers, woodmen, yardmen, and switchmen were involved in servicing and fuelling the locomotive, making up the train, and switching onto sidings to permit two-way traffic on the single-track railways of the time. Gangs of labourers worked under the direction of the engineering staff to maintain the track and roadbed and to clear ice and snow in the wintertime. Labour was required at stations for baggage and freight handling under the supervision of the stationmaster, who sold tickets, made out way-bills and receipts, and operated the telegraph at the smaller depots; at the bigger ones he would be assisted by clerks and operators. Passengers and employees alike passed under the watchful eye of the railway police force, whose members worked undercover on occasion to trip up defaulting agents or dishonest conductors.

Company headquarters boasted large central office staffs organized in various departments, overseeing operations and maintaining accounts. By 1861, the Grand Trunk's 223 locomotives travelled a third of a million miles each month; the smaller Great Western used 94 locomotives to travel 1.8 million miles in 1861, transporting half a million tons of freight and more than half a million passengers. This required a large amount of clerical labour, not only because of the sheer volume of business that had to be recorded, checked, and cross-referenced, but also because of the primitive techniques available for the purpose.[4]

But the railway companies were more than high-volume transportation companies. They also operated the country's largest and most complex manufacturing facilities. By 1857, the Grand Trunk and the Great Western, along with some of the smaller railways, possessed the capacity to build as well as repair their thousands of cars. By the end of the decade, they had upgraded their engine-repair facilities so that they could build locomotives as well. The same shops produced much of the hardware and machinery required for other aspects of the railway's operations: castings for bridges, say, or machinery for grain elevators. A large and diversely skilled work force was necessary for the shops. Thus by 1857, the Great Western's locomotive and car shops at Hamilton, Ontario, employed about 600 tradesmen and labourers, along with about 125 more in London, Ontario.[5]

Managerial control of the work process in this new industry was, from the start, a prime objective of the investors and officers who directed the companies. Complex organizational structures were established almost from the outset of rail operations. While these were intended in the first instance to co-ordinate multifarious operations and help control costs, they inevitably involved the institution of fairly sophisticated supervisory techniques. The general principles underlying railway organization included a careful division of responsibilities and the distribution of authority along with complex reporting procedures and swift discipline for all derelictions of duty.[6] Railway companies required much of their workers by way of loyalty, obedience, and care. Generally speaking, discipline – the habituation of the worker to the new mode of production – is a pervasive problem of industrialization. But for at least three related reasons, the problem of discipline assumed a special urgency on the railways.

First was safety, an anxious concern not only because of the inexperience or recklessness of workers, but also because of the inadequacies of the companies' equipment. Accidents caused injuries, deaths, lawsuits, and unplanned capital expenditure, so the railway companies, as well as the government, were keen to reduce their frequency. Second was the special significance of the clock in railway operations, where effective scheduling was necessary not only to avoid accidents but to meet the competition of other lines, make the necessary connections in a proliferating network of traffic and timetable agreements, and reduce the impact of heavy, fixed expenses by operating the company's equipment at optimal levels of efficiency. Finally, the problem of discipline was exacerbated by the spatial dispersion of the work force and by the fact that many of those whose work it was most crucial to regulate closely were beyond the reach of direct supervision.

Structural factors and self-conscious managerial policies conditioned the railway companies' attempts to regulate and discipline their employees. At its most immediate and overt level, discipline amounted to the enforcement of company rules, backed up by the authority of the state. But punitive measures must be placed in the broader context of a second level of discipline inherent in the conditions of working life – job hierarchies, pay structures, opportunities for advancement – that played their part in regulating workers' behaviour, and on labour-market conditions that placed structural limits on managerial autocracy as well. Finally a third, still broader, context of discipline requires discussion: the emergent culture of the railways' skilled workers, who reacted to managerial paternalism with a complex blend of deference and resistance.

PUNITIVE DISCIPLINE

The driver is, in fact, while his train is in motion, the sole, and almost the irresponsible Arbiter of the fate of all those entrusted to his care. It is most important ... to teach this class of men, that they cannot always elude responsibility and punishment.[7]

The most explicit manifestations of manage ment's effort to discipline the work force were the elaborate rule books that employees were required to carry with them at all times, on pain of a fine to be deducted from their wages. These rules were something more than the mere domestic regulations of private companies: they could be enforced judicially by the state. By their private acts of incorporation (and, after 1851, by the Railway Clauses Consolidation Act[8]), railway companies, like other corporations, were empowered to make regulations for the appointment and direction of their employees. Unlike most other corporations, however, they could look to the public courts to have these rules enforced. For example, the Great Western's revised Act of 1853 provided that fines levied by the company in accordance with its by-laws could be collected, "upon proof of the offence," by process before a justice of the peace, with the power to seize and sell property, or, failing sufficient goods to pay the penalty and expenses, by imprisonment not exceeding one month.[9] The Act for the Punishment of the Officers and Servants of Railway Companies, passed in 1856 following the report of a legislative inquiry into Great Western accidents, empowered magistrates to fine employees up to $100, and to imprison them for up to five years if, by their breach of company rules, they had put persons or property at risk. Otherwise, they could be fined one month's pay by the court, and the employer could dock a second month's pay.[10]

Indeed, not satisfied with these methods of publicly enforcing private laws, the legislature also supplied rules and regulations of its own making. The Railway Clauses Consolidation Act required, among other things, that railway servants wear badges indicating their office, made it a misdemeanour for conductors or enginemen to be drunk on duty, and provided penalties for conductors who permitted freight cars to be coupled in rear of passenger coaches, and for enginemen who failed to ring a bell or sound a whistle at level crossings.[11] The rule books themselves varied in length, from the Montreal & Champlain Railroad's two printed columns to the forty-four-page version published by the Great Western in 1854; but whatever the peculiarities of procedures on the various roads, they all prescribed much the same set of general regulations. The Grand Trunk's version is typical:

Each person is to devote himself exclusively to the Company's service, attending during the regulated hours of the day and residing wherever he may be required.

He is to obey promptly all instructions he may receive from persons placed in authority over him and conform to all regulations of the Company.

He will be liable to criminal punishment for disobediences or negligence of an order, and dismissal for misconduct, incompetency, using improper language, cursing or swearing while on duty.

He is not on any occasion to receive a fee or reward from any person without the sanction of the Company.

No instance of intoxication will be overlooked; and besides dismissal, the offender shall be deemed guilty of a misdemeanor.

Any case of rudeness or incivility to passengers will meet with instant dismissal.

Every person must appear on duty clean and neat.

No person is allowed under any circumstances to absent himself from duty, without the permission of his superior officer, except in case of illness, and then notice is to be immediately sent to his immediate superior officer.

No person is to quit the Company's service without fourteen days previous notice; and in case he leaves without such notice, all pay then due will be forfeited.

The Company reserves the right to deduct from the pay such sums as may be awarded for neglect of duty as fines and for rent due to the Company.

Should any person think himself aggrieved he may memorialize the Board, but the memorial must be sent through the head of his department.[12]

These general rules were followed by descriptions of signals and other operating features of the line, and then by detailed regulations for different groups of workers. In 1854, for example, the Great Western listed 38 rules for enginemen, 22 for conductors, 27 for track-repair crews, 20 for station-masters, and shorter codes for baggagemen, brakemen, porters, gravel-train conductors, drawbridge tenders, switchmen, and signalmen. Clerks were covered by a separate code in 1854, and telegraph operators got a rule book of their own in 1857.[13]

Of course, it is one thing to publish rules, and quite another to enforce them. There is some evidence that rules were not always routinely applied.

Punishment seemed, at least on occasion, to vary less with the responsibility of the transgressor than with the difficulty of replacing him were he to be dismissed. In one instance, when an accident was blamed on the combined negligence of a conductor, a stationmaster and a porter, the conductor was suspended for ten days, the stationmaster fined a week's pay, and the porter fired. "The punishments and penalties employed on a railroad should, as for the discipline of all other large bodies of men, be clearly defined and invariable," the commissioners on GWR accidents urged. "As the matter now stands, they are arbitrary, uncertain, partial and ineffective. The man who is suspended for a fortnight or mulcted of a week's pay, may, if he is a favourite at head quarters, have all his arrears made good at the end of the month. The dismissed man is the only man who is really punished."[14]

However unevenly, though, discipline *was* enforced. Intoxication or negligence resulting in accidents usually led to dismissal, even in the face of petitions for mercy signed by fellow workers or local residents.[15] Dismissal was also meted out for "repeated absence and other irregularities," and, in another instance, for "grossly offensive language ... addressed to the Vice President."[16] The threat of dismissal was also employed frequently, as when the Great Western's Finance Committee warned a clerk that it "would insist at all times on obedience to its orders, unless the parties disobeying were prepared to back up their disobedience ... by the resignation of their situation."[17] Nor were the railway companies reluctant to go to the public authorities to have their rules enforced. To take a single example among several to be found in the police-court columns of local newspapers, the Great Western brought a complaint against the engineman on one of its gravel trains for disobeying orders and running his locomotive on the main line when a freight train was due. The magistrates sentenced him to pay a £4 fine or spend a month in jail.[18]

But using the courts to enforce discipline was not without its difficulties. Jurors were often unwilling to convict workers, who may have been their neighbours, and they exhibited an unfortunate tendency to blame the company itself when accidents could be traced to defective equipment. Great Western managing director Brydges complained to the accident commission about what transpired when he laid manslaughter charges against a section-gang foreman to whose alleged carelessness and disobedience an accident had been attributed: "He was tried and acquitted [by the jury] in the face of a very strong charge against him by Chief Justice Robinson." The commissioners subsequently recommended that "all cases affecting such Companies ... should be removed to the jurisdiction of tribunals remote from the operation of local or personal influences."[19] But perhaps the greatest difficulty in prosecuting serious charges was simply laying hands on the miscreants. Switchmen in particular learned early to head for the hills – or the United States – whenever anything untoward happened in their bailiwicks.[20] In at least one such case, the Great Western offered a thousand-dollar reward for the apprehension of a conductor who had taken flight following a serious accident. The directors' zeal may have been especially aroused, though, by the fact that warrants had been sworn against each of them charging personal criminal responsibility for the accident.[21]

Needless to say, lesser penalties than dismissal and the laying of criminal charges were commonplace. The Great Western's outside locomotive paysheets show, for example, that three of the company's forty-eight enginemen were stopped fines ranging from 10s. to 12s. 6d. ($2–2.50) in October 1855.[22] The rule books made extensive provisions for the levying of fines. A Great Western engineman could lose a day's pay for failing to arrive at work at least one hour before his starting time, was subject to a "heavy" fine or dismissal for permitting unauthorized persons to ride on the engine, and could be docked one dollar for "getting off his Engine when alone to hold the Switches." Besides these strictures, peculiar to his occupation, he was also subject to the general rule that punishment could be expected for disobedience, neglect of duties, incompetence, negligence, misconduct, intoxication, swearing, smoking, incivility, rudeness, absence, and failure to keep a copy of the timetable and the rule book on his person.[23]

HIERARCHY AND MOBILITY

It would be a mistake to conclude that such overt instruments of discipline as rules and punishments were the only, or even the most important, mechanisms for optimizing the loyalty, obedience, and care of the railway work force. Disciplinary consequences could also flow from the conditions of railway employment itself. Railway workers were relatively well paid by mid-nineteenth-century standards. More important, theirs were steady, year-round jobs in what was very much a seasonal economy. While skilled railway workers in the shops and running trades were more likely to keep their jobs in periods of declining revenues or seasonal slumps in traffic than less-skilled labourers in station service and maintenance of way, railway workers in general enjoyed substantially greater regularity of employment than workers with similar levels of skill in the larger economy.[24] Some of the dimensions of and reasons for this distinction will be explored in the next section; here it is enough to note that for many railway workers the prospect of regular employment must have supplied a powerful incentive to good behaviour.

Indeed, many of the conditions of railway employment could be seen in a double light, as meeting some impersonal objective need, and as contributing toward employee discipline. This was true, for example, of company housing, for as a Great Western foreman put it, workers "should be provided with comfortable dwellings so as to keep a man near his work, and to make him feel that he has something to lose if he does wrong."[25] Railway managers' efforts to promote a sense of corporate identification included the provision of uniforms and the promotion or support of such early industrial welfare initiatives as insurance plans and company social gatherings. But the disciplinary core of the railways' paternalistic labour practices was the detailed reproduction of job hierarchies and the promise of career mobility. Workers were expected to be loyal, not merely to avoid discipline, or to keep good jobs, or even to show themselves deserving of promotion to better ones. Workers were expected to be loyal because it was in the nature of the hierarchical relations they and their employers took for granted; and workers could expect to be rewarded for their loyalty for the same reason.

In fact, there was not a single job hierarchy on the railways, but several. One reasonable indicator of a job's relative ranking is pay. While really adequate longitudinal data are lacking, good information on particular groups of workers at various moments in the decade is available. It points up the great diversity of railway work and the coexistence of various pay structures: piecework, trip rates, day rates, and weekly, monthly, and yearly salaries. In terms of pay at least, this diversity is reducible to a series of distinct hierarchies existing roughly in parallel, representing occupational grades through which mobility occurred. The pay structure shows railway work to have been organized as a series of discrete ladders, each with a relatively small number of rungs. In the minds of those involved, however, the ranking scheme may have been far more finely detailed, so that the number of rungs increased manyfold: was it a step up to go from cleaning a freight locomotive to a passenger engine, even with no change in pay? Whose heart sank and whose spirits rose when, in December 1857, the Great Western moved agent Shaw from Waterdown to Wellington Square, and agent Parsons from Wellington Square to Waterdown? Whatever the specific answers to these questions might be, there seems little doubt that railway workers possessed an elaborate conceptual map of job strata that is only crudely represented in the pay figures.

There is a rich source of information about the Great Western shopcrafts in a series of manuscript paysheets covering most of 1854 and 1855, and comparable data for the Grand Trunk shops in 1859.[26] These are summarized in table 1. With the exception of some of the Great Western bolt makers, who were on piecework, all the shop workers were paid by the day. Two features of the Great Western paysheets suggest that the organization of work more closely resembled the industrial than the artisanal model. First, the car-shop work force included a large and undifferentiated group of workers, the car builders, who accounted for almost half the total employment in the shop. While their pay varied, more than half received a single rate, $1.75 a day. Second, the range of pay *within* occupational groups may indicate something about the organization of work. In most categories of employment, the

TABLE 1

Shopcrafts and Rates of Pay (Halifax cy. equivalent)

	G.W.R. Hamilton Car Shops, Jan. 1855				G.W.R. Hamilton Loco Shops, Mar. 1855			
	No.	High	Low	Mean	No.	High	Low	Mean
Belt maker					1			1.25
Blacksmith (or "Smith")	7	2.00	1.50	1.79	10	2.25	1.50	1.88
Blacksmith App/Asst	12	1.13	1.00	1.07				
Boiler maker					9	2.73	1.62	2.08
Boiler maker Asst					12	1.50	.38	.85
Bolt maker	4	(3 on piecework)		1.32				
Brass founder								
Brass turner					1			1.60
Car builder	59	2.13	.60	1.57				
Car builder's lad	1			.33				
Car greaser								
Car inspector								
Car repairer								
Carpenter					8	2.00	1.60	1.74
Carter					1			2.25
Copper smith					2	2.25	2.00	2.13
Copper smith Asst					2	.85	.50	.68
Examiner	10	2.00	.70	1.11				
Fitter	4	1.25	1.13	1.22	29	2.25	1.65	1.89
Fitter Asst					10	1.50	.60	1.14
Glazier								
Hammerman					16	1.25	1.00	1.14
Iron founder								
Iron founder App/Asst								
Labourer	16	1.50	1.00	1.13	12	1.25	1.00	1.07
Labourer (stores)	13	1.25	.50	.98				
Machine man					9	2.00	.50	1.15
Machine man's lad					1			.50
Machinist	3	2.00	1.75	1.92				
Mason					1			1.75
Millwright					1			2.25
Moulder					1			2.00
Moulder Asst					2	1.00	.50	.75
Oiler	1			1.10				
Painter					3	1.50	1.00	1.23
Patternmaker	2			2.25	2			2.00
Petty stores (keeper)					1			1.10
Planer	2			1.25				
Pool keeper					1			1.10
Pressman								
Sawyer	1			1.50				
Springmaker								
Stationary engineman					1			1.20
Striker								
Tinsmith								
Tinsmith Asst					1			1.00
Turner	8	1.13	.50	.69	8	2.25	1.00	1.97
Upholsterer								
Watchman	2	1.15	1.00	1.08	1			1.15
Total:	144				146			

[1]Shopcrafts only.
[2]These figures, reported for comparison purposes by the Grand Trunk, seem to include the Great Western's locomotive shopcrafts only, and not the car-shop workers.

G.T.R. Loco Dept, Oct. 1859[1]				G.W.R. 1859 (G.T.R. figures)[2]		
No.	High	Low	Mean	No.	Mean	
						Belt maker
53	2.22	1.00	1.67	20	1.90	Blacksmith (or "Smith")
						Blacksmith App/Asst
12	1.90	1.20	1.62	13	1.95	Boiler maker
13	1.15	.40	.84	17	1.07	Boiler maker Asst
						Bolt maker
4	2.00	1.00	1.40			Brass founder
						Brass turner
						Car builder
						Car builder's lad
24	1.38	.50	.93			Car greaser
6	1.75	1.20	1.46			Car inspector
65	1.75	1.00	1.27			Car repairer
94	1.90	.35	1.20	10	1.27	Carpenter
						Carter
5	2.00	1.25	1.71	4	1.95	Copper smith
6	1.15	.80	.89			Copper smith Asst
						Examiner
82	2.15	.75	1.66	75	1.69	Fitter
33	1.25	.30	.67	27	1.03	Fitter Asst
1			1.80			Glazier
						Hammerman
2	1.80	1.50	1.65	1	2.00	Iron founder
3	1.00	.40	.80			Iron founder App/Asst
59	1.30	.50	.95	23	1.11	Labourer
						Labourer (stores)
29	1.70	.35	1.01	6	1.26	Machine man
						Machine man's lad
						Machinist
						Mason
						Millwright
						Moulder
						Moulder Asst
						Oiler
34	1.75	.40	1.31	4	1.44	Painter
4	2.00	.60	1.76	3	2.25	Patternmaker
						Petty stores (keeper)
						Planer
						Pool keeper
4	1.50	1.00	1.12			Pressman
4	1.35	1.00	1.09			Sawyer
5	1.80	1.25	1.59			Springmaker
9	1.50	.70	1.28			Stationary engineman
72	1.38	.40	1.01	29	1.22	Striker
2	1.60	1.40	1.50	3	1.45	Tinsmith
2	1.00	.80	.90			Tinsmith Asst
26	1.90	1.10	1.63	14	1.78	Turner
2	1.30	1.20	1.25			Upholsterer
29	1.40	.90	1.09			Watchman
684				249		Total:

majority of workers received similar rates of pay, with one or two being paid at noticeably higher rates, and perhaps a few at significantly lower ones. This seems to suggest organization on a "lead hand" basis, as much in the traditional crafts (blacksmiths, for example) as in the relatively unskilled occupations (examiner, labourer). Nonetheless, these data quite clearly indicate the existence of a hierarchy of craft in the shops, and the insertion of new occupations into the pay structure.

Similar information is available for the Great Western's "outside loco-motive" work force, comprising enginemen, firemen, engine turners (hostlers), and labourers engaged to clean locomotives, cut and store wood, and pump water. With some minor exceptions, outside labourers received $1 a day in 1854–5. A few enginemen were paid monthly ($50–$60), but the majority were paid by a combination of trip and day rates. In June 1854, enginemen received $2.25 or $2.50 per trip (amounting to a day's work), and 33 or 38 cents for every additional hour they were detained on the line. Their standard day rate for work in the engine sheds was $2. Firemen received half the enginemen's rate, but without the detention allowance: a few were paid by the month at $30. Firemen could consider themselves enginemen in training, and when they were called upon to drive, they received the engineman's trip rate. Both groups were reimbursed for the cost of lodgings. Finally, engine turners were paid by the month, $45 at Hamilton and $40 at the other depots. The railway's managing director estimated that enginemen averaged $70 "more or less" a month, and firemen $30–$40, but the paysheet evidence suggests this estimate was high.[27]

Conductors, baggagemen, and brakemen, employed by the railways' traffic departments, constituted a separate occupational hierarchy in their own right. In December 1856, the Grand Trunk employed 49 conductors at monthly salaries ranging between $40 and $60, 20 baggagemen at $30–35, and 78 brakemen at $30–32. The Great Western paid similar rates.[28] The traffic departments also included employees at stations. In December 1856, the Grand Trunk's 112 station and freight agents received yearly salaries ranging from £25 to £350. The Great Western's 39 stationmasters made between £90 and £200. Salaries varied with the importance of the station; the men in charge of the terminal depots earned the most. Agents at the larger stations were assisted by additional clerical workers, who possessed numerous special titles – first clerk, ticket clerk, lost-baggage clerk, freight clerk – and who in some cases supplemented their incomes by serving as telegraph operators as well. Clerks made between £50 and £150, so that their earnings were in many cases greater than those of agents at the smaller stations.[29]

Clerical salaries in the railways' head offices were similar to those on the line. For example, in 1857 the Grand Trunk's audit department employed an inspector and chief clerk at £200 each, two freight officers at £175 each, a ticket printer at £160, six passenger clerks with salaries ranging between £50 and £150, three freight clerks at £50, £70, and £100, and an assistant printer and a boy, each making £30.[30]

The data on occupational groups and rates of pay are summarized in table 2. While there are obvious difficulties with this presentation – it compares different railways at different points in time; it assumes employees worked full days and months; and it fails to show distributions over the ranges (although means are provided where available) – it nevertheless manages to suggest some interesting relationships. First, it appears that the majority of railway workers' pay fell within the range of $1–2.50 per day. Second, it appears that workers with a particular level of skill or responsibility within one occupational group received roughly the same pay as workers at a comparable level in other groups, although the form of payment varied by occupational group, rather than by grade. Thus enginemen were roughly equivalent to conductors, to agents at the larger stations, to senior clerks, and to skilled tradesmen. Firemen, brakemen, and (on the GWR) minor station agents were roughly comparable in terms of pay to labourers: the latter differed, we may surmise, less in terms of pay than in terms of the opportunity structure. Firemen were engineers in training; brakemen could aspire to become baggagemen and ultimately conductors; minor station agents could look forward to more responsible postings. So far as we know, however, outside labour did not have access to similar promotional opportunities.

Occupational mobility often required geographic mobility as well. As one GTR manager reminisced, railway officers were like Methodist preachers – they were movers.[31] Railway records are filled with instances of job transfers, especially in the salaried occupations. In many cases, though, it is impossible to know whether people were being moved up, down, or sideways.[32] All the same, many employees moved with a purpose: consider the case of John Porteous, who "in all his movements had one object in view, and that was to make a *step higher!*"

In October, 1854, he joined the Great Western Railway at Hamilton, Ont., as billing and corresponding clerk in the freight department; six months afterwards he was doing the same kind of duty at Suspension Bridge. In 1855 he was corresponding clerk at Windsor, then promoted to the position of freight cashier and accountant at the same station. In November, 1857, his health giving way, he resigned and left for Scotland, but returned to Canada in July, the following year, when Mr. Brydges appointed him cashier and accountant of the Detroit, Grand Haven & Milwaukee Railroad at Milwaukee, Wis. In 1863 he removed to Portland, Me., to hold a similar office on the Grand Trunk Railway there. On the death of Mr. Graham, the Portland agent, in November of that year, Mr. Porteous succeeded him as freight agent at that important depot. In this position he remained until April, 1876, when Mr. (now Sir Joseph) Hickson sent him to England to establish the Grand Trunk agency at

TABLE 2

Occupational Groups and Rates of Pay (estimates based on 26-day month)

$/Month	$/Day	GWR Loco Dept 1854	GTR Loco Dept 1859	GTR Traffic Dept 1856	Station Agents
					▲$117
75	2.88				
70	2.69	● Brydges's est. of avg. engineman's pay			
65	2.50		◄ (70% at this rate)		
60	2.31				
55	2.12	Enginemen			GTR 1856 / GWR 1857
			Enginemen		
50	1.92			Conductors	
45	1.73				◄ (mean)
40	1.54	Turners	● (1% of Firemen)		◄ (mean)
35	1.35				
30	1.15		● (99% of Firemen)	Baggagemen ● Brakemen	
25	.96	Firemen	Cleaners		
20	.77				
15	.58				
10	.38				
5	.19				

Sources: As in table 1.

Clerks on Line	Outside Labour	GWR Car Shop 1855	GWR Loco Shop 1855	GTR Shopcrafts 1859
				● Blacksmith (top rate)
		● Patternmaker (top rate)	● Boiler maker (top rate)	
			● Boiler maker (mean)	
		● Machinist (mean)	● Fitter (mean)	
	◀ (mean)		● Carpenter (mean)	● Pattern maker (mean)
				● Fitter, Blacksmith (mean)
GTR 1856	GWR 1857	● Car builder (mean)		
◀ (mean)				
				● Carpenter, Car repairer (mean)
		● Labourer (mean)	● Hammerman (mean)	● Machine man (mean)
				● Labourer, Striker (mean)
			● Boiler maker's Asst (mean)	● Boiler maker's Asst (mean)
		● (lowest rate)		
			● (lowest rate)	
				● (lowest rate)

Liverpool. On Mr. Porteous' return to Montreal he was appointed assistant general freight agent of the G.T.R. on January 1st, 1877, and when the late Mr. P.S. Stevenson resigned the general freight agency, on account of sickness, Mr. Porteous succeeded him on July 1st, 1878, being the fourth G.F.A. since the opening of the line. This position he held until December, 1886, when he resigned to accept that of general manager of the through freight department of the Central Vermont Railroad, with headquarters at Boston ... On the first of February, 1892, Mr. Porteous was again further promoted to the general managership of the National Despatch Freight Line, with office at Boston, which position he still retains.[33]

Mr Porteous's brilliant career is interesting for several reasons. We pass no comment on the happy accidents of sickness and death that made for its advancement at crucial stages. But note how narrowly constricted was the chain of opportunity that took him so far. Porteous's career path barely took him out of the freight office. And this, it seems, was typical of railway careers: firemen might become enginemen, brakemen could become conductors; junior clerks aspired to become station agents or better; and shop workers might become lead hands, foremen, or, albeit rarely, locomotive or car superintendents, but the lines *between* the occupational grades were infrequently crossed.[34]

RECRUITMENT AND RETENTION

The material basis for railway company paternalism was the scarcity of skilled labour and the companies' urgent desire to protect their heavy investment in recruitment and training. Particularly (although by no means exclusively) in the 1850s, with the start-up of operations on an unprecedented scale, railway companies were faced with the task of recruiting large numbers of specialized personnel whose required skills were usually scarce to the point of non-existence in the local labour market.

The Grand Trunk addressed this problem by hiring the bulk of its original work force in Britain, through the agency of its contractors, Messrs Peto, Brassey, Betts, and Jackson. It is not known just how many of the 4,000 masons, carpenters, quarrymen, enginemen, fitters, and other skilled tradesmen (as well as "large drafts" of navvies, or unskilled construction labourers) who contracted to come to Canada on five-year engagements in the spring of 1854 actually arrived and set to work in building the line. Nor is it certain how many of them remained to operate the road once construction was complete; the likelihood is that many did. The Grand Trunk also recruited all its senior operating officials in Britain, initially on five-year contracts.[35]

The recruitment practices of the Great Western are obscured slightly by the company's defensive reaction to contemporary criticisms that it had too many Englishmen and Scots on its line. Of its 36 enginemen in November 1854, however, 23 had British experience and only 7 American. Of the enginemen, 8 came from a single English line, the London and North Western, which had also provided the company's managing director, C.J. Brydges. Indeed, all the GWR's senior officers were recruited in Britain, as were at least a dozen station employees. Brydges reported in 1854 that of 77 stationmasters and other station employees who had been in Canada less than three years, "some came out from Railways in the old country, without knowledge of the Company or its officers, and upon making application for employment, were, upon being found suitable, taken on."

The Great Western reported 212 station employees in all, of whom only 13 had been born in Canada. Similarly, while Brydges claimed that the company had not "brought out" any conductors or baggagemen, only 13 per cent of them were Canadian born, and another 25 per cent American. Finally, of the "large staff of mechanics employed at the different workshops ... a different class of men to any previously in the country," Brydges reported that "about twenty-five have been brought out by the Company, and most of the remainder have been men who have been taken on as ordinary workmen and gradually trained for the duties they now fulfill."[36] The local labour market presumably furnished the bulk of the company's demand for unskilled labourers and "ordinary workmen." Nonetheless, it appears from statements made by the shop workers themselves that the majority were first-generation immigrants from Britain, whether or not the company had directly recruited them there.

The railway companies' investment in recruiting and training skilled and specialized workers had direct implications for discipline. Good pay, welfare schemes of one sort and another, and a host of measures intended to build up loyalty to the company served to protect the proprietors' investment in manpower. At the same time, of course, the magnitude of that investment materially limited managerial autocracy. We have already suggested that scarce workers might only receive a reprimand in circumstances where unskilled labour would be fired. Beyond this, the railway companies strove to protect their investments by restructuring operations to provide work for engine crews and shop workers during slack times. Both the Grand Trunk and the Great Western began to manufacture their own cars in the mid 1850s, and their own locomotives by the end of the decade, in large part because it was better business to keep their shops working in slack periods than to lay off workers whom it could be difficult to replace when time improved.[37]

This policy is illustrated by the Great Western's aggregate payrolls, reported half-yearly from July 1854 on. These accounts report the wage-bill for five groups of occupations: enginemen and firemen; conductors, baggagemen, and brakemen; porters, policemen, and switchmen; locomotive-shop workers; and car-shop workers. Our preliminary analysis of these figures suggests that less-skilled workers, particularly those not involved in shop work or locomotive running, were far more susceptible to displacement in periods of economic downturn than were their scarcer co-workers.[38]

Following several years of rapid growth, the Canadian (as indeed the whole North Atlantic) economy suffered a sharp recession in the latter part of 1857. However, the Great Western's traffic receipts and net revenue had already begun to fall off quite steeply the previous year and only recovered with the general strengthening of the economy in 1859. Overall, the railway's payroll components follow this trend. A period of rapid growth, associated with the economic boom and the beginning of railway operations, is followed by a period of decline and, by the end of the decade, recovery. While this cycle can be identified to some extent for each of the components, the extent of its influence differs markedly among the different categories of employment. At one extreme, the payroll for porters, switchmen, and policemen soars dramatically in the earlier period and plummets in the later one. These workers were particularly vulnerable to market fluctuations because they were unskilled, paid at day rates, and the company had a minimal investment in their recruitment and training. Porters in particular were vulnerable to lay-off as the volume of passengers and freight declined between 1856 and 1858.

At the other extreme, the curve for car-shop payrolls is practically flat throughout the period. The locomotive-shop payroll climbed rapidly to mid 1857 and then levelled off. The payrolls of the remaining two occupational groups – engineers and firemen, and conductors, baggagemen, and brakemen – responded more moderately to the business cycle. While the more skilled of these employees represented a substantial investment in recruitment and training, they could not be fully employed in a period of declining train mileage. These data suggest that unskilled railway workers were exposed to a classical labour market during the decade; that the shop workers were protected by inelastic demand; and that the skilled workers in the running trades were cushioned by relatively inelastic supply.

In the Great Western's locomotive department, for example, outside labourers, the lowest-paid workers on the line, were the chief target of early cost-cutting efforts. The men who worked the GWR's water pumps were the first victims: when steam pumping engines (which could also be used to saw wood) were introduced between July and December 1854, sixty jobs were eliminated.[39] By contrast, the scarcity of qualified enginemen and firemen, and the substantial investment the railway had incurred in recruiting and training them, meant that they must be retained at almost any cost:

The running of engines for gravel and wood trains whilst the line was being completed and ballasted, were of great benefit to this department, inasmuch as they found profitable employment during the summer months for a large number of engineers and firemen which it was absolutely necessary to retain on the staff for working the heavy traffic during the fall and winter, but as this opportune employment is now at an end, the Locomotive Department labours under a very great disadvantage because we cannot possibly discharge our steady and experienced men at each recurrence of slackness in traffic.[40]

This labour-market dualism was not purely a function of skill level, however, but depended on occupational grade as well. So long as the railway companies were committed to making work in the shops so as to retain skilled workers, there would be work for unskilled shop workers as well. This apparent dualism was undermined in several of the grades by the structures of occupational mobility. The line was drawn not so much between the skilled and the unskilled, but between the unskilled in outside labouring jobs (who lacked access to a mobility ladder) and the remainder of the work force.

DEFERENCE AND RESISTANCE

Railway managers liked to talk about "the existence between all classes of the Company's servants, of that spirit of unanimity and cordiality which is so indispensible to railway working."[41] There is evidence that sentiments like these were more than mere anodynes. During this decade in which the railways were a new industry just beginning operations, managers and skilled workers (at least) in each of the companies considered themselves members of a single community, although by no means a community of equals. This community was structured on paternalistic lines, but the paternalism was moderated – again, in the case of the skilled workers at least – by a good deal of pride and self-respect. This pride in craft and occupational solidarity could prompt Grand Trunk shop workers to hold an indignation meeting in support of their employer, and against newspaper charges that the company's cars were of shoddy construction.[42] It could equally prompt organized resistance when management overstepped itself. If we are to understand the two principal occasions of industrial conflict in railway operations during the 1850s, we have first to examine the strands that defined and knit together this railway community.

It was a paternalistic community, in which "every man should be taught to feel that he is cared for by his superior and that his good conduct will be noticed and rewarded."[43] The material basis for paternalism has already been described: it consisted in the imperfections of the labour market for the key shopcrafts and running-trades workers, in the companies' heavy investment in recruiting and retaining these scarce workers, and in the imperative of maintaining discipline in far-flung enterprises where direct supervision was impossible. This structural imperative to paternalism was expressed in the provision of company housing, the uneven enforcement of company rules, the relatively high rates of pay enjoyed by skilled workers, and their substantial job security. It was reflected, too, in the silver medals distributed by the Grand

Trunk's directors to the "best men for economy, regular running, care and freedom from accidents," in the various incentive schemes whereby workers took a share of savings earned through greater productivity, and in the schools and churches erected by the companies for their workers' families.[44]

There were cultural links to knit the community together as well. Perhaps most significant was the fact that many managers and skilled workers were recent immigrants from Britain (and from England in particular) and may indeed have worked together on British railways. Certainly there was no end to the protestations of loyalty at the various festivals and dinners where the community congregated. Many a toast was drunk to the army and navy, the fatherland, the queen and royal family – and on at least one occasion during the Crimean war, to the emperor and empress of France as well.[45] A substantial proof of allegiance came in 1855, when the Great Western's employees subscribed more than £800 to a Patriotic Fund to support the war in the Crimea.[46] Another tie binding railway workers and managers together was common defence against often-hostile public and press. Just as general manager Brydges defended the character, sobriety, and competence of Great Western employees before the Accident Commission, so the workers did their part by rallying behind the company, telling the directors that "in all their trials they could count upon the united support of the employees, whenever anything was wanted from them, to maintain the high character of the road."[47]

Labour/management reciprocity extended to community affairs quite removed from the workplace. In Hamilton, for example, the Great Western's management could count on worker support at the polls for its electoral interests; the workers could similarly count on the managers to intervene on their behalf when they became embroiled in a dispute with the directors of the local Mechanics Institute.

In the 1857 election, both the Grand Trunk and the Great Western urged their employees to support candidates sympathetic to company interests. The Great Western posted notices in the shops that managing director Brydges would speak on behalf of a local candidate, and the men were invited to "volunteer" to come hear him. Election day was declared a holiday in the shops, where the men were marshalled and marched to the polls. Great Western workers also intevened in the elections in Galt and Essex. The politics of paternalism though, were not entirely dissociated from the coercion of property. After the election, a disgruntled partisan alleged that "McGregor the artisan" had been fired, despite four years' service, simply for refusing to vote for the company's candidate.[48] Such charges were a common theme in the abuse heaped upon the railway and its employees by newspapers on the other side of the political divide. The Great Western mechanics' answer came at their annual festival in 1857, where a locomotive-department worker insisted before the whole assembly that "the Great Western mechanics could compare favourably with those who aspersed them … He thought it right that the mechanics should do their duty to the Company, and then they would earn the respect of all."[49]

The dispute at the Hamilton and Gore Mechanics Institute arose when the Great Western workers attempted to transform the middle-class library and social club into an institution that would be more responsive to their needs. In 1854, the railway's board of directors had agreed to contribute £100 to the institute on condition that membership privileges be extended to its employees. By December of the following year, the railway workers had accumulated so long a list of grievances about the institute's management that they met to consider establishing an alternative institution of their own. They complained about high dues, the irrelevance of most of the literature stocked by the institute to the mechanics' concern with "scientific" matters, the speakers who were being brought in, and the complete absence of classes in mechanical principles and applications for workmen and their sons. The institute's president attended the meeting to defend his policies, but Brydges spoke up for the workers, urging the institute to recognize the validity of the grievances and to compromise. The meeting closed with "three hearty cheers" for Brydges, "the workmen's real friend." Two months later, the institute amended its by-laws, reduced its fees, and elected Brydges to its board. By 1857, classes were being held in Mechanical and Architectural Drawing (23 participants), Mathematics, Writing and Arithmetic (30 participants), French, and "Mutual Improvement, or Debating Class." All were taught by Great Western employees, and many of the students came from the local railway shops. The Great Western directors continued their annual grant in support of membership fees until 1866, when the company's mechanics built their own reading room.[50]

Democracy, progress through science, and education as the means to self-improvement were recurrent themes in the culture of the railway community. All these were celebrated regularly at the annual mechanics' festivals and at the numerous testimonial dinners mounted to honour the companies' officers. These gatherings, where elaborate speeches and toasts accompanied dinner, and music and dancing followed, were organized by workers' committees with the active support and participation of management. Typically, the hall would be decorated with portraits of managers, banners inscribed with the names of such "mechanical heroes" as Watt, Arkwright, and Fulton, slogans proclaiming "Success to Canadian Enterprise," pictures of locomotives, and the insignia of various fraternal organizations.[51]

These dinners both expressed and fostered the solidarity and values of the railway community. Managers would often use these occasions to advance corporate welfare proposals, as in 1857, when Brydges promised company support for an employees' sick fund, or 1858, when he urged the creation of a mutual benefit society and made another proposal that spoke to a key artisanal value: "A great many of the youths employed at the shops were destitute of the benefit of having received instruction in the first rudiments of a common education; and it was proposed to establish a School at the Works, for the purpose of instructing those youths; and it would give him and the Directors the greatest possible pleasure to aid and carry this suggestion into execution."[52]

The testimonial dinners honoured upward mobility and workplace harmony. When the Great Western's locomotive superintendent left the company to join the Buffalo and Lake Huron Railway (incidentally taking a number of fitters with him), 150 subscribers presented him with a silver tea service and a ring, as well as a dinner in his honour. "Mr. Yates is one of our own class," announced the evening's master of ceremonies, "having graduated amongst us, and we are now about to award him a diploma and spend a pleasant evening." On another occasion, 200 workers presented a retiring shop foreman with a purse of $200, "as a mark of our respect and esteem, and in acknowledging the power that was vested in you we all believe you used that power with mildness and affability." The community sometimes assembled on more solemn occasions. Following the Desjardins Bridge disaster of 1857, which claimed fifty-nine lives, the Great Western workers subscribed for a monument to the engineman and fireman, "a marble column upon the top of which stands a very pretty model of a locomotive," suitably inscribed:

> Life's railway o'er, each station past,
> In death we're stopped and cease at last
> Farewell dear friends, and cease to weep
> In Christ we're safe, in him we sleep.[53]

The paternalistic solidarity of the railway community was threatened by strikes only twice during the decade. This was in marked contrast to the railways' experience during their construction phase, which had seen an almost unbroken succession of strikes, riots, and other "ructions" by navvies and labourers, usually in response to wage reductions, changes in working hours, defaults by contractors, or frustration at the unavailability of work.[54] It was this pattern of construction-labour relations that led Pentland to classify the railways as "modern" market-oriented employers.[55] The experience of operations, as we have already suggested, was markedly different. What is particularly interesting about the two upheavals of the 1850s is that the paternalistic railway community seems to have survived them intact.

The strike on the Great Western began in November 1856, when a new locomotive superintendent, Alexander Braid, dismissed a popular shop foreman named Stephenson, apparently in order to replace him with a personal favourite. When Braid told the shop workers, who had convened to demand an explanation, that Stephenson "was in the habit of being drunk in his shop," the men denounced this as a "monstrous fabrication" and struck work, vowing not to return until Braid himself had been dismissed. The enginemen and firemen threatened to strike in sympathy with their fellows in the shops. Brydges received the shop workers' grievance committee "in the courteous manner which characterizes that gentleman," expressed his regret at the strike, and agreed to reinstate Stephenson, although not to dismiss Braid. He also promised that no one would be discharged on account of the strike, reassured the deputation that a rumoured wage cut would not take place, and reaffirmed the practice of paying men who arrived at the shops a little late on Saturday for three-quarters of a day's work, rather than just half. Finally, he compromised the men's demand for free passes by agreeing to let them ride at half fare.[56] Once again, Brydges was hailed as the workmen's friend. Subsequently the mood was one of forgiveness. Braid was eventually welcomed back at the Mechanics Institute, and when he left the company in 1858, he was treated to a testimonial dinner where the men presented him with a $500 silver tea service.[57]

There are several versions of the 1859 conflict on the Grand Trunk. George Reith, the railway's new general manager, was on a tour of western U.S. railroads when he learned that wages elsewhere were lower than on the Grand Trunk. Without consultation, he apparently wired Montreal that all wages and salaries were to be reduced 10 per cent forthwith. The Toronto *Leader* claimed that Reith expected to earn a bonus by his cost-cutting measure; in any event, the Grand Trunk's employees got wind of the order and threatened to resign en masse. Their strike threat worked. The Grand Trunk's president convened the board of directors, announced that neither he nor the vice-president had been consulted about the cut, and reported that GTR wages were in fact lower than those paid on the Great Western or the Northern. The board rescinded Reith's order, effectively dismissing him. Reith managed to arrange a £4,000 settlement from the English directors of the Grand Trunk, a rather less-appropriate testimonial than the one sent him by a group of American railway executives – a large tray and goblets, made of tin. The Grand Trunk workers memorialized the event in a song that denounced Reith's attempted "piracy" while reaffirming their affection for other Grand Trunk officers:

When rose-lipped June, enraptured, bent
To sip the falling dew,
A Reith conceived the foul intent
To clap on us the screw
Of ten per cent. But where's the man
Who speeds the rail along
But will take up, with heart in hand,
The chorus of my song?

May he who dares, with pirate hand,
Our "little all" assail
Storm-tost, behold no more the land,
But perish in the gale.
When honest bluntness is our theme,
To Bidder we recur;
For manliness, the very *name*
Of Shanley we revere;
But when we think of every ill
That pirates can bequeath,
Each object serves our minds to fill
With reveries of Reith.[58]

How are these events to be interpreted? Some might see in these conflicts the early stirrings of class consciousness among the railway workers. There is some authority for this view: one of the Hamilton strikers declared "that it was all very well to say that they were independent of the Great Western Railway, but they should reflect that capital always tyrannized over labour." His view did not go unchallenged, though, for another rose to say that he "had had much to do with strikes in the Old Country, and had come to the knowledge of the fact that tyranny of the employee over the employer was as possible and hateful as that of the employer over the employee." Still others were content to urge their fellows to act "like men," to avoid "sacrificing their dignity."[59] Taking it all together, it seems a more convincing view that these events arose not out of class consciousness, but out of something antecedent, albeit related to it: an artisanal ideology compounded of pride in craft, personal dignity, and democratic aspiration, but shaded for all that by a sense of rank and mutual obligation. This was an artisanal view that did not look to petty proprietorship as the ultimate expression of success in work, but rather accepted the critical features of paternalistic employment relations in the large corporation, combining independence and deference to find its place in the railway community.

DIMENSIONS OF PATERNALISM

As H.C. Pentland has argued, the persistence of the "traditional" personal relation of worker and employer into the industrial age was a function of the underdevelopment of the labour market. It was a strategy whereby employers confronted the material reality of labour shortage and the seasonality of labour requirements in an attempt to ensure that workers would be available when required. In strictly economic terms, Pentland's personal labour relation amounted to the employer's assumption of some significant portion of the cost of supporting the worker and his family in periods of underemployment – a cost that is assumed wholly by the worker in the fully-formed classical labour market, and is partially socialized (with the burden falling on workers generally) in the welfare state.

But the personal labour relation clearly carried implications beyond the narrowly economic. The assumption of the worker's overhead costs rarely (if ever) took the indirect form of simple cash transfers. Instead, the employer effectively substituted his own decisions about consumption for those of the worker. Where few employees were involved, they might be taken into the employer's household, eat at his table, wear his family's cast-off clothing. Where the work force was larger, the employer might choose for and on behalf of his employees by supplying company housing, subsidizing prices in a company store, and arranging for the provision of doctors or schools. Apprenticeship, with its requirements of maintenance and training, placed the employer formally in loco parentis; so, too, may the general employment relationship justifiably be characterized as paternalistic to the extent that the employer undertakes to supply the material, political, cultural, or moral-cum-spiritual maintenance of the work force. In this more general sense, then, paternalism may flow not only from a rational calculation that market forces are inadequate or unreliable guarantors of employee loyalty or efficiency, but from ideological and broadly cultural wellsprings too. And in this more general sense, paternalism may persist and develop even after the demise of its original progenitor, the personal labour relation.

Employment in railway operations in the 1850s was clearly transitional with respect to both the personal employment relation and paternalism. More precisely, it can be located on the boundary between the paternalism of the personal labour relation and the newly emerging corporate paternalism of what would be known a half-century later as business's "welfare work."[60] Railway workers were bound by ties of personal loyalty, dependence or deference to particular foremen, supervisors, or managers, depending upon their position in the hierarchy. Such ties counted for much in an employment structure geared to personal mobility. But at the same time these personal relations were located in an increasingly impersonal corporate structure that centralized authority and operated according to imperatives quite independent of personality, for all that the "railway service" claimed the personal loyalties of its servants. This could lead to conflict, as the Braid and Reith affairs showed, but the relative decline of the personal labour relation did not mean an end to paternalism.

The crucial feature of paternalism in the 1850s was the railway companies' commitment to providing slack-time employment for the shopcraft and running-trades workers. Rapid growth associated with start-up combined with the scarcity of experienced workers in these trades to strengthen their position and provide them a base from which to proclaim their artisanal pride and independence, and to join with management in designing the institutions of community – all this, of course, shaded by deference and an acknowledgment of hierarchy, but not determined by it. By the mid 1870s, however, the underlying structure of paternalism would change markedly. Pressed by financial crises and conscious of the development of a better-stocked labour market, a new generation of corporate managers would abandon the old commitment to slack-time employment and embark on a policy of lay-off and retrenchment. The paternalism of the later 1870s would have two faces: first, the moral regeneration of railway labour through company-sponsored temperance and bible movements and the organization of the Railway YMCAs, and second, superannuation and accident insurance schemes intended, at least in part, to offset more directly the successes of the Railway Brotherhoods in unionizing important segments of the work force. While its form and content varied with the relative strengths of employers and particular groups of workers, and with the nature of the institutions they created, paternalism was to persist as a characteristic feature of railway labour relations well into the twentieth century.

NOTES

Research for this paper, and for the larger Canadian Railways Industrial Relations History Project of which it forms a part, has had the generous support of the Social Sciences and Humanities Research Council of Canada. At various times this project has benefited from the research assistance of Rose Hutchens, David Sobel, Lynne Brenegan, and Robert Nahuet.

1 For example, W.T. Easterbrook and Hugh G.J. Aitken, *Canadian Economic History* (Toronto 1963), ch. 14, "The Coming of the Railway."

2 Arthur Lower states that John Egan, "King of the Ottawa," employed 3500 men in timber making in 1854. They were distributed among a hundred establishments, however, with little imperative to close co-ordination, and can hardly be considered a single work force. *Great Britain's Woodyard: British America and the Timber Trade* (Montreal 1973), 166.

3 Occupational terminology varied, with the English terms gradually giving way to American ones over the period. For clarity's sake, we have adopted the better known terms: engineman instead of engine-driver; brakeman instead of brakesman or breaksman; conductor instead of guard; cleaner instead of wiper.

4 J.M. Trout and E. Trout, *The Railways of Canada* (Toronto 1871), 83, 100.

5 Public Archives of Canada, RG 30, *Canadian National Railways* (henceforth CNR) contains papers of most of the railways that eventually became part of the CNR system. CNR 2, 606 (2 March 1855) and 2, 635 (30 March 1855); Hamilton *Spectator*, 15 September 1855. For a detailed account of this aspect of railway operations, see Paul Craven and Tom Traves, "Canadian Railways as Manufacturers 1850–80," Canadian Historical Association, *Historical Papers* (1983), 254–81.

6 For studies of the development of railway management in the United States and Britain, see Alfred D. Chandler, Jr, *The Railroads* (New York 1965), and *The Visible Hand* (Cambridge, Mass. 1977); T.R. Gourvish, *Mark Huish and the London and North Western Railway: A Study of Management* (Leicester 1972). The "general principles" of management were set out by Daniel C. McCallum, superintendent of the New York and Erie Railroad, in that company's annual report for 1855 (see Chandler, *The Railroads*, 102).

7 The commissioners appointed to inquire into a series of accidents and detentions on the Great Western Railway, *Report*, Journals of the Legislative Assembly of United Canada, 18 Vict. App. YY, 1855 (henceforth *Accident Commission*). The Accident Commission report is imperfectly paginated.

8 14 & 15 Vict., c. 51.

9 16 Vict., c. 99, sect. XI.

10 19 Vict., c. 136.

11 An amending Act of 1853 (16 Vict., c. 169) made it a misdemeanour punishable by up to a year's imprisonment at hard labour to tamper maliciously with or damage railway property or cause any stoppage of operations. If damage to property carried on the road, or injury to persons, ensued, the offence became a felony punishable by not less than one and not more than two years in the penitentiary; while if loss of life was involved, the offence became manslaughter and the offender liable to from four to ten years in the penitentiary.

12 CNR 1000, 570f (1857).

13 Great Western Railway, *Rule Book*, 1854; CNR 2, 103 (June 1854); CNR 2, 1201 (1857). In the absence of other detailed information, these codes of rules are frequently the best available approximations to a description of the work process for various occupations in this period.

14 *Accident Commission*.

15 CNR 6, 768 (1857); CNR 6, 758 (1857); CNR 1000, 129 (1857).

16 CNR 6, 813f (1858).

17 CNR 5 (5 June 1855).

18 Hamilton *Spectator*, 11 November 1854.

19 *Accident Commission*.

20 Toronto *Globe*, 18 October 1853.

21 CNR 2, 445f (1854).

22 CNR 6394 (1854–5).

23 Great Western Railway, *Rule Book*, 1854.

24 This is admittedly impressionistic for the 1850s, since too little detailed quantitative work has been done on real incomes and regularity of work in a broad cross-section of occupations in the period to substantiate the information. By the late 1880s, we find explicit acknowledgments of the greater regularity of work on the railways (although many of the other working conditions characteristic of the 1850s no longer obtained), for example, in the testimony of David Cashion, a moulder in the Grand Trunk's Hamilton works, before the Royal

Commission on the Relations of Labour and Capital (Ontario evidence, pp. 784–6).

25 *Accident Commission*, 119.

26 The 1854–5 Great Western paysheets are in CNR 6394. The Grand Trunk figures are reported in its locomotive superintendent's report, appended to the railway's *Annual Report* for 1859.

27 *Accident Commission*, and see table 2.

28 Special Committee appointed to inquire and report about the condition, management, and prospects of the Grand Trunk Railway Company, *Report*, Journal of the Legislative Assembly of Canada, 20 Vic., App. 6, 1857 (hereafter GTR *Report*); *Accident Commission*.

29 GTR *Report*; CNR 6, 795 (1857).

30 These are yearly salaries in Halifax currency. GTR *Report*; CNR 5, Finance Committee, 7 December 1854; 5 and 10 October 1854.

31 Myles Pennington, *Railways and Other Ways* (Toronto 1894), 186.

32 CNR 6, 791 (1857); 6, 796 (1857). Railway company rules typically required that employees reside wherever they were ordered.

33 Pennington, *Railways*, 186f. Porteous seems to have followed Brydges from the Great Western to the Grand Trunk; this was not an uncommon route for career moves in an industry where paternalism was accompanied by patronage.

34 One of the methods used to supply work in slack periods was to send enginemen and firemen into the shops for part of their working time; this meant that there was more interchange between the shopcrafts and the footplate trades than might otherwise have occurred. One machinist who became a fireman in the late 1850s transferred back again when his fiancee said she would not marry him unless he quit the road and went back to his trade (University of Western Ontario, Spriggs Collection, box 4312, W.K. Baines to Spriggs, 13 Feb 1934).

35 Toronto *Leader*, 30 March, 26 May, and 13 July 1854; GTR *Report*, 218; Pennington (the Grand Trunk's first goods manager) reports that James Hardman, John Roberts, S.P. Bidder, and he all came to Canada on five year contracts (*Railways*, 81).

36 *Accident Commission*; A.W. Currie, *The Grand Trunk Railway of Canada* (Toronto 1957), 163.

37 For details, see Craven and Traves, "Canadian Railways as Manufacturers."

38 This analysis is described in detail in our working paper, "Labour and management in Canadian railway operations: the first decade," presented to the Commonwealth Labour History Conference, Coventry, England, in September 1981. It remains tentative, however, until data covering a substantially longer time series are analysed.

39 CNR 1, 58 (26 September 1854), report of R.W. Harris to shareholders; CNR 1, n.p. (24 August 1854), report of G.L. Reid, chief engineer, to shareholders.

40 CNR 1, n.p. (17 August 1860).

41 The words are Walter Shanly's, quoted by Pennington, *Railways*, 124.

42 Montreal *Gazette*, 10 May 1856.

43 Quoted by Pennington, *Railways*, 87.

44 Grand Trunk, *Annual Report* (1859), 26; Montreal *Gazette*, 10 August 1853.

45 Montreal *Gazette*, 8 January 1855.

46 Hamilton *Spectator*, 23 May 1855.

47 *Accident Commission*; Hamilton *Spectator*, 23 January 1860, copying the London *Prototype*.

48 Hamilton *Spectator*, 12 December 1857, 13 January 1858, 4 January 1858; Toronto *Globe*, 8 January 1858.

49 Hamilton *Spectator*, 1 January 1858.

50 CNR 2, 59 (1854). Hamilton *Spectator*, 7 December 1855; 4 and 5 February, and 3 March 1856; 28 February 1857. CNR 6, 891 (1858); Bryan Palmer, *A Culture in Conflict* (Montreal 1979), 51. Workers on the Grand Trunk met at the Montreal Mechanics Institute in 1856 to plan their involvement in the upcoming festivities to celebrate the opening of the line. In 1857 they established the Grand Trunk Literary and Scientific Institution, and by 1859 it had opened a reading room at Point St Charles (Montreal *Gazette*, 22 October 1856; Montreal *Pilot*, 16 June 1857; Toronto *Globe*, 17 May 1859).

51 One of the Great Western workers' grievances against the Mechanics Institute was that in 1854 its directors refused to rent them the hall for the first festival on the pretext that there would be dancing (Hamilton *Spectator*, 7 December 1855). For accounts of various festivals, excursions, and other celebrations, see, for example, Toronto *Globe*, 11 February 1860; Hamilton *Spectator*, 7 January 1857, 23 January 1860; Montreal *Pilot*, 22 August 1859.

52 Hamilton *Spectator*, 25 February 1857; Hamilton *Times*, 9 January 1858.

53 Hamilton *Spectator*, 13 March and 5 October 1854, 27 September 1856, 21 February and 9 September 1857; Montreal *Pilot*, 29 December 1856, 22 July 1856; Hamilton *Evening Times*, 17 May 1861; Pennington, *Railways*, 126n.

54 These strikes took the typical form of "collective bargaining by riot," and represented the continuation of the labour struggles of the 1840s in canal building onto the railways in the 1850s. For a discussion of the canal navvies' battles, see Ruth Bleasdale, "Class Conflict on the Canals of Upper Canada in the 1840s," *Labour/Le Travailleur* VII (1981): 9–39.

55 This analysis suggests that the labour-market situation on the railways corresponded in many respects to what Pentland described as "personal labour relationships," particularly for those workers whose skills were relatively scarce. Pentland looked at labour relations in railway *construction* and concluded that the railway companies were modern, capitalistic employers; that is, that they took advantage of the evolving classical labour market to depersonalize employment relations. However true this may have been of relations with navvies in construction (and with unskilled outdoor labour like the porters discussed above), it would seem that personal labour relationships characterized the railways' relations with the majority of their operating personnel. We return to the question of paternalism in

the concluding section of this essay. H.C. Pentland, *Labour and Capital in Canada 1650–1850*, ed. Paul Phillips (Toronto, 1981).

56 Hamilton *Spectator*, 7 and 8 November 1856.

57 Hamilton *Spectator*, 25 February 1857, 21 April 1858.

58 Pennington, *Railways*, 151; Toronto *Leader*, 29 November 1860; CNR 1000, 193f (1859); CNR 1003, 50–3 (1859); Pennington, 357: the song is signed "Philip Dormer, Fireman," and Pennington ascribes it, somewhat uncertainly, to a "rhymster of Maine." Bidder and Shanley preceded Reith as GTR general managers.

59 Hamilton *Spectator*, 8 November 1856.

60 These considerations apply to all groups of workers, with the partial but significant exception of outdoor labour. See Canadian Pacific Railway Company, *Welfare Work* (n.p.; n.d.: circa 1909), and more generally, Paul Craven, *"An Impartial Umpire": Industrial Relations and the Canadian State 1900–11* (Toronto 1980), 100–5; and Tom Traves, *The State and Enterprise: Canadian Manufacturers and the Federal Government, 1917–31* (Toronto 1979), chapter 5.

GREGORY S. KEALEY

Work Control, the Labour Process, and Nineteenth-Century Canadian Printers

In the nineteenth- and early twentieth-century Canadian labour and socialist movement, printers held pride of place. From D.J. O'Donoghue, "father of the Canadian labour movement," through stalwart Canadian presidents of the International Typographical Union (ITU), John Armstrong and W.B. Prescott, to socialist leaders such as Toronto's Jimmy Simpson, Winnipeg's Arthur Puttee, and Vancouver's R.P. Pettipiece, printers played prominent roles in the Canadian working-class world.[1] And for every printer who became a labour leader, there were probably ten others who became successful in some other walk of life – journalism, publishing, and politics representing only three of the most popular paths. The printers, then, represent the ultimate respectable Victorian craftsman. Indeed, they can be studied as the extreme example of the successful skilled workers who to a large degree maintained their societal positions, despite the onslaught of the Industrial Revolution. By studying printers and their responses to the changing nature of both their work and their workplaces over the course of the century, we can begin to evaluate the role of the successful skilled worker in capitalist transformation.

Printers are a particularly suitable choice for study because rich primary sources exist that allow us to penetrate at least some of the "mysteries of the craft." As well, there is a large secondary literature on both sides of the Atlantic, beginning with the very earliest academic studies of labour. In Canada, the richest extant data cover Toronto – the centre of the English-Canadian publishing industry and a city that possessed a vibrant newspaper press. Much of the material in this paper is drawn from Toronto sources, but other Canadian cities are also considered.

The study of Canadian printers in the nineteenth and early twentieth century divides into three distinct periods of workplace struggles defined by the interaction of labour and capital. The first period, up to mid century, was typified by handicraft production and small combined newspaper and "job" (mixed printing) shops with low levels of capitalization. Relations within the printing industry closely resembled Richard Price's notion of "autonomous regulation."[2] A second period, from the 1850s to the early 1890s, was ushered in by the arrival of the daily paper, rotary presses, and a growing division of labour between pressmen and compositors. In this period, the union and its importance grew, capitalization rose, and competition intensified. This second period might be typified as one of "union regulation," as the typographical unions became ever more crucial to the process of workplace struggle. Finally, from the early 1890s, with the introduction of the linotype machine through to the eight-hour struggle of 1905–7, a third period emerged in which a binational system of collective bargaining commenced and the local unions became increasingly subservient to the international union. At the same time, capitalists began effectively to mass their forces in city-wide and national associations. While it would be anachronistic to see this as a full-fledged "modern industrial relations system," we can nevertheless assert that the constituent ingredients were by then present, including an ever-increasing state role.

HANDICRAFT AND AUTONOMY

A history of Canadian printers in the first half of the nineteenth century, the period of autonomous regulation, commences in the 1820s, when Canadian print shops began to grow beyond simple artisan shops in which a master printer might utilize an apprentice or a combination of a journeyman and an apprentice.[3] By the 1820s the combined newspaper and job shops of the emerging Canadian cities began to bring small numbers of journeymen together in one shop and increasingly to allow the master, now a proprietor, to spend most of his time on journalism and politics. Indeed, some of the new enterprises of the late 1820s and 1830s placed men in charge of shops who were not members of "the art preservative," as printers described themselves. In these cases, journeymen were hired as foremen to run the practical side of the business.

What work did printers perform in these early shops? Printing involved two separate processes that in these early years were both carried out by the same individual: typesetting and presswork. Setting type or composing had not changed since Gutenberg and would not until the early 1890s. Composition involved taking a single piece of type from the case, placing it in a composing stick, and thus – letter by letter – spelling words with the appropriate spacing and line justification (insuring equal line length by either spacing-out or spacing-in through the addition or deletion of various slugs and leads). When the composing stick was filled with a few lines, they were transferred to a galley. When the galley was completed, it was run on a proofing press to take a single impression. After proof-reading, corrections were made and the galley was ready for the press. This second process, presswork, involved two printers working jointly – one inking, while the other screwed and pulled. The latter job involved considerable strength and both jobs were dangerous in the period of wooden presses whose screws occasionally broke, injuring the printers.

Thus, in the early years of the nineteenth century, printing remained a handicraft. Yet changes were already under way that heralded the industrialization of printing. The iron press was in the process of replacing wood, rollers instead of balls began to be used for inking, and experiments with horsepower and steam-power were commencing.[4]

In the smaller British North American towns, newspaper shops would change very slowly, but already by the 1830s in the growing cities, print shops were increasing in size and number. More important, it was also becoming clear that not all journeymen could aspire to be masters. As non-printers began to take on employers' roles as newspaper editors and publishers, the older craft solidarity of master and journeyman weakened. By the 1830s, then, printers for the first time began to identify their interests as distinct from those of their masters and from the trade at large. As a result, the first printers' unions emerged in the British North American colonies.[5]

The language of these early unions' statements of principle suggest how tenuous was this break. In Quebec, for example, printers formed their first union in 1827 and in 1836 defined their intent largely in terms of the improvement of the craft and declared their commitment to "the welfare of employer and employed."[6] In Toronto, the printers' initial public announcement pinpointed many persistent themes of nineteenth-century printers' unionism:

Owing to the many innovations which have been made upon the long established wages of the professors of the art of printing, it was deemed expedient by the journeymen printers of York, that they should form themselves into a body, similar to societies in other parts of the world, in order to maintain that honourable station and respectability that belongs to the profession.[7]

Drawing on the strengths of informal craft custom derived from both the Old World and colonial America and on the established practices of the previous thirty years of printers' unionism in England and the United States, Toronto printers quickly established a standard rate, an unemployment benefit, a tramping benefit for fellow craftsmen who chose to move on in search of work, sick benefits, a card system, rules governing apprenticeship, and apprenticeship limitation. They also initiated attempts to influence hiring by insisting on priority for unemployed union members. The major conflicts of the period revolved around apprenticeship; the Toronto Typographical Society (TTS) petitioned the legislature in 1836 "for the better regulation of apprentices in the art of printing."[8]

At first, Canadian publishers appeared to welcome the new unions and their rules. In most cases. practical printers themselves, they willingly accepted the printers' proud avowals that "the object of this society was for the interest of the employer as well as the employed." In October 1836, however, Toronto printers demanded a $1 increase on their scale and the strict enforcement of their apprenticeship limitation clause. Employer/employee unity broke down and, when the masters refused the increase, the union struck. The strike met vigorous employer opposition and the men were forced to return to work under a general amnesty without gaining their objectives, although some printers did receive the higher rate. In this case, employer solidarity, the defection of at least one union foreman, and the combined ability of masters, "rats" (the printers' term for scabs), and apprentices to continue to produce the weekly papers helped defeat the union.[9]

Although attempts were made at inter-union communication, these first printers' unions in Quebec (1827), Toronto (1832), Montreal and Hamilton (1833), and Halifax (1827) were intensely local[10] (see appendix 1). The Toronto Typographical Society's early years can thus be used as an example of this early phase of class struggle in the printing trade. After a seven-year hiatus, the Toronto union re-emerged in early 1844. In the interim, the old union scale "had in the main been upheld," thus suggesting that much of the early printers' strength lay in informal work groups. The impetus for reorganization came not from any immediate desire to press new demands, but from the arrival of George Brown who attempted to organize the Printing Employers Association with the general aim of reducing wages to the level of the provincial towns. Brown's interest in cost cutting apparently arose from the expense of importing Toronto's first cylinder press for the *Globe* office. The new machinery created initial financial difficulties for him, and, as an improving capitalist, he continued to try to reduce his labour costs. Brown's familiarity with the newest in machine presses was evident in his position as Canadian agent of H. Roe & Co. of New York, the major producer of the machinery.[11]

Another ongoing dispute between masters and men continued to focus on apprenticeship, which apparently provided the more traditional masters with their major saving. "This growing evil," as the union described "the mania for taking boys" in 1845, confounded the printers, for "it is a matter where the right of capital is so nicely balanced against the interest of labour that it requires a delicate and skillful touch to turn the scale in our favour." This "delicate touch" continued to escape the union and the most frequent grievance arising throughout the 1840s revolved around the terms and limitations of apprenticeship.[12]

Brown and his fellow employers slowly but surely were transforming the old handicraft trade into a new industry. Printers took note of these alarming developments and reorganized. Soon after Brown's arrival, the printers noted that "when clouds appear, wise men put on their cloaks." Thus, under a new motto "United to support, not combined to injure," the TTS explained that "as far as the scale of prices is concerned, they believe in adhering, taking all things into view, to what had hitherto been considered the customary rates in the city for piecework and weekly wages." In the wording of the union's statement, "everything calculated to give offence to the employers was studiously avoided." Brown's initial attempt at rate cutting failed because he was unable to carry the other Toronto employers with him. And a few months later, the union formally pre-empted another possible means of cutting labour costs by resolving that "when a compositor is employed by the piece he shall not allow the foreman, or other person, paid by the week, to make up his matter and take the 'fat' of the same." In this way, they prevented any master from reducing costs by taking the "fat" (in printers' parlance, the material most easily and thus quickly composed) "for the office," that is, to be set by a printer on a weekly wage as opposed to the more customary piece rate of the trade. In addition, for the first time, an overtime rate was demanded and won for night composition after 7:00 p.m. These gains led one year later to a renewed assault on the union by George Brown who, after filling his shop with boys, began to hire journeymen printers below scale. When the union expelled those working under the scale, Brown fired his union printers, including the TTS president, asserting, "I will not be dictated to by the Society as to what wages I must give men belonging to it. I will not be compelled to pay every man $7 a week." The union declared the *Banner* a rat office, and published "A Plain Statement of Facts," which made clear their continuing belief in the customary wage:

For a number of years a certain scale of prices has prevailed in this city which was considered perfectly fair and reasonable by all the employers ... and which continued in operation without exception until [Brown's arrival] ... who has ever since been unremitting in his liberal endeavours to reduce as low as possible that justly considered fair and equitable rate of remuneration due to the humble operative ... The printers of Toronto are but acting on the defensive and contending for no additional remuneration – nothing exorbitant or unreasonable – but, on the contrary, are only endeavouring to maintain that which is considered by all the respectable proprietors, as fair and just reward for their labour and toil. "The labourer is worthy of his hire."[13]

The Toronto union had other problems in the late 1840s. It experienced low attendance at meetings, probably owing to the continued relative autonomy of individual office work groups. This problem was overcome in three ways in the late 1840s, however, and did not recur subsequently. First, in 1848 the benevolent aspects of the society were consciously expanded to increase its stability. Second, the following year, foremen became full members instead of sustaining their previous honorary status – an extremely important development given the foreman's control over hiring. (This rule, later imbedded in the International Typographical Union's Book of Laws, proved central to union power.) Finally, Brown and the other master printers provided additional impetus for union growth in 1847 when, after a meeting with the journeymen to discuss craft matters, they presented a plan for a reduction in the wage scale that the printers successfully resisted.

By the late 1840s, then, handicraft printing had begun its slow evolution toward full-fledged industrial production. Clearly differentiated groups of workers and employers had emerged and confronted each other over the latter's attempts to cut their costs of skilled labour. But the labour process itself was still largely unchanged. With his agency for the most advanced technology, George Brown represented the future, but the new world of printing remained no more than a dim cloud on the printers' horizon. Symbolically, the Toronto printers greeted the new decade with one of their frequent dinners, which still involved masters and men united in a celebration of "the art preservative."

THE ROTARY PRESS, THE DAILY NEWSPAPER, AND LOCAL UNION RULE

In the years from 1850 to 1890, Canada experienced an industrial revolution. For printers, however, as for many groups of craftsmen, industrialization proceeded unevenly. By the late 1840s, an important component of the printing trades was about to join the ranks of industry. City newspaper production, based on growing urban markets, would be transformed in the following decades by steam-powered cylinder and rotary presses and the arrival in Canada of the daily paper.[14] Yet, only urban newspapers purchased the new machine presses, while in the book and job segments of the industry and in the country newspaper offices, the old presses would hold on for decades to come. At the same time, the evolution of the labour process within each sector was equally uneven. Typesetting remained unchanged in its reliance on skilled printers, and the stark contrast between the pressmen with his massive machines and the compositor with his case and composing stick demonstrates well the uneven transition from handicraft to industry within printing. The divisions between these two groups of workers continued to increase, and the "all-round" printer started his journey towards obsolescence.

For both employers and employees, the uneven development of the industry would make the achievement of unity difficult, and thus keep the battles between them surprisingly equal. Only later, as the division of labour advanced and the industry sorted itself out into trade segments, would capital unite. Equally, only after the workers themselves divided into the newly created component crafts would the possibility of a new unity present itself.

The cities led the way in these dramatic developments. In Toronto the first steam-powered press was introduced at the *Christian Guardian* office in 1851.[15] Two years later, George Brown continued his role as an innovator by bringing to the *Globe* Toronto's first rotary presses. The huge increase in the pace of production that resulted allowed newspaper publishers to produce dailies in place of the older tri-weeklies, semi-weeklies, and weeklies. In 1860, the *Globe* added a second large, double-cylinder press and new American folding machines. The increasing size of the firm was reflected in its incorporation a few years later as the Globe Printing Company on a limited liability basis. In 1868, a new building was purchased large enough to house the paper's two massive new Hoe Lightning four-feeder presses. The demands of the daily papers for quicker production led to the introduction of new improved web presses (roll fed, rather than sheet fed) at the Montreal *Star* in 1875, and at the Toronto *Globe*, *Mail*, and *Telegram* in 1880. By 1881 the *Globe* had the most sophisticated plant available.[16]

These new presses and the daily papers they made possible transformed the scale of newspaper production and dramatically raised capitalization levels. Between the 1850s and the 1880s, these pressures brought about a "fierce struggle" to extend circulation and eliminate competition that culminated in numerous newspaper failures and mergers, especially in the depressions of the late 1850s and the 1870s. Historian Paul Rutherford has described the industry as reaching the status of "ruthless" form of "big business" by the 1860s. The increasingly separate book and job branch of the industry also faced a crisis in the 1870s owing to "ruinous competition," which led Theodore L. De Vinne, a leading New York employer, to express concern about "the menacing aspects of the future" for the industry. In Ottawa in particular, the problem was cutthroat competitive bidding for government printing contracts.[17]

These developments in the printing industry after 1850 had profound implications for the work force. In the first place, they drove a wedge between the compositors, whose handicraft skills remained intact, and the pressmen, who had become machine-tenders. A printer told a royal commission in the 1880s that he was familiar with small presses, but knew nothing of the large rotaries, which he described as "out of the line of the usual printer's work."[18] Although this division had been developing for years, the crisis came to a head in the 1870s and led initially to separately chartered pressmen's locals of the ITU (Ottawa 1880; Toronto 1883; Montreal 1887). In 1889, however, after years of tension, the pressmen seceded to form the International Printing Pressmen's Union (IPPU). This split led to years of inter-trade wrangling, although a modicum of pease resulted from the so-called Tri-Partite Agreement of 1895, which conceded local jurisdiction over pressmen to the IPPU and of bookbinders to the International Brotherhood of Bookbinders. All pledged to work together in an Allied Printing Trades Council in each city that would control the union label.[19]

Second, the growing separation of the book and job sector of the industry from newspaper publishing grew more apparent in the 1870s, as newspapers increasingly abandoned their job shops. This separation carried serious implications for printers because the branches emphasized different skills. Most job shops demanded more varied skills that more closely resembled the talents of the old-time, all-round printer, whereas the urban daily newspapers were increasingly specialized. The built-in variation in pay scales, whereby newspapers paid by the piece and job shops by the week, led increasingly to quite separate negotiations and different scales for the two branches of the industry.

In the newspaper offices, rising capitalization and vigorous competition led publishers to pursue cost-cutting tactics, especially in the still labour-intensive typesetting work. In the labour/management strife that ensued, masters viewed the conflict specifically in terms of workplace control: "The simple truth of the matter is the journeymen insist upon ruling editors, publishers and anyone connected with the establishments, especially in the morning paper offices. The dictation has reached the point where it becomes intolerable; and the employers, one and all, have resolved to submit to it no longer, be consequence what it may."[20]

The printers fought back by strengthening their union organization. In the wake of the 1854 strikes in Toronto and Quebec, they first canvassed the idea of a broader, Canada-wide organization, but without any success.[21] Eventually, the continental labour market in which Canadian artisans worked led Canadian printers to join the National Typographical Union in the United States. Saint John led the way in 1865, and locals in Toronto, Montreal, Ottawa, Hamilton, Halifax, London, St Catharines, and Quebec followed in quick succession (see appendix 2). The new Canadian membership brought a change in the name of the central organization to the International Typographical Union. Not surprisingly, these centres of printers' unionism coincided almost completely with the urban areas where daily papers had caught on: Montreal had eight; Halifax, Saint John, Toronto, and Quebec four each; and Ottawa, Hamilton, London, and St Catharines three each. (The lone exception to this pattern was Kingston, which had two dailies in 1872, but no ITU local until 1886). After encountering difficulties in the economically depressed 1870s (the Saint John and Halifax locals lapsed briefly), the ITU's Canadian membership rebounded with new vigour in the 1880s, and new locals were added in Ontario and the West.

These local unions sought to consolidate and defend craft control of the labour process through carefully policed "laws." As a Toronto printer explained in the 1880s, all matter in union shops was distributed equally: "Whatever may be first on the hook is given to the first men calling for it." Foremen, who were union members, had complete control over hiring. A wage scale was not reached by bilateral negotiation: the union men would simply "discuss it in the union first and then change the scale," the Toronto printer noted.[22] In 1878, the Toronto local further developed its organization by empowering a three-man "Guardian Committee" to act as a secret body to deal with "unfair" shops and printers who violated union rules.[23]

These unions' power lay not only in their members' valuable skills, which could be withdrawn from any printing offices that refused to accept union standards of employment, but also in the newspapers' susceptibility to public pressure owing to their dependence on circulation revenue. In 1853, the Toronto printers initiated a provocative and innovative strategy by appealing for broad support in *An Address to the Working Classes of Canada*. This general indictment of the Brown family's labour policies over its ten years in Canada concluded with a warning:

WORKING MEN, OF WHATEVER CALLING! ... Beware of the *Globe* – put no faith in its proprietor: The oppressor of the Journeymen Printers is the oppressor of the journeymen of every other trade. It is necessary, then, to say that George Brown *is the enemy of the working classes generally.*[24]

This kind of appeal was particularly effective in the midst of the newspapers' competitive battles in the 1880s, when printers first introduced boycotts against Toronto and Halifax newspapers, a tactic imported from the Irish struggles and popularized by the Knights of Labor throughout North America.[25]

In their confrontation with the ITU locals, the publishers resisted not only new wage demands, but also any restrictions on their ability to make use of their employees' labour-power. The most famous episode of industrial conflict in the period involved the question of shorter hours of work, which the Toronto union first raised in 1869, partially echoing the militant American movement spearheaded by the National Labor Union, in which the ITU was active. In 1872, a major struggle pitted the Toronto printers against George Brown and a hastily organized Master Employers' Association. The issue was the nine-hour day, and Toronto printers provided the cutting edge for the larger movement. This strike is almost as famous as the Winnipeg General Strike in Canadian history and need not delay us here, except to note that the issue revolved around control and authority, not wages. The printers sought a 10 per cent increase on piece rates and a 10 per cent decrease in hours in book and job shops. The masters indicated their willingness to concede the former, but with Brown's leadership resisted shorter hours and "the tyrranical thralldom of the Typographical Society." The strike became a political cause célèbre, especially when Brown decided to prosecute the leadership of the union for conspiracy. Great political advantage accrued to the Conservatives owing to their major Toronto newspaper's support of the printers, and to the Macdonald Tory government's passage of a Trade Unions Act to legalize unions. The strike resulted in a split decision: the printers won the nine-hour day in most Toronto job and bookshops, but the union temporarily lost its position in some of the Toronto newspaper offices.[26]

Often in the years after 1850, Canadian printers fought more defensive battles, as their employers resorted to a variety of managerial innovations to chip away at craft control. After an 1853 strike in Toronto, the workers' recriminations against the great innovator, the *Globe*, brought these practices to light. "Anything but full employment had been the order of the house," since piece hands were often kept standing idle and week hands were frequently laid off for half and even quarter days, "a practice unknown in any other office, probably in America," the printers complained. Compositors were often kept at work until 3:00 or 4:00 a.m., only to find that there was no work for them the next day, "thus impairing their health and turning the hours of repose into those of labour." The printers also warned that apprentices suffered "gross injustices" at the *Globe* since they were subject to arbitrary dismissal and, in addition were not instructed in the secrets of the craft. Finally, against Brown's vow not to pay men of unequal merit the same rate, the union requested that he convert his shop from weekly pay to piece rates, as was the norm in other Toronto newspaper offices, and provide them with sufficient work.[27] In a similar vein, Saint John printers lost a strike in 1859 over the limitation of apprenticeships,[28] and in 1873 the Ottawa Master Printers declared that foremen must leave the union, that the open shop must prevail, that departing journeymen must give two weeks notice, and that no printer could leave work without the consent of the employer.[29]

Newer managerial tactics were even more threatening. One major change was the development of night work in order to produce morning papers. Toronto printers denounced this "unnatural" system of work in 1853, and the struggle against it continued the following year, when their demands included another advance in the overtime rate and, for the first time, pay while standing idle. The newspaper proprietors protested that these demands were a hidden attempt to abolish night work, but their compromise offer, which was eventually accepted in the major print shops, conceded differential rates for night work, but not its abolition, as the union had demanded the year before. Employers offered small advances with higher pay for night work while abolishing charges for overtime. In effect they moved toward a clearly recognizable shift system that entrenched night work in the industry.[30]

Another innovation in the 1850s that had serious long-term implications was the recruitment of women as compositors in a strike-breaking role. Toronto publishers used them in the 1854 strike, as did London employers in 1856.[31] Boys and country printers continued to be used as well; in fact, a Toronto printer argued in the 1880s that the steady influx of young, country printers who "go and come like swallows" and often were not properly trained constituted the biggest problem facing that city's printers. But unionized printers' ire singled out employers who resorted to using women as "rats." By the 1880s, women, nonetheless, had only a limited role in the industry, mostly performing recognizably inferior work owing to their lack of training and their usually short time at the case. While welcome to join the union and entitled to equal pay, they seldom fulfilled the five-year initiation requirement to demonstrate competency. There were, however, two women in the Toronto union by 1887.[32]

In the 1870s and 1880s, new attacks were launched on compositors' customary prerogatives. In most offices, for example, the "fat," especially advertisements, had been distributed in various ways devised by the printers themselves to preserve equitable pay. These devices were necessitated by the standard piece rates of the newspaper branch of the industry. Innovative cost-cutters continued to fight for the right to keep the fat "for the office," that is, to give it to less efficient compositors paid by the week. Similar struggles occurred over the ITU's "matrix law," whereby the union demanded that either all material published in a newspaper had to be typeset on the premises, or else the compositors had to be paid as though it had been. This rule prevented publishers from using various kinds of pre-set plate matter to fill their pages while avoiding composition costs. In the 1880s, numerous agencies sprang up to provide precisely these services to newspapers in the form of so-called boilerplate. The ITU fought plate matter from its inception, while profit-conscious employers tried to introduce it continuously.[33] When the Royal Commission on the Relations of Capital and Labour visited Saint John in the late 1880s, it discovered an ongoing fight over fat and plate matter. "I do not agree that the printer is entitled to the fat matter," one proprietor explained. "I think that a man who has control of a business like a newspaper, who has all the care and responsibility of the concern, should have something to say in the matter." He frankly admitted that taking the fat was an economy measure caused by increasing competition, as was the use of plate matter, which he viewed as "a kind of improved machinery."[34] In 1887, the Saint John local lost a major strike against the city's three newspapers over the use of plate matter,[35] and the St Catharines printers' defeat in three unsuccessful strikes in an eighteen-month period in the late 1880s over the same issue led to the local's demise.[36] A similar issue emerged in an unsuccessful strike against the Toronto *World* in 1888, when its proprietor refused to abide by a union rule that any additional insertion of an ad, if it was changed at all, was to be paid for again in its entirety.[37]

The years between the 1850s and the 1880s, then, saw the struggles between the skilled printers and their employers intensify. On the one hand, the workers had tightened the bonds of unity by joining the ITU and adopting its increasingly rigid set of "laws" governing the trade; on the other, their bosses, caught in cutthroat competitive battles, relentlessly attacked craft control over the labour process. There was no final victory in this trench warfare. In 1884, the Toronto *Mail* was still blustering that it "purported to resume the control of the necessary and proper economies of our own business, which had largely passed into the hands of the Printers Union";[38] and three years later the manager of the Saint John *Sun* was still muttering about management's right of "using their own property as suits themselves" and refusing to "submit to dictation on the subject."[39] In some cities, the printers had suffered severe defeats, but in Toronto at least, they maintained much of the workplace control (which David Montgomery and others have associated with the autonomous workman) that was now increasingly centred in the union. Certainly their maintenance of craft control should belie any lurking romantic notions of conflict-free handicraft based on "customs" and "traditions." There were customs, but they were established in the rough-and-tumble of class conflict. None was safe from the encroachment of improving employers.

THE LINOTYPE AND THE TRIUMPH OF THE INTERNATIONAL UNION

Two related changes took place in the labour process and work relations of the Canadian printing industry at the close of the nineteenth century – mechanization and bureaucratization. One brought machinery into the composing room, the bane of the improving-employers' life, which Theodore De Vinne (the F.W. Taylor of printing) once described as "the great sinkhole" where "the profits of the house are lost."[40] The second drew Canadian printers and their unions into much more centralized structures of collective bargaining.

The industry, especially the newspaper sector, was reaching much larger proportions by the 1890s. The first step toward concentration of capital appeared when the Southams of the Hamilton *Spectator* purchased the Ottawa *Citizen*, which they combined with their huge job shops in Toronto and Montreal.[41] Monopoly capitalist strategies thus began to figure even in the newspaper business, formerly a bastion of competition in limited markets. This trend toward concentration was also evident in the founding in 1889 of the McKim advertising agency as a central clearing house for the placing of national and regional newspaper advertisements.[42] Even more important, however, was the growth of national and continental employers' associations.

Across North America two of these organizations emerged in the late 1880s. The United Typothetae of America (UTA), covering the book and job branches of the industry, met for the first time in 1887 "to resist the demands of the International Typographical Union for the nine-hour day." While often split between what Clarence Bonnett called "negotiatory" and "belligerent" factions, the UTA was generally at war with the ITU. Encouraged by an initial victory in 1887 in defeating the union's campaign for shorter hours, the UTA proceeded to refuse any conference with the ITU and planned further assaults on long-standing union rules – control of foremen, limitation of apprentices, the holding of union meetings during business hours, the closed shop, the matrix law, priority laws, and other examples of union power. The UTA dealt the ITU another strike defeat in Pittsburgh in 1891–3 and won smaller victories in a number of local struggles, including Montreal and Ottawa, where Theodore De Vinne's "Printers' Protective Fraternity" provided strikebreakers. The ITU's continental alliance with the bookbinders' and pressmen's unions in 1895, however, convinced the UTA of the need for compromise, and in 1898 the Syracuse Agreement was signed, covering both Canada and the United States. The other continental employers' association, the American Newspaper Publishers' Association (ANPA), also founded in 1887, tended towards a "negotiatory" position, and after 1900 entered into elaborate international arbitration agreements with the ITU and other printing trades' unions.[43]

Canadian publishers and printers joined both the UTA and the ANPA, but they also had an organization of their own that shared a similar history. The Canadian Press Association (CPA) had been founded in 1859, but through its first three decades it functioned primarily as a social club for small-town newspaper publishers. The Toronto press, for example, maintained its splendid isolation from the CPA for many years. By the late 1870s, however, more interest was being expressed in the business side of newspaper publishing, and the trend continued in the 1880s. By 1888, the CPA had established its aim as "the principle of improving the prosperity of the newspaper industry." Complaining of too much competition, of the growth of advertising agencies and their commissions, and of declining subscription rates, the publishers piously pronounced that "a newspaper, to be a power for good, must make money." Not surprisingly, then, topics at conventions in the early 1890s included typesetting machinery and myriad discussions of managerial strategy. These interests intensified early in the twentieth century and in 1905, a Daily Newspapers Section of the CPA was created. This body would be a major actor in the renewed struggle over shorter hours.[44]

Meanwhile, union centralization was growing as a result of the union's failure to implement shorter hours in the trade in 1887. The creation of the UTA as an employers' association with clear anti-union aims and its success in defeating the ITU shorter-hours strikes in 1887 created an impetus for union reform. These institutional changes, which had been proposed earlier but rejected by the membership, brought in full-time officers, an international strike fund, and executive control over the decision to strike. The appointment of district organizers led to the development of specialists in bargaining who travelled from city to city as union trouble-shooters. The much-vaunted local autonomy of the typographical unions, especially big-city locals like

Toronto Local 91, was considerably eroded in this process. By the turn of the century, a pattern of large-scale binational negotiations was established, with provisions for international arbitration.[45]

The significance of these binational developments was accentuated for Toronto printers because of their almost unique status of already having won the nine-hour day in 1872. One of only three ITU locals on the continent with this contract provision, the Toronto local was understandably less than enthusiastic about an expensive struggle against the UTA, especially when in 1891 it was refused international sanction for a proposed struggle to increase the Toronto wage scale. The events of the 1880s and 1890s signalled a real decline in local union power that, in the Toronto case, would be damaging to its interests in the future. This conflict between the local and the International was mediated for Toronto printers by the presence of W.B. Prescott, (a stalwart of the Toronto local) as ITU president from 1891 to 1898.

After 1887, union/management negotiations in Toronto were qualitatively different. Instead of the unilateralism of the autonomous regulation period, or even the tentative consultation of the period of union regulation, this period witnessed the establishment of full-scale collective-bargaining procedure. The union appointed a scale committee that, in effect, became a bargaining team. The committee formulated its demands and communicated them to the newly formed Toronto Printing Employers' Association. Meetings took place in which the masters presented their counterproposals in a bargaining environment. The committee then consulted the union on the revised set of proposals. Details on the 1887 negotiations are scant, but in 1890–1, this process took a full eleven months before the International refused to sanction a strike – a far cry from the immediate stikes called earlier in the century.[46]

These new, more centralized structures of capital and labour were soon tested in two major confrontations, first over the introduction of typesetting machinery and then over the eight-hour day. The major technological innovation, which finally ended the remaining handicraft skill of typesetting, was Otto Mergenthaler's invention of the linotype machine. Extraordinary efforts at designing a mechanical device to set type had continued throughout the nineteenth century, but the increased flurry of experimentation in the 1870s and 1880s that culminated in the new machine enjoyed considerable attention and enthusiastic support from the increasingly profit-conscious employers. Especially crucial in the newspaper industry, above all at the big-city dailies, where speed was of the essence, the machine spread across Canada in the 1890s. Initially, it appeared to represent an answer to employers' major problems: the physical limitations on production resulting from hand composition and the union's ongoing control of the composing room. As it turned out, only the first problem was overcome, since the ITU locals won control over the operation of the machines. Guided by central ITU policy, union strategy was not to resist their introduction, but to insist that only practical printers should run them.

The challenge of the linotype came first in the large cities, and the Toronto experience illustrates the union's success in integrating the machinery into its shop-floor control patterns. The *Globe* bought the first typesetting machine in 1891, and the union immediately began to prepare a new scale of wages for machine operators, simultaneously pushed by the *Mail*'s complaint that the union was forcing it to acquire machines because union printers were working too cheaply on the *Globe*'s machines. The employers responded that new scales were premature, since they were still unsure of the machines' capacities. But the union proceeded unilaterally to declare a new wage rate, which would be a time rate rather than the customary payment by the piece. The men wanted to avoid the speedup that might result from piecework on the new machines. In September, the newspaper publishers eventually agreed to an acceptable scale. Only the *News*, and a few months later the *Presbyterian*, forced the printers out on successful strikes to resist the introduction of piece rates. Even the *Telegram*, the only non-union office remaining in Toronto, came to terms and became a strict union office after almost twenty years of resistance. All Toronto newspapers, in fact, were union shops, as were most book and job shops, and estimates of union organization in the 1890s ranged between 85 and 90 per cent of the industry. Union members were to learn on the machines at a rate of $12 a week for six weeks and then $14 a week after demonstrating their proficiency, which was set at a low level of 2,000 ems per hour or 100,000 ems per week. Thus, by the early 1890s, the union had achieved almost complete organization of the industry and had won control over the use of the new machines, thanks to the combination of the printers' shop-floor and union strength, the skill requirements of the new technology, and the employers' evident desire to stabilize costs in the industry.[47]

The other great struggle of the period, for the eight-hour day, was co-ordinated even more tightly from ITU headquarters and highlighted the change that had taken place from autonomous control through union power to the triumph of centralization. After the "armed truce" of the 1898 Syracuse Agreement, which brought the nine-hour day a year later, both sides spent the following years "preparing and hoarding for a great struggle over the eight-hour day and the closed shop." In 1902, the ITU set up an International Eight-Hour Committee, which called on all locals not to sign contracts dated beyond 1 October 1905 unless they contained eight-hour clauses. The UTA, meanwhile, refused all attempts at compromise and discussion, instead insisting that the ITU cease to control foremen, an ITU rule dating from the 1850s. When, in 1903, the pressmen's union accepted a Typothetae guarantee of union scale and union conditions in return for the open shop, the war became inevitable. The fight commenced in September 1905, when the ITU called out all locals without the eight-hour day and not under contract in support of its embattled Chicago, Detroit, and San Antonio locals. This call pulled out some 88 locals and 3,000 printers, and the number increased by January 1906, the original date proposed for the strike. Unlike many strikes where victory or defeat are quick and clear, the strikes dragged on for almost three years. The 1907 ITU convention dismissed its Eight-Hour Committee with victory in sight, but the various strike assessments, while diminished after October 1906, were not completely lifted until the end of February 1908. The magnitude of the strike may perhaps be illustrated by the total of $4,163,970.64 that the ITU estimated it spent in winning the eight-hour day. And win it did, although at great cost. Even the UTA conceded defeat when, in February 1908, it quietly dropped the 54-hour-a-week phrase from its official policy. By that date the association had shrunk to half its pre-strike size, since each city employer's group was forced to resign when it capitulated to the ITU.[48]

The major struggle in Canada had taken place in Winnipeg, but there had been battles in several other centres. Only in Winnipeg and Saint John did resistance amount to much. After the ITU walked out in September 1905, the Winnipeg branch of the Typothetae fought long and hard, and resorted to the importation of English printers. The fact that these compositors were induced to migrate without being given information of the strike in progress created a furore that eventually led to a polite condemnation from the Department of Labour, penned by the inimitable W.L.M. King. The department officially listed the strike as over in November when the Typothetae members filled their shops with the unwitting Brits, but the strike continued and in January most of the English printers left work and joined the ITU. By June 1906, the local labour press reported all union printers at work in eight-hour shops. The Typothetae's open-shop drive had failed in Winnipeg.[49]

The Saint John local pressed its demand for eight hours in early December 1905 and succeeded with the newspapers but not with the job shops. After a short strike, most of the employers conceded, one of them muttering that it was "outrageous that an employer can be held up by his workmen and forced to grant whatever they have in mind to ask whether he feels like doing so or not." By April the last holdout conceded defeat and Saint John, too, was an eight-hour city.[50]

The other Canadian eight-hour strikes were minor affrays. In Hamilton and Halifax, brief strikes took place to force small recalcitrant shops into line. In London, it took only a one-day strike to gain the shorter day in all but one shop, while in Regina, one week proved enough to muscle one newspaper into line. The strike in Guelph, however, was more interesting. There, an agreement had been reached in summer 1905 that the printers would receive the eight-hour day on 1 January 1906, as long as the ITU did not change its position. As it turned out, later representations from the Daily Newspaper Section of the CPA to the ITU executive in September 1905 led to an agreement for an 8½-hour day on 1 January 1906 and a further reduction to eight hours on 1 July 1907. This settlement prevailed in many Ontario localities, including Guelph. Guelph printers, however, who had won an eight-hour Saturday three years before, could not believe that this meant an increase in Saturday hours for them until July 1907, and when the employers tried to enforce this increase, they struck. The employers appealed to the ITU executive, which responded by ordering their Guelph members back to work. Centralized power clearly cut in both directions.[51] This was also apparent in other Canadian jursidictions. In Hamilton, a revolt against the 10 per cent levy on the union membership to finance the eight-hour fight led to the suspension of the local's charter for three months in 1906, while in Ottawa, the relatively privileged Government Printing Bureau printers led a major secession movement away from the ITU in protest over the extra assessment.[52]

In Toronto the scene proved even more complicated. Because they were tied into a three-year contract that did not expire until 1 June 1907, the city's printers were on the sidelines of the initial struggle. When, in early summer 1907, they began to negotiate, they demanded both eight hours and wage increases. The talks soon deadlocked and International vice-president J.W. Hays arrived in Toronto to intercede. Hays met with the local's scale committee and was filled in on their negotiating stance and on the fact that any agreement had to be ratified by the membership. He proceeded to settle for far less than they sought and signed the contract. In the ensuing tumult, the International president backed Hays and asserted that the International must support such a contract signed in good faith. The infuriated Toronto union threatened mightily, but eventually backed down before the International, which two months later claimed with a straight face that the Toronto agreement was a great victory. Sanctity of contract, bureaucratic dirty tricks, refusal of membership ratification rights, all came with what American writers of the J.R. Commons school liked to term "the high-water mark of typical American unionism."[53]

Both union control of the linotype in the 1890s and the shorter-hours victories of 1898 and 1906–7 were at best ambiguous triumphs. In their wake came a vastly more centralized, bureaucratized ITU – a union that increasingly defied rank-and-file control. This conflict would come to a head in the major confrontation between the New York Typographical Union "Big Six" and the ITU leadership in 1919, when the New York local broke openly with the ITU and took their members out in the so-called Vacationist Movement, after refusing to accept an international arbitration agreement. While eventually defeated in 1919 with the active support of the ITU leadership, rank-and-file printers had had enough, and in 1920 the old leadership was thrown out and replaced with the more militant "Progressives" led by John McParland.[54]

Although wages varied throughout Canada printing centres, other general patterns appeared in the 1880s and 1890s, including the surrender of local control to the international union and successful control of the linotype. By this period the seeds of twentieth-century developments were evident for labour, capital, and, in a muted fashion, the state. In the years after the eight-hour struggle, the ITU would grow even more powerful; the UTA – created first to battle labour and then later to conciliate it – would struggle vigorously for the open shop in 1921; and the Canadian state would extend its experimentations with developing a legal structure to contain and mediate class conflict.

Although the periods of handicraft and of autonomous control were long gone, printers continued to hold considerable power at the workplace – a power that had been maintained despite extensive mechanization, an ever-increasing concentration and centralization of capital, and the emerging machinations of a far-from-neutral state.

Printers, the labour aristocrats of Victorian and Edwardian Canada, won many victories in their struggles with capital. In the first period of autonomous control, they benefited greatly from their rare skill and from the deep divisions that kept their partisan employers from uniting against them. The industrialization of printing brought power presses into the system, and an increasing division of labour both within the structure of the industry (newspapers versus book and job work) and between two distinct groups of printers (compositors versus pressmen). Nevertheless, more formalized union control, derived partially from the traditions of autonomous control, was established through ever more frequent struggles between printers and their employers. The latter still laboured under significant divisions and it was only in the late 1880s that they created continent-wide associations to battle the international union. The following two decades of warfare saw two significantly different employer strategies emerge. The newspaper branch of printing, buoyed by the extraordinary expansion of the dailies made possible by the linotype and the new national advertising revenues of the emerging monopoly sector, largely pursued a policy of peace. After testing the ITU on the machine question, they settled into a "negotiatory" stance that led to a series of international arbitration agreements governing the major city dailies of the continent after 1900. Meanwhile, the United Typothetae of America, born in the struggle against shorter hours, pursued a holy war for the open shop. Engaged in an intensely competitive branch of printing, the Typothetae's members felt they could not afford the concessions that the newspaper publishers extended to the ITU. Without doubt the ITU benefited from this divergent employer strategy, although they increasingly did so by winning victories for the elite of their members – newspaper compositors – at the expense of other printers. The result of these struggles in the printing industry was a set of work relations governed by a rigid bureaucratic code of rules and regulations consolidated in contracts and watched over by a more centralized union bureaucracy.

Printers, then, entered the twentieth century with much of their power and control intact. Canadian printers were not unique in this achievement; it was shared by printers internationally. How do we account for their relatively unusual success in withstanding the onslaught of capital, unleashed in the massive restructuring of labour processes and of the working class? No single explanation will suffice. Printers combined their old craft customs with a vigorous trade unionism to defend their position. They also achieved control of the new technology of the typesetting machine by cleverly acceding to a process of reskilling and demonstrating their willingness to work the new machines. In addition, their literacy, general standing in the community, and leadership in the broader trade-union movement all provided extra clout in bargaining. And finally, in the newspaper industry, the employers' dependence on intensely competitive local markets led to their placing a high premium on stability. In this, printers resembled building-trades workers who also maintained strong craft traditions during this period.

There can be little doubt of the necessity of viewing working-class history through the lens of changing work relations. The eminently historical character of contemporary work relations demonstrates in important ways that they are not "inevitable and eternal," as they too often appear. "Technological determinism" and "iron laws of bureaucratization" must be debunked through a historical understanding of capitalist decision making about machines and workplace arrangements. Most important, this history must emphasize the role played by working-class resistance in the evolution of the capitalist work process. As Jonathan Zeitlin has argued in his stimulating study of British compositors and engineers, changes in the labour process are "the outcome of a complex process of struggle and negotiation which cannot be deduced from a unilinear view of capitalist development."[55]

Late nineteenth-century labour militants like George McNeill understood this struggle. Writing at the height of the "Great Upheaval," he noted that printers were "pioneers in testing and enforcing 'usages and customs' in trade unionism."[56] Yet the firmament of McNeill's America was transformed in the two decades following 1886. For printers, the major symbol of monopoly capital's brave new world was undoubtedly the typesetting machine. For Hamilton printer-historian Frank Kidner, alias "Red-Ink," this new world called forth a compendium of printers' lore. Nostalgically he worried about the passing of "the old order of things" with its "race of printers full of quaint conceits and eccentricities," and he despaired of the new technology:

Ye printers dear, what's this I hear; the news that's goin' round?
A grand machine, to take your place, has surely now been found.
It'll set the type quite neatly, at a most tremendous speed,
And the clever printer man, they say, we shall no longer need.

Nostalgia and despair, however, were not Red-Ink's final reflection, nor should they be ours:

But the summer time will come again and winter's winds will blow,
And many a harvest time will come again and go,
Ere the thing of cranks and gearing takes the place of pen and ink,
Or supplants the toiling typo, with his power to *work* and *think*.[57]

APPENDIXES

APPENDIX 1
Preliminary List of Nineteenth-Century Local Printers Unions

Quebec	1827–; 1836–44; 1855–
Toronto	1832–7; 1844–
Montreal	1833–?
Hamilton	1833–?; 1846–?; 1852–3; 1854–
Halifax	1837–?
Kingston	1846–?
London	1850–?
Saint John	1856–9
Victoria	1863–?
St John's	1883–

APPENDIX 2
Canadian ITU Locals to 1908

Local number	City	Date initial organization	Subsequent organization
85	Saint John	1865	surrendered 1878; rechartered 1881
91	Toronto	1866	
97	Montreal	1867	see locals 145, 176
102	Ottawa	1867	
129	Hamilton	1869	suspended 1906; reinstated 1906
130	Halifax	1869	surrendered 1879; rechartered 1883
133	London	1869	
145	Montreal (Jacques Cartier)	1871	
147	St Catharines	1870	surrendered 1875; rechartered 223, 1887; surrendered 1891; rechartered 1901

Local number	City	Date initial organization	Subsequent organization
159	Quebec (French)	1872 ⎱	amalgamated as local 302, 1893
160	Quebec (English)	1872 ⎰	
176	Montreal (English)	1871	
191	Winnipeg	1881	
201	Victoria	1884	
204	Kingston	1886	suspended 1906
51	Brantford	1886	surrendered 1889?; rechartered 273, 1890; surrendered 1898; rechartered 378, 1900
171	Calgary	1887	failed, 1888?; rechartered 449, 1902
226	Vancouver	1887	
227	Peterborough	1887	suspended 1891; rechartered 279, 1893; surrendered 1894; rechartered 248, 1902
253	New Westminster	1889	suspended 1894; rechartered 264, 1899; surrendered 1903; rechartered 632, 1908
258	Guelph	1893	suspended 1896; rechartered 391, 1901
143	Belleville	1896	suspended 1898; rechartered 257, 1901; suspended 1902
280	Sherbrooke	1896	suspended 1900
317	Nelson	1896	suspended 1898; rechartered 340, 1899
335	Rossland	1896	
257	Brandon	1896	suspended 1898; rechartered 656, 1905; surrendered 1906
317	Woodstock	1899	suspended 1900; rechartered 1902; surrendered 1906
337	Nanaimo	1899	surrendered 1905
358	Greenwood	1899	suspended 1906
366	Berlin	1899	surrendered 1905
139	Stratford	1901	
393	Brockville	1901	suspended 1906
411	Galt	1901	
157	Sydney	1901	suspended 1903;
459	St Thomas	1901	suspended 1906; reorganized 1908;
460	Chatham	1901	surrendered 1906
464	Charlottetown	1901	suspended 1903
467	Dawson	1901	surrendered 1906
296	Lindsay	1902	surrendered 1906
550	Windsor	1902	suspended 1907; rechartered 553, 1907

Local number	City	Date initial organization	Subsequent organization	
604	Edmonton	1903	surrendered 1906; rechartered 1907	
421	Sarnia	1904	surrendered 1905	
579	St Hyacinthe	1904	suspended 1906	
539	Pt Arthur	1904	surrendered 1906; rechartered 575	
647	Sault Ste Marie	1905	surrendered 1906	
417	Ft William	1905		
627	Moose Jaw	1905		
657	Regina	1905		
664	Fredericton	1905		
666	Moncton	1905	suspended 1906	
663	Saskatoon	1906		
540	Cranbrook	1907		
541	Vernon	1907		
551	Lethbridge	1907		
5	Toronto (mailers)	1894		
27	Winnipeg (mailers)	1905		
6	Ottawa (newspaper writers)	1902	suspended 1903	
10	Montreal (newspaper writers)	1904	suspended 1906	
23	Winnipeg (German-American)	1906		
5	Ottawa (pressmen)	1880	surrendered 1890	⎫
10	Toronto (pressmen)	1883	surrendered 1890	
30	Montreal (pressmen)	1887	suspended 1892	⎬ IPPU
7	Ottawa (pressfeeders)	1889		
7	Toronto (pressfeeders)		surrendered 1890	
1	Toronto (web pressmen)	1894		⎭
4	Ottawa (bookbinders)	1889	suspended 1893	IBB
21	Toronto (stereotypers)	1893		⎫
33	Montreal (stereotypers)	1898		⎬ ISEU
50	Ottawa (stereotypers)	1901		
59	Winnipeg (stereotypers)	1901		⎭
9	Montreal (photo-engravers)		suspended 1899; rechartered 1901; suspended 1903	⎫ ⎬ IPEU
20	Toronto (photo-engravers)		suspended 1901	⎭

IPPU	International Printing Pressmen's Union, 1889
IBB	International Brotherhood of Bookbinders, 1893
ISEU	International Stereotypers and Electrotypers Union, 1902
IPEU	International Photo-Engravers Union, 1902

Source: ITU, Proceedings.

APPENDIX 3

Tentative List of Canadian Printers' Strikes to 1908

1836	Toronto	1888	Saint John		Vancouver
1853	Toronto		Ottawa	1899	Toronto
1854	Toronto		Hamilton		Halifax
	Quebec		Quebec		London
1856	London		St Catharines (2)		Ottawa
1859	Saint John	1889	Vancouver		Winnipeg
1866	Quebec		Halifax	1901	Montreal (3)
1869	Ottawa	1890	Toronto	1902	Toronto
	Montreal		St Catharines		Halifax
1870	Ottawa		Montreal	1903	Montreal
1872	Hamilton	1891	Toronto	1904	Quebec
	Montreal (2)	1892	Vancouver		Montreal (2)
	Toronto		Ottawa (2)		Winnipeg
1873	Ottawa		Toronto (2)	1905	Winnipeg (2)
1877	Ottawa		Saint John		Edmonton
1878	Toronto		Halifax		Halifax
	Montreal	1893	Toronto (2)		Saint John
1879	Stratford		Vancouver	1906	Saint John
1880	London	1894	Winnipeg		Winnipeg (2)
	Montreal	1895	St John's		Montreal
1881	Saint John		Toronto		London
1882	Montreal	1896	Toronto		Guelph
	Winnipeg		Winnipeg		Regina
1883	Toronto		Vancouver		Hamilton
	Montreal (2)	1897	Rossland	1908	Saint John
	Ottawa		Winnipeg		Winnipeg
1884	Toronto		Calgary		Halifax
1885	Winnipeg	1898	Winnipeg		Vancouver
1887	Vancouver		Brandon		

Sources: ITU, *Proceedings*; *Historical Atlas of Canada*, vol. 2, thanks to Bryan Palmer; *Historical Atlas of Canada*, vol. 3; research.

NOTES

My thanks to Doug Cruikshank for research assistance, and to Russell Hann whose insights into the transformation of the nineteenth-century newspaper industry have been particularly stimulating. In addition, I would like to thank this volume's editors for their scrupulous and rigorous efforts. An earlier version of this paper was presented at the Commonwealth Labour History conference, University of Warwick, 2–4 September 1981.

1 On O'Donoghue, see Gregory S. Kealey, *Toronto Workers Respond to Industrial Capitalism* (Toronto 1980), passim, and Gregory S. Kealey and Bryan D. Palmer, *Dreaming of What Might Be: The Knights of Labor in Ontario* (New York and Cambridge 1982), passim; on Armstrong, see Kealey, *Toronto Workers*; on Simpson, see Gene Howard Homel, "James Simpson and the Origins of Canadian Social Democracy" (PHD dissertation, University of Toronto 1978); on Puttee, see A. Ross McCormack, "Arthur Puttee and the Liberal Party, 1899–1904," *Canadian Historical Review* (hereafter CHR) 51 (1970): 141–63, and his "British Working-Class Immigrants and Canadian Radicalism: The Case of Arthur Puttee," *Canadian Ethnic Studies* 10 (1978): 22–37; on Pettipiece, see McCormack, "The Emergence of the Socialist Movement in British Columbia," *BC Studies* 21 (1974): 3–27, and his letters to the *Typographical Journal* 24 (1904), 304–5, 646; 28 (1904): 292; 26 (1905): 576; International Typographical Union (hereafter ITU), *Proceedings*, 1908.

2 Richard Price, *Masters, Unions and Men* (Cambridge 1980); see also his "The Labour Process and Labour History," *Social History* 8 (1983): 57–76, and "Rethinking Labour History: The Importance of Work," in James E. Cronin and Jonathan Schneer, eds, *Social Conflict and the Political Order in Modern Britain* (New Brunswick, NJ 1982).

3 On early Canadian printing, see H. Pearson Gundy, *Early Printers and Printing in Canada* (Toronto 1957); Eric Haworth, *Imprint of a Nation* (Toronto 1969); Carl Benn, "The Upper Canadian Press, 1793–1815," *Ontario History* 70 (1978): 91–114; and similar literature for other Canadian regions.

4 Rollo G. Silver, *The American Printer, 1787–1825* (Charlottesville, Va. 1967), passim. See also Lawrence C. Wroth, *The Colonial Printer* (Charlottesville, Va. 1964).

5 Note, for example, the prominent treatment given printers in Eugene Forsey, *Trade Unions in Canada* (Toronto 1982), 9–31.

6 Ibid., 14–15.

7 On the early years, see John Armstrong's serialized history of the Toronto Typographical Union published in the *Toiler* (Toronto), and conveniently available in a scrapbook in the Robert Kenny Papers, University of Toronto Archives. See also Sally F. Zerker, *The Rise and Fall of the Toronto Typographical Union, 1832–1972* (Toronto 1982), ch. 2, and Forsey, *Trade Unions*, 18–28. Quotation as rendered by Armstrong from original minute book, 12 October 1832.

8 John Armstrong's serialized "History" (n. 7 above).

9 For a curious view of this strike, see F.H. Armstrong, "Reformer as Capitalist: William Lyon Mackenzie and the Printers' Strike of 1836," *Ontario History* 59 (1967): 187–96. For anyone who finds this persuasive, see also Paul Romney,

"William Lyon Mackenzie as Mayor of Toronto," *Canadian Historical Review* 56 (1975): 416–36.

10 Forsey, *Trade Unions*.

11 John Armstrong's serialized "history"; Toronto Typographical Union (hereafter TTU), minutes, Ontario Archives; *Globe* (Toronto); Zerker, *Rise and Fall*, ch. 3; Forsey, *Trade Unions*, ch. 1; on Brown, see J.M.S. Careless, *Brown of the Globe*, 2 vols (Toronto 1959–63), I; on the press, see Paul Rutherford, *A Victorian Authority: The Daily Press in Late Nineteenth-Century Canada* (Toronto 1982).

12 On the pervasiveness of the apprenticeship question, see John R. Commons, ed., *A Documentary History of American Industrial Society* (Cleveland 1910–11), VII, 109–31.

13 TTU, minutes, 2 July 1845.

14 Rutherford, *Victorian Authority*, ch. 2–3.

15 Elizabeth Hulse, *A Dictionary of Toronto Printers, Publishers, Booksellers, and the Allied Trades, 1798–1900* (Toronto 1982), x–xi.

16 For details on the *Globe*, see Careless, *Brown*, passim. See also Rutherford, *Victorian Authority*.

17 Rutherford, *Victorian Authority* and idem, *The Making of the Canadian Media* (Toronto 1978), 9; ITU, *Proceedings*; *Printers' Circular* (Philadelphia) 4, no. 10 (December 1869): 373; 7, no. 7 (September 1872): 253–4; 8, no. 7 (September 1873): 248.

18 Canada, Royal Commission on the Relations of Capital and Labour, *Report* (hereafter RCRCLR): *Ontario Evidence* (Ottawa 1889), 36–51.

19 For an excellent history of the pressmen, see Elizabeth Faulkner Baker, *Printers and Technology: A History of the International Printing Pressmen and Assistants Union* (New York 1957).

20 *Globe*, 2 July 1853.

21 Hamilton Typographical Union, minutes, Special Collections, Hamilton Public Library.

22 RCRCLR, *Ontario Evidence*, 36–51.

23 TTU, minutes, 1878–80.

24 This pamphet, partially damaged, is held in the pamphlet collection of the Ontario Archives.

25 Kealey and Palmer, *Dreaming of What Might Be*.

26 Despite the fame of the strike, Paul Craven's recent discovery of the court records in the Criminal Assize Clerk's Files at the Ontario Archives promises new insights.

27 *Address to the Working Classes in Canada*. On the many strikes of the 1850s, see Paul Appleton, "The Sunshine and the Shade: Labour Activism in Central Canada, 1850–60" (MA thesis, University of Calgary 1974); and Bryan D. Palmer, *The Working-Class Experience: The Rise and Reconstitution of Canadian Labour, 1800–1980* (Toronto 1983), ch. 2.

28 *Daily Sun* (Saint John), 28 February 1898, in Canada, Department of Labour, vertical file, RG 27 (3126), file 1, Public Archives of Canada (PAC).

29 *Printers' Circular* 4, no. 10 (December 1869): 373; 13 no. 7 (September 1873): 248.

30 *Globe*, 28 June, 2 July 1853; 2, 7, 8, 9, 12, 16, 23 June 1854.

31 Appleton, "Sunshine and Shade."

32 RCRCLR, *Ontario Evidence*, 36–51.

33 ITU, Executive Council, *A Study of the History of the International Typographical Union, 1852–1963*, 2 vols (Colorado Springs 1964), II, section III (hereafter ITU, *Study*).

34 RCRCLR, New Brunswick, 179–86.

35 Saint John Typographical Union, minutes, New Brunswick Museum; Richard Rice, "History of Organized Labour in Saint John, New Brunswick, 1813–90" (MA thesis, University of New Brunswick 1968), ch. 5.

36 ITU, *Proceedings*; Kealey and Palmer, *Dreaming of What Might Be*, 370–71.

37 *Globe*, 26, 27 July, 8, 15 August 1888; *Typographical Journal*, 15 September 1889; *Mail*, 17 August 1889.

38 For a full discussion of the Toronto context, see Kealey, *Toronto Workers*.

39 Quoted in Rice, "Organized Labour in Saint John," 152.

40 Quoted in Baker, *Printers and Technology*, 69.

41 Charles Bruce, *News and the Southams* (Toronto 1968).

42 H.E. Stephenson and Carlton McNaught, *The Story of Advertising in Canada* (Toronto 1940), 19.

43 On the employers' associations, see Clarence E. Bonnett, *Employers' Associations in the United States* (New York 1922), especially chs 8–9; Leona M. Powell, *The History of the United Typothetae of America* (Chicago 1926); Charlotte E. Morgan, *The Origin and History of the New York Employing Printers' Association* (New York 1930); Selig Perlman and Philip Taft, *History of Labour in the United States, 1896–1932* (reprint, New York 1966), 51–60.

44 A.H.U. Calquhoun et al., *A History of Canadian Journalism ... 1859–1908* (Toronto 1908); W.A. Craick, *A History of Canadian Journalism, II: 1919–1959* (Toronto 1959).

45 ITU *Study*, II, section III, ch. III.

46 Zerker, *Rise and Fall*, ch. 6.

47 For a detailed discussion of these struggles, see Kealey, *Toronto Workers*, ch. 6.

48 ITU, *Proceedings*, 1905–8.

49 Ibid.; *Typographical Journal*, 1905–8; *Labour Gazette*, 1905–8, especially W.L.M. King, "Investigation of Alleged Fraudulent Practices in England to Induce Printers to Come to Canada," VI (1905–6), 1122–30; *Clarion* (Winnipeg), 4 November 1905 (clipping in Russell Papers, Public Archives of Manitoba).

50 *Daily Sun* (Saint John), 1 January 1906. (My thanks to Robert Babcock for this source.)

51 *Labour Gazette*, 6 (February 1906): 918–19.

52 ITU, *Proceedings*, 1907.

53 Perlman and Taft, *History*. On the strike, see TTU, *Minutes* and Zerker, *Rise and*

Fall, ch. 8. While Zerker's account is factually correct, the attribution of the difficulty to the 49th parallel is indefensible. Needless to say, major American locals were also being victimized. The greatest conflict of this kind would come later in 1919, when the ITU turned its full power against New York's "Big Six" to destroy the so-called Vacationist Strike. Nationalism is too simple an answer. See my review in *Canadian Book Review Annual* (1982), 337–8.

54 ITU, *Study*, section III, ch. IV.

55 Jonathan Zeitlin, "Craft Control and the Division of Labour: Engineers and Compositors in Britain, 1890–1930," *Cambridge Journal of Economics* 3 (1979): 263–74, quotation at 272.

56 George McNeill, *The Labor Movement* (New York 1887), 189.

57 "Red-Ink" [Frank Kidner]. *"Pi": A Compilation of Odds and Ends Relating to Workers in Sanctum and Newsroom Culled From the Scrap-book of a Compositor* (Hamilton 1890), 215–16.

DAVID FRANK

Contested Terrain: Workers' Control in the Cape Breton Coal Mines in the 1920s

The strikes of coal miners have a prominent place in modern labour history. "Eclatantes, massives, spectaculaires," Michelle Perrot has written, "les grèves minières attirent tous les regards."[1] Work stoppages, however, are exceptional events in labour history, for strikes represent only one type of episode in the continuum of events at the workplace. And although it is often noted that the coal miners have gone on strike more frequently and more effectively than other workers, historians have devoted relatively little attention to the importance of the workplace in explaining the shape of conflict in the coal industry.[2]

The coal miners' workplace loomed large in the events of the 1920s in industrial Cape Breton, the location of the largest coalfield in eastern Canada.[3] A study of this period of intense class conflict confirms the importance of the theme of "workers' control" in analysing what Eric Hobsbawm has described as "the conditions of working class effectiveness."[4] A persistent local tradition of workers' control enabled the coal miners to adopt resourceful tactics in the strikes of the time and encouraged them to seek radical solutions to the problems of the coal industry. This study also suggests that it is important to distinguish at least three meanings of a term like "workers' control": (1) *organic control*: common attitudes and practices of the coal miners' daily work life favoured the growth of a limited but significant tradition of workplace authority; (2) *tactical control*: at key moments in the strikes of the 1920s, the coal miners exploited the unusual physical conditions of their workplace in order to strengthen their effectiveness in confrontations with their employer; (3) *strategic control*: the militancy of the coal miners in the 1920s also included strong sympathies for ideals of industrial democracy, public ownership, and other alternatives to capitalist domination of the coal industry.

In 1920, the formation of the British Empire Steel Corporation seemed to promise an era of harmonious labour relations in the coal mines; indeed during the construction of the merger that year, promoter Grant Morden boasted that the new corporation planned to include labour representatives on the board of directors.[5] Within a few short years, however, Besco was notorious for its wage-cutting policies. Only the 1920 agreement was concluded without a strike, and the following years would be remembered as "labor's war." By 1925, Besco president Roy Wolvin made no secret of his desire to eliminate the United Mine Workers (UMW) from the coalfield and described the union as "a body whose object is to secure possession of our corporation's property, whether by nationalization (with or without compensation) or Workers' Control."[6]

From its beginning in 1920, the new corporation was concerned about an existing pattern of workers' control in the mines. The terms of the "Montreal Agreement" in fall 1920 included new clauses designed to limit the coal miners' authority within the workplace. A section entitled "Management of Mines" stated: "The right to hire and discharge, the management of the mine and the direction of the working force are vested exclusively in the company, and the United Mine Workers of America shall not abridge this right." Elsewhere the contract also specified: "Employees shall perform such work as the management may direct." Another clause stated that work stoppages were to be considered violations of the agreement: "It is distinctly understood that no other grievance shall be considered where men suspend work to enforce adjustment and employees shall not be sustained in such course." The only exceptions to this provision were to be in the case of the employers' failure to pay wages or in the case of unsafe conditions in the mines; even the traditional right to stop work for accidents and miners' funerals was to be negotiated by a committee. Finally, a clause headed "Duties and Limitations of the Mine Committee" subordinated the miners' pit committees to a formal grievance procedure culminating in arbitration. This section of the contract ended on a hopeful note: "Miners to continue to work from the inception until the final adjustment."[7]

When delegates from the local unions met to review the new contract in November 1920, there were vocal objections to these clauses. Peter McMahon, a union leader at Dominion No. 1, claimed the agreement would set the miners back to a time when they were unable to protest dismissal of their fellows. Another delegate protested that the union's closed shop was endangered and that local grievances would not be settled if the right to stop work was sacrificed. Delegates rejected the contract by a vote of 76:20.[8] A stormy referendum campaign followed in which the district officers were vigorously assailed at local union meetings for betraying the miners' interests. On one occasion, at a meeting in New Waterford, union vice-president Robert Baxter and secretary-treasurer J.B. McLachlan, both men with established reputations as radical union leaders, were pelted with a shower of eggs. McLachlan argued persuasively that the evils in the contract were exaggerated and that the wage advances were substantial ones. He also stressed another gain: "Now we have the operators locked into a pledge to meet with us at end of contract. That is something we never had before." In the end, the officers prevailed, and the new contract was approved by a vote of 6,499 to 4,490.[9]

The controversy over the Montreal Agreement suggests the importance of an organic tradition of workers' control in the mines. Formally, the coal miners were entitled to little authority within the workplace. Under the Coal Mines Regulation Act, each colliery was under the "daily personal supervision" of the mine manager. In practice, however, the mine was not entirely an autocracy; Ian McKay has very usefully compared the government of the mine to a constitutional monarchy in which managers and miners exercised reciprocal rights.[10] Certainly mine managers readily recognized that the organization of work relations in the mines and the physical conditions of the workplace limited the effectiveness of managerial authority and inspired a powerful sense of independence in the individual mineworker. A wise mine manager knew that the best approach to a coal miner was a deferential one. As J.R. Dinn of Glace Bay reminded members of the Mining Society of Nova Scotia: "If the official is in the habit of approaching a man in an unbecoming manner, using a gruff and harsh voice, the man naturally becomes discontented and careless, due to the fact that he resents this treatment."[11]

Although the coal industry was a founding force in the Industrial Revolution, the coal mines had escaped – as late as the 1920s – some of the characteristic effects of industrialization. From the surface, the coal mines appeared to resemble huge underground factories or "Great Black Cities." The employment of capital and technology on a large scale permitted the operation of the large collieries that typified the Cape Breton coalfield and in some cases extended more than two miles from the shoreline. About 10 per cent of the annual coal production was consumed in generating power for colliery operations. Powerful surface engines hauled as much as 18,000 tons of coal from the deeps every day; great fans propelled millions of cubic feet of air into the distant workings; and for every ton of coal that arrived at the surface, powerful pumps removed seven tons of water from the mines. But from the depths of the coal mines, where the great majority of coal miners worked, the industry resembled not so much a factory as the scattered settlements of a rough, primitive, and often pre-industrial countryside. The coal miners' workplace was unusual in many ways. The miners worked in a labyrinth of dark slopes, tunnels, and caverns located hundreds of feet below the surface of the land and the ocean. In their travel to work and in their daily tasks, the coal miners confronted harsh physical conditions: rough footing, steep grades, a low roof, dripping water, narrow passageways, pools of stagnant water and mud, cold rushing air currents, clouds of bitter smoke and choking coal dust, falling stone and coal overhead, fatal pockets of methane gas embedded in the seams, and finally, an almost universal darkness.[12]

The most important factors shaping the organization of work in the coal mines in the 1920s were the restricted scope of mechanization at the coal face and the persistence of the room and pillar system of mining. In the 1920s, the coal industry suffered from a significant technological lag. The most arduous and time consuming of operations – the loading of coal – proceeded entirely by hand, "as in the days of the Duke of York." Although coal-cutting machinery was employed extensively after the 1890s, loading operations did not become the subject of innovation until the 1920s. Longwall mining allowed the extraction of 100 per cent of the coal and simplified mine operations, but in most of the Cape Breton mines the depth of cover was not sufficient to permit the introduction of longwall mining before the 1920s.[13] Room and pillar remained the dominant system of mining. In the decades after the 1920s, the gradual mechanization of loading and the general introduction of longwall mining profoundly transformed the shape of the coal miners' workplace. But in the 1920s, despite the advance of machinery and adjustments in the division of labour, the Cape Breton mines remained largely hand powered, labour intensive, and tradition bound in organization.

In the work force at the mines, about four in five workers were employed underground. More than half the underground miners worked directly at the coal face; in the isolated 20-foot-wide "rooms," the miners, usually working in teams of two, extracted the coal from the seam and loaded it into wooden boxes. Another large group of workers transported the coal, first by horse and then by mechanical haulage, to the surface. Other mineworkers maintained roadways, airways, roof supports, tracks, pumps, fans, engines and other equipment, cleared fallen stone and coal, carried supplies and tools, opened new sections, and performed other tasks. The labour-intensive nature of mine operations is illustrated by the fact that, in the years 1913 to 1924, for the Dominion collieries the cost of labour-power ranged from 53.23 to 65.03 per cent of the cost of producing a ton of coal, and normally exceeded 60 per cent.[14] The number of coal-cutting machines in the Dominion collieries in 1923 was approximately equal to the number of pit horses at work in the mines.[15] By the 1920s, machinery occupied an accepted place at the coal face, but only partially affected the organization of work. At the coal face and on each level, the number of men employed in hand-powered operations greatly exceeded the number of those running machines.[16]

Coal mining also remained dangerous work. Accidents were a constant factor in the miner's working life, and the comment "Nobody I know escaped injury in the mines" was a common recollection. The published Mines Report ceased to include information on non-fatal accidents in 1919, but reported 294 accidents in 1917 and 362 accidents in 1918. In the years 1917–26 a total of 207 men and boys died in the collieries of the Dominion and Scotia companies

in Cape Breton.[17] Almost one-third of the total belonged to a group of 65 men
and boys who died in an explosion in No. 12 colliery, New Waterford, on 25
July 1917. This was the largest disaster ever to strike the Cape Breton mines
and the explosion dramatized the price of coal for a generation of miners.[18]
Most of the deaths, however, resulted not from major calamities but from the
daily toll of fatal accidents. More than 40 per cent of the total were caused by
falls of stone, coal, and timber from the roof and walls of the mines. The
various haulage operations were also a major cause of deaths during this
period and accounted for almost 20 per cent of the total: men were struck, run
over, or crushed by moving coal cars and boxes.

A close relationship existed between the physical conditions of the mines
and a vigorous workplace culture. "Being down in the mine is a different
world there altogether," reflected one miner, "not just simply the physical
environment but the feeling of the men." The coal miners' ability to master the
unusual conditions of the mines was a continual source of pride. Coal miners
often recalled the wide range of instinct and experience that assisted the miner
in his work. "Pit workers tell of 'getting a feeling' that makes them stop and
investigate," wrote Stuart McCawley; "it may be a change in the air pressure,
a queer odour, a crack or creep in the rock." The days before the advent of
longwall mining and mechanized loading were recalled as a time when the
miners took great pride in their work. "It was a trade. Coal mining was a trade
then," recalled one man, and another added: "We built up a certain pride. This
is my mine. This my section of the mine. And you prided on that."[19]

Some sections of the Coal Mines Regulation Act did recognize the miners'
special interest in their workplace. The coal miners had the right "at their own
cost, from time to time" to appoint two men to inspect conditions in the mine.
When the manager prepared the required "Special Rules" for his colliery, he
was required to post these prominently and for two weeks the miners had the
right to propose changes to the Mines Department. Another provision stated
that officials could not search employees for matches, tobacco, pipes, and
other contraband materials unless they also allowed themselves to be
searched. A separate section of the act ensured the status of the checkweighman, who guarded the miners' interests at the scales at each colliery. Paid by
the miners through deductions from their earnings, the checkweighman ran
for annual election; he was often likely to be a miner injured in a mine accident
or a worker blacklisted by the company.[20]

Although not recognized in legislation, the pit committee also embodied
the coal miners' workplace authority. This committee was usually a
three-man body elected by the union members at each colliery. The
committee represented the men at inquiries into accidents, and the constitution of UMW District 26 provided that committees conduct regular inspections
of the mine.[21] The pit committee's most important function was to adjust
disputes and grievances as they arose in the course of the day, or as they were

TABLE 1
Strike Activity, 1917–1926

Category	1917	1918	1919	1920	1921	1922	1923	1924	1925	1926	Total
Wages				5	2	1 D		D	D	3	14
Non-industrial		D		4 D		1	2 D (D)	(D)		(D)	13
Production relations	2	3		7	3	8	4	5		5	37
TOTAL	2	4	–	17	5	11	8	7	1	9	64

D district strike.
(D) incomplete district strike.

presented at the local union meeting. While the individual workman dealt directly with the overman or the underground manager, the committee negotiated directly with the mine manager. The rapid settlement of grievances was crucial to the coal miners. Innumerable conditions affecting the miner's earning power were beyond his control: wet places, narrow seams, weak roof, fallen coal, insufficient boxes, poor air pressure. "If you didn't get your 10 or 12 or 15 tons a day, you didn't get a pay day," explained one miner. A common coal-town greeting referred to this constant worry: "How're you gettin' your coal out?" Each week the miners crowded into their union halls to hear pit committees and local officers report on their negotiations with the mine management. Though the coal miners shared many common grievances, what is most notable is the amazing diversity of grievances among the coal miners. One former local union leader has recalled that this was a large factor in the vitality of the miners' union in the 1920s:

When you went to a local union meeting after the contract was signed, what were you dealing with? The different conditions in the hundreds and hundreds of places in the pit ... As a rule there were enough grievances coming out of the pit to give us a big meeting. When you had big meetings you could talk about a lot of things, put a lot of things over. So that's why we had big meetings those days, and good meetings they were.[22]

An analysis of the pattern of strike activity in the mines also reveals some of the scope of this organic tradition of workers' control. Although the large coal-miners' strikes of the 1920s in Nova Scotia won national attention and accounted for more than 2.1 million striker-days, most of the coal-miners' strikes were short, localized confrontations that received little notice in official publications such as the *Labour Gazette*. In the years 1917–26, a total of 64 strikes were found. Most of these were short, one-to-three-day stoppages, originating in local issues and usually culminating in a complete shutdown of the mine. In the information summarized in table 1, the individual strikes were grouped in three principal categories, according to the type of issue precipitating the strike.[23] Wage disputes were only one cause of conflict and accounted for only 14 strikes of the total number. A second group of 13 strikes originated outside the workplace and illustrated the miners' assumption that they enjoyed the right to close the mines on a variety of appropriate occasions: these included elections, circuses, May Day, political protests, and sympathetic strikes.[24]

The largest group of strikes involved disputes over the relations of production within the mines. At stake here was the authority of the mine managers to control the organization of work in the mines. Resistance to formal time discipline appeared on several occasions: miners insisted that "as soon as the men had done their work they would be free to go home"; they also objected to a new checking system governing access to the mines.[25] In protests involving the use of mine machinery, the men protested the shortcomings of the older "puncher" machines in order to protect their earning power and to enhance efficiency in mine operations.[26] The most common strikes involved challenges to work assignments and discipline in the mines: the miners protested the transfer of men to lower-paid duties, demanded extra hands in work crews, and objected to the employment of a mine official guilty of "neglect of duty and uncalled for conduct." In strikes against the dismissal of individual mineworkers, the miners defended workers accused of "shirking" their duties, violating regulations, refusing reassignment in other tasks, quarreling with (and in one case assaulting) an official, and otherwise "not doing a fair day's work." In all but two of these cases the miners were successful in defending the discharged men.[27] The miners were also notably effective in protecting the status of the union at the workplace, which was the issue in six strikes. These stoppages strengthened the position of the pit committees, maintained mine examiners within the union, and enforced the closed shop when groups of new recruits appeared at the pitheads.[28]

Although the outcome of workplace disputes was not always known, few defeats were reported, and it seems clear most of these "unofficial" strikes enjoyed some measure of success. The miners expected at least a compromise: we hear this assumption most clearly in the description of one dispute as a protest against the "company's alleged red-tape system and failure on the part of the mine officials to meet the men half way."[29] By tying up the mine, the miners served notice that officials were exceeding the acceptable bounds of their authority. By choosing to take action on such occasions, the miners were able to exercise a continual restraining influence on managerial authority in the workplace.

As in the controversy over the Montreal Agreement in 1920, there was evidence in several of these strikes of tensions between local protests and district authority. Most of these local strikes took place without the authorization of the district executive. At times, the union officers advised local strikers to return to work without achieving their aim. For instance, in the aftermath of the 1922 district strike, mineworkers tied up the four northside pits to support the beleaguered local railway brotherhoods. The district officers commended the men's solidarity, but stated that under the new settlement, they must return to work.[30] However, it would be difficult to characterize the district officers as loyal exponents of "industrial legality." The controversy over the Montreal Agreement led the officers in 1921 to propose amendments to the "Management of Mines" clauses and the elimination of arbitration of grievances. When a contract was finally signed in 1922, the document included no detailed terms apart from wage rates, a feature that enabled union officers in 1923 to claim that the sympathetic strike in support of the Sydney steelworkers was not a violation of contract.[31] It is clear that the district officers often threw their support behind protests originating in local workplace actions. In one notable example, some 2,000 men in four neighbouring pits went on strike to protest the discharge of nine surface workers. The executive endorsed the action and helped bring the strike to a successful conclusion.[32]

While company officials responded to the miners' organic control of the workplace by attempting to limit the mineworkers' authority through contract clauses and disciplinary measures, union leaders attempted to harness workplace protests to the more general goals of the union. Probably the most controversial workplace actions undertaken by the coal miners in the 1920s were the "strike on the job" and the "100 per cent" strike. These forms of protest could only be understood and accepted among workers who shared common assumptions about their right to exercise a powerful latent authority within their workplace. This type of concerted workplace action designed to achieve major union objectives involved a second form of workers' control, which may be described as tactical control.

This approach was closely associated with the radical leadership of the union in the early 1920s. Among these leaders the dominant figure was the secretary-treasurer, J.B. McLachlan, whose formative experiences in the Lanarkshire coalfields in the 1880s inspired him to apply the residual wisdom of the "independent collier" to the new circumstances of mass trade unionism and monopoly capitalism in the early twentieth century. In 1921, as the second confrontation with the Besco management approached, McLachlan drew a vivid picture of workers' control in the Lanarkshire pits:

The writer worked in Lanarkshire, Scotland, the home of Robert Smillie, when the Lanarkshire Miners' union was organized, and of course as the miners had never heard of this thing called "recognition," it never occurred to them to consult the operators at all in securing many of the things which they wanted. They simply went ahead and legislated for themselves without ever once consulting the operators. Here are three things which they did: – Inaugurated an eight hour working day from bank to bank, instituted a five day working week and set the exact number of pounds of coal any one man could dig. When these things were done, the men simply assumed the attitude the operators had taught them in the days when they had no union. These old country operators felt very important and they used to say, when troubles occurred between them and the miners, "We have nothing to discuss, we have nothing to arbitrate," and so the miners occupied the trenches dug by the operators and refused to arbitrate or discuss the amount of work that they would perform.[33]

Restriction of output was under discussion as early as May 1920, when company officials were refusing to meet with the union to negotiate the new contract. McLachlan himself proposed a 50 per cent reduction in output in order to hurry the operators to the bargaining tables. Similar suggestions were advanced in the Phalen local at Dominion No. 2, where a local officer threatened "systematic holidaying" or "other means to curtail the output of the mine."[34] The extent to which this tactic was practised in 1920 cannot be measured, but in the first three months of 1922, restriction of output played a crucial part in the first major wage struggle of the 1920s.

Following a one-third wage cut in January, in February the miners rejected the findings of a conciliation board by a vote of 10,305 to 468, and in March they rejected a compromise negotiated by the union officers by a vote of 8,109 to 1,352. In the absence of support for strike action from the international office of the UMW, the coal miners turned increasingly to restriction of output in these months. By mid February, a reporter for the Halifax *Herald* found that "Fabian tactics [had] spontaneous growth, arising with the men themselves as their method of expressing dissatisfaction with the wages now in force ... Beyond question, it has operated to cut down production in some mines by something like 50 per cent."[35] A miner who worked at No. 5 colliery recalled how the slowdown was organized:

All the men agreed in the local union to load six boxes of coal, that'd be leaving off four boxes. We generally loaded ten ... The driver took his time and the man that was working at the face took his time ... And the shiftman had his coat on, the man who was putting up the timber. And he seen a light coming, he'd get up and he'd start to move around ... We all endorsed it and put it into effect. And it was effective ... There were only a couple of mines in the district that were kind of slow in endorsing this slowdown, but before it went into effect too far the whole district endorsed it, and they had it going for months. And the company hollered. They were getting hurt.[36]

Originating as a spontaneous workplace protest against the wage reduction, the slowdown was eventually recognized as official district policy in the wage struggle. Following the rejection of the proposed contract in a referendum vote on 14 March, McLachlan issued a formal circular appealing for general adoption of the slowdown: "War is on, and it is up to the workers in the mines of the British Empire Steel Corporation to carry that war into the 'country' of the enemy. There is only one way to fight this corporation and that is to cut production to a point where they cannot any longer earn profits." Joint meetings of locals in the Glace Bay and New Waterford districts endorsed the policy, and after a stormy meeting in which the executive was equally divided, on 23 March the district executive also endorsed the slowdown.[37]

Though controversial, "striking on the job" proved effective in the limited purpose of gaining reconsideration of the coal miners' case against the wage reduction. In a furious exchange of telegrams, McLachlan defended the morality of the tactic against Minister of Labour James Murdock, a former officer of the Brotherhood of Railway Trainmen, who charged the miners were "un-British, un-Canadian and cowardly to pretend to be working for a wage rate in effect while declaring to the world that only partial and grudging service will be given." It was the federal government rather than the corporation that finally took action. McLachlan twice addressed appeals to the House of Commons and the dramatic protest attracted national attention to the crisis in the coalfields. An emergency debate took place in the Commons on 30 March, and as the minority Liberal government faced criticism from all sides, the government agreed to the unusual step of reconvening the conciliation board.[38]

The second major form of tactical workers' control adopted by the coal miners in the 1920s was the withdrawal of maintenance men from the mines. In the "100 per cent" strike, the removal of men from the colliery powerhouses, pumps, fans, engines, and other equipment exposed the mines to the dangers of accumulated gas and water. Again, this tactic was strongly endorsed by McLachlan. Rejecting the traditional UMW policy of supplying maintenance men during strikes, in July 1922 McLachlan urged the miners to "forget all the ethics that they had been taught about the property of the owners."[39] When the 1922 strike began at midnight on 15 August, pumpsmen, enginemen, firemen, and other maintenance workers joined the walkout. Stablemen removed pithorses from the mines, and crowds of strikers marched to the power plants at Waterford Lake and No. 2 colliery and shut down these operations. Similar tactics were employed in July 1923, when the miners struck in support of the Sydney steelworkers. Strikers dumped coal on the railway tracks and aggressively patrolled entrances to the yards. When the company requested that men be supplied to lift coal from the No. 2 bank, where the coal pile was reaching high temperatures, the union officers refused the request.[40] These dramatic shutdowns prompted John Moffatt, the former leader of the Provincial Workmen's Association, to object: "No greater tragedy has ever occurred in Canadian history, and it is being conducted with a callous recklessness that savors of madness."[41] In contrast, the local worker-poet Dawn Fraser mocked the company's powerlessness:

> Now, where these tactics are employed,
> Of course, the mine will be destroyed,
> The master class will lose their hold,
> The capitalists will lose their gold.
>
> Then Roy the Wolf began to weep,
> His tears fell fast, his groans were deep –
> "I don't care what you do to me,
> But, oh! protect my property!"[42]

In fact, the effects of a complete cessation of maintenance work were not tested, for a "white collar brigade" of officials and office staff were permitted access to the mines to perform some essential duties.[43]

As a tactic, the dramatic protest was only partly successful. In 1922, Nova Scotia Premier G.H. Murray speedily concluded an agreement for the resumption of maintenance work and appointed a new conciliator, who engineered a new agreement eliminating about half the original wage cut. The premier's rapid intervention, more than seven months after the dispute began, appeared to result mainly from the dramatic workplace actions employed by the miners in 1922. The following year, however, the "100 per cent" tactic was superseded by other events in the determining the outcome of the strike. McLachlan and union president Dan Livingstone were arrested on criminal charges in connection with the circular calling the strike, and ten days later UMW president John L. Lewis revoked the district charter and suspended the executive for calling a strike in violation of contract. The steelworkers' strike was broken, and newly appointed provisional officers organized the mineworkers' return to work.

The administration of District 26 under the trusteeship revealed a less sympathetic attitude on the part of union officers toward workplace action. In January 1924, the miners once more battled wage reductions. Headed by Silby Barrett, a defeated rival of McLachlan and Livingstone, the provisional executive negotiated an agreement covering maintenance work at the mines, and the 25-day strike progressed "in an orderly and lawful manner."[44] Included in the new agreement was a clause entitled "Maintenance Men During Suspension of Mining" that repudiated the "100 per cent" strike as a violation of the agreement. Although the contract included small increases in the miners' rates, the contract was rejected in a referendum vote; this result was ignored by the provisional executive. The Glace Bay Gazette noted that miners particularly objected to the restoration of clauses specifying managerial authority: "They are regarded as 'too binding' and as tending to deprive the miners of their accustomed liberty of action in the pits. We do not pretend to understand the real significance of the objectionable clauses. Probably they were designed to bring about a better state of discipline in the mines, by all accounts an object greatly to be desired."[45]

And yet, when the long struggle against Besco was renewed in 1925, once more the withdrawal of maintenance men was a notable feature of the confrontation. Endorsed by the again autonomous district in a convention in November 1924, the withdrawal of maintenance men at the beginning of the long strike in March 1925 carried no element of surprise.[46] When Wolvin protested the policy, he won little sympathy from John L. Lewis, who replied that this was "a blunder only exceeded by the action of the British Empire Steel Corporation in locking out their employees and attempting to have them starved into a wage reduction." Following a trip to Nova Scotia in April, Lewis dropped his opposition to the "100 per cent" tactic entirely and approved the payment of limited relief funds to the strikers. At first no picketing took place at the collieries, and officials and office staff performed minimal duties without obstruction. For the first two months of the strike, despite the withdrawal of maintenance men, attention focused not on the workplace but on the struggle of the union, town councils, and citizens' committees to provide adequate food, shelter, and clothing for the population. Donations poured in from across the country, but there was no progress toward a settlement.[47]

By the third month of the strike, the miners, fearing defeat, began to adopt more aggressive measures at the collieries. Union locals in Glace Bay placed pickets at the mines, preventing officials from entering the yards. Other locals rejected proposals to implement "100 per cent" picketing throughout the district. But at the end of the month, the strike reached a critical turning point. Refusing to meet the union's elected officers on the grounds that four executive members were "communists," the corporation offered separate settlements to several union locals; these involved acceptance of the wage reductions and abolition of the union check-off. On 1 June 1925, the union executive offered to submit the dispute to arbitration by the minister of labour, but this concession was rejected by the corporation. In this context, on 3 June, the executive returned its attention to the workplace and announced a policy of "100 per cent" picketing. The temporary work crews met obstruction at the collieries and in the next few days more than thirty arrests took place.[48]

The sharpest conflict came in the New Waterford district, where a struggle for control over the company power plant precipitated the climax of the strike. As the Waterford Lake power plant supplied both the collieries and the community with power and water, this installation had been excepted from the original withdrawal of maintenance men. But in accordance with the new district policy, on 4 June the miners shut down the Waterford Lake power plant and ejected company officials from the building. One week later, early on the morning of 11 June, a force of about 60 company officials and company police surprised the miners' pickets and recaptured the plant. When the news reached town, the coal miners assembled on the ballfield and some 800 men trekked through the woods to the scene. They were met by company policemen, mounted on horseback and firing handguns. Several miners were shot and one of their number, William Davis, was killed. In the short, pitched battle the police were routed, and those who did not escape into the woods or across the lake were marched into town and beaten and bloodied in the street. On the following nights, a wave of property violence swept through the coal towns: company stores were raided and burned, and several colliery buildings were also destroyed.[49]

Again, workplace action proved the turning point in the strike. The federal government moved swiftly: as in previous years, the Canadian army was rushed to the coalfields, and federal officials attempted to bring the corporation and the union to a settlement. Ultimately, following a provincial election, it was the newly elected Nova Scotia premier, E.N. Rhodes, who achieved a temporary agreement bringing the five-and-a-half month strike to an end. The Rhodes settlement, which included the appointment of a royal commission to investigate conditions in the coal industry, was approved by the miners in a referendum vote and by the corporation board of directors. Yet even as work resumed on 8 August, another walkout took place as the miners attempted to prevent the corporation from applying a blacklist in the rehiring process. Following another intervention by Premier Rhodes, work resumed on 10 August.[50]

In the major strikes of the 1920s, the struggle for control over the miners' workplace was clearly an influential factor. Workplace action exploited the unusual physical conditions of the coal mines in order to increase the pressure on employers and governments, and the structure of tactical workers' control seems to have had unusual effectiveness in animating the dialectic between state and capital. The slowdown proved effective in bringing about government action in 1922; it reappeared in the aftermath of the 1925 strike and was again adopted in a rank and file revolt in 1941. And the withdrawal of maintenance men in 1922 and 1925 precipitated the turning point in each of these long strikes. This structure of tactical control was never without limits or controversy. In 1923, the union was torn apart by internal controversy, and workplace action had little effect on the outcome of the strike. Furthermore, this form of workers' control was also potentially divisive. Slowdowns threatened the earnings of contract miners and subjected ideals of manliness, honesty, and hard work to severe tests. Similarly, the "100 per cent" strike endangered the miners' workplace and thereby seemed to contradict their traditional concern for safe conditions in the mines.

Most of the workplace struggles of the 1920s were defensive actions in which the mineworkers exercised partial or temporary control over the workplace. But the coal miners also sought to permanently transform the government of the mines in order to win greater control over their workplace. This search for alternatives to capitalist domination of the coal industry expresses the meaning most commonly associated with the slogan "workers' control," a programmatic sense that may be conveniently described as strategic control.

The quest for strategic control was rooted in the existing practice of workplace authority, but in the crisis at the end of World War I, this tradition converged with more ideological traditions articulated by local radicals and socialists. This convergence was by no means unique to Cape Breton, for similar developments were taking place in the politics of both the Miners' Federation of Great Britain and the United Mine Workers of America in these years. Indeed, in 1920, District 26 president Robert Baxter was alert to this context: "Nationalization of all coal mines will be the only cure for the miners' troubles, which exist over the world today."[51]

The organic roots of the search for strategic control were perhaps most evident in the miners' continual concern over safety conditions in the mines. When pit committees in the 1920s challenged the accuracy of government reports on safety conditions,[52] or when the miners sought to retain mine examiners within the union's jurisdiction, or when they campaigned for the election of mine inspectors by the underground work force, the mineworkers were seeking to increase the extent of formal workers' control within the mines. Justifying the election of mine inspectors, for instance, union leaders argued: "The miners on their part have their lives and their own safety to consider and for this purpose they want a mine inspector whose duty would be solely to see that life and limb are safe ... in other words, the miners think they have the right to have, to some extent at least, a voice in the management of the mines." Resisting company attempts to remove mine examiners from the union, the miners protested (successfully until 1928): "Our reply is that inasmuch as the members of this union have their lives at stake if the mine examiners fail to carry out their duties faithfully, that it is to their special interest to give these men the support of this union in their efforts to enforce the special rules."[53] And when McLachlan argued for public ownership of the mines before the Duncan Commission in 1925, he rested his case on these grounds: "The workers have put too much into these mines. Three lives in every thousand. That is more than all the millions they [the operators] have put in. Over a period of years they have put the money in, the workers have put their blood in it."[54]

The goal of public ownership of the coal industry won unprecedented support in the 1920s. The theme had been prominent in the early campaigns of labour and socialist candidates in Cape Breton, where a common refrain was "the democratic organization and management of industry by the workers."

And when Big Bill Haywood toured industrial Cape Breton in 1909, "his picture of the coal miners under an industrial democracy brought forth hearty and spontaneous cheers of the workers."[55] At the convention of the Amalgamated Mine Workers in November 1918, the delegates endorsed the principle of public ownership in two resolutions and urged the government to "nationalize all industries and their operation for the benefit of the country instead of for private enrichment"; similar declarations were endorsed at subsequent miners' convention.[56] The continual re-election of radical union officers like McLachlan, and the sweeping successes of the Independent Labour Party in the mining district, also reflected the existence of wide support for the goal of public ownership of the coal industry.

What is most notable about the quest for strategic control in the 1920s is the timing: discussions became most vigorous in moments of crisis; the process of continual class conflict stimulated the convergence of organic and ideological traditions of workers' control. In the early months of 1922, for instance, Besco officials frequently cited the troubles of the coal market to justify the unpopular wage cut; in response, resolutions from the union locals and commentaries in the *Maritime Labor Herald* charged the corporation with mismanagement, inefficiency, high salaries, incompetence, and overcapitalization. The alternative was the inauguration of "industrial democracy": the mines would be placed "in control of the miners under public ownership and supervision by the Government of the Province." In February 1922, the district convention once more endorsed nationalization of the mines, and in the provincial legislature, labour MLA Forman Waye introduced a resolution demanding that unless Besco signed a contract "that will ensure wages which will allow a decent Canadian standard of living," the government would take steps "to cancel their coal leases and operate mines for the benefit of the people of the Province." In June 1922, W.U. Cotton, editor of the *Maritime Labor Herald*, urged the coal miners to begin the election of candidates for mine managers and other company positions; they would serve, not in office, but as "a constant reminder to the owners that the miners were out, not merely to get a little more money while living under industrial tyranny, but were out also to take over the operation of industry under democratic methods." (Later Cotton also wrote an extended plan for government ownership of all elements of the coal trade "as a public monopoly, to be operated for service and not for gain.")[57]

This analysis of the miners' search for workers' control also enables us better to understand the authenticity of the so-called "red" declarations adopted by the coal miners' district convention in June 1922. One of these soon became notorious, for it included the statement "that we proclaim openly to all the world that we are out for the complete overthrow of the capitalist system and capitalist state, peaceably if we may, forceably if we must ..." With its echoes of Chartism and Bolshevism, the declaration accurately reflected the revolutionary sentiments of leaders such as McLachlan. But the main part of the policy committee report, from which these lines were drawn, was devoted to a brief analysis of the economic condition of the coal industry that stressed the problems of overexpansion, idle time, and wage reductions, all of which were common to coal miners far beyond Cape Breton Island in the 1920s. The report noted that these were "a result of the efforts of 'Captains of Industry' to run the coal business."[58] Seen in the context of the campaign for public ownership, the radical declarations endorsed at the district convention must also be understood as part of the search for alternatives to capitalist domination of the industry.

Discussions of the need for strategic control again reached a peak with the restoration of district autonomy in 1924 and the advent of the 1925 strike. In 1924, the *Maritime Labor Herald* installed the slogan "Nationalization of Industry with Workers' Control" on its front page, and this weekly appeal no doubt helped explain President Wolvin's particular animus toward the weekly newspaper. In discussions of the impending wage cut, an observer in the Sydney *Post* invoked the wisdom of an earlier day: "As an old miner in Cow Bay used to quote, 'Cut the bosses, And cut the costes'."[59] The mine committees represented one "embryonic" form of workers' control, but in the hard winters of 1924 and 1925, the coal miners also explored another form of direct action. Along the shores, at abandoned mine sites and even on the ballfields, miners opened shallow "bootleg" pits to mine coal from the outcroppings of the coal seams in violation of coal company leases. Company officials took "illegal" miners to court, earning condemnation from at least one union local for their "inhuman and uncharitable actions." Yet the practice continued to flourish in hard times.[60] Meanwhile, under McLachlan's editorship, the *Labor Herald* published a series of editorials entitled "Let the Miners Run the Mines" and "More Power to the Mine Committees." The emergent strategy of workers' control was closely linked to the existing organic elements, such as the pit committees: "The workers have in embryonic form a species of control which they understand and support and can be induced to extend. Elected representatives of the men at each mine and plant should strive to increase their powers in questions of safety, hours worked, appliances used, mines opened and closed, men hired and fired."[61] From the hearings of the Duncan Commission in the fall of 1925, it was clear that the issue of strategic control was a prominent concern of the corporation and the coal miners alike. An exchange between President Wolvin and a Reserve Mines coal miner, James Clarke, was charged with the tensions of the 1920s:

Q: Did you approve of the nationalization of mines?
A: Yes, sure I approve of it yet.
Q: You think the workmen could run the mines better than the Corporation?

A: Oh, I think that, I feel positively sure of that.

Q: It is a great thing to have confidence.

A: That is right too. I believe it is the workmen that is running it now. I notice any time the workmen stops the mine stops.

Q: You are absolutely right. That is what I like to bring out, you have been running the mine since 1921?

A: Yes, when she was not working we owned it, at least the Provincial Government told us we owned it when she was producing nothing, but the minute she started to produce they took it from us again.[62]

In the summer of 1922, the *Maritime Labor Herald* had sounded an optimistic note: "Within seven years from the present time, the miners of Cape Breton and the steelworkers of Sydney will be in control of the mines and steel works." The prediction proved overconfident; indeed in 1926, the Duncan Report evaded the issue and contained no reference to public ownership. But although delegates to the district convention in January 1926 were divided over the report's wage schemes, they once more endorsed nationalization of the coal mines. Commented the *Canadian Mining Journal*: "The only question receiving unaminous endorsement was the nationalization of coal mines, but like the soldier's song, it has a long way to go."[63] In the 1920s, the coal miners shared aspirations for greater control over their workplace than they were able to achieve at the time, but the refrain continued in the 1930s and 1940s. Ultimately, the goal was achieved in the 1960s, though the circumstances and the results were vastly different from those the mineworkers had envisaged in the 1920s.[64]

A great deal has been written about the origins of public ownership in Canada, but very little attention has been paid to the role of Canadian workers in creating support for public ownership.[65] Yet, as David Montgomery has reminded us, notions of public ownership and workers' control were not simply political or ideological ones; they had organic roots in the workplace experience of many workers. Such was the case in the history of the Cape Breton coal miners. Perhaps their experience was in some ways an anomalous one, for in the coal industry the advance of machine power and rigorous work-discipline followed an uneven pace: large-scale capital and technology coexisted alongside relatively traditional, hand-powered, and labour-intensive operations. These conditions permitted the persistence of a vigorous workplace culture among the coal miners. While the labour-intensive quality of the industry tempted employers to seek large savings in their wages bill, the coal miners resourcefully exploited the peculiarities of their workplace to strengthen their resistance. These conditions enhanced working-class effectiveness in the coal industry, making the coal mines, in that apt phrase, a "contested terrain." Meanwhile, under conditions of intense class conflict, existing traditions of workers' control were transformed. At a time when the Canadian labour movement was generally in retreat after the defeats of 1919, the coal miners in the 1920s pursued an aggressive strategy designed not only to defend their economic position and protect their union, but also aiming to transform the structure of control in their industry. It was the beginning of the coal miners' lasting political commitment to the goal of public ownership in the coal industry. Whatever the ambivalence of the ultimate outcome, we are reminded that support for public ownership originated, in part, in the battles of Canadian workers for more responsible forms of industrial organization.

NOTES

1 Michelle Perrot, *Les ouvriers en grève, France 1871–1890* (Paris 1974), 367.
2 The most influential study focused on geographic and community factors, arguing that coal miners, like other resource workers, formed "isolated masses, almost a 'race apart' "; see Clark Kerr and Abraham Siegel, "The Inter-industry Propensity to Strike – An International Comparison," in Arthur Kornhauser, Robert Dubin, and Arthur M. Ross, eds, *Industrial Conflict* (New York 1954). This hypothesis has been severely criticized, most notably by Edward Shorter and Charles Tilly in *Strikes in France, 1830–1968* (Cambridge 1974), who tend to stress the importance of political and ideological factors in explaining strike patterns. Carter Goodrich's classic study, *The Miner's Freedom* (Boston 1925), was perhaps the first attempt to explore the relationship between the spectacular upheavals of the coal-miners' strikes and the more obscure everyday workplace practices of the coal miners. Important recent studies include Keith Dix, *Work Relations in the Coal Industry: The Hand-Loading Era, 1880–1930* (Morgantown 1977) and Royden Harrison, ed., *Independent Collier: The Coal Miner as Archetypal Proletarian Reconsidered* (New York 1978).
3 For general introductions to the events of this period, see Dawn Fraser, *Echoes from Labor's War: Industrial Cape Breton in the 1920s* (Toronto 1976) and Paul MacEwan, *Miners and Steelworkers: Labour in Cape Breton* (Toronto 1976). A comprehensive outline of the major events is provided in Don Macgillivray, "Industrial Unrest in Cape Breton, 1919–1925" (MA thesis, University of New Brunswick 1971).
4 E.J. Hobsbawm, *Labouring Men: Studies in the History of Labour* (London 1964). The theme has been brilliantly applied also by David Montgomery in the studies collected in *Workers' Control in America: Studies in the History of Work, Technology, and Labour Struggles* (Cambridge 1979).
5 *Press Opinions of "Empire Steel"* (n.p. 1920), 7. On the context of economic difficulties in the industry and financial mismanagement, see David Frank, "The Cape Breton Coal Industry and the Rise and Fall of the British Empire Steel Corporation," *Acadiensis* 7, no. 1 (Autumn 1977): 3–34.

6 Nova Scotia, Royal Commission on Coal Mining Industry [Duncan Commission, 1925], "Minutes of Evidence," 4290.

7 *United Mine Workers' Journal*, 15 November 1920.

8 Sydney *Post*, 18, 19, 20 November, 1 December 1920.

9 Sydney *Post*, 1, 17 December, 19 November 1920. McLachlan added: "It took a lot of work to build up District 26, but the biggest fool in the district can tear it asunder in two weeks."

10 Ian McKay, "Workers' Control in Springhill, 1882–1927" (paper presented at the annual meetings of the Canadian Historical Association 1981), 27.

11 J.R. Dinn, "The Human Element in the Prevention of Accidents," Canadian Institute of Mining and Metallurgy and the Mining Society of Nova Scotia, *Transactions* 26 (1923): 498 (hereafter *Transactions*); added Dinn: "For the production of any commodity, the primary essential factor is labor."

12 Canada, Dominion Bureau of Statistics, *Coal Statistics for Canada, 1927* (Ottawa 1928), 40, 45; Alex L. Hay, "Coal-mining Operations in the Sydney Coal Field," American Institute of Mining and Metallurgical Engineers, *Technical Publication No. 198* (New York 1929), 7, 33; Dinn, "A Contrast of the Physical Conditions in United States and Cape Breton Coal Mines," *Transactions* 28 (1925): 510; *Canadian Mining Journal*, 15 April 1911, 241.

13 H.B. Gillis, "The Use of Mechanical Loading Machines in Mines," *Transactions* 24 (1921): 310, 315–6; Hay, "Coal-mining Operations," 16–17.

14 *Report of the Royal Commission on Coal Mining Industry in Nova Scotia* [Duncan Report], supplement to the *Labour Gazette* (January 1926): 23.

15 In 1923 the number of horses in the collieries of the Dominion Coal Company was 528 and the number of coal-cutting machines was 534; in the collieries of the Nova Scotia Steel and Coal Company there were 139 horses and 83 machines; Nova Scotia, *Journals of the House Assembly, 1923*, "Mines Report."

16 In 1921 the underground work force in the Nova Scotia coal industry numbered 9,830 men. Of these, 4,647 men worked at the coal face (handcutters and helpers 2,362, machine cutters 1,068, loaders and helpers after machines 1,217) and 2,123 men were engaged in haulage operations (790 by horse, 1,333 by mechanical haulage). There were 1,504 men employed in ventilation, road making, timbering, pump operations and other tasks, and 1,132 men engaged in other labour. Supervisory officials numbered 424. See Canada, Dominion Bureau of Statistics, *Coal Statistics for Canada, 1922* (Ottawa 1922), 38.

17 Data on the causes of mine fatalities in the Dominion and Scotia collieries on Cape Breton Island was generated from *Nova Scotia Mines Reports*, 1917–1926: falls 84, gas and dust explosions 67, haulage 40, machinery 8, other 8. In the years 1920–23, the Duncan Report (17–18) noted that the annual fatalities in Besco mines averaged 2.11 per 1,000 employees; in the same period, the rate in the United States was 3.8 per 1,000 men and in Britain 1.0 per 1,000 men. The years from the mid 1890s to the mid 1930s revealed no substantial improvement in fatality rates in Nova Scotia: in 29 of the 40 years, the rate exceeded 2.0 per 1,000

and in another 8 years it exceeded 3.0 per 1,000; see *Nova Scotia Mines Report* (1939), 140, and C.O. Macdonald, *The Coal and Iron Industries of Nova Scotia* (Halifax 1909), 190–1.

18 A monument was erected in New Waterford and the anniversary was commemorated each year. The explosion left a legacy of controversy. Although a government report assigned no responsibility for the disaster, a coroner's jury found "gross irregularity" in the operation of the mine and found officials "guilty of gross neglect"; a grand jury later indicted three officials for manslaughter and the coal company for "causing grievous bodily harm" to its employees, but there were no convictions. *Canadian Mining Journal*, 15 August, 1 October, 15 December 1917. See also "Mine Explosion in New Waterford, 1917," *Cape Breton's Magazine*, no. 21 (1978): 1–11.

19 Murdoch Clarke interview, 1976; Stuart McCawley Scrapbook, Miners' Memorial Museum, Glace Bay, p. 75; Angus F. MacDonald interview, 1975.

20 Nova Scotia, *Statutes of Nova Scotia*, 1918, "Coal Mines Regulation Act," sections 5, 24, 50 (rule 5), 53, 43. Following the 1923 strike, for instance, a deposed and blacklisted union leader, William Carey, was elected checkweighman at Florence colliery; Sydney *Post*, 26 November 1923.

21 District 26, United Mine Workers of America, *Constitution* (n.p. 1920), see article II, section 6, and article XVI. For a study tracing the gradual restriction of the authority of the pit committee, see Evelyn Preston, "The Pit Committee in the Illinois Coal Fields" (MA thesis, University of Wisconsin 1923).

22 Angus F. MacDonald interview, 1975.

23 The problems of analysing strike activity are considered in Shorter and Tilly, *Strikes in France*; and an important contribution to the discussion of strike activity among coal miners is Jon Amsden and Stephen Brier, "Coal Miners on Strike: The Transformation of Strike Demands and the Formation of a National Union," *Journal of Interdisciplinary History* 7 (Spring 1977): 583–616. See also Craig Heron and Bryan Palmer, "Through the Prism of the Strike: Industrial Conflict in Southern Ontario, 1901–1914," *Canadian Historical Review* 58 (December 1977): 423–58.

24 The data discussed here and presented in table I was generated from the columns of the local press and from the records of the Department of Labour (RG 27), Public Archives of Canada (PAC). A more detailed account of this research is to be found in David Frank, "The Cape Breton Coal Miners, 1917–1926" (PH D dissertation, Dalhousie University 1979), 236–48.

25 Sydney *Post*, 29 April 1920; PAC, RG 27, vol. 327, F. 171, 172; Sydney *Post*, 7 April 1924; Sydney *Post*, 15 September 1920; PAC, Arthur L. Sifton Papers, "RCMP Secret Weekly Summary," no. 43, 30 September 1920; Sydney *Post*, 23 October 1922; *Maritime Labor Herald*, 28 October, 4 November 1922.

26 *Labour Gazette* (June 1923): 609, PAC, RG 27, vol. 331, 31.

27 Sydney *Post*, 25 August 1920; 19, 25 September 1922; *Maritime Labor Herald*, 16 September 1922. *Canadian Labor Leader*, 20 July 1918; PAC, RG 27, vol. 327,

F. 4; vol. 332, F. 9; F. 16; vol. 333, F. 47, Sydney *Post*, 19, 22 July, 1924; *Labour Gazette* (February 1922): 187; PAC, RG 27, vol. 305, F. 2; Sydney *Post*, 4 June 1920, 7 October, 1922; *Maritime Labor Herald*, 28 January 1922; *Labour Gazette* (December 1924): 1033; PAC, RG 27, vol. 330, F. 21; RG 27, vol. 333, F. 73; Sydney *Post*, 28, 29 October 1924; *Labour Gazette* (May 1926): 436–7; ibid. (July 1926): 649–50; ibid. (December 1926): 1192.

28 *Labour Gazette* (May 1918): 332, PAC, RG 27, vol. 307, F. 9, Halifax *Herald*, 27 April, 26 August 1918; PAC, RG 27, vol. 307, F. 18; Sydney *Post*, 2, 9 August, 14 July 1920; *Labour Gazette* (August 1926): 762–3; ibid. (September 1926): 861.

29 Sydney *Post*, 26 August 1920.

30 Sydney *Post*, 6, 7, 8, 9 September 1922.

31 District 26, United Mine Workers of America, "Proceedings, 1922," 7; *Maritime Labor Herald*, 14 October 1922, 17 February 1923.

32 *Labour Gazette* (July 1923): 729; Sydney *Post*, 13, 14, 15, 16 June 1923; Montreal *Star*, 15 June 1923; PAC, RG 27, vol. 331, F. 70, 71.

33 *Maritime Labor Herald*, 12 November 1921.

34 Sydney *Record*, 29 May 1920; Sydney *Post*, 16 June 1920. On restriction of output, see R. Page Arnot, *A History of the Scottish Miners from the Earliest Times* (London 1955), 17; John R. Commons, "Trade Union Regulation and Restriction of Output," *Eleventh Special Report of United States Commissioner of Labor* (Washington 1904); and S.B. Mathewson, *Restriction of Output among Unorganized Workers* (1931; Carbondale, Ill. 1969).

35 Halifax *Herald*, 27 February 1922.

36 Joseph Nearing interview, 1975.

37 *Maritime Labor Herald*, 18 March 1922; Sydney *Post*, 20–24 March 1922.

38 Canada, *Debates of the House of Commons, 1922*, 512–4, 497–545.

39 *Maritime Labor Herald*, 29 July 1922.

40 Sydney *Post*, 17 August 1922; Sydney *Record*, 17 August 1922, Montreal *Star*, 18 August 1922; Sydney *Post*, 4, 5 July 1923.

41 *Canadian Mining Journal* (25 August 1922).

42 Fraser, *Echoes from Labor's War*, 54.

43 Sydney *Post*, 6 July 1923.

44 Ibid., 16–21 January 1924; PAC, RG 27, vol. 332, F. 2.

45 *Besco Bulletin*, no. 20 (1925); Glace Bay *Gazette*, 26 April 1924.

46 Sydney *Post*, 22 November 1924. See, for instance, the ongoing agitation in the *Maritime Labor Herald*, 3 January 1925, and company plans to prepare for a prolonged shutdown, Sydney *Post*, 8 January 1925.

47 Beaton Institute of Cape Breton Studies, C.B. Wade, "History of District 26, United Mine Workers of America, 1919–1941," unpublished manuscript, 1950.

48 Sydney *Post*, 5, 6, 8, 9, 10 June 1925; *Labour Gazette* (July 1925): 661–2.

49 Sydney *Post*, 13 June 1925; Wade, "History of District 26."

50 *Labour Gazette* (August 1925): 771–2; Wade, "History of District 26."

51 Sydney *Post*, 2 September 1920. For analysis of the nationalization campaigns

among the coal miners in Britain and the United States, see Frank Hodges, *Nationalisation of the Mines* (London 1920); Ken Coates, ed., *Democracy in the Mines* (Nottingham 1974); and Arthur C. Everling, "Tactics Over Strategy in the United Mine Workers of America: Internal Politics and the Question of the Nationalization of the Mines, 1908–1923" (PH D dissertation, Pennsylvania State University 1976).

52 *Maritime Labor Herald*, 3 June 1922, 19 July 1924.

53 *Eastern Federationist*, 8 March 1919; *Canadian Mining Journal* (27 April 1923): 329; ibid. (11 May 1928): 394–5; *Minutes of First Annual Convention of the Amalgamated Mine Workers of Nova Scotia* (hereafter AMWNS) (Sydney 1917), 12–3; *Proceedings of* AMWNS, *Second Convention, 1918* (Sydney 1918), 14.

54 Duncan Commission, "Minutes of Evidence," 1175.

55 *Cotton's Weekly*, 23 December 1909. See also David Frank and Nolan Reilly, "The Emergence of the Socialist Movement in the Maritimes, 1899–1916," *Labour/Le Travailleur* 4 (1979): 85–113.

56 AMWNS *Proceedings, 1918*, 56.

57 *Maritime Labor Herald*, 21, 28 January, 4, 18, 25 February, 17 June 1922; *Labour Gazette* (March 1922): 308–9; *Maritime Labor Herald*, 1 July 1923.

58 "Minutes, Third Annual Convention of District 26, United Mine Workers of America, 20–24 June, 1922," 23–5. The text of this report also appeared in the *Maritime Labor Herald*, 1 July 1922.

59 Sydney *Post*, 5 March 1925.

60 Ibid., 3 March, 29 December 1925; Miners' Memorial Museum, Glace Bay, clipping, 1932, Stuart McCawley Scrapbook, 202.

61 *Maritime Labor Herald*, 7, 14, February 1925.

62 Duncan Commission, "Minutes of Evidence," 235.

63 *Maritime Labor Herald*, 15 July 1922; *Canadian Mining Journal* (12 February 1926): 174–5.

64 C.B. Wade, "Coal Should Be Public Utility," *National Affairs Monthly* 4, no. 10 (November 1947): 334–43; Allan Tupper, "Public Enterprise and Social Welfare: The Case of the Cape Breton Development Corporation," *Canadian Public Policy* (Autumn 1978): 530–46. On the parallel struggle for public ownership in the Cape Breton steel industry, see "Report on Sydney Steel," *Canadian Dimension* (February–March 1980): 33–52.

65 Herschel Hardin, *A Nation Unaware: The Canadian Economic Culture* (Vancouver 1974); Montgomery, *Workers' Control in America*.

VERONICA STRONG-BOAG

Keeping House in God's Country: Canadian Women at Work in the Home

Women in the home make up the largest single group of Canadian workers. Over the years, Canadian women have both concentrated their efforts in this setting as full-time housewives and, at the same time, have assumed its responsibilities as a double shift alongside employment in field, shop, office, and elsewhere. To be sure, cottage industry or domestic production has often involved male participation, and in the pre-industrial world many artisans worked at home. Nevertheless, opportunities for men have always been better in the primary-resource sector, trade, industry, and the professions, and over time, fewer and fewer families were able or willing to commit all male or even female labour to the domestic environment. In general, Canadian women have been assigned the overriding obligation of tending the hearth fires while men have sought their primary duties elsewhere. The absence of male adults for longer or shorter intervals,[1] together with the late nineteenth-century drain of child workers into compulsory schools and into new jobs in factory, shop and office, left women increasingly isolated in the home. Domestic tasks were overwhelmingly reckoned to be in the first instance theirs, however inequitable the result. It is this fundamental fact that has shaped women's experience of paid and unpaid work over the course of Canada's development.

Women's efforts as housewives and domestic servants have been hailed as natural, divinely inspired, and biologically determined. Their labour has often been credited both by anti-feminists and by feminists in the nineteenth and twentieth centuries[2] as the critical guarantor of peace, order, and good government, but has rarely been subject to systematic analysis. Like the Canadian Shield or the northern winter, homework in all its numerous and changing guises has been largely taken for granted as part of the natural backdrop against which important "man-made" history, like railway construction or dominion/provincial relations, has occurred. Apart from essentially token acknowledgments of women's contribution, the discussion of work in Canada has taken the location and the sex of its subjects as public and most often male. The phenomenon of work within the home has been neglected, both as relatively insignificant and essentially uninteresting. The result has been studies that treat the dynamics of the waged-labour economy in isolation from the operations of a domestic economy to which they are inextricably tied. Not surprisingly, the world of work is imperfectly understood.

Fortunately, guides to the landscape of domestic work are now appearing in European, American, and, slowly, Canadian literature. Scholars in women's history and women's studies in particular are beginning to document the nature and, just as important, the meaning of domestic work.[3] In particular, recent literature points to the contradictions between the low status accorded the housewife and the significance of her role in the maintenance of the structures of social and economic power. Scholars are unanimous in rejecting the view that work within the home is either minimal or in decline and in insisting that domestic labour of all kinds lies at the core of human relationships and is crucial to the functions of the political economy of societies at every stage of development. Men in their roles as husbands, fathers, brothers, and sons are identified as deriving direct and substantial benefits from women's paid and unpaid work in the home. The allocation of domestic responsibilities overwhelmingly to women frees men to explore a wider range of social, economic, and political avenues. These other activities are then rewarded with benefits for the most part superior to those offered for work in the home. The fact that women are assigned pre-eminently to the domestic sphere also encourages employers to pay them lower wages and offer them fewer opportunities. Their work in the marketplace has been conveniently viewed as something of an aberration, expandable and contractable at the whim of state, business, and family necessity. Over the long term, only women's domestic labour has received full social sanction. Approval, however, rarely brought with it any serious attention to the exact nature and extent of women's work within the home. Omission and misinformation have been the ready substitutes.

This paper takes up the task of identifying the broad contours of Canadian home labour by characterizing the range of jobs included within this descriptive category and pointing to the difficulties of capturing the content and consequences of activities whose nature is essentially dynamic; the paper examines the history of domestic labour in Canada. In all cases, the terms domestic work and labour and homework and labour are used interchangeably. Although the former is often used to refer especially to women's work in the family context and the latter to mean commodity production or waged labour by family members within the home, distinctions between the two are frequently blurred. Work of all types within the home has generally been a seamless web of effort in which female labour, both paid and unpaid, is central and dominant.

To appreciate the substance and significance of women's work within the home, it is necessary to be able to descríbe it more precisely. Two characterizations of female domestic labour by Canadian sociologists are useful introductions to the problem. Pat and Hugh Armstrong's assessment of the post-war period in *The Double Ghetto* divides "the complex of tasks performed by women in the home ... into four categories: housework, child care, tension management and sexual relationships."[4] A somewhat different schema is presented in Meg Luxton's study of a Manitoba resource town in *More Than a Labour of Love*. Here we are presented with "four related but distinct work processes performed by the housewife":

The first involves looking after herself, her husband and other adult members of the household ... the dominant requirement is that the labour power of the wage earner be reproduced on a daily basis ... The second component of domestic labour is childbearing and childrearing ... The third ... is housework ... all those activities ... that are necessary for maintaining the house and servicing household members. The final component of domestic labour involves the transformation of wages into goods and services for the household's use. This process of "making ends meet" involves money management and shopping. Sometimes it also requires that women take on additional work to bring more money into the household.[5]

While raising many significant questions, neither of these categorizations, both designed to deal particularly with urban Canada in the last half century or so, seems entirely satisfactory in encompassing the full range of work in Canadian homes, rural and urban, rich and poor, over a long time period. They fail either to give proper attention to the paid work of the landlady, seamstress, word processor, and the like, or to acknowledge women's special responsibility for the care of dependent adults, especially the aged and those with handicaps.[6]

For purposes of discussion, a third method of conceptualizing labour within the home is proposed here; it shifts and enlarges the definitions of the Armstrongs and Luxton. This system of classification introduces five essential work processes that may vary, often enormously, over time and space. The first, *housework*, would include the maintenance of the physical premises, the transformation of wage income into goods and services, including shopping and money management, and the production of goods and services for family use, notably in gardening, cooking, sewing, diet planning, decorating, and cleaning. The second, *reproduction and care of dependent children*, would include pregnancy, and the socialization, nurture, and management of children. Youngsters in receipt of care enter the family not only by birth but by adoption, fostering, indenture, or a host of more informal arrangements. Relationships and female responsibilities vary just as tremendously. The third, *care of working adults*, would include physical assistance, tension management, and, in some instances, sexuality, the object being to maintain adults as effective productive members of their society whether as housewives, wage-earners, or agricultural, commercial or industrial entrepreneurs. The fourth, *care of dependent adults*, would include maintenance and management of adults who, by reason of physical or mental handicap, cannot contribute fully to their own support. The fifth, *paid work within the home*, would include a wide range of activities by which women add to family income through domestically based activity. It would cover such paid labour as, for example, laundry, sewing, typing, and taking in boarders.

All five categories encompass interrelated and sometimes simultaneous tasks. Just as frustrating schematically, homes range enormously in the degree to which they incorporate these activities. Housewives and families frequently have a certain margin of choice. Such discretionary power in the organization of domestic labour is very much influenced by factors like class, race, and ethnicity. In some communities – the Hutterites, for example – women have traditionally allocated little, if any, time or energy to the purchase of consumer goods. In contrast to many other Canadians, especially those in today's cities, Hutterite women have placed greater emphasis on gardening, food processing, and clothing manufacture.[7] Yet, even within such an ethnically homogeneous community, variables can appear. Between 1960 and 1970, for example, the Jasper Hutterite colonies saw "concerted campaigns by women" to introduce consumer items such as vinyl, electric floor polishers, and indoor plumbing.[8] For some, at least, the costs of maintaining any ethnic "hard line" in the domestic realm were just too high. Although ethnic, class, or racial identities can provide powerful encouragement for a certain type of domestic orientation, opportunity is, over time, the major factor. The choices of a welfare mother in Vancouver's False Creek Flats in the 1950s or the wife of a seasonally employed day labourer in Bytown's shanties in the 1850s were severely limited. Not for them the choices between a host of products or activities.

Yet, for all the restrictions they encountered, women from every background often evidenced considerable imagination in finding ways to cope with inadequate resources. As the case of an early twentieth-century Labrador woman makes clear, devising solutions could be critically important:

She could not nurse her babies. She had to get a bottle for them. What she used for food was flour. She took the dry flour and packed it in white cloth and boiled it for four hours. When she took it from the cloth it was like a piece of chalk ... She would take a piece and grate it up and make a pap like a real thick gravy. She boiled it again and added sugar, a little butter and a little salt. She raised eight children like that until they were ten months old ... Some of them grew up to be old men and women.

Such ingenuity was matter of factly summed up by a niece: "When put to the test we could always manage."[9] The sheer variety of ways by which resourceful women could come out on top underscores the inappropriateness of any wholesale characterization of housewives as victims. They could be and often have been powerful survivors.

Coming to terms with women's work within the home is complicated by the fact that jobs within these five categories are not always acknowledged as work either by housewives or by the society at large. Reference to love or instinct, for example, clouds any understanding of process, product, and power, resulting in dismissal of much of the reality of women's lives. Given these difficulties, measurement of domestic work can pose something of a dilemma. Luxton's reminder of the Marxist distinction between two types of time is helpful in this regard: "Production time measures the duration of a task from start to finish; labour time measures the specific period during which the worker is actually expending labour."[10] Child care, for example, involves specific allocations of labour time at various intervals, but the production time in terms of creating a healthy, functioning adult is the child's lifetime itself. Production time sets up a central dilemma for those involved in home labour: the normal state of work is unfinished; the worker is always on call.

The division of domestic labour into its component parts helps bring these distinctions to life, for despite all myths to the contrary,[11] the home and all within it are in a constant state of transformation and transition. The home is a world in motion. This tendency to change springs from three fundamental processes. The first is the production of goods and services both to be used by the family and to be bartered or sold beyond its confines. A sequence of stages marks production, whether it be of a cake, perhaps from grinding flour to the last touches of icing, or expediting human excretory processes, perhaps from buying to placing to dumping to washing a bedpan. Technology may transform the steps or the process itself, but there is no magic art that, for example, creates in a single step nicely mannered children, a good-tempered husband, or a well-laid table. There would be no need for marriage manuals, child psychologists, or cooking lessons if such processes were natural, obvious, or always simple. It may be love that spurs the creation of the baby's sweater and booties, but it is skilled labour that guides the mother's ever-busy hands. The impact of technology here is critical. The application of hand or water or electric power, for example, helps determine processes and skills, the precise sequence and nature of which contribute to the home's overall dynamism.

The second force for change comes from the character of the human group living within the home. Here it is important to distinguish between the *household*, which may include kin and non-kin living in the same residence, and the *family*, which refers solely to individuals related by blood and marriage whose relationships "transcend the residential unit."[12] The changing balance and connection between these two groups can be very critical in shaping domestic labour demands. The presence, for example, of boarders, like hired help, has clear implications for the housewife's role. Similarly, the existence of a larger supportive kin group external to the home but available for assistance in child care or medical emergencies can be influential. Household organization and family structure are, in turn, best understood as intimately related to a cycle of family development "that occurs through the addition, aging, and loss of family members."[13] As Tamara Hareven and others have convincingly demonstrated, treating the "family as a process over time rather than a static unit at certain points in time"[14] is essential if we are to understand the shifting constellation of family and household members. We need to think of "family time" as an independent cycle including such changes as "marriage, child birth, maturation and leaving home."[15] To give only one example, taking in boarders may be a special feature of households headed by the widowed or couples whose children have left home.[16]

Third, just as domestic labour is intimately tied to "family time," it is wedded as well to "social time," that is, to the "changing institutional conditions in the larger society, namely: occupational structure, migration, settlement patterns, and changing policies and legislation governing family behaviour."[17] The dynamics of commercial or industrial capitalism, in short, help set the stage for the performance of family roles. While there is no simple cause and effect relationship, a range of opportunities for waged labour, education, or leisure help determine who is at home, who is available, and who is responsible for domestic work. The wage-earning options offered the housewife in the marketplace are an important variable here. State policies can be a vital determinant of options. For instance, the introduction of compulsory schooling by drawing children of useful age out of the home helped concentrate responsibilities on the mother-wife. And the two world wars disrupted home life by draining away men to the front and opening up more positions in waged employment for women. However much the family may aim to segregate itself – as in some religious communities, for example – isolation is never complete. Ties to the world beyond may be rejected; they may at times appear as gossamer – but they set conditions fundamental to the domestic experience.

The rhythms of production, of family and household composition, and of the dialectic of family and social time create a world in motion, however imperceptible the beat may be to the casual observer or the nostalgic memory. Portraying the entirety of these mutually interacting systems is a monumental task. Without sensitivity to the dynamic quality of this world, however, it is impossible to conceptualize adequately any part of the fabric of domestic labour that maintains the home. The ways in which housework, reproduction and child care, the care of working adults, the care of dependent adults, and paid work within the home have evolved in Canada are intimately related to shifts in these three fundamental rhythms.

Before dealing more precisely with domestic labour, one major disclaimer is necessary. The experience of homework, like the exact make-up of the rhythms just described, has varied, sometimes dramatically, between classes, regions, town and country, and ethnic and racial groups. These differences mean, in effect, multiple worlds of domesticity. The contours of many of these worlds have yet to be mapped, even in their broadest outlines. That is the task of the future. The task here, less ambitious by far, is to highlight some characteristics of domestic work experience. Since information is not equally available on all five categories of homework, there has been no attempt to make the treatments precisely analogous. They should be seen as snapshots – sometimes aspiring to the status of moving pictures – of a complex and interrelated set of functions. Moreover, although women's work as servants and as housewives is distinct in a number of critical respects, it also reveals substantial similarities. Accordingly, for the purpose of this overview, differences between their activities are not distinguished. That is a separate and important issue.

HOUSEWORK

In the course of Canada's history, the two most significant and related trends in housework have been the shift from production to consumption and the technological transformation of the home, especially the kitchen. These changes have been gradual, beginning among the wealthier inhabitants of towns in the eighteenth century, and are still far from complete in many poorer residences today. The result is the simultaneous presence of both old, sometimes very old, and right up-to-date forms. One and the same family may encompass arrangements legitimated by custom and others without precedent.[18] The result belies simplistic notions of progress.

Women in the home have traditionally been producers of household commodities, such as food, clothing, and linen. Even today, there are those who argue that wives and mothers can improve their family's lot, and incidently prove their own femininity, by returning to the homemade rather than the store-bought. Slowly, however, except in cases of economic necessity or some cultural imperative to the contrary, homemakers have turned to the purchase of many foods, furnishings, and services. They have done so for a variety of reasons. Foremost is the pressure of convenience. About 1750, for example, some women embraced "une modification majeure du travail domestique" when purchases of cooking stoves freed them from bending over open hearths or fires.[19] This move to more sophisticated cooking and heating arrangements was repeated in a host of environments by subsequent generations of Canadian pioneers. Open-hearth cooking, with its implications for "single pot" meals,[20] took a long time to disappear from Canadian homes. Its memory is still resurrected nostalgically in camp-fire cookery. As two more examples also make clear, technological choices shaped, when they did not determine, daily routines. Catharine Parr Traill's advice to the prospective soap-maker on the early nineteenth-century frontier sets out the complex procedure by which settlers gained necessities:

Soap is made from a union of the lye of wood ashes, and any sort of grease, the refuse of the kitchen; even bones are boiled down in strong lye, and reduced ... The careful Canadian housewives procure a large portion of their soap-grease from the inside, and entrails of the hogs, and other beasts that are killed on the farm ...

The ashes should be put into the leech barrel, and pounded down with a long beetle. You may distribute the lime as you fill it up, or dissolve the lime in a pail of boiling water, and pour on after the barrel is filled up, and you commence running the lye.

Make a hollow in the top of the ashes, and pour in your water; as it soaks in, keep adding more; it will not begin to drop into the trough or tub for many hours; sometimes, if the ashes are packed down tight, for two or three days; but you must keep the hollow on the top of the barrel always supplied with water – soft water is best, if you are near a creek, or have a rain water tank (which is a great convenience to a house), and the water you run your leech with should be kept hot at first.[21]

Not surprisingly, soap was an early and much prized commodity on store shelves.

Close to a century later, another literary-minded, immigrant housewife, Kathleen Strange, complained of the labour demands of a laundry:

Washing! What a job that always was. Usually it took me the entire day. In summer I washed outside; in winter down in the basement. The boiling, sudsy water had to be carried in pails from the stove to wherever my tubs were set. More than once I burned myself severely, spilling water on unprotected hands and legs ...

At the beginning I had washed by hand, rubbing laboriously on a board and earning for myself a frightful backache.

Her exertion was somewhat abated with the purchase of "an American ... portable contraption, consisting of two vacuum cups set on two steel arms, which one clamped to the edge of an ordinary washtub and which, when worked with a handle, pressed up and down and round and round on the clothes. I ... found it a great help. But it still necessitated a lot of elbow grease."[22] Not surprisingly, the prospect of respite from such arduous, time-consuming, and fatiguing tasks spurred purchases of bakery goods, ready-made clothes, dairy products, washing machines, and electric stoves. At the last case makes clear, however, labour was not so much eliminated as reshaped.

The attraction of store clothing, dinners-to-go, or similar "easy" items became especially noticeable when women were trying to juggle the responsibilities of work in the home and the paid labour force. The marked expansion of ready-to-serve foods and fast-food outlets in the 1970s[23] was a clear response, in part at least, to the greater numbers of wage-earning women. The appeal of convection and microwave ovens is much the same. Revealingly enough, ads for such innovations often played on women's sense of unease about the transformation. "Add and stir" mixes, for example, insisted that greater convenience in no way undermined the "home-made" quality of new products. At issue here, among other things, was the need by women (in the paid labour force, in particular) to reduce the time and energy required for domestic tasks while still satisfying related emotional demands from family members. Food preparation, for example, is intimately associated with uxorial and maternal love and nurture. Given its symbolic significance, women tend to reduce their labour for the household with great circumspection. This hesitation and resulting sense of inadequacy are all the more understandable in light of the advice offered by self-appointed counsellors, like this example, which appeared in a Canadian labour journal: "It pays to wash over the kitchen floor frequently; some people do it only once or twice a week, but when you realize that microbes live in dust and particularly the sort of dust that congregates where food has been spilt, it is wise to wash it over every day – it will only take you five to seven minutes."[24]

Much of the trend to consumption centred on the acquisition of new technologies. The kitchen has been at the heart of this development. Traditionally, food preparation areas had been characterized by relatively few gadgets, casual planning, and generally limited facilities, but the 1920s and 1930s saw a heavy emphasis on industrial-like efficiency, high technology, and strict hygiene.[25] The attempt at transformation occurred simultaneously with the reluctant recognition that few families would be able to delegate kitchens and chores to hired help. When the female householder of the middle class was acknowledged as chief cook and cleaner, the kitchen became more thoroughly integrated into day-to-day routines. The emergence of the breakfast nook, just like the reduced status of the formal dining room, reflected a marked shift of responsibility to the middle-class housewife. An enthusiasm for domestic work, which had been contradicted by decades of determined searching for ideal servants, was increasingly fostered by repeated emphasis on the important, indeed rewarding, skills associated with the modern kitchen.

Good management was essential to success. As one exponent of mobilizing kitchen equipment into work centres pointed out in 1937: "The kitchen being the factory of the house, should be planned like any other factory!"[26] Wasted motions, with the fatigue they engendered, could be avoided when appliances, counters, cupboards, and sinks were placed at the correct height and location. The kind of haphazard arrangements that had been acceptable for the domestic servant would no longer be tolerated in increasing numbers of twentieth-century homes.

TABLE 1
Refrigeration Facilities in Occupied Dwellings in Selected Cities over 30,000, 1941

City	Tenant/Proprietor (T/P)	Refrigeration facilities			
		Mechanical	Ice	Other	None
Halifax	T	17.2	47.5	0.3	35.0
	P	36.8	42.5	0.4	20.3
Montreal	T	24.2	65.8	4.9	5.1
	P	32.6	59.0	3.8	4.6
Ottawa	T	47.8	42.1	0.9	9.2
	P	54.9	38.2	0.4	6.5
Toronto	T	42.8	44.5	0.2	12.5
	P	46.5	43.4	0.1	10.0
Winnipeg	T	45.9	30.8	0.3	23.0
	P	41.0	37.3	0.1	21.6
Edmonton	T	26.2	16.2	0.6	57.0
	P	25.9	19.4	0.4	54.3
Vancouver	T	27.8	12.5	1.4	57.0
	P	29.6	16.1	0.9	53.4

Source: Canada, Census, 1941, table 17a, "Refrigeration facilities in occupied dwellings, cities of 30,000 and over," IX, 81.

Kitchens advertised after World War I included a number of built-in features. Where formerly a separate cabinet unit was purchased as a distinct piece of kitchen furniture, to be augmented by open shelving and a simple basin, permanent units and fixtures became the order of the day.[27] Since new, smaller appliances such as egg cookers, fruit juicers, timers, and waffle irons had to be put away when not in use, space became a premium in most homes. Such items began to appear in Eaton's catalogues in the 1920s and 1930s, long before the majority of Canadians ever possessed the storage room that such purchases, together with store-bought food and clothing, required. No wonder, then, that updating houses, notably kitchens, by the addition of significant cupboard area, became a major and continuing refrain of both popular and professional architectural guides.

Small appliances were increasingly popular, but the mechanical, especially the electrical, refrigerator was the most significant addition to the preferred world of the middle-class housewife between the wars. As table 1 indicates, many urban families had committed resources to this major purchase by 1941. Menus, food preparation, and shopping shifted substantially in response to its presence. Of course, the routines of poorer and rural Canadians continued to be served by the ice-box, the cold cellar, and more make-shift arrangements until after World War II. Also increasingly popular was the clothes washer operated by electricity, gas, or propane. The hard labour associated with hand washes could be forever banned, as one 1920 article entitled "Make Blue-Monday a Workless Washday"[28] suggested. The third major item to attract wide attention was the cooking stove. In some ways, the 1920s and 1930s seem the heyday of Canadian stoves, which came in a wide and colourful variety of shapes and sizes. Like the early kitchen cabinets, they frequently encompassed a range of functions including storing water, heating rooms, and housing utensils. Stainless steel and enamel additions also saved time spent in blacking and cleaning older cast-iron models. The greatest savings accrued, however, to men and boys whose job it had largely been to chop, stack, and carry wood, coal, or peat for cooking. No comparable tasks remained with electric, gas, or propane models. In contrast, any potential for releasing women from labour was largely lost when new purchases allowed and indeed promoted – with the encouragement of manufacturers and nutrition experts – more elaborate menus with their longer preparation time.[29] Little wonder, then, that books and newspaper columns on cooking became standard fare for housewives who could no longer automatically look to their predecessors for guidance.

The addition of these major appliances, as well as a host of smaller rivals, including the electric ironer, the floor polisher, and vacuum cleaner, regularly advertised with the benefit of "Easy Payment Terms" during the inter-war years,[30] promised to mechanize domestic operations in ways reminiscent of factories. If the housewife could not supervise servants scrubbing the week's wash, she could supervise a mechanical replacement. Like employees in favoured sectors of the economy, the lucky housewife could increasingly perform her work in clean, sanitary, and efficiently organized surroundings, perhaps even to the tunes of a new radio or still later to the visual messages of the television. Despite the fact that such changes in setting and tools improved the work situation without eliminating the need for house labour or female responsibility for it, Canadian women were in the main convinced of the potential benefits. The consumer market for household appliances opened up in the 1920s, receded during the depression and war, and then expanded in the late 1940s and beyond, as it became clear that the domestic world could share in the technological advances that had transformed industry. The growing power of the mass media meant that the lives of Canada's working-class and farm women did not go untouched by dreams of new consumer goods. For them, the familiar world of backbreaking labour could not change fast enough.

Consumer demand was not an autonomous creation of domestic need. Early in the twentieth century, "captains of consciousness" emerged to channel desires for domestic improvement into business profits. Popular media fueled by entrepreneurs anxious for increased sales, along with press agents increasingly adept at manipulating demand, encouraged women to seek higher levels of domestic and personal consumption.[31] The emergence of consumer credit on a significant scale after World War I, and even more widely after World War II, also influenced the judgment of novice buyers.[32]

New goods and services promised a transformed life-style in which the female body and mind would be liberated for higher, or at least less onerous, forms of activity. One 1939 ad for Heinz spaghetti played on this theme with its patronizing claim:

Unexpected things are forever happening to the best of housewives. You're milling around in the millinery department or seeing the news reel over – when suddenly dinnertime sneaks up on you! It's *home on the run* – and thank Heinz for those tins of rib-lining, soul satisfying cooked spaghetti on your pantry shelf! ... *It brings a man home on the run!*

Consumers, however, were not as gullible as such ads might suggest. In 1940, a University of Toronto psychologist observed that "even ... middle-aged women are beginning to be more skeptical and the day is coming when the millions of dollars spent in advertising such dishonest claims will not sell the goods."[34] Moreover, for every innovation in selling, Canadian women learned new forms of resistance, such as comparison shopping. But such activity required skill, energy, and time,[35] as did meeting the new demands for higher standards of hygiene, design, and comfort, or enhanced child care. Like the stevedore who could rely increasingly on mechanization to reduce the weight he had to heft, the housewife did not see an end to labour itself.

The slow, uncertain, and still incomplete shift to consumption and modern technology contributes a major variable to the performance of housework. The timing and impact of these developments, and for that matter their predecessors, need serious attention. Only this can convey the complexity of a picture that in the 1980s still sees some housewives coping with cold-water flats or rural shanties, while others are learning the skills of computerized budgeting and microwave cookery. The survival of older forms of domestic work and the appearance of new ones raises substantial questions about obsolescence, progress, and inequity.

REPRODUCTION AND CHILD CARE

Like housework, reproduction and child care have enjoyed continuing, albeit fluctuating, public attention. Authorities have sometimes included advertising agents and their employers, but professionals in such fields as religion, health, psychology, education, and social welfare have exercised more formal influence. Churches of every faith have often had a good deal to say about parental conduct. Bringing up children in "the nurture and admonition of the Lord" has been regarded as serious business, best conducted with clerical supervision.[36] One advocate of the Church of England, for example, reminded "Christian parents" that they should "seize every suitable opportunity of making Christian impressions upon the minds of the children entrusted to them."[37] Instruction could cover even the smaller details of personal life: in 1742 Quebec bishops were troubled by mothers' practice of sleeping with their children.[38] The authority of religious counsellors has fluctuated a good deal over time and place. Certainly by the end of the nineteenth century, their voices formed only one part of a chorus that greeted Canadians embarking on parenthood.

Doctors, teachers, dentists, and a host of other secular experts crowded forward to champion their own form of expertise. Not all were new to Canadians. By the end of the nineteenth century, however, older services, in medicine, for example, were becoming more technical, more specialized, and in general less comprehensible and less controllable by the average user. Newcomers in psychology, dietetics, and social work also promised improved means of dealing with the problems, among others, of health, child management, sexuality, and personality. These modern counsellors, armed with higher degrees and professional certification and monopoly, were often intimidating, all the more so when they regularly looked to evidence of family failure for their raison d'être. Difficulties as varied as vitamin deficiency, juvenile delinquency, job absenteeism, dental decay, and marital discord became choice targets for study and correction. By the twentieth century, the association of professionals with public schools, social-welfare agencies and departments, hospitals, clinics, and penal and reform institutions brought many Canadians into contact with such taskmasters. Over time, it grew harder to ignore directives that often bore the state's stamp of approval.

Nevertheless, reception of these new authorities was just as mixed as that which has greeted the clergy. One British Columbia mother typified the sceptical consumer: "Although I grew up in a big family I didn't really know anything about child rearing – except the basics. But then, who does? Certainly not the people who write those silly psychological books on child care."[39] Not all potential clients were as confident, outspoken, or independent. Eager to reduce infant and maternal mortality[40] and anxious about maternal responsibility for social maladjustment,[41] mothers were susceptible to pressure from well-meaning, if sometimes self-serving, advisers who urged them to reject midwives, home births, folk remedies, and care by "rule of thumb." Only recently have outspoken and organized protests against the hegemony of the professionals appeared, notably in health care, as with the resistance to the medicalization of childbirth and the authority of the psychiatrist.[42]

Volumes like William A. McKeever's *Training the Girl*, Alan Brown's *The Normal Child: Its Care and Feeling*, Federal Ministry of National Health and Welfare's, *The Canadian Mother and Child*, and especially Benjamin Spock's, *Baby and Child Care*[43] form part of an extensive library of advice literature, itself supplemented by radio, film, and television. By the middle of the twentieth century, few Canadian homes remained untouched. Domestic labour, and the labourer herself, could not help but be affected. Consider, for instance, the extremely popular *The Canadian Mother and Child*, which refers quite matter of factly to "The Expectant Mother's Job" in one chapter title. Here the worker is urged to maintain a high level of efficiency and morale through subscribing to a proscribed set of up-to-date procedures and principles. Still another chapter dwells on "Relaxation and Posture" in much the same way. Occupational hazards such as emotional and digestive upsets, varicose veins, muscle cramps, hemorrhoids, vaginal discharges and bleeding, and toxemia are also described, just as they should be by any employment counsellor. The eleven-step "Procedure for Boiling Formula in a Saucepan and Pouring into Sterilized Bottles" testifies to the effort at regulation that characterizes much professional advice. Alternate job descriptions are routinely condemned, as in the reminder not to "try out fancy theories learned over the back fence or other unreliable sources. There are good books on the subject of bringing up your child."[44] Women's traditional networks of information are thus subtly and not so subtly discounted.[45]

Technological innovation has also had its role to play in modifying the mother/child relationship. The appearance of items as diverse as soothers, playpens, breast pumps, backpacks, disposable diapers, jolly jumpers, and intercoms could signal shifts in the duration and character of contact. Access to an automobile has had, for some families, an especially dramatic effect. Listen, for example, to a Packard ad from the 1930s:

... Believe me, the hands that rock the cradle are the hands that hold the wheel these days!

I taxi my husband to and from trains. I jitney the children to and from school, to and from riding club, to and from the movies. I dash to the stores and the bank – and struggle with traffic and parking.

I seem to spend half my life in a car.[46]

As suggested by this copy and the accompanying two pictures, one featuring a woman whose authority is signalled by car keys, modern equipment was susceptible to a variety of uses. On the one hand, it might give women new physical mobility; on the other, it presented new possibilities for employment. Women seized both opportunities.

Options in child care were also enhanced by women's better access to reliable and safe forms of birth control. This is one part of the explanation for the decline in Canadian family size since about 1870. Fewer children may not only free women's time, but also change the quantity and quality of attention given individual offspring and others within the family.[47] The consequences of the unavailability of good contraceptive technology have been painful, as one personal account from the 1970s indicates: "I wanted an abortion because my husband was irresponsible and didn't have any intention of working steady. How I hunted for a doctor to do an abortion! I couldn't find one – I was scared to try too much for fear of killing myself. I ended up with two unwanted children. After my second contraceptive failure, they put an IUD in me, which has worked for me. My "ex" finally got tired and left. Now I sit on welfare, bitter at being trapped and in poverty."[48] Not surprisingly, in view of child-care's heavy labour component and the economic implications of too many mouths to feed, women like this witness have been eager consumers and suppliers of birth-control information. Inasmuch as it has been possible, given deficiencies in materials and the indifference or opposition of church and secular authorities, women have struggled not to be the victims of their capacity to bear children.

What we need to understand better is the complex interplay between a women and the expectations of the larger society regarding children and mothering. We need to know, too, how the experience of first and subsequent births changes the type and quantity of labour devoted to the family as a whole and its individual members in particular. The sex of children is another unappreciated factor. For much of Canada's history, girls, as in McKeever's *Training the Girl*, have been regularly and early called upon for household duties to a degree rarely matched by boys. The nature and meaning of such practices should be deliberately addressed in any discussion of reproduction and child care.

CARE OF WORKING ADULTS

Just as women are crucial in assuring the production in children of new members of the labour force, they also help to guarantee the industry of adults. By offering a home, they remunerate (as mere money cannot) workers for their toil. Within the home, family members are prepared psychologically and physically to take up roles, however burdensome, in productive labour. The varieties of support and nurture are numerous, from going without food in order to give more to a wage-earner, to providing sex on demand to men frustrated by lack of power elsewhere,[49] to entertaining employers or employees, to providing volunteer services as a confirmation of a bread-winner's status. The housewife is also responsible for maintaining her own productivity in the home and, when necessary, the marketplace. This may require anything from purchasing a suitable wardrobe to packing lunches to juggling schedules.

The type of assistance given a husband, for example, has varied a good deal. In the middle-class suburb of Crestwood Heights, "no partner is more important to the career than the wife."[50] Women's sociability, deferral of consumption, housekeeping, sacrifice of a husband's assistance, and emotional support all promote male employment hopes. While in many ways self-evident, this contribution was rarely acknowledged explicitly by the suburbanites interviewed in this mid 1950s study. In contrast, the mutual dependence of male and female roles is captured very neatly in a later investigation of Saskatchewan farm and ranch families. While undeniably pre-eminent in the management and maintenance of the agricultural enterprise, a substantial number of husbands "are dependent upon wives for help in bookkeeping, letter-writing, and dealing with bureaucratic agencies."[51] Women also manage social commitments extending beyond the work group, thereby confirming and furthering a family's status and influence in the community. Their role in the economic and social functioning of the farm or ranch is visibly pivotal.

Luxton's interviews with working-class wives in Flin Flon also identify female labour as critical. At the end of each workday men must be restored for the toil of the mines. The effect of this industry on women's organization of domestic routines can be profound, as one case illustrates:

If a man is engaged in shift work, the household then operates around two, or sometimes three, often contradictory schedules. It is the woman's task to service each routine and to prevent each of them from coming into conflict. This process is well illustrated by one housewife's day. The woman gets up at 7:00 a.m., feeds the baby, then gets the three older children up, fed and off to school by 8:45 a.m. Meanwhile her husband who is on the graveyard shift (midnight to 8:00 a.m.) comes in from work and wants a meal, so once the children are fed she prepares his dinner. Then he goes to bed and sleeps until about 6:00 p.m. During the day she must care for the toddler, do her housework, feed and visit with the older children who come home for lunch from noon to 1:30 p.m. and return again at 4:00 p.m. All this occurs while "daddy is sleeping" and the noise level must be controlled to prevent him from being disturbed. At 5:00 p.m. she makes supper for the children and at 6:00 p.m. she makes breakfast for him. By 8:30 p.m., when the children are in bed, he is rested and ready to socialize while she is tired and ready to sleep.[52]

Not surprisingly, marital relations in this northern Manitoba town fluctuate in response to the needs of the major bread-winner. If his day goes badly, a husband's anger and frustration can be reaped by the family in terms of alcoholism, wife battering, and absent fathering. The benefits of his work may be there as well, of course, but these, too, are somewhat unpredictable in shaping women's labour at home. What is clear, however, is that legal recourse for domestic, on-the-job violence has usually been wanting.[53] More positively, women have found solutions individually in deserting violent spouses and collectively in transition houses and organizations such as Women Against Violence Against Women.[54]

The needs of the "working" wife – significantly in 1979 a majority of married women were for the first time engaged in the paid labour force[55] – also have to be accommodated. This may present difficulties. Some men, for example, regret or resent the loss of personal services wives have often rendered.[56] In contrast, women have not yet won the right both to time for self-maintenance and care and to assistance, emotional and otherwise, from husbands. One study of Halifax couples in 1971–2, for example, concluded that "it is noticeable that married employed women with young children, a group that does carry heavy work responsibilities, spend less time on other forms of maintenance than anyone else."[57] The commonly told anecdote about mothers resorting to locking themselves in the bathroom in order to get any time at all alone sums up the general dilemma. It gives special meaning to the expression "a room of one's own"!

It is clear, too, that the structure of the economy at large is absolutely fundamental in shaping the nature and extent of obligations. In an earlier stage of industrial capitalism, for instance, some of the parents and grandmothers of those businessmen and housewives in *Crestwood Heights* might well have lived together on the premises of their tailoring or merchandising operations. Ranching and farming couples often share significant knowledge, sometimes expertise, in the family enterprise. The juxtaposition of activities in a shared physical setting has enormous implications both for women's involvement in paid labour and for men's engagement in domestic life. In contrast, the first generation of women to arrive in Flin Flon, between 1927 and 1939, had to cope with a waged-work situation that drew husbands away, often for months at a time. Pioneers were isolated with children and frequently detached from the day-to-day demands of their husbands' exertions. For them and their daughters, the passage of time has meant more regular contact with spouses, their needs and demands. The implications of such variations in development need to be seriously considered when any attempt is made to describe the housewife's days.

CARE OF DEPENDENT ADULTS

Not all adults are able to support themselves. Handicaps of very kind disqualify many from participation in productive labour. In Canada's history some of these – the aged, the physically infirm, those with mental handicaps – have spent their days in houses of industry, poor law institutions, homes for the aged, asylums for the retarded, and hospitals for the insane. Many die soon after the onset of their infirmity and thus demand little of anyone's attention. Some scavenge precariously for themselves. What of the others? Historians have been interested in the evolution of social-welfare policy to deal with such human problems.[58] Institutionalization or placement in a substitute home has been, however, only one possible response. For example, in nineteenth-century Canada, "Even with the construction of new asylums and additions to old ones, the supply of unwanted and mad relatives appeared endless."[59]

TABLE 2
Percentage of Total Population Aged 65 and over,
by Sex, Canada, 1901–1981

	Female	Male
1901	2.5	2.6
1911	2.3	2.4
1921	2.3	2.4
1931	2.7	2.8
1941	3.3	3.4
1951	3.8	3.9
1961	3.9	3.7
1971	4.5	3.6
1981	5.5	4.2

Source: F.T. Denton and B.G. Spencer, "Canada's
Population and Labour Force: Past, Present and Future,"
in V.W. Marshall, ed., *Aging in Canada* (Toronto 1980),
10–26 and Statistics Canada, *A Profile of Canada, the
Provinces and the Territories from the 1981 Census:
Selected Facts on Population, Families and Dwellings*
(Ottawa n.d.).

Refuges for the elderly were similarly overcrowded. For those who could
not work nor cause others to work for them, the past offered few agreeable
options. Their situation in the present and the future also causes anxiety. The
survival of those, who, by medical intervention or social improvement, live
longer lives than ever before, for example, raises the question of their care.
Since 1921, Canada's population has been aging. There are now more "young
old," over 65 years of age, and "old, old," over 75, than at any previous time
in Canada's history. The rising proportion of the elderly in the population as
whole, as set out in table 2, creates a heavy level of dependency for the
society. That weight of responsibility is not, however, spread evenly. Men
over 65, for instance, are much more likely to have a spouse as care-giver than
women of the same age. Wives are there to nurse ailing older husbands, but
when widowed, they are likely to be on their own.[60]

In all periods of Canadian history some families have harboured their
vulnerable members. Seventeen years of increasing effort by Doris Shipley
to dress, feed, and maintain her aged mother-in-law Hagar in Margaret
Laurence's *The Stone Angel* (1964) found real-life equivalents. The facts of
sex and marriage assigned Doris a role that was clearly both uncongenial and
unrewarding. Even when substantial affection existed, care-givers must have
welcomed at least the occasional remission from their duties. The inauguration of pensions of all kinds, like visiting nursing and homemaking services,
recognized the presence of dependent adults in the family home just as much
as they offered individuals the chance to live alone. The so-called "normaliza-

tion" thrust of many of today's care programs is another policy decision that often retains people in the family. The result, commonly, is to increase demands on some female relative. The operative assumption is that women's commitment to waged labour and independence is less pressing and sacrosanct than men's.

Again, overall patterns in the case of adult dependency have yet to be systematically identified. While there is agreement that the extended family rarely lived together in one home in the past, little is known about the exceptions or about the existence of dependency in adults of the parent/child generations. Only slowly are we beginning to learn how families and the housewives who service them viewed dependent adults, not to mention how they treated them in the privacy of their own homes. Even the fragments we have, as with the apparent cruelty of the Inuit in abandoning older relatives, frequently need re-examination.[61] One fact can, however, be largely taken for granted: given their primary obligation for homework of all kinds, women have figured most prominently in the care of adult dependents. Jane Synge's interviews with Hamilton workers reveal some of the personal consequences of assistance to aged parents. One farm woman born in 1892 recalled how the death of her father brought the burden of a mother and two aunts.[62] Responsibility seems to have fallen first on the unmarried. Another female respondent of the same age summed up the situation facing many daughters:

In those days, there were a lot of girls stayed home, I mean in the class I was, helping mother. If there was more than one, one nearly always stayed home. That was one of the things I was afraid of. I'd never have much money though I'd be taken care of. My parents would get old and I'd be afraid to leave them.

We saw that happen so often when I was young, where the unmarried daughter was sort of left in a bad spot. But it seemed to be sort of taken for granted. There seemed to be in every family an unmarried aunt who was available to come and that sort of thing.[63]

In the event of no suitable single candidate, married children, usually daughters first, would be expected to offer bed and board. Such assistance sometimes received economic recompense, as with cases where a farm or a house was turned over to the nurturant children. Costs could still be high. A poem by P.K. Page captures powerfully how one hard-bitten old sea captain "made his one pale spinster daughter grow / transparent with migraines – and how his call / fretted her more than the waves."[64] There is little that can satisfactorily recompense for this kind of "job stress." Women finding themselves in custody of insane or retarded siblings, children, or spouses had, one would think, even less to expect in terms of material repayment. In any case, with or without reward, the labour, both physical and psychological, remained and needs to be integrated into any discussion of domestic work.

PAID WORK WITHIN THE HOME

Not all labour within the home has been unpaid. Until the 1920s, of course, waged domestic service composed the largest single category of female employment. Probably still more significant numerically have been housewives' efforts to augment family income through home industry or service. Taking in boarders, caring for children, selling liquor, offering medical help, baking, sewing, laundering, and a host of other activities have regularly been resorted to in efforts to bring in essential cash.[65] These activities often revealed considerable entrepreneurial ability. In a not untypical example, one Athabaskan woman from the Northwest Territories took full advantage of new demands for her services. She recalled her response to the arrival of the American army to build the Alaskan Highway in the 1940s.

Those soldiers had no place to wash their clothes. One day one of them came to see me, asked if I could wash some of his clothes for him. He say he'd pay me. I had scrub board so I said I would charge him so much for socks, so much for shirts, so much for pants, like that … Then he tell his friends I guess. Soon I'm doing for them.

I got old wooden washing machine – the crank kind. You turn handle to make work. Gee it was funny – those kids like to turn handle to play so they help me. Soon I got my sister to help me. First I just give her socks to wash. We iron everything, pack it up for them just like laundry.

I save $250 from the money I make. Then … buy gasoline washing machine. Then I really can do lots. Have seven or eight lines of wash – one for each person's clothes – I can do between seven and ten piles a day …

You know, between September and March I made $3500 …[66]

A sense of pride and self-confidence came hand in hand with more material benefits.

Such money-making efforts have been the particular preserve of poorer women, but they have by no means been limited to them. Housewives whose husbands earned good money have also used their skills to guarantee greater comfort and advantages for family members. Others, particularly those with artistic and literary ambitions, have found precious reward for their talents. For Nellie McClung and the scribbling sisterhood, for example, the opportunity to establish individual work regimes within the home has been heaven sent.[67] The numbers engaged in home-based industry have fluctuated considerably and have rarely been captured adequately by the census. Still, there is no doubt that in especially hard times, such as the 1930s and the 1980s, still more women search out homework solutions to an inadequate family income. Proper acknowledgment of such efforts has also been hindered until very recently by the dichotomy too many commentators assume to exist between paid and domestic work. Right up to the present, many housewives toil at home to produce cash or its equivalent in barter. Time spent in housework, child care, and the care of working and dependent adults has been influenced by an essentially economic calculus that frequently had to take into consideration the need for paid labour as well.

One early twentieth-century adviser pointed out the key to the viability of such additional initiatives: "To unite her home-making and her other employment successfully, the girl should learn how to organize her time. A girl, for instance, might look after poultry whie she waits for the kettle to boil. The same time might be taken for work in the garden. Heat that is used to cook dinner will help to can or preserve. The day's work should be planned if time is to be put to the best use."[68] As this advice suggests, money-making homemakers have often to be something of time and motion experts.

It is sometimes argued that paid homework offers substantial advantages to women who can find no ready substitutes for their unpaid domestic labour. The recent entry of word processors into the private home has been justified in just this way. The pressures of meeting yet more external deadlines and standards can, however, be destructive both to women and their families. A new study of industrial home sewing in Canada[69] enumerates many of these difficulties. Piecework rates set the pace, not the labourer herself. The experience of one young mother of two pre-schoolers illustrates the dilemma facing many homeworkers:

Her doctor finally ordered her to stop sewing at home because it was causing too much stress for her ... She would try to do everything. She would jump from the machine, feed the baby, quick sew a zipper, stir the pot on the stove, rush back to her machine, rush back to change the baby and keep on sewing. She would eat her own sandwich while she kept sewing. The doctor told her she would get an ulcer if she kept it up. He said that if you work in a factory you only do one thing at a time – and you take time off to eat your lunch.[70]

Certain groups of women – recent immigrants, racial and ethnic minorities, mothers with young children – have been especially vulnerable to such up-to-date versions of the old putting-out system.

Their home-bound exertions would have been fully familiar to a host of predecessors. Women in Victorian Canada bought pedal sewing machines on the instalment plan to add to meagre family incomes through piecework. Throughout the 1920s and 1930s, home knitting and the attendant purchase of knitting machines were regularly extolled as women's contribution to family expenses.[71] The first provincial programs of mothers' allowances in the same years counted on clients maintaining financial sidelines as a way of escaping "pauperization" and bridging the gap between privation and some small modicum of comfort.[72] It was very carefully emphasized, however, that these remunerated labours were not to distract women from their major obligations as mothers. Nor, incidentally, in a patriarchal and class society were babysitting, laundering, sewing, or other tasks expected to offer women real financial security after offspring were grown. The record of such efforts is still far from complete, but it is clear that, at least for women and one suspects for the great majority of men, the home was never a sheltered "haven in a heartless world."[73] There is no sharp division between work outside the home and that within it. In particular, the continuing existence of paid homework as a significant phenomenon testifies to the essential untidiness of human endeavours and their resistance to neat categorization and compartmentalization.

A world of human emotion – love and hate – is invoked by the word home. Those associations, powerful inducements both to action and forgetfulness, frequently obscure the dynamic reality of domestic labour that lies at their core. It is primarily women's toil in housework, in reproduction and child care, in caring for working and dependent adults, and in paid homework that underpins the larger system of socio-economic relationships, whether it be as in Canada's history, commercial, industrial, or financial capitalism. Yet central as it is to appreciating what exactly women, men, and children have experienced and felt, domestic labour in all its forms, its processes, and its relationships is far from being completely understood. A good beginning is made, however, in raising questions that examine, break down, and situate the multitude of tasks which go to make up the home and women's work. In other words, the world of home labour should be treated with the same seriousness and respect now being accorded to labour in public settings. Such recognition will help restore awareness of the complications of woof and warp that unite the various worlds of labour How tightly they are woven together is evocatively set out in one poem by Bronwen Wallace entitled "Overtime No. 3":

After about a week
of steady overtime when
I've had it with trying
to keep the kids quiet and
watching supper shrivel
on the stove and being
afraid to tell him about
the dent in the front fender
Just about the time I figure
the overtime will barely cover
a divorce

it's payday

He comes in more quietly than usual
I make coffee and we talk
for awhile
then just before he goes to bed
he hands me the cheque
as if it had my name on it too.[74]

It is long past time that the history of work, like that cheque, had the housewife's name on it, too.

NOTES

My thanks to Anita Fellman, Angus McLaren, Arlene Tigar McLaren, and Mary Lynn Stewart-McDougall for their comments on an earlier draft of this work.

1 For a valuable discussion on the significance of the recurring pattern of male adults absent from Canadian homes, see Isabelle St Martin, "Family Separation: The Case of the Women Left Behind," (MA thesis, Concordia University 1980).

2 See, for example, the importance attached to the home and the functions performed within it by Stephen Leacock, "The Woman Question," *The Social Criticism of Stephen Leacock*, edited and introduced by Alan Bowker (Toronto 1973) and Nellie McClung, *In Times Like These*, introduced by Veronica Strong-Boag (Toronto 1972).

3 Among the important non-Canadian readings are the contributions of Ann Oakley, notably *Woman's Work. The Housewife, Past and Present* (New York 1974) and *The Sociology of Housework* (New York 1974); Barbara Ehrenreich and Deirdre English, especially "Microbes and the Manufacture of Housework," in *For Her Own Good* (New York 1978); Ellen Malos, ed., *The Politics of Housework* (London 1979); Kathryn Kish Sklar, *Catharine Beecher, A Study in American Domesticity* (New York 1973); Theresa McBride, *The Domestic Revolution: The Modernisation of Household Service in England and France 1820–1920* (London 1976); and Dolores Hayden, *The Grand Domestic Revolution: A History of Feminist Designs for American Homes, Neighborhoods, and Cities* (London 1981). The essential recent Canadian work must include Joy Parr, ed., *Childhood and Family in Canadian History* (Toronto 1982); Penney Kome, *Somebody Has To Do It. Whose Work is Housework?* (Toronto 1982); Pat and Hugh Armstrong, *The Double Ghetto. Canadian Women and their Segregated Work* (Toronto 1978); Meg Luxton, *More Than a Labour of Love. Three Generations of Women's Work in the Home* (Toronto 1980); Beth Light and Alison Prentice, eds, *Pioneer and Gentlewomen of British North America 1713–1867* (Toronto 1980); Seena B. Kohl, *Working Together: Women and Family in Southern Saskatchewan* (Toronto 1976); Laura Johnson, *The Seam Allowance: Industrial Home Sewing in Canada* (Toronto 1982); and S.J. Wilson, *Women, the Family, and the Economy* (Toronto

1981). It would also be profitable to consult somewhat older publications such as S.D. Clark, *The Suburban Society* (1966); John R. Seeley, R. Alexander Sim, and E.W. Loosley, *Crestwood Heights. A Study of the Culture of Suburban Life* (Toronto 1956); Edwin C. Guillet, *Early Life in Upper Canada* (Toronto 1933) and *Pioneer Arts and Crafts* (Toronto 1940); Isabel Skelton, *The Backwoodswoman* (Toronto 1940); and Anthony Adamson and Marion MacRae, *The Ancestral Roof: The Domestic Architecture of Upper Canada* (Toronto 1963). These volumes, together with items referred to especially under "Material History," in Beth Light's and Veronica Strong-Boag's *True Daughters of the North. Canadian Women's History: An Annotated Bibliography* (Toronto 1980) and the entries in the only Canadian bibliography on domestic labour itself, "A 'Round the Clock Job: A Selected Bibliography on Women's Work at Home in Canada" (Ottawa 1983) by Kathryn McPherson encourage a more informed understanding of the nature of domestic labour and introduce some of the key theoretical issues.

4 Pat and Hugh Armstrong, *The Double Ghetto* (Toronto 1978), 55.

5 Luxton, *More Than a Labour of Love*, 18–19.

6 Both as health professionals and para-professionals (nurses and nursing assistants in particular) and as homeworkers, women (much more than men) are likely to care for adults – spouses, parents, other relatives, or strangers – who are aged or have handicaps and consequently are not producing members of their society. On this, see Diane de Graves, "Women Caring for Women," *Resources for Feminist Research* 11, 2 (July 1982): 212–13 and Nina Chappell, "The Future Impact of the Changing Status of Women," *Canada's Changing Age Structure: Implications for the Future*, a Research Symposium sponsored by Continuing Studies, Simon Fraser University, 20–23 August 1981.

7 For a discussion of Saskatchewan Hutterite women see J.W. Bennett, "A Comparison: Hutterite Women and Their Families," in Kohl, *Working Together*.

8 Ibid., 123.

9 Elizabeth Goudie, *Women of Labrador* (Toronto 1973), 46.

10 Luxton, *More Than a Labour of Love*, 20.

11 One thinks especially of the influence of that "classical family of western nostalgia" or the stable extended family so aptly summed up by W.J. Goode, *World Revolution and Family Patterns* (New York 1963), 6 and passim.

12 Tamara Hareven, "The Family as Process: The Historical Study of the Family Cycle," *Journal of Social History* 7 (1973–4): 323.

13 Glen Elder, "Family History and Life Course," *Journal of Family History* (1978): 279.

14 Hareven, "The Family as Process," 323.

15 Ibid., 325.

16 Ibid., 324. In contrast, Michael Katz in *The People of Hamilton, Canada West* (Cambridge and London 1975) sees boarding as more a reflection of "convenience, price, and the presence of friends living there or nearby" (37) rather than as

related to the family life cycle. He does, however, discover many widowed land-ladies.

17 Hareven, "The Family as Process," 325.
18 See R. Samuel, "Workshop of the World: Steam Power and Hand Technology in Mid-Victorian Britain," *History Workshop* 3 (Spring 1977): 6–72 for an excellent discussion of how old and new processes can be incorporated simultaneously and indeed profitably in industry. The home was also a centre where alternate technologies were tested and developed, either to be rejected or incorporated. The result was a workplace like industry – both tied to the past and looking to the future.
19 Micheline Dumont, Michele Jean, Marie Lavigne, and Jennifer Stoddart, *L'Histoire des femmes au Québec depuis quatre siècles* (Montréal 1982), 102.
20 For a fascinating discussion of "single pot" cooking, see Ruth Schwartz Cowan, *More Work for Mother: The Ironies of Household Technology from the Open Hearth to the Microwave* (New York 1983), 21–2.
21 Catharine Parr Traill, *The Canadian Settler's Guide* (Toronto 1969), 167–9.
22 Kathleen Strange, *With the West in Her Eyes. The Story of a Modern Pioneer* (Toronto and NY 1937), 220–1.
23 See M. McKinley, "Albertans Flee Their Kitchens," *Alberta Report* 9 (22 March 1982): 28–9; R.W. MacNaughton, "Fast Food Still on the Move," *Financial Post* 73 (21 April 1979): 13, "Mac's Stores Moves into Fast Food," *Marketing* 84 (21 May 1979): 2; "Le Croque-bec, un fast-food de chez nous," *Commerce* 81 (octobre 1979): 118–19; R.L. English, "Baby Boomers and Over-60s Dictate Sophisticated Packaging," *Financial Post* 74 (15 March 1980): 53.
24 "Taking the Work Out of Housework: In the Realm of the Home," *Canadian Congress Journal* (May 1929): 39.
25 See, for example, the attitudes revealed in B. Evan Parry, "Plan for Use Sequence," *Canadian Homes and Gardens*, Jan.–Feb. 1937, 59 and "The Builder Looks at Plumbing," ibid., Jan. 1931, 66.
26 Parry, "Plan for Use Sequence."
27 See, for example, for the inter-war years, the trend to built-in features for Canada's model kitchen revealed in the pages of *Chatelaine, Canadian Homes and Gardens*, and the *Journal* of the Royal Architectural Institute of Canada. *Eaton's Catalogue* documents a corresponding reduction in the number of ads for separate kitchen cabinets.
28 *Western Home Monthly*, May 1920, 25.
29 On aspects of this transition, especially the shift from the hearth to iron to stainless-steel stoves, see Cowan, *More Work for Mother*, especially ch. 3.
30 See BC Electric's ad promoting clothes washers, *Western Woman Weekly*, 22 May 1920, 9.
31 For an appraisal, if uncritical, of the development of Canadian advertising, see H.E. Stephenson and C. McNaught, *The Story of Advertising in Canada* (Toronto 1940), especially chs 9 and 15. For an up-to-date, provocative, and important

study of the pressure to consume, see Stuart Ewen, *Captains of Consciousness* (New York 1976).

32 See, for example, the high percentage of credit-to-cash sales in the Canadian retail trade reported in Canada, *Census*, 1931, v. 2, table 813, "Canada, the Provinces and the Territories – Retail Merchandise Trade, 1930, Credit Business," 69.

33 "Home on the Run," *Saturday Night*, 4 March 1939.

34 K. Bernhardt, "A Criticism of Marketing Techniques," in Jane McKee, ed., *Marketing Organization and Technique* (Toronto 1940), 93.

35 For a useful discussion of misleading advertising, product adulteration, short weight, and the absence of generally accepted product standards, see Canada, Royal Commission on Price Spreads, *Report* (1935), ch. VIII.

36 For a description of one denomination's attitudes to children, see Neil Semple, "'The Nurture and Admonition of the Lord': Nineteenth-Century Canadian Methodism's Response to 'Childhood,'" *Histoire sociale / Social History* 14, no. 27 (mai/May 1981): 157–75.

37 Adam Townley, *Seven Letters on the Non-Religious School System of Canada and the United States* (Toronto 1885), as cited in A.L. Prentice and S.E. Houston, eds, *Family School & Society* (Toronto 1975), 137.

38 See Dumont, Jean, Lavigne, Stoddart, *L' Histoire des femmes au Québec*, 71.

39 Phyllis Knight and Rolf Knight, *A Very Ordinary Life* (Vancouver 1974), 164–5.

40 On the campaign, see Suzann Buckley, "Ladies or Midwives? Efforts to Reduce Infant and Maternal Mortality," in L. Kealey, ed., *A Not Unreasonable Claim* (Toronto 1979).

41 See Ontario, Department of Labour Papers, general subject files, v. 2, "Mothers' Allowances 1919" for persistent stress on a woman's major responsibility for social order through good child rearing.

42 For some of the arguments in favour of home births, see Sheila Kitzinger's popular *Birth at Home* (NY and Melbourne 1979), especially chs 1 and 2. For a critique of psychiatric hospitals and the treatment of women in particular, see Helen Levine, "The Personal is Political: Feminism and the Helping Professions," in Angela Miles and Geraldine Finn, eds, *Feminism in Canada* (Montreal 1982).

43 McKeever (New York 1914); Brown (Toronto 1926); National Health and Welfare (Ottawa 1940); Spock (New York 1946).

44 *The Canadian Mother and Child* 3rd ed. (Ottawa 1972), 122.

45 For more on this subject in the inter-war years, see Strong-Boag, "Intruders in the Nursery: Childcare Professionals Reshape the Years One to Five, 1920–1940," in Parr, ed., *Childhood and Family in Canadian History*.

46 "Listen to the Plea of the Family Taxi-Driver," *Canadian Homes and Gardens*, Oct.–Nov. 1936, 48.

47 See Margrit Eichler, *Families in Canada Today: Recent Changes and Their Policy Consequences* (Toronto 1983), especially 245–6.

48 Canada, Committee on the Operation of the Abortion Law, *Report*, 1977, personal account 3, on 178.

49 The identification of sexuality as part of services rendered in domestic labour has been somewhat controversial. Its significance is nevertheless addressed in much of the recent literature. See, for example, Luxton's chapter on "Wives and Husbands" in *More Than a Labour of Love*. Naturally, not all sexual exchange falls into the definition of labour. Two critical distinctions between work and non-work for housewives would surely be reciprocity of pleasure and the absence of coercion of any kind.

50 Seeley, Sim, and Loosley, *Crestwood Heights*, 135.

51 Kohl, *Working Together*, 71.

52 Luxton, *More Than a Labour of Love*, 47.

53 See Gillean Chase, "An Analysis of the New Sexual-Assault Laws," *Canadian Woman Studies/Les cahiers de la femme* 4, no. 4 (Summer/August 1983): 53–4.

54 For some discussion of these solutions, see Marry Lassance Parthun and Gloria Hart, "Domestic-Violence Intervention: A Generic Service Model," ibid., 73–4; Marsha Endahl, "The Silent Crime and the Beginning of Change," ibid., 78–80; and Jan Lancaster and Ajax Quinby, "Vancouver's Munroe House: A Second Stage Transition House," ibid., 56–7.

55 Eichler, *Families in Canada Today*, 44.

56 See, for example, the remarks by a 45-year-old businessman searching for a new partner in Judith Finlayson, "Companion Wanted," *Homemaker's*, May 1983, 32. Male response to spousal employment is both controversial and evidently in transition. See also Eichler, *Families in Canada Today*, 46, 189–90.

57 Susan Clark and Andrew Harvey, "The Sexual Division of Labour: The Use of Time," *Atlantis* 2, no. 1 (Fall 1976): 60.

58 See, for example, Richard Splane, *Social Welfare in Ontario 1791–1893* (Toronto 1971).

59 Cheryl L. Krasnick, " 'In Charge of the Loons': A Portrait of the London, Ontario Asylum for the Insane in the Nineteenth Century," *Ontario History* 74, no. 3 (Sept. 1982): 145.

60 See Sharon McIrvin Abu-Laban, "The Family Life of Older Canadians," in Victor W. Marshall, ed., *Aging in Canada* (Don Mills 1980), 128–9.

61 For an explanation stressing the significance of a cosmology that viewed death in a special light, see Lee Guemple, "Growing Old in Inuit Society," ibid.

62 Jane Synge, "Work and Family Support Patterns of the Aged in the Early Twentieth Century," ibid., 139.

63 Quoted in Synge, "Work and Family Support," 143.

64 "A Portrait of Marina," in M. Wilson, ed., *Poetry of Mid-Century 1940/1960* (Toronto 1964), 178.

65 See Light and Prentice, eds, *Pioneer and Gentlewomen of British North America*, especially 144–60 for an indication of the type of paid labour performed by early Canadian housewives.

66 As quoted in Julie Cruikshank, *Athabaskan Women: Lives and Legends* (Ottawa 1979), 52–3.

67 For an indication of such freedom, guaranteed often by the presence of a maid-of-all-work, see N.L. McClung, *The Stream Runs Fast* (Toronto 1945).

68 Marjory MacMurchy, *The Canadian Girl at Work: A Book of Vocational Guidance* (Toronto 1919), 81.

69 Laura C. Johnson, *The Seam Allowance: Industrial Home Sewing in Canada* (Toronto 1982).

70 Quoted in ibid., 80.

71 See, for example, the ad from the Auto Knitter Hosiery Company, "And I make $4.00 a Day Besides Doing All My Own Housework," *National Home Monthly*, January 1925, 29.

72 See Strong-Boag, "'Wages for Housework': Mothers' Allowances and the Beginnings of Social Security in Canada," *Journal of Canadian Studies* 14, no. 1 (Spring 1979): 27.

73 For an argument based on a faith in a time when the family did fulfil such a function, see Christopher Lasch, *Haven in a Heartless World. The Family Beseiged* (New York 1977).

74 Tom Wayman, ed., *Going for Coffee: An Anthology of Contemporary North American Working Poems* (Vancouver 1981), 164.

MERCEDES STEEDMAN

Skill and Gender in the Canadian Clothing Industry, 1890–1940

Today to produce one garment you need fifty machines, because you don't have a pool of skilled help. You have what you call sectionalized production where you take girls, mostly women, housewives, and you teach them to sew one operation so to produce one coat, you have to have fifty or sixty machines. It's not just the machines, you have to have the managerial know-how to break garments down, how to do time-motion study and besides, you need many, many other technical equipments.[1]

Louis Poslun's years of experience in Tip Top Tailors gave him a clear sense of how to deskill a labour process by breaking production down into simple mechanized operations and closely monitoring workers. Yet the process of deskilling entails other dimensions as well. Skill is intricately tied to the gender of the worker, and the notion of skill in the clothing industry often had less to do with the job itself than with the sex and the bargaining position of the worker in the production process.[2]

This essay explores the complex role of women in the Canadian clothing industry – from the time of the small shop of the custom tailor to the era of the huge mass-production factory.[3] It argues that the role of women was conditioned by a sexual division of labour that was organized and reorganized to reflect the patriarchal structures dominant in Canadian society. That is, the basis of women's work in the clothing industry lay in the social view that their ultimate destiny as wives and mothers made them peripheral to the paid work world. Moreover, women's demands and struggles for changes in their conditions went largely unsupported by male workers and trade unionists who saw women's entrance into the work force as a threat to their jobs. Ultimately, these attitudes intersected with the desires of employers for a cheaper and more flexible labour force to create a significant gap between the lives of women and men in the needle trades.[4] Women were drawn into the struggles of the male-dominated unions against the evils of sweatshops and the breakdown of skilled jobs, thereby gaining experience as trade unionists and a new status in the industry itself. And unionization did limit the exploitation of both women and men. But throughout these struggles, there remained a clear conception of the divisions between the jobs of women and men.

EVOLUTION OF THE INDUSTRY

Men's and women's clothing has always been turned out by separate, distinctive trades within the garment industry, each with its own organization of production. In the men's sector, garments not made in the home were originally produced in custom tailor shops, where one man made up the whole garment. In the United States and Canada, factories appeared as early as the 1830s to produce ready-made clothing and gradually expanded over the next half century, as retail merchants who had been importing clothing turned to manufacturing, and custom tailors began to employ their journeymen during the off season to make up extra suits. In these "factories," manufacturers would typically have the material cut on their premises and then distribute the cut bundles to individual homes or contract shops to be sewn up. The preponderance of outside help is suggested in the dispersal of workers at the H. Shorey Company of Montreal: 130 inside hands and 1,400 outside hands are listed on the 1892 payrolls.[5] The growth of this system of production was connected to the arrival of the increased number of Jewish immigrants who entered the trade as workers and contractors in the main garment centres – Montreal, Toronto, Hamilton, and Winnipeg.[6] According to R.P. Sparks, founder of the Canadian Association of Garment Manufacturers, this early ready-made clothing was "of the roughest sort, principally because of the lack of suitable machines to eliminate hand-sewing operations." It was only in the 1890s that "the production of machine-made clothes on a large scale became a reality."[7] As the demand for men's suits became steadier after 1900, more and more of the outwork was moved inside larger, integrated factories.

The evolution of ready-made women's clothing was similar to the one in men's garments, but somewhat slower in displacing custom dressmakers and tailoresses.[8] The ready-made industry began in the 1890s with the production of cloaks and suits; the heavy material used made the process similar to that in the men's suit industry. The women's cloak and suit industry reached a peak of prosperity in 1909–13 when it was controlled by several large manufacturers, but after World War I, many smaller shops were set up in a more fragmented market. By the 1930s, Sparks estimated that there were 188 such manufacturers in Canada.[9] The forerunner to the dress industry was the manufacturer of shirtwaists or slips, two of whom existed in Montreal in 1900. Within five years, the "whitewear" (underwear) branch of the trade in Canada had doubled, and was estimated to be "six times what it was six years ago."[10] It was the popularity of the simple housedress in the twentieth century, however, that expanded factory production of women's clothing. In

Canada, the predominance of the custom dressmaker had passed by 1910, and by the 1920s, mass production of dresses was well established.[11]

In many ways, the women's cloak and suit industry was similar to that of the men's sector, as production runs were long and the whims of style and fashion appear not to have been quite so capricious. In the dress sector, however, the dictates of fashion were much stronger. Different styles were produced for different periods of the year, and the seasonal nature of the trade became much more pronounced. Indeed, it was the dictates of short seasons, combined with the larger variety of styles and the different materials used, that created the industrial necessity for shorter runs of individual garment styles. In order to meet these demands, dress factories remained small, specializing in a specific grade of garment, and were often in existence only for the extent of one season. As a result, contracting out parts of the garment was not common. One worker described the situation: "Because what do you need? You buy a machine and you have a corner in your basement and you start working and you enslave yourself day and night and when you have a little cash you rent a dump some place and you open up a shop."[12] The precarious nature of dress manufacture meant that the life expectancy of the majority of firms in business during the period under discussion would be less than seven years.[13]

Throughout this period the technological base of the whole industry remained relatively limited. The most important innovation had been the invention of the sewing machine in 1849.[14] By the turn of the century, the most common sewing machine in use in Canada was the Singer 95K10 with a stitching speed of 2,500 stitches per minute. This was slowly replaced by a single needle cockstitch machine with a speed of 3,500 stitches per minute that compelled operators to turn out more garments.[15] From the beginning, the demand for more material by sewing machine operators had led to a transformation in cutting tools: from short knives to long knives, to electric rotary knives, to the band-saw cutting machines of the 1920s that made it possible to cut 500 layers of cloth at one time.

Other technological innovations included devices for automatically cutting and stitching buttonholes that reduced the time for this work on suits and coats from 3 hours and 20 minutes to 17.5 minutes.[16] In the 1930s, basting and tacking machines replaced many operations done by hand. Other operations were also mechanized, as an American writer noted in 1935: "Folding, shaping, and creasing of every description are machine operations. Collar point forming, shaping and turning are now done entirely by machine to a point where workers are no longer needed even for the purpose of applying heating irons to the material, as formerly."[17] Sewing machine modification allowed for the simplification of complicated sewing jobs: sewing sleeve linings at cuffs, attaching waistbands to pants, serging pockets and side seams on pants, and so on. All served to increase the number of garments produced.

Most new machines took the work away from the finishers who had sewn by hand: buttons, tacking, facings, linings, and collars were now all done by special machines.[18] By the late 1930s, in fact, hand finishing had disappeared from the larger shops in Montreal, although the more fragmented dress industry, there and in Toronto, remained mostly untouched. As one Montreal pensioner from the dress shops remembered: "For the operator, automation in the [dress] industry makes no difference. You can't divide the work. A dress is a dress. You can't have a special machine break down the work."[19]

Each of these changes was accompanied by an extension of the division of labour. At first, tailors maintained control over production of the more complex garments, such as the suit jackets and coats: they gave out the vests, pants, and linings to be made up by women workers. Initially this division of labour served to enhance the position of the skilled tailors, but as the factory system developed, they lost their ability to intervene in the process of breaking down skills in the factories and contract shops. The sewing machine, equally adaptable to tenement or factory, allowed manufacturers to farm out those garments that required straight stitching. As the factory system expanded at the turn of the century, it was these simple garments that became its major products: pants, vests, shirts, and uniforms. Once these commodities were no longer under the jurisdiction of the skilled tailor, it became much easier for the capitalists in the trade to use less-skilled workers inside the factory proper.

The rigid control over the craft was thus broken, and "section work" was easier to establish. By 1920, divisions in the labour process in the production of men's suits and coats were extremely complex, as illustrated in the list of vocational opportunities provided by the industry: cutters of various grades, trimmers, fitters, fitters' helpers, thread markers, pocket operators, helpers, lining makers, sleeve makers, canvas makers, edge tapers, operators-joiners, lapel and collar makers, buttonhole makers (by machine and hand), edge basters, lining basters, shoulder and undercollar basters, top-collar basters, head tailors, armhole sergers, finishers, button sewers, brushers, bushelers, seam pressers, edge pressers, off pressers, and basting pullers.[20] Production divisions within the dress industry were considerably simpler: cutters and trimmers, machine operators, finishers, and pressers. Hand sewing was initially present in this trade, but gradually disappeared in the 1930s in all but the high-grade dresses.

In general, then, the needle trades evolved from the custom tailor shop, to partial factory production with outworkers in contract shops and private homes, to full-scale production under one factory roof. Yet the movement was quite uneven and created a great variety in the mode of production right through to the 1930s. The common characteristics of all clothing production in Canada, however, were the intense competition between small-scale manufacturers, the rather limited technological base, and, perhaps most important, the systematic exploitation of a seemingly endless pool of cheap, female labour.

THE SEXUAL DIVISION OF LABOUR

Needlework has been a traditional female domestic craft for centuries, and it was commonplace in nineteenth-century Canada for working-class and farm women to make all the family clothing. Some women also ran their own custom tailor shops, handling most tasks themselves, including the most skilled cutting work. In the artisanal workshops of male tailors, however, women and girls joined the family production unit mainly as helpers and finishers. Thus, custom tailors and the first manufacturers had a ready supply of knowledgeable and skilled women workers available, but they used this labour only for jobs designated as least skilled, like sewing up pants or stitching lining into men's suits. As women were drawn into the industry through homework and contract shops, they continued to work primarily as finishers, button sewers, and lining makers, both by hand and on sewing machines. Sometimes, during rush seasons, women in the home would be given much more skilled work on coats and cloaks, but their wages rarely reflected this level of competence, and such work remained exceptional.

The most important factor in accounting for the role of women in the emerging clothing industry was their position in the family. Confined to the household by social custom and social duty, women (particularly married women), were blocked from long-term participation in work outside the home. Thus, it was perhaps inevitable in the transition from the custom tailor shop to the fully integrated clothing factory, that employers utilized this vast and vulnerable population to turn out certain garments in the home. "The work suits women because they can carry on household work at the same time," a defender of the system argued; "several are mothers of families who eke out their husband's wages in this way; others are obliged to be at home to care for aged or sick relatives."[21] Their isolation from other homeworkers placed them in a weak bargaining position and allowed the contractor, in most instances a middleman between the retailer and the worker, to maintain a downward pressure on their wages. In 1890, Mackenzie King observed that "the fact remains that the price which has been paid to women homeworkers on government clothing, was itself clearly insufficient to constitute a living wage ... Many of these women were compelled to toil fifteen hours a day, or even longer on government work in order to gain a living."[22] Indeed, whether on government work or not, women's wages in all categories of work were lower than men's. In 1920, female factory operators received $12.00 per week on average for a 45-hour work week, while males received $24.65 for the corresponding work.[23] The presence of cheap female labour in the home had the effect of depressing the rates of pay of women who worked in the factory. Yet for the men in the industry, no comparable group served to depress their wages.[24] The use of young women as poorly paid or underpaid "learners" was a common practice. Since learners in the trade were almost exclusively female, employers depended heavily upon them to reduce further the wages of women in the trade.[25]

The low wages earned by women made it virtually impossible for them to live independently. Even after the introduction of minimum wage laws for women in Quebec in 1919 and Ontario in 1920 that required companies to restrict the pool of underpaid or free female labour to under 20 per cent of female employees,[26] employers were nonetheless able to use cheaper female labour on a casual basis during rush seasons, often hiding the wage violations within the books of the firm. A 1934 report on minimum wage violations itemized three types.

There are three chief types of incorrect wage statements: (1) The wages are actually put down incorrectly. This can be done if the firm actually keeps two sets of books, one for the inspectors, and one for the firm. (2) The wages are down correctly, but there are employees unlisted. The firm puts in its wage sheet that the employees listed are getting more than they actually receive. A variation of this is where two girls pay is in one envelope. This is very common in the clothing trade, where one finds in the wage lists "so-and-so and helper." (3) The most common method of violation, is incorrect time-keeping. In the wage statement returned, the hours are put down as much less than the girls actually worked. It is very easy to do this in such an industry as the cloak making trade where very few firms even possess time clocks.[27]

In essense, then, women's position in the home as the family caretakers became not only the principal justification for making extensive use of them as homeworkers, but also paved the way for their social and economic subordination in the contract shops and the larger factories. The women who entered the factories were, for the most part, young, unmarried – mainly French Canadian (popularly known as "midinettes") and immigrants – who did this type of work to help support their families up to the point when they became wives and mothers themselves.[28] In short, the transformation from custom tailor shop to factory tied the requirements of industrial capitalism to the family economy.[29] According to historian Christine Stansell, "The confinement of women workers to their households gave rise to a specific psychology of female subordination in their relations with employers as well as to a particular organization of labour. The outside system masked women's involvement in wage labour; they appeared to be peripheral to industrial production and their identity as workers seemed secondary to their roles as wives and mothers."[30]

An essential and structural feature of this sexual subordination and segmentation was the inability of women to gain entry to the skilled jobs, especially cutting and pressing. After the invention of the modern cutting knife in 1876, for example, few women became cutters.[31] The new knives allowed the cutter to slice through many layers of cloth, and thus made the work heavier than it had previously been. The cutter's skill was considerable, for the cost of production could be seriously affected by the laying out of the pattern. "The cloth is laid out on long table," investigators for the Ontario Department of Labour observed. "It must not be stretched too much or left too loose, or the fit and the style of the garment will be spoiled." Women were considered incapable of "standing and reaching across wide tables ... even when the materials are light."[32]

In this instance, technological innovation seemed to pose as the major obstacle to women's continued involvement in skilled work in the needle trades. Yet, the observation of the authors of the Department of Labour report that a great number of elderly men were engaged as cutters belies this explanation. In fact, definitions of skill were strongly influenced by the gender of the worker in that sector. Work on men's clothing was deemed to be more skilled work, while dressmaking, an almost entirely female occupation, was considered "light," unskilled work – despite the fact that, as an Ontario factory inspector pointed out in 1912, it could be "hard and exacting" and that a female operator made virtually the whole dress, without the extensive subdivision of labour in the men's clothing sector.[33] A 1920 Ontario government report on vocational opportunities in the garment industry specifically referred to the job by the sex of the worker, noting that "cutting for the most part is a man's occupation," and that "even in the women's factory clothing the majority of those designated as trimmers are men and boys." The report also pointed out that "men for the most part do the operating [sewing] in the case of very heavy materials and women when the fabrics are lighter," and that "men do not infrequently operate on coats and women more often do the stitching in the case of vests, trousers and skirts."[34]

A further manifestation of the sexual division of labour was the particular susceptibility of women workers to the speed-up devices of their employers. In fact, as most women were sewing-machine operators,[35] and as employers were aware that the major cost in garment production rested in this aspect of the labour process, speed-up was an issue of special relevance to women workers. As one Montreal dress manufacturer explained, "It was skill and the speed of the operator which determined how many garments were made and the resulting price and profit."[36]

The most important device for speeding up production was piecework. As homemakers and as contract shop workers, women were likely the first pieceworkers and were too isolated and vulnerable to fight this system of payment.[37] Thus, when women entered the factories, the piecework system came with them. Under this system, women worked harder in order to gain the extra wages. But, as one Ontario factory inspector noted, women's extra efforts to increase their speed and add to their earnings succeeded "until the employer awakens to the fact that he is paying them as much for five days as he formerly did for six." The employer would then cut the price to the original level, and the cycle continued. He concluded that "the natural tendency of piecework is to cause the worker to work harder and harder, until they work their lives out for no benefit for themselves."[38] According to a turn-of-the-century American study, the advantage of a piecework system was "the incentive that it offered to greater intensity of effort."[39] Wages had originally been paid by the week, but as the making of coats became increasingly sectionalized in the late nineteenth century, the weekly wage came to be tied to a set number of coats. From the turn of the century, there was a general tendency in the trade to move to piecework in all sectors of production. "At first this method was used to make cheap everyday garments," an Ontario factory inspector observed in 1910, "but now it is extending to the better grade fabrics as more buyers are developing."[40]

Certain jobs within the industry, however, remained untouched by the piecework system – notably the male jobs of cutter and high-grade presser. The men working in these jobs used their unions to ensure that the introduction of piecework rates never affected their work situation by making the work lighter. A retired factory worker described the position of the cutters in the 1930s: "They always worked time work and they had a set price. They were the aristocracy of the trade. The cutters, no matter how slow it was, used to hang around the shop and get paid for it." In contrast, she noted, "when you work piecework, if you haven't got a dress to make, you don't get paid."[41] Decisions concerning who had work and who sat idle were arbitrary and remained contentious issues until the late 1930s, when the unions were able to win control of work allocation within the factory. Women pieceworkers were more vulnerable even in this system because of their youth and their status as subordinate labour in the factory system. The piecework system also caused antagonism among the workers, and haggling with employers over prices and the divisions of work made the atmosphere intolerable.

Piecework thus institutionalized the intensity of work familiar to women from experiences in their homes and in the contract shops. In combination with the seasonal nature of the industry – thirteen-hour days and sixty-hour weeks were still common in the 1930s during rush periods – factory life became exhausting and dangerous to their health. The H.H. Stevens's Royal Commission on Price Spreads heard testimony from one Eaton's employee who exclaimed that "we were badgered, and harrassed and worried ... We were told to work and work so hard at these cheap rates to make the $12.50 [minimum wage] and you were threatened if you didn't make $12.50 you would be fired."[42] An examiner at Eaton's spoke of the effect of speed-up: "Well, the girl that worked beside me was away for two months with nervous exhaustion. I would go around to the operators, you know, if I had to take work back to them or anything. Many times, I would go back to find them crying ... they were generally in a very highstrung condition."[43]

The pace of work at Eaton's was part of a generally harsh industrial environment. In 1911, the firm described the life of operators in their factory. Operators wasted scarcely a second and sewing machines were kept running almost steadily all day long. This pace was matched by a rigid discipline: "A striking illustration of habit of swift co-ordinate action may be witnessed in the Eaton's operating rooms where the gong rings to cease work for the day. Instantly the power is shut off, and the girls lay aside their work for the night. Another gong rings and they stand up beside their chairs. A third bell clangs and with a simultaneous crash every chair in the room is upturned on the tables out of the way of the sweepers.[44]

Since the system of speed-up placed the responsibility for output on the shoulders of the individual worker, workplace discipline was important. Elaborate rules and fines were imposed on operators. Manufacturers fined operators if empty spools of thread were not returned to the foremen, if improper language was used in the shop, and if goods were damaged. As a means of regulating quality, examiners returned work that they considered of poor quality to the operator, who then had to repair the work for free.

In sum, the consolidation of the sexual division of labour had important consequences for women and the development of the industry. With regard to women, even while they became more and more prominent in the factories, they languished in the lowest-paying operator's jobs.[45] Moreover, as these jobs were now classified as unskilled – the jobs a women could do – employers were able to cheapen their labour costs considerably. With these changes in the sexual division of labour, skills had been downgraded, section work standardized, and piecework accepted for all the tasks performed by machine operators.[46] The subordination of women was fully consolidated.[47]

WOMEN'S RESPONSE

The powerful forces arrayed against women working in the clothing industry made collective responses extremely difficult. When women did oppose changes in the labour process, the patterns of resistance reflected the specific problems created by a predominantly female work force. The women's youth and inexperience, and the patriarchal perceptions of their position as wage-earners, all served to make organizing more difficult. Male trade unionists took for granted the women's inferior, transient status in the industry, but, at the same time, recognized that they needed the support of female workers in their fights against long hours, low wages, subcontracting, piecework, and other injustices. This ambivalence is evident in two crucial areas – participation in union affairs and the struggle over particular workplace issues affecting women.[48]

The garment industry has a long but chaotic history of unionization. Four different modes of organization appear between the 1890s and the 1930s. The first was pure craft unionism. Independent organizations of custom tailors existed in Canada prior to the 1890s, but the first significant unionizing effort was under the auspices of the Journeymen Tailors Union of America, which had 38 locals in Canada by the 1890s, 28 of them in Ontario.[49] Since these craftsmen saw the new factory employees as a threat and were unwilling to accept them into their ranks, however, the workers in the new ready-made industry found it necessary to create their own union, the United Garment Workers of America (UGWA). Its first Canadian local was established in Toronto in 1894, and in 1899 the first separate women's local was organized in Winnipeg.[50] This union's jurisdiction encompassed all workers in the ready-made men's wear section of the industry, and adopted a cautious strategy of relying on the union label, rather than workplace militancy, to wrench concessions from employers. A 1914 internal dispute over these conservative policies resulted in a breakaway union, the Amalgamated Clothing Workers of America (ACWA), which quickly dominated the men's sector of the trade.[51] By the early 1920s, Canadian membership had peaked with 9,750 members and then dropped to a low of 4,300 in 1926. This union was characterized by a greater willingness to use the strike weapon, but also, in the late 1920s, by an eagerness to establish elaborate collective-bargaining procedures that would stabilize wages and working conditions across the industry. Lasting success eluded the union in Canada until 1935, when provincial legislation in Ontario and Quebec helped to bring about union recognition and established common wage rates for the men's clothing industry in each province. By 1938, union membership had peaked again at 11,155.[52]

In the women's garment industry, unionization proceeded at a slower pace. The earliest unions were in the cloak trade, and organizational efforts by the International Ladies Garment Workers' Union (ILGWU) began soon after the union's inception in 1900. The Canadian locals fought several bitter strikes, but were quite unstable. They disintegrated between seasons, and declined when strikes were settled. Not until the mid 1930s did they successfully establish locals in the dress sector.[53] In general this union's mode of organization parallelled that of the ACWA.

In 1928, a new organizing strategy emerged in the form of the Industrial Union of the Needle Trades Workers (IUNTW), founded in Montreal by the communist activists in the ILGWU. Eventually joining the communist-led Workers Unity League, this new organization sought to broaden the base of the trade-union movement in the clothing industry by unifying workers into an industry-wide union. It battled for several years with the ILGWU for control of the industry in Toronto and Montreal.[54] After calling an unsuccessful strike in Montreal in 1934, the IUNTW gained momentum and ultimately organized most of the dress sector.[55] But early in 1936, it followed other affiliates of the Workers Unity League back into the mainstream international unions, in this case the ILGWU.[56]

The strategic position of the cutters and pressers within the labour process made them the key to union success, and it was this layer of work force, along with the skilled tailors in the men's clothing and women's cloak sectors, which dominated the union leadership. One old-timer recalled: "The pressers first organized a pressers club in 1932. All men, and then little by little, they started to organize the shops. In the shop, the cutter and the presser can do a lot of things to work with the operators and they have influence on the rest of the shop to organize."[57] Women workers, however, remained for many years peripheral to union development.[58] Most of their union experience came through participation in strikes, and as a result they often drifted away from the union when the excitement of the strike subsided. They had little influence on union policy or in the day-to-day activities of the unions before the 1930s. In the era of the United Garment Workers, the pattern of sidelining women workers was perhaps most marked, as a 1913 strike of men's clothing workers in Hamilton revealed.

On 15 April 1913, the tailors in Hamilton's four largest firms led 2,000 garment workers out on strike for higher wages. On the first day of the strike, headquarters was packed with strikers, but the men and women met separately, with Margaret Daley of the United Garment Workers' New York office looking after the women. Most of the 500 women who joined the picket lines that day were new union members. A press report of the women's participation reflected the patronizing attitude expressed toward the women's trade-union consciousness: "The girls and women, apparently not realizing the seriousness of the strike and seemingly enjoying it greatly, gathered in the streets. One good looking young woman cried, 'I was never in a strike before,' and she shoved into a crowd of girls on John Street, 'It's lots of fun isn't it.' 'It won't be so funny when we don't get our paycheques on the weekend,' said another, then they all laughed."[59] The women arranged the entertainment, "so they will be provided with some form of amusement during the continuance of the strike."[60] The press also noted that in one shop the "girls" had gone back to work and the union was going to talk to them. By 26 April, the union had won a partial victory, which would have been impossible without the full participation of the women. Yet the union local disintegrated shortly afterward.[61]

Attitudes changed little in the 1920s. The male cutters and pressers provided the patriarchal figures for union activity in the dress trade, which was otherwise dominated by women. Organization in Montreal was under the guidance of "father figures" in the union movement. "For many reasons, we feel like proud parents," Sam Liberman of the Montreal Cloakmakers Union, ILGWU, reminisced. "We fought side by side and encouraged the midinettes in their early struggle for recognition. When they were hungry, we fed them, although we were pretty lean ourselves; when they were discouraged, we played big brother, often hiding our own scars, and our own trembling hands."[62] The skilled men called the strikes and asked the women to join them, but little effort was made to educate them about the union. Until the late 1930s, none of the unions in Canada had women on the staff; their executive membership was largely male and the business agents were all men. On a few occasions female organizers arrived from New York to work with the women, as did Margaret Daley in 1912 and Rose Pesotta in Montreal in 1934, but these visits were rare. Since women were not usually at the meeting where key decisions were made, business agents and executive board members could continue to overlook women's concerns. A close study of the meetings of operators, finishers, and drapers locals in Montreal and Toronto shows little female participation. Women seemed to turn up to meetings either to defend themselves in shop-floor disputes or to plead with the executive to excuse them for not paying union dues promptly.[63]

In Montreal the gap between the Yiddish-speaking union executive and the "midinettes" made unionization in the dress sector difficult. As early as 1904, the Montreal ILGWU locals spoke of the difficulty of organizing "the French Canadian girls."[64] In 1914 and 1916 requests were made to the General Executive Board for a French-Canadian organizer in Montreal, stating, "If not for the French workers, whom we are powerless to organize, the locals would be in excellent condition."[65] In 1928, the ILGWU was roughly 45 per cent Jewish, and the ACWA approximately 60 per cent.[66] By 1932, the ILGWU was still convinced that the dress industry "presents practically an unorganizable field as it is employing nearly exclusively French Canadian women" and "a concentrated movement to organize all the French speaking people in the dress trade is still a long distance."[67]

The Industrial Union of the Needle Trades Workers was nonetheless soon doing the job for them. The success of this left-wing union lay partly in its more democratic structure for shop-floor participation. In an IUNTU shop there was a steward and a shop committee, which embraced all occupational groups in the shop. Each craft in the shop had its own local, but in the shop they met as one unit. These committees dealt with the daily running of the shop, and handled grievances, distribution of work, and piece rates. For pieceworkers in the dress trade, such a union presence was essential for dealing with the disputes over work allocation and over prices on short runs of garments.[68] The shop committee thus provided an immediate union presence in the competitive world of speed-up that kept most workers in a state of tension much of the time.

These shop committees were largely female, and through them women workers managed their own social concerns. In fact, the shop chairlady often played the role of mother to the young girls in the shop. One informant discussing her position as shop chair in a Toronto dress factory recalled assisting young girls with menstrual problems or emotional crises when they occurred on the job.[69] Women who served as chairs were on the executive board of the IUNTW, which gave them a greater voice in union affairs. In contrast, the ILGWU shop organization was less democratic and more emphasis was placed on the occupational divisions within the shops. Although there were shop-price committees and chairladies, much of the price settlement in that union relied on negotiations between the business agent and the manufacturer, and the at-large election of the executive board gave workers less direct influence in union affairs. For the women in the IUNTW, a strong shop-floor organization increased their commitment to the union. When the organization disbanded, their union activism decreased, and it took several years for the ILGWU to gain the confidence of its new membership.[70]

For most of the period, then, unionism in the industry was male dominated and reflected the concerns of the more traditional skilled elements of the work force. More important, however, the presence of these unions reflected the ideological hegemony of patriarchy in the workplace. Union treatment of young women as "daughters" – as helpless victims of the exploits in the trade – meant that the union saw little place for them in the development of collective bargaining in the industry. In struggling against the evolving labour process in the needle trades, male unionists concentrated on eliminating those forms of production that were identified with degradation and exploitation, particularly homework and contract work. They led many tumultuous strikes against these conditions and for higher wages, and at least in the area of eliminating housework, they showed some success over the long term.[71] Alterations in the production process often led to walkouts by union members; a notable example occurred at the Eaton factory in Toronto in 1912, when 65 men in one department resisted the introduction of a new machine that would replace female finishers and require the tailors to do the extra work with no increase in wages. Eaton's held firm, and the huge strike that ensued had petered out by the summer, despite strong support from the rest of the Toronto labour movement.[72] The willingness of the male garment workers to fight for issues of primary concern to women workers, however, was lukewarm at best. The readiness of manufacturers to use less-skilled, lower-paid women against male labour in the industry heightened the men's uneasiness about women's role in the needle trades.

In 1913, for example, a Montreal manufacturer, was training young women in various branches of garment production in order to replace men working at these jobs. The firm kept an outside shop in Joliette, where 300 women earned $3–6 a week, while its unionized shop in Montreal had men working for $15–20 a week for the same work. When the company threatened to send its work to the outside shop unless the men accepted a wage reduction, the men refused, claiming that they had no objection to women working but did oppose the extremely low wages paid. The strike put 1,000 union members (half of them women) out on the street, as two more shops walked out in sympathy, but it had collapsed by the end of the year.[73] That company continued to be a thorn in the side of the union for many years because it persisted in using cheap outside labour to undercut the workers in their Montreal establishment. In 1927, the left-wing Toronto magazine, *Woman Worker*, pointed out how this problem of pitting one sex against the other plagued the industry: "At this time there are clothing manufacturers who have made up their minds to smash the needle trades unions ... they told the organized workers they will not pay the union rate of wages. This means they have shut out the organized workers. They have taken in their places unorganized workers and these unorganized workers are women."[74]

As we have seen, piecework was crucial for women workers. The unions' record in resisting this aspect of the labour process proved weak and uneven. The early unions' inability to curb homework and contracting out (where piecework payment was established) hampered their ability to control the wage-incentive system in the inside shops. Since piece rates were usually applied to women's jobs, the male unionists were also constrained by their confusion over the status of women in the industry. In many cases, unions were willing to accept piece rates in the factories as long as they were limited to the operators' jobs – work usually performed by women. In general, the union battles against the introduction of piecework varied from sector to sector, from city to city, and from job to job. In the dress industry, where women made most of the garment, piecework was the established method of production from the inception of the factory system, although a small number of jobs within the industry remained on time rate well into the 1970s. In the cloak and men's clothing sectors, however, making up of the garment remained under the control of the tailors, who were unionized and better able to fight the introduction of piecework. In parts of these sectors, the battles against piecework were hard and furious, while in other parts the union fought for increases in piece rates rather than for their abolition.

In Winnipeg in 1910, for example, the Journeymen Tailors struck successfully for a raise in piece rates, while in the same year, tailors in another shop walked out for four days, saying, "We refuse to return to work under the new and proposed piecework system." They also won.[75] A year later, sixty women and forty men of Hamilton's United Garment Workers local used a strike to convince their employers "that the piecework system was not wanted in this city, and that garment workers did not want to work under such conditions, as they found it impossible to earn a living by piecework." Their bosses agreed and the workers returned to time work.[76] In 1912, the UGWA led 4,500 Montreal garment workers from twenty leading manufacturers into the streets, carrying "red flags and other Socialist emblems," and demanding a forty-nine-hour work week, regulation of apprenticeships, and the abolition of piecework. The strike ended six weeks later with a partial victory, but piecework remained a contentious issue.[77]

The Amalgamated Clothing Workers Union fared no better. In 1917 they took the same workers out on strike for shorter hours, increased wages, weekly rates instead of piecework, but ended up again in a compromise.[78] The Amalgamated wrestled with their position on piecework into the 1920s, when, under Sidney Hillman's "labour statesmanship," the union worked out a standard piece rate based on the division of the garment into its "basic body" parts.[79] This union-sanctioned form of scientific management became the standard for all wage negotiations in the trade.

The ILGWU was similarly unsuccessful in curbing payment by the piece. In 1918, it tried to reintroduce payment by the week into its contracts, arguing that "the hurry and rush and the overtaxing of strength, which is so natural under the piecework system, will disappear together with the idea that in order to secure larger earnings they must drive their machines with all the energy left in them."[80] In the 1920 convention, the General Executive Board took a stand to abolish all piecework.[81] Yet, in Toronto in 1921, manufacturers faced with a weak union of cloakmakers reintroduced piecework and threatened lockouts if the unionists refused to comply.[82] By 1925, the Montreal local had shifted to demands for price committees to set piece rates, rather than for their abolition.[83] In 1928, the union stated its conclusions that "in the development of this system of jobbing-subcontracting, a condition developed which made the desired results of the week-work system ineffective."[84] The Industrial Union of the Needle Trade Workers took up the battle cry in 1929, and struggled for the eradication of piecework.[85] But the system faced no more challenges once that union merged into the ILGWU. After 1934, clothing manufacturers and union officials appealed to the government to intervene, to help regulate the baser forms of competition and exploitation in the needle trades. The first step in that direction came under Quebec Labour Minister J. Arcand, who introduced the Collective Labour Agreements Act (CLAA), which allowed the lieutenant governor in council to issue a decree extending the provisions of any collective agreement to the entire industry in a designated region of the province.[86] The organized needle trades in Montreal jumped at the opportunity to register their contracts in the men's suit and women's cloak trade under the new act and talks took place between state officials, union representatives, manufacturers, and their lawyers.

The first union/management negotiations under the CLAA took place in Montreal's men's suit and cloak sector. Under the leadership of Bernard Shane, the ILGWU demanded a differential pay for men and women – a demand readily accepted by all parties. Shane then took this agreement to Toronto to get inserted into the contract the clause whereby the rate of "skilled female operators shall be 20 per cent below the skilled male operators" while that of "female semi-skilled operators shall be 10 per cent below the semi-skilled male operator's minimum." Not surprisingly, Toronto manufacturers had no trouble accepting this clause. Toronto unionists, on the other hand, were opposed to its adoption. Undaunted, Shane pressed ahead, arguing that the "female operators in Canada are far below in their skill, especially in production, in comparison with the men operators." His views must have prevailed, since ILGWU member H. Langer came to understand that "there are few girls, either in Toronto or Montreal, that can compare to the minimum of a skilled male operator."[87] In the end, the Toronto people "toned down the clause" so that it would not apply to section operators and all parties were happy with the arrangement.[88]

With the passage of the CLAA and the Ontario Industrial Standards Act of 1935, the perpetuation of wage discrimination based on the sex of the worker employed was ensured. In addition, state sanction of wage rates based on the price per piece legitimized piecework wages in the trade.[89] Henceforth, union contracts in the industry began with the understanding that the piecework system would remain in place. All that was left to argue about was the price per piece and the question of who had the right to determine it. Through the active participation of the state apparatus, the final chapter in the history of occupational segregation and exploitation of women in the trade had been written.

The period from the 1880s to the 1930s was crucial for women's industrial work experience, for it was then that the sexual division of labour within the needle trades was formalized. Occupational segregation by sex, with its corresponding lower wages, defined women's place within the labour force and assisted in the way skill was defined in specific jobs in the trades. Inferior workers making inferior wages were seen as doing work that required little or no skill, reinforcing for the women who did this work the peripheral nature of their position in the industry.

Women's work experience continued to reflect their position within the family unit and to reinforce their dependence upon it. Wages paid to women were never enough to allow them economic independence from the family unit. Their work experience remained peripheral to their adult lives, since they entered the trade in their teens and left in their early twenties. Yet the structural impact of their presence has had an ongoing impact on the definitions of skilled work and the sexual divisions of labour in the trades. Manufacturers made decisions to use female labour to cheapen labour costs, and in the process certain jobs became entrenched as women's jobs. As this happened, these employers helped to perpetuate the traditional patriarchal power relations between the sexes because women's jobs were seen as secondary to those done by men. And women's and men's jobs remain to this day separate worlds within the needle trades.

By the end of the 1930s, trade unions had integrated women, had managed to limit the use of contractors and homeworkers, and had improved the condition of work in the trade. Yet in the process of this struggle, they had acceded to manufacturers' demands to perpetuate a sexual division of labour that persisted in linking skill level to the gender of the worker and obliged women to remain the junior partners of the needle-trade community.

NOTES

1 York University Archives, interview, Louis Poslun, 1972.
2 For a general discussion of Canadian and American women's work experience, see V. Strong-Boag, "The Girl of the New Day: Canadian Working Women in the 1920s," *Labour/Le Travailleur* 4 (1979): 152–58; G. Cuthbert Brandt, "Weaving It Together: Life Cycle and the Industrial Experience of Female Cotton Workers in Quebec, 1900–1950," ibid. 7 (1981): 113–26; W. Roberts, *Honest Womanhood* (Toronto 1976); L. Woodcock Tentler, *Wage-Earning Women: Industrial Work and Family Life in the United States, 1900–1930* (New York 1979); *Women at Work: Ontario, 1850–1930* (Toronto 1974); C. Stansell, "The Origins of the Sweatshop: Women and Early Industrialization in New York City," in M. Frisch and D. Walkowitz, eds, *Working-Class America* (Urbana 1983), 78–103; M. Dumont et al., *L'histoire des femmes au Québec depuis quatres siècles* (Montréal 1982), 204–9, 272–6. A. Coote and B. Campbell, *Sweet Freedoms: The Struggle For Women's Liberation* (London 1983), 48–80; C. Cockburn, *Brothers: Male Dominance and Technological Change* (London 1983); A. Coyle, "Sex and Skill in the Organization of the Clothing Industry," in J. West, ed., *Women, Work, and the Labour Market* (London 1982), 10–25; A. Phillips and B. Taylor, "Sex and Skill: Notes Toward a Feminist Economics," *Feminist Review* 6 (1980): 79–88.
3 The sketchy evidence on factory developments in the Canadian clothing trade has been supplemented with evidence from the British and American needle trades. On Canada, see Canada, Royal Commission on the Relations of Capital and Labour, *Report: Evidence – Ontario* (Ottawa 1889); W.L.M. King, *Report to the Honourable Postmaster General on the Methods in Canada in the Carrying Out Government Clothing Contracts* (Ottawa 1898); A.W. Wright, *Report upon the Sweating System in Canada* (Ottawa 1896); G.J.J. Tulchinsky, *The River Barons: Montreal Businessmen and the Growth of Industry and Transportation, 1837–53* (Toronto 1977), 219–20; R.P. Sparks, "The Garment and Clothing Industries," *Manual of the Textile Industry of Canada* (Montreal 1930). For American sources, see J. Hardy, *The Clothing Workers: A Study of the Conditions and Struggles in the Needle Trades* (New York 1935); W. Carsel, *A History of the Chicago Ladies Garment Workers' Union* (Chicago 1940); L. Levine, *The Women's Garment Workers: A History of the International Ladies Garment Workers' Union* (New York 1924); J. O'Neal, *A History of the Amalgamated Ladies Garment Cutters'*

Union, Local 10 (New York 1927); C.J. Stowell, *The Journeymen Tailors' Union of America* (Chicago 1918); J. Seidman, *The Needle Trades* (New York 1942); M.H. Willett, *The Employment of Women in the Clothing Trade* (New York 1902); J. Pope, *The Clothing Industry in New York City* (New York 1905); C.B. Kidwell and M. Christman, *Suiting Everyone: The Democratization of Clothing in America* (Washington 1974). On the British industry, see M. Stewart and L. Hunter, *The Needle is Threaded* (London 1964). With regard to Canadian production, clothing manufacturing ranked seventh in a list of twenty-three in 1870; it was third by 1900 and had declined to eighth by 1929, ninth by 1939 (G. Bertram, "Economic Growth in Canadian Industry, 1870–1915: The Staple Model and the Take-Off Hypothesis," *Canadian Journal of Economics and Political Science* 29 [1963]: 159–84). Since the manufacture of clothing tends to be concentrated in cities like Toronto and Montreal, it is probably more useful to examine the position of the industry locally. In 1871, the Toronto clothing industry led the city in number of workers employed, in value of production, and in the numbers of women it employed (G.S. Kealey, *Toronto Workers Respond to Industrial Capitalism, 1867–1892* [Toronto 1980], 28). By 1931, Toronto's 36 establishments in men's clothing accounted for 82.9 per cent of the capital investment in all clothing production in the province (Canada, Dominion Bureau of Statistics [hereafter DBS], *Report on the Men's Factory Clothing Industry in Canada* [Ottawa 1931], 4).

4 In specific centres, women outnumbered men, even in the early years of the trade. In 1881, 7,193 women, as compared to 1,748 men, worked in the garment industry in Montreal (S. Cross, "The Neglected Majority," *Histoire Sociale / Social History* [November 1973]: 223). By 1901, the first year in which census data actually separated factory production from tailoring and dressmaking, women in men's and women's factory production numbered 2,802 in Ontario and 1,301 in Quebec, compared to 834 men in Ontario and 702 in Quebec (Canada, *Census* [Ottawa], 1901, III, 26–27, 32–33).

5 Stansell, "Origins of the Sweatshop"; Cross, "Neglected Majority," 211. Evidence for the numbers of homeworkers is hard to establish. Mackenzie King reported at length on its prevalence in his study of government contractors (see his 1898 *Report to the Honourable Postmaster General*). The 1901 Canadian census estimated 6,650 outworkers in the ready-made clothing industry in Ontario and 2,738 in Quebec. A 1916 report on Toronto tailoring trades estimated that of 40 custom tailors, 17 had some sewing done in their shops and sent the rest out, while 21 had no sewing at all done in their shops; 38 tailors employed an estimated 110 homeworkers, along with 67 men and 43 women inside their shops (Public Archives of Ontario [hereafter PAO], RG 7 (Deputy Minister of Labour, general subject files), series 2, box 1, "Information re tailoring in a small district in Toronto"). As late as the 1920s, a researcher discovered that the number of Quebec garment workers should be revised upward from the official government figure of 5,340 to 6,500 to include the contract shops. A well-informed manufacturer

estimated a work force of 7,500–8,000 for the city of Montreal alone. If we take these calculations seriously, then a third of the labour force was in fact hidden from the statisticians (V. Shlackman, "Unemployment in the Men's Clothing Industry in Montreal" [MA thesis, McGill University 1931], 12; see also, M. Davidson, "Montreal's Dominance in the Men's Clothing Industry" [MA thesis, University of Western Ontario 1969], 30).

6 In 1891, the Jewish population of Canada was 6,414 but by 1911 the number had increased to 75,681. Of the Jewish immigrants arriving between 1901 and 1910, 7,855 settled in Montreal and 7,427 in Toronto. A large percentage of them started their work life in the garment trades, where they could work in their own language (see J. Seidal, "The Development and Social Adjustment of the Jewish Community in Montreal" [MA thesis, McGill University 1939]).

7 R.P. Sparks, "A 20th Century Expansion: The Growth of Clothing Manufacture in Canada," *Manual of the Textile Industry* (1936), 96.

8 Strasser offers an explanation for the late development of the women's ready-made clothing industry: "Always excluded from the sewing circles and quilting bees, men increasingly wore clothes made in the public world, not the private ... women's clothing remained the product of the private home and the independent seamstress, although paper patterns, which made it possible to sell the design of a garment separately from the garment itself, brought international fashion even to the frontier home by the mid 1870s" (Susan Strasser, *Never Done: A History of American Housework* [New York 1982], 134). Seidman estimated that the women's cloak manufacturer began around 1840 in the USA, although the industry did not reach prominence until the close of the century (Seidman, *Needle Trades*, 20–2).

9 Sparks, "Garment and Clothing Industries," 120. See also *Industrial Canada* (June 1905): 759. In 1916, the ILGWU reported that "there is in Montreal, quite a large trade of waists and dresses employing approximately 3,000 women" (International Ladies Garment Workers' Union [hereafter ILGWU], *Proceedings* [1916], 47). In 1891, the census recorded 22,686 dressmakers in Canada; by 1911 the number had risen slightly to 27,747, but by 1921 had fallen to 17,933, and by 1931 to 10,411 (Canada, *Census*, 1891, II, 186–8; 1911, VI, 34; 1921, IV, 18; 1931, VII, 64; and Sparks, "Garment and Clothing Industries," 123).

10 "Wearing Apparel," *Industrial Canada* (June 1905): 759.

11 In 1925, women's ready-made clothing ranked fifteenth in the list of manufacturers for the province of Quebec; in 1928 it was tenth, 1934 sixth, and 1936 fourth (*Canada Yearbook* [Ottawa] [1937]; see also Sparks, "Clothing Canadians," *Manual of the Textile Industry in Canada* [1936], 99).

12 Quoted in S.C. Berson, "The Immigrant Experience: Jews in the Clothing Trades, 1900–1930" (MA thesis, University of British Columbia, 1979), 230.

13 H.H. Stein, "Dress and Sportswear Trade Problems," *Manual of the Textile Industry in Canada* (1951), 215.

14 Seidman, *Needle Trades*, 14–22; Levine, *Women Garment Workers*, 5; Willet, *Employment of Women in the Clothing Trade*, 32–44; Hardy, *Clothing Workers,*

22; M. Berg, *Technology and Toil in Nineteenth Century Britain* (London 1979), 225–31; Strasser, *Never Done*, 138–44; Kidwell and Christman, *Suiting Everyone*. Canadian evidence on the introduction of the sewing machine into factories is sketchy. They were almost certainly in use by the 1860s. The first sewing-machine manufacturer, Hamilton's R.M. Wanzer, produced 1,000 machines a week in 1861. Charles Raymond of Brantford began producing machines in his factory in 1870 (J.J. Brown, *Ideas in Exile: A History of Canadian Invention* [Toronto 1977], 177; see also O'Neal, *History*, 391, 403; interview, M. Reid, Industrial Division, Singer Sewing Manufacture Ltd, Montreal, 1979). It is important to note that "most sewing innovations have centred around eliminating the most skilled part of the work; guiding the material through the machine at an extremely fast pace. Sewers only spend 20 per cent of their time actually sewing; the rest is spent handling the garment" (L. Lampere, "Fighting the Piece-Rate System: New Dimensions of an Old Struggle in the Apparel Industry," in A. Zimbalist, ed., *Case Studies in the Labor Process* [New York 1979], 263).

15 By the 1950s, two new models had pushed that figure up to 6,000 stitches per minute (interview with Reid). For a history of the Singer machine, see R. Brandon, *Singer and the Sewing Machine: A Capitalist Romance* (London 1977).

16 The effects of these technological changes on the speed of production was expressed well by Amalgamated Clothing Workers' president Sidney Hillman when he testified at a 1932 government hearing: "It takes 50 per cent of the people to produce as many garments today as it did in 1915" (Hardy, *Clothing Workers*, 200; see also ILGWU, *News History, 1900–1950*).

17 Hardy, *Clothing Workers*, 197–98.

18 By the late 1930s, hand finishing had disappeared from the large shops in Montreal (interview with Reid). For further discussion of industrial changes, see H.I. Safa, "Runaway Shops and Female Employment: The Search For Cheap Labor," *Signs* (Winter 1981): 418–33; Lampere, "Fighting the Piece-Rate System."

19 Interview, M. Leblanc, Montreal, 1981.

20 Ontario, Department of Labour, *Vocational Opportunities in the Industries of Ontario: Bulletin 4 Garment Making* (Toronto 1920), 3.

21 Wright, *Report on the Sweating Trades*, 47.

22 King, *Report to the Honourable Postmaster General*, 20.

23 Canada, *Census*, 1921, IV, 148–55.

24 Tentler, *Wage-Earning Women*, 23.

25 One contractor described the system of learners in 1898: "These learners, usually girls, are kept at some trivial and easily mastered work, such as pulling out basting threads, sewing on buttons or running up seams on a sewing machine, and then, when the term for which they had agreed to work without wages expires, they are discharged." The government commissioner commented that "it is not easy to determine just what effect the existence of such an 'apprenticeship system' may have upon the wages, but the effect must be detrimental" (King, *Report to the Honourable Postmaster General*, 47).

26 *La Gazette du Travail* (April 1919): 530–1; *Labour Gazette* (April 1921): 589. Minimum wages for women were calculated at $12.50 a week on the basis of estimates made for costs of living for a single girl for a week in the city of Toronto.

27 PAO, RG 7, I.M. Lunn, "Report on Minimum Wage Violations" (February 1934), 9–10.

28 Between 1881 and 1911 the French-Canadian population in Montreal increased from 78,684 to 345,144. Davidson, "Montreal's Dominance of the Men's Clothing Industry," 43. Between 1901 and 1920, 14,972 immigrant Jews arrived in Montreal (table VIA, Judith Deidal, "The Development and Social Adjustment of the Jewish Community in Montreal" [MA thesis, McGill University 1939]).

29 Working-class family income came from a multitude of sources: homework, the outside wages of family members, lodgers' rent, and the unpaid labour of women involved in home production. As a result, women's position in this economy often dictated that money they earned came from sources not readily identified by historians. However, see, for example, B. Bradbury, "The Family Economy and Work in an Industrial City, Montreal in the 1870s," Canadian Historical Association, *Historical Papers* (1979), 71–96; and Sally Alexander, "Women's Work in Nineteenth-Century London," in J. Mitchell and A. Oakley, eds, *The Rights and Wrongs of Women* (London 1976). The interrelationship between family and work is well documented in T.K. Hareven, "Family Time and Industrial Time," *Journal of Urban History* (May 1975): 365–89; and Brandt, "Weaving It Together."

30 Stansell, "Origins of the Sweatshop," 95.

31 Levine, *Women Garment Workers*, 9. There is some debate as to the extent of women's employment as cutters in the early years. Pope states in *The Clothing Industry* that women worked as cutters, but offers no source for his observation. Levine accepts this statement in *The Garment Workers*. Edith Abbott, however, suggests in her study, *Women in Industry* (New York 1910), 225, that such work was always done by men. Pope elaborates on the changing function of the cutter in the shop: "With the rise of the wholesale manufacturer there appeared at once a differentiation of functions; the old cutters became the foremen and had general charge of the manufacture, and in their place grew up a new class of cutters who did nothing but cutting, and a class who gave their full attention to designing" (Pope, *The Clothing Industry*, 22).

32 Ontario, Dept of Labour, *Vocational Opportunities*, 5.

33 Ontario, *Report of the Inspectors of Factories* (Toronto 1912), 57.

34 Ontario Dept. of Labour, *Vocational Opportunities*, 5, 8, 10–12. See also, H. Mitchell, "Wages in the Textile Industries, 1922–1928," *Industrial Canada* (April 1929): 63.

35 In 1911, women made up 52 per cent of the workers in clothing factories. By 1921 they comprised approximately 74 per cent of the clothing factory employees, and by 1931 their proportion was level in factory employees; by 1931 their proportion was levelling off at 79 per cent. These figures, however, understate the number of

women in the trade because they exclude dressmakers, tailors, and custom shops. The 1911 statistics also exclude shirtmakers, half of whom were female (Canada, *Census*, 1911, III, 26–7; 1921, IV, 100; 1931, VII, 625). In contrast, male cutters outnumbered women two to one in 1931, and in Ontario and Quebec alone, by three to one. In Quebec the male dominance in the cutter's job was even more pronounced: six to one in the men's suit and coat industry; and 291 to eight in the dress industry, where women's employment was the highest and the fabrics lighter and easier to handle (ibid., 646–49, 660–61).

36 Interview, William Malus, Montreal, 1980.
37 Pope has suggested that piecework was present in the outside shops as early as 1777 in the USA (*The Clothing Industry*, 124).
38 Ontario, *Report of the Inspectors of Factories*, 1910.
39 Willett, *Employment of Women in the Clothing Trade*, 37.
40 Ontario, *Report of the Inspectors of Factories*, 1910.
41 Interview, Eva Shanoff, Toronto, 1974.
42 Royal Commission on Price Spreads, *Evidence* (Ottawa 1934), 50–65, 4482.
43 Ibid., 50–65, 4521.
44 *News* (Toronto), June 1911 (clipping in Eaton's Archives).
45 DBS, *Report on the Men's and Women's Clothing Industry in Canada*, 1918–38.
46 Direct labour costs in the production of cloaks were estimated by T. Cohen in 1937: in the cheaper range of garments, cutting represented 3 per cent of the total cost; operating 11–13 per cent; pressing 2–4 per cent; and finishing, 5–6 per cent. These estimates help us to understand the importance of the sewing operation to the total labour cost. It is understandable that manufacturers saw to it that this cost be kept to the minimum by hiring females at lower rates (ILGWU Archives, Dubinsky correspondence, Toronto Cloakmakers Joint Board, T. Cohen to D. Dubinsky, 20 January 1939).
47 In an interview, one official of the Singer Machine Manufacturing Company commented on women's positions and wages in the firm: "They'll [the women] do it, depends how hungry they are" (interview with Reid).
48 For an excellent discussion of the AFL and CIO responses to women in the union movement, see R. Milkman, "Organizing the Sexual Division of Labor: Historical Perspectives on 'Women's Work' and the American Labor Movement," *Socialist Review* 10 (1980): 95–150. For further discussions of the problems of organizing women during this period, see A. Henry, *The Trade Union Women* (New York 1915); N. Andrews, "Organizing Women," American Federationist (1929): 36; Roberts, *Honest Womanhood*; R. Pesotta, *Bread Upon the Waters* (New York 1940); Tentler, *Wage-Earning Women*, 58–83; R. Baxabdall et al., *America's Working Women* (New York 1976), 115–25, 167–209; A. Schofield, "Rebel Girls and Union Maids: The Women Question in the Journals of the A.F.L. and I.W.W., 1905–1920," *Feminist Studies* (Summer 1983): 335–58; C. McLeod, "Women in Production: The Toronto Dressmakers' Strike of 1931," in *Women at Work*, 309–29; L.A. Tilly, "Paths of Proletarianization, Organization of Production,

Sexual Division of Labor, and Women's Collective Action," *Signs* (Winter 1981): 416–17.

49 Stowell, *Journeymen Tailors' Union*.

50 E. Forsey, *Trade Unions in Canada, 1812–1902* (Toronto 1982), 259–65.

51 Amalgamated Clothing Workers of America (hereafter ACWA), Montreal Joint Board, *From Drudgery to Dignity (1915–1955)* (Montreal 1955). Between 1900 and 1914, 40,000 clothing workers took part in 158 strikes. One of the largest took place in 1912, when 4,500 workers walked out for nine weeks, for a 49-hour work week, the abolition of piecework, and the regulation of the apprentice system in the trade. The strike was a partial victory (see Canada, Department of Labour, *Strikes and Lockouts, 1901–1916* [Ottawa 1917]; *Globe* [Toronto], 10 June 1912; Berson, "Immigrant Experience," 212–13).

52 Brecher, "Patterns of Accommodation," 174; T. Copp, "The Rise of Industrial Unions in Montreal, 1935–1945," *Relations industrielles* (1982): 845–6; E. Lorensten and E. Woolner, "Fifty Years of Labour Legislation in Canada," in A.E. Kovacs, ed., *Readings in Canadian Labour Economics* (Toronto 1961), 119–20. The legislation in Quebec was the Collective Labour Agreements Act and in Ontario, the Industrial Standards Act.

53 The ILGWU was initially established in Montreal in 1904 and worked to establish a local in Toronto later that same year. Its existence was short-lived, however, (ILGWU, *Proceedings*, 1904, 12; June 1908, 16). By 1914, the union had 4,000 members in Canada, and by 1920 the eleven Canadian locals had 3,702 members; by 1928 their membership had dropped to 656 in eight locals. However, by 1938 the union had gained some control over the dress industry, with sixteen locals and 8,307 members (ILGWU, *News History*; *Canada Yearbook*, 1920, 530–31; 1930, 620; 1940, 771).

54 In the Toronto dress strike of February 1934, the Industrial Union had actually won a partial victory for its members. The ILGWU in Toronto was involved in a strike in the cloak industry at the same time, and the two unions spent a considerable amount of their time fighting one another, as they had in the dress strikes of 1931 and 1932 (see McLeod, "Women in Production"). Bernard Shane, the ILGWU organizer in Montreal, was vehemently anti-communist and kept the New York office in touch with relations between the two unions. During the 1934 dress strike, he wrote about the ILGWU's collaboration with the manufacturers to force a settlement in the communist-led strike (ILGWU Archives, Dubinsky correspondence, B. Shane to D. Dubinsky, 25 August 1934). After the Industrial Union's victory (in spite of the ILGWU meddling), Shane denounced "the treachery committed by the so-called leaders of the strike, acting in the most irresponsible way" (ibid., 5 September 1934). See also I. Angus, *Canadian Bolsheviks: The Early Years of the Communist Party of Canada* (Montreal 1981), 274–88.

55 For the Toronto strike see *Mail and Empire*, 22 January 1934; *Labour Gazette* (1934): 107–9, 193. For the Montreal strike see ibid. (1934): 814, 905, 907; interview, J. Gershman, Toronto, 1972.

56 "A Program for Action for the Needle Trades," *Canadian Labour Monthly* (December 1938): 33–4; Communist Party of Canada, *Canada's Party of Socialism: History of the Communist Party of Canada, 1921–1976* (Toronto 1982), 85–7; Interview, J. Gershman.

57 Interview, I. Shanoff, Toronto, 1974.

58 See Canada, Department of Labour, *Labour Organizations in Canada* (Ottawa), 1914, 1915.

59 Hamilton *Spectator*, 15 April 1913.

60 Ibid., 17 April 1913.

61 Ibid., 26, 28 April 1913.

62 ILGWU, Montreal Joint Board, *Les Midinettes, 1937–1962* (Montreal 1962), 93.

63 For examples, see ILGWU, Toronto Joint Board, minutes, 1928–39.

64 ILGWU, *Proceedings*, 1904, 12.

65 Ibid., 1914, 11.

66 Seidal, "Jewish Community in Montreal," 187.

67 ILGWU, *Proceedings*, 1932, 47. Rose Pesotta, in *Bread Upon the Waters*, described the ILGWU Montreal campaign to organize the dressmakers. She outlined some of the problems in organizing the young French-Canadian women, in particular the obstructive role of the Roman Catholic church.

68 Interviews with I. Hertzman, Montreal, 1979; R. Kamarofsky, Winnipeg, 1983; E. Newmark, Toronto, 1974; J. Gershman; E. Shanoff; and M. Dolgoy, Toronto, 1983, who was particularly helpful. I am also indebted to David Montgomery for insights on the subject of union shop-floor organization.

69 Interview, E. Shanoff.

70 In 1937, Toronto had over 2,000 workers in 60 shops when unionization brought them into Local 72, ILGWU. In Montreal, the 4,000 dressmakers were organized into Local 262. See ILGWU, *News History*.

71 On 8 March 1912, for example, the Toronto Journeymen Tailors' Union went on strike to control contracting out and to fight low wages paid to women – an effort that won praise from Toronto labour leaders for "their demands to put female labour on equality with male labour for similar work" (Public Archives of Canada [hereafter PAC], MG 28, I 48, Toronto Trades and Labor Council, minutes, 7 March 1912). The garment unions did not always have the full support of the Canadian labour movement in these efforts; in 1915, for example, the executive of the Trades and Labor Congress of Canada passed on to the government the Journeymen Tailors' resolution against homework, but attached an editorial comment: "It would be a very great hardship in many persons to prevent them from working in the making of clothing in their homes" (PAO, RG 7, series 2, box 3, "Ontario Executive Report to the Trades and Labor Congress of Canada" [1915]). Only in the 1930s did contracts begin to state boldly that "no work shall be given to be manufactured or worked upon at home."

72 Eileen Sufrin, *The Eaton Drive: The Campaign to Organize Canada's Largest Department Store, 1948 to 1952* (Toronto 1982), 27; S.A. Speisman, *The Jews*

of Toronto: A History to 1937 (Toronto 1979), 193–4; ILGWU, *Proceedings*, 1912, 77–8.

73 *Labour Gazette* (1913): 422, 726; 1914, 947, 1079.

74 *Woman Worker*, July 1927.

75 *Labour Gazette* (1910–11): 38.

76 Hamilton *Spectator*, 31 May 1911; *Labour Gazette* (1910–11): 1435.

77 *Globe*, 10 June 1912; Dept of Labour, *Strikes and Lockouts*.

78 ACWA, Montreal Joint Board, *From Drudgery to Dignity*.

79 The erratic treatment of the piecework issue by union officials prior to the standardization of the price system is illustrated by the method of negotiation used in the Toronto local. In the ACWA's first Toronto contract in 1919, piecework was forbidden. Yet by 1925, the local union business agent was telling manufacturers that "the Amalgamated was committed to piecework as a whole, because it is in operation in most of the markets, but has not entertained the proposition here." Later that year, the Toronto local agreed "that any association house may have the privilege of installing the piecework system in any shop or section thereof" (Men's Clothing Manufacturers' Association, Toronto, minutes, 25 March, 27 April 1925). A Montreal ACWA member recalled a similar capitulation: "Montreal was a week work industry. Everybody was working by the week, not the section, not the garment. Hillman began to develop in those days the theory that section work pricing will solve all the problems. He wanted to kick out the week work system from Montreal ... One of the issues that separated the right and the left was the question of week work and piecework" (ILGWU Archives, interview, N. Breslow).

80 ILGWU, *Proceedings*, 1918, 39.

81 Ibid., 1920.

82 Ibid., 1934.

83 Montreal *Gazette*, 3 February 1925.

84 ILGWU, *Proceedings*, 1928, 165.

85 Interview, J. Gershman. See also "A Program of Action for the Needle Trades," *Canadian Labour Monthly* (December 1930); Communist Party, *Canada's Party of Socialism*, 85–7.

86 Copp, "The Rise of Industrial Unionism in Montreal, 1935–45."

87 ILGWU Archives, Dubinsky correspondence, B. Shane to D. Dubinsky, 21 October 1935.

88 J.L. Cohen Papers, PAC, MG 30, A94, vol. 3, file 2181A.

89 Brecher, "Patterns of Accommodation," 123.

GRAHAM S. LOWE

Mechanization, Feminization, and Managerial Control in the Early Twentieth-Century Canadian Office

The focal point of the electronics revolution now overtaking industrial societies is the automated office. Through the application of silicon-chip technology, it has been possible to fuse two powerful mediums: computers and telecommunications. This hybrid technology will undoubtedly have a far-reaching impact on all forms of information-processing work. Changes will be most dramatic in the clerical sector, and much speculation revolves around the office of the future.[1] As we look ahead, however, we can benefit from a glance over our shoulder in order to draw lessons from the past. While the electronic office appears to be a radical departure from earlier phases of automation and mechanization, closer scrutiny reveals basic continuities in the evolution of office technology since the turn of the century. Indeed, the office underwent several mini-revolutions following the introduction of typewriters, calculating machines, and Hollerith punch-card equipment. Electronic information processing has built upon the changes wrought by these early technologies, but they have received surprisingly little scholarly attention. This essay examines the origins of modern office technology, concentrating on the mechanization of the Canadian office roughly between 1900 and 1930. It locates mechanization within a complex web of occupational and organizational changes in the office, especially the shift to a female labour pool and the development of various managerial control strategies.

The revolution in administration sparked by the post-1900 rise of corporate capitalism in Canada created an unprecedented demand for clerical workers.[2] In 1891, clerks represented only 2 per cent of the total labour force; by 1931, their relative share had grown to 6.7 per cent. Much of this increase in office employment is accounted for by the recruitment of women into newly created menial administrative jobs. Thus, between 1891 and 1931, the female proportion of total clerical employment soared from 14.3 to 45.1 per cent.[3] By the beginning of the depression, the female clerk was a defining feature of the Canadian office.

These changing patterns of clerical employment reflected the growing importance of administration in expanding twentieth-century industries. In manufacturing, for example, the ratio of supervisory and office employees to production workers rose steadily after 1905, through to the 1930s.[4] According to Paul Craven, this increasing administration/production ratio marked a fundamental reshaping of industry along modern corporate lines and a concomitant expansion of managerial functions.[5] The office's new role was certainly not exclusive to the manufacturing sector. The railways were Canada's largest employers during this period, and their central office staffs continued to grow during the 1920s, even though employment in railway operations declined.[6] The development of numerous service industries also created a large white-collar work force outside manufacturing. For instance, Sun Life Assurance Co. grew from a staff of 21 in 1890 into an insurance giant, employing 2,933 people in head office by 1930.[7] Similarly, in banking, the Bank of Nova Scotia expanded its staff from 81 in 1882 to 2,251 by 1927.[8] And in the public sector, the federal civil service increased its employment from 20,016 in 1912 to 32,885 by 1931.[9] In short, the mechanization of clerical work was part of a massive restructuring of the means of administration that saw the large-scale recruitment of women into newly created routine clerical tasks and the application of tighter managerial controls. By the 1930s, these interwoven trends had laid the foundations for successive waves of technology. It is thus appropriate to launch our inquiry by examining the two major thrusts of early twentieth-century workplace rationalizations, namely cost accounting and scientific management.

RATIONALIZING CLERICAL LABOUR: MACHINES AND MANAGERIAL CONTROL

Cost Accounting

The introduction of cost-accounting techniques had a direct impact on office procedures. Basically, all accounting schemes involve clerical work. The last quarter of the nineteenth century witnessed a "costing renaissance" in the industrial world, as businessmen grappled with declining profits, rising costs, keener competition, and larger-scale operations.[10] American factory engineers made an important contribution to modern management practice by developing cost accounting into a sharp instrument for eliminating production inefficiencies.[11] Their careful systems for controlling inventory, as well as material and labour costs for each job, and using job cards and time clocks laid the foundations for Frederick W. Taylor's scientific management. In fact, many of the so-called "new management" schemes around the turn of the century were accounting systems to monitor overhead costs.[12] But advances in this area were rapid and by 1905–10, prime cost accounting, which measured materials and direct labour costs, had reached its modern form. In short, cost accounting offered managers a more straightforward solution than Taylorism to rising costs, lagging productivity and inefficient work organizations. Sound management was often equated with cost accounting, as the authors of a 1925 textbook on the subject stressed: "Organization, management and cost accounting are so intimately related that it is almost impossible to consider them separately."[13]

Canadian businessmen were well aware of the advantages of a thorough cost-accounting system. After 1900, major business publications such as the *Monetary Times* and *Industrial Canada* regularly featured articles on the topic. In one of the first articles to appear, *Industrial Canada's* readers were told how cost accounting facilitated more accurate estimates of production costs, better scrutiny of management techniques, and more efficient production methods.[14] It was not long before the connection was made between accounting for costs and greater control over the labour process. A prerequisite for an effective accounting system was a careful record of workers' production, allowing management to keep workers and machinery continually busy.[15] The diffusion of these techniques is indicated by the professionalization of accountancy. The Canadian Accountants Association was founded in 1908 by employees engaged in accounting and office management in large corporations.[16] Cost accounting became a specialized function, leading to the formation of a Cost Accountants Association of Canada in 1920. The *Monetary Times* welcomed the new association in an editorial, proclaiming that the "new science of cost accounting" was essential for all businesses.[17]

Even though some cost accountants laid claim to a distinctive expertise quite separate from Taylorism and the broad scientific-management movement, all these strategies shared common concerns. For example, the Taylorite's preoccupation with efficiency was no less muted in discussions of accounting: "The secret of efficiency, after all, is costs. A knowledge of what any item in a factory costs to make and to market, the knowledge of costs generally is the cornerstone of a knowledge of business."[18] The theme of managerial control was also pervasive. Indeed, a costing system was often the means for achieving this goal. We thus find the *Monetary Times* arguing that "cost systems are an essential part of modern scientific business management. For the capital invested in a business proves just as efficient as are the brains employed to handle it; and the best guide for brains is analysis. That is the function of a cost system – to give the manufacturer a detailed knowledge of his business – and to give him this detailed information regularly and automatically."[19] Stated in this way, cost accounting may be seen as a major force within the battery of scientific-management schemes that transformed the office into the hub of a production-control system.

What precisely was the impact of cost accounting on clerical work? Clearly the advent of any accounting system induced office growth simply by proliferating information. A prominent Canadian accountant was therefore quick to remind businessmen in 1906 that the increase in clerical staff and office expenses resulting from the installation of a costing system would be more than offset through savings in the factory.[20] In practice, however, this often was not the case. By the 1920s, cost-accounting experts acknowledged that administrative overhead had not been adequately examined, urging that it be computed as a percentage of the cost of each article produced.[21] The problem of administrative inefficiency was particularly acute in strictly white-collar organizations. We must note, however, that efforts to devise more effective costing systems reaped secondary benefits for management in terms of more rationalized office routines. The development of more sophisticated accounting systems usually went hand in hand with mechanization. As we will see below, Hollerith technology was often introduced into offices as part of a drive to improve accounting procedures.[22] This was especially evident in the telephone utilities' efforts to devise a national, standardized accounting system during the 1920s. The development of this uniform system resulted in more centralized, routinized, and mechanized accounting departments – or, in the words of Bell Telephone's comptroller, "efficient administration."[23]

Scientific Office Management

The interaction between technology and a more professional, "scientific" approach to office management can be traced back to the World War I period. When the sprawling office bureaucracies of the 1910s and 1920s saddled management with escalating administrative costs, scientific management offered a ready solution. Introduction of machines was high on the list of recommended reforms. W.H. Leffingwell, a prominent expert on office efficiency, informed Canadian and American life-insurance managers that – of fifteen different office work arrangements – manual clerical procedures had the lowest efficiency rating, while office machines had the highest.[24] But Leffingwell emphasized that cost reductions required more than just mechanization. He proposed that office management become a profession based on the precepts of science, offering seven prerequisites for achieving this: office work must be organized the way factory workers would be organized to produce a commodity; waste must be eliminated; the office must be under a system of production control; methods ensuring maximum effort must be implemented; clerks must be properly trained; measures of a fair day's work on each clerical task must be known; and the office manager must procure a solid day's work from each clerk.[25] Essentially this was a prescription for Taylorism in the office.

Office managers attentively listened to claims by efficiency experts that Taylorism could yield cost savings, higher productivity, and increased efficiency. During the emergence of the modern office, there was an abundance of literature on work rationalization available to the "progressive" office manager. Lee Galloway, an influential writer on office management, established the organic link between mechanization and the Taylorite's concern with efficiency.[26] Galloway stressed the control functions of the office and argued that accurate information was essential for good management, but so too was a reduction of the office costs incurred by processing this information. Both ends could be achieved, he claimed, by modelling office organization after the factory: "Much of the routine work of the office employee resembles in one respect that of the factory. The tasks of both frequently entail reproductions of copies from a model. Work of this kind can be done equally well by machines at a great saving in labour and cost."[27] Galloway attempted to convince managers that this principle was especially applicable to typing work, providing a step-by-step plan for setting up a central stenographic department.[28]

The factory ideal could not, however, be fully achieved. Galloway put his finger on the fundamental difference between office and factory when discussing the problem of measuring clerical work in standardized units: "There is no more difficult problem in the whole field of office management than the determination of standard units of measurement whereby the output and efficiency of a department may be measured."[29] Solutions to this problem have evidently proved to be elusive. According to a 1971 estimate in an office-management textbook, the average firm receives only one-half value for clerical salaries because of difficulties in monitoring clerical costs.[30] The authors of the text advocate staff reductions through work measurement, much along the lines initially set down by Taylor. Taylor's definition of scientific management as "management based on measurement plus control" guides the book's discussion of how to apply time-study techniques to the office.[31] Yet, even the most carefully planned measures of clerical tasks may be insufficient in face of the abstract nature of office production: "Inefficiency in the office is not always obvious. Much of the waste and inefficiency in clerical procedures is hidden. It is seldom as perceptible or dramatic as the scrap pile or the shutdown machine."[32]

It is uncertain just how widespread the application of scientific management was in the office during the decades leading up to the depression. A substantial body of published material was available on the subject by the 1920s in the U.S. and Canada. And organizations such as the National Association of Office Managers, formed under the banner of Taylorism, reflected the institutionalization of a new orientation to office management.[33] Nonetheless, the diffusion of full-blown scientific-management programs was probably limited. This was certainly the pattern in the factory, where no more than 200 firms implemented Taylor's comprehensive package of reforms during his lifetime.[34]

Taylorism did chalk up some important successes in Canadian shops and factories, the most notable being Henry L. Gantt's reorganization of the Canadian Pacific Railway's Montreal shops.[35] Yet even here, Taylorism was not fully accepted. Like their U.S. counterparts, Canadian businessmen preferred to borrow bits and pieces from the wide variety of efficiency schemes in vogue at the time. This eclectic approach to scientific management was evident in the clerical operations where applications reflected the overriding concern, especially among managers of large offices, that administrative inefficiencies would detract from the control functions residing in the office. Interestingly, some of the most dramatic rationalization measures were introduced into public bureaucracies. The federal civil service was completely overhauled after World War I by a team of Chicago efficiency experts.[36] A merit-based job and salary-classification scheme was introduced in a drive to replace favouritism and patronage with efficient bureaucratic regulations. The need for a "scientific promotion system" based on the efficiency ratings of employees was also implemented by provincial governments. The Ontario civil service commissioner became a convert to the ideology of the new cadre of management experts. "Every office of the government should be so organized that all its activities will function smoothly and efficiently – with speed, accuracy and dependableness," he wrote. "An efficient office controls and co-ordinates its activities and conserves time and energy."[37]

Similar views were articulated by managers of large corporate offices. An influential business publication, *Industrial Canada*, mirrored businessmen's heightened concern over rising office costs. Even advertisements for basic office equipment were infused with the spirit of Taylorism. One ad for a special records desk pictured a male manager standing over a busy female file clerk with a caption warning against "the costly wastefulness of misdirected efforts – the work-day weariness of futile steps."[38] A regular feature in *Industrial Canada* during the 1920s was an "Office and Finance" section. The type of advice offered can be represented by an article entitled "The Intelligent Revision of Office Methods,"[39] which documented how managers could eradicate sources of inefficiency using a standard scientific-management strategy: measure work flows, analyse tasks, and then outline the simplest work method on instruction sheets. Although such articles were not as numerous as those pertaining to factory or shop management, they nonetheless document a trend toward more rationalized administration.

THE MECHANIZATION OF THE
CANADIAN OFFICE

One of the basic principles underlying the application of machinery to clerical work resides in Charles Babbage's conception of the division of labour.[40] Briefly stated, the capitalist can utilize machine technology to simplify, standardize, cheapen, and regulate the productive process. With respect to clerical work, mechanization strengthens managerial control by providing more and better information on which to base decisions, and through the closer regulation of clerical work in an attempt to reduce office overhead. The first process is amplified in an IBM sales brochure used in the 1930s:

The moment a business grows beyond the point where one man can carry all its essential facts in his head, a need begins for mechanical methods of organizing these facts so that the business can be effectively managed. With each successive increase in the size of a business, the demand for more speed, economy, and precision in dealing with the increasing array of essential facts becomes more insistent.[41]

And once the machine is operating, its regulation of the work process exerts additional control. The worker's relationship to office machinery is defined largely by rules that the technology embodies. Charles Perrow elaborates:

Any machine is a complex bundle of rules that are built into the machine itself. Machines insure standardized products, thus eliminating rules regarding dimensional characteristics. They insure even output time; they also indicate precisely what kind of material can be fed into them. The larger the machine, presumably the more people it replaces, and this eliminates rules about how workers are to interact and cooperate and coordinate their activities.[42]

In short, mechanization should be seen as a central component of managerial strategies to rationalize work. Office mechanization progressed through three distinct stages, each precipitating dramatic changes in the nature of office work.[43] Mechanical innovations were thus cumulative and interconnected, building not only on previous technologies but also modifying the way tasks were organized and regulated. Only through the planned integration of machines and organizational changes could managers come close to achieving factory standards of control and efficiency.

The first stage involved the typewriter and the adding machine. Both had become standard fixtures in most large offices by World War I, supplementing traditional office methods by helping clerks to perform their tasks with greater speed and accuracy. Clerks were still able to determine the sequence and the pace of the work process. Adding machines augmented the bookkeeper's skills in carrying out computations. Typewriters were largely "programmed" in their operations by the typist, even if used continuously. When the single machine was integrated into a system with other machines, a second stage was reached. In the highly rationalized typing pool or accounting office, machines facilitated the mass production of standardized information. By World War I, many adding and computing machines had become multi-purpose, giving rise to full-time machine-operator jobs.

The apex of mechanized office technology was reached with the introduction of punch-card equipment. This third stage of mechanization was a watershed in the modernization of the office. Indeed, the origins of the automated office may be traced back to the punch-card technology invented by Dr Herman Hollerith. An integrated series of Hollerith machines recorded, classified, and analysed data contained on the punch cards. Hollerith machines interacted with bureaucratization and the rise of scientific approaches to office management during the 1920s. In this context, Holleriths "greatly accelerated the trend toward functional specialization. Many more special-purpose machine-operating jobs evolved, placing women filling these jobs in a relationship to technology similar to the mass-production factory worker. Work in these jobs is repetitive, mechanically paced, and minutely sub-divided."[44] Hollerith operators were small in number, but they nonetheless formed the core of the office machine-minders. References to the "office-as-factory" most accurately apply to this group of female operatives. While this epithet is equally appropriate for the typing pool, mechanized information processing reached its height when punch-card technology entered the office. Documenting the application of the typewriter, adding and calculating machines, and Hollerith equipment in the Canadian office between the turn of the century and the 1930s will help to understand more fully the evolution of office mechanization through the three stages discussed above.

Typing

The typewriter is now virtually synonymous with the office. Its impact on the recording and communicating functions of the office have been truly revolutionary. The first typewriter with any commercial potential was patented in the United States and manufactured by E. Remington & Sons, a firm of New York gunsmiths. The major drawback of the Remington was that typists could not see their work because of the awkward position of the carriage. This problem was corrected with the introduction of the Underwood upright in 1897. In 1901, over 500 Underwoods were used in Canadian business schools to train the first wave of a new cadre of female office workers.[45] A Canadian advertisement for the Underwood upright in 1905 described the machine as a necessity for modern business.[46] The following year there were over 8,000 Underwoods alone in offices across the country; the railways and the federal government were their largest users.[47] By 1909, Underwood was reporting average daily sales of about 300 typewriters.[48] A general indication of the growing market for typewriters during the post–World War I era was the large number of ads for various models displayed in management publications such as *Industrial Canada* and the *Monetary Times*. Capitalist industrial development and the attendant communications requirements helped to make the typewriter a standard fixture in offices. We consequently find the Underwood Typewriter Company reporting net Canadian earnings of $2,130,846 in 1918.[49] Such rapid diffusion of this basic office technology carved a major niche for women in clerical occupations. Indeed, Christopher Latham Sholes, whose version of the machine was first to find a viable commercial market, proclaimed: "I feel that I have done something for the women who have always had to work so hard."[50]

New production technologies usually spawn organizational changes to take advantage of the way machines accentuated the division of labour. In this respect, the typewriter contributed to the internal differentiation of the clerical work force, as well as to the rationalization of employment conditions. The impact of the typewriter was especially evident in the specialization and fragmentation of typing activities. In 1920, the Ontario civil service listed three distinct grades for stenographers and an equal number for secretaries.[51] The profusion of job classifications created by the typewriter is well illustrated by the campaign that the National Office Management Association (NOMA) launched after World War II. Guided by scientific management, NOMA articulated the type of skill-based job hierarchy that had existed for decades in many large offices:

What the NOMA wants the world to understand is that "secretary" is a specific job classification. It should not be confused with "typist," "junior stenographer" or "stenographer," for properly speaking, a "secretary" is more than these. A "typist" of either sex knows the touch system but not shorthand. A "junior stenographer" knows shorthand as well as typing and can take and transcribe dictation. A "stenographer" is proficient in all these skills and also knows letter forms, the various office systems and clerical tasks, like filing, related to the job. Finally, a "secretary" knows everything a senior stenographer knows and can also relieve the boss of some of his routine work. Above this is the "private secretary" who works directly with an executive. This is the top of the line for a typewriter operator.[52]

In a 1937 study, the International Labour Organization identified four main changes in offices that had resulted from mechanization: (1) a high degree of division of labour involving elementary, repetitive, and monotonous operations; (2) an increased pace of work; (3) the standardization of work methods;

and (4) improved methods of work preparation and supervision.[53] The typewriter had a limited impact in these respects prior to the reorganization of typing work into central pools. The introduction of just one machine into an office furthered the division of labour by creating a new occupation – the typist. Several machines facilitated a finer breakdown of work, allowing each typist to perform one particular kind of task. Hence, in insurance companies, we begin to find job titles such as loans typist, policy typist, and renewal typist before World War I.

The typewriter quickened the pace of work, since new office productivity standards were based on the machine's capabilities. And because machines turned out a uniform product, they facilitated the standardization of forms and recording methods. Furthermore, the operation of a typewriter was easier to regulate by a set of rules and procudures than was the work of the copyist. Yet without a conscious plan to merge typewriter technology with a more streamlined organizational design, management could only reap partial benefits. The full power of the typewriter to rationalize office production was unleashed only with the creation of centralized typing pools.

Typists occupied the lowest rung of the typewriter-based hierarchy mentioned above. These women became the most numerous of the new machine-related workers and performed increasingly routine tasks. Given these characteristics – and the associated problems of regulating the work flow of many typists dispersed throughout a large office – managers began to create centralized pools even before World War I. Typing pools resembled paper-generating assembly lines. Fewer typists could produce more, mainly because the flow of work was closely monitored: "Standards will be set, tasks will be assigned and controlled with the same precision and definiteness as in the scientifically managed factory."[54]

Some of the larger bureaucracies, such as Sun Life, centralized their typing facilities as early as 1911. The most immediate benefit to management was the elimination of costly slack periods, a major problem when each department had its own typists. The introduction of dictating machines around this time meant that the pool supervisor could allot correspondence. When correspondence work slowed, the typists were assigned tasks such as updating mailing lists or typing forms to maintain a steady work flow. As offices expanded, so did the typing pools. Sun Life employed 87 female typists in its stenographic department by the 1930s.[55] In 1935, the Canadian Pacific Railway amalgamated the 20 stenographers and typists from two auditor's departments into a separate office, equipped with dictaphones, under the direction of one supervisor. This reorganization was highly successful, at least from management's perspective:

In addition to a reduction in the personnel as a result of the increased efficiency obtained by eliminating time occupied in receiving dictation and interruptions, a flexibility is obtained which enables the handling of special work and peak loads which was not possible when operators were located in separate offices. To the dictators there is a greater convenience ... There is no waiting for a stenographer. The employees displaced have been relocated in positions vacated by clerks pensioned or resigned.[56]

The typewriter, especially in a central pool, introduced a new element of stress into clerical work.[57] Manual typewriters required considerable muscular exertion to operate. Operators frequently suffered from stiff finger joints, sore hand muscles, as well as backache and general muscular fatigue after a day at the keyboard. Furthermore, the perpetual clatter of machines in a busy typing pool caused psychological strain. These negative side effects of the typewriter suggest that the machine introduced certain similarities with factory work. But the most significant change was the diminished level of control that pool typists exercised over their work.

By the end of World War I, efficiency experts had seized on the typewriter as a vehicle for implementing production-control systems into the office. Because type is more easily measured than handwriting, "scientific" managers established production quotas and efficiency ratings. For example, Leffingwell calculated that a square inch of pica type was the equivalent of ten words. By placing a square-inch grid over typed work, a supervisor could determine the quantity of output. This provided a basis for production bonuses and piece rates in the office. Leffingwell elaborates on how managers used the typewriter to promote greater efficiency in office work:

In one very large company, having more than 1,000 office employees, the manager is proud of the fact that he has eliminated 21 key-strokes on each letter, and thereby saves 620 strokes of the typewriter operator each day – each operator writes a daily average of 30 letters. This is equal to 10 lines, or 100 words a day. Multiplied by 100 operators, it is a saving of 1,000 lines or 10,000 words a day. Again, multiplied by the working days in a year – 300 – this means a saving of 300,000 lines annually, or 3,000,000 words, with a cash value of perhaps $2,000 a year. An excellent saving to be sure.[58]

This office was not an aberration in the mind of some over-zealous efficiency expert. While it is uncertain whether any Canadian office managers went to such extremes, Leffingwell's approach embodies an ideal that guided attempts to increase the efficiency of typing operations. Similarly, managers gained tighter regulation over work activities by replacing multi-function stenographers with single-function pool typists. The combination of mechanization and organizational changes set a pattern for future developments. Recent innovations in word processing are essentially logical extensions of the typing pool. C. Wright Mills argued that the "office-machine age" only develops when "the machinery and the social organization of the office are fully integrated in terms of maximum efficiency per dollar spent."[59] The evidence just presented indicates that far from having to wait until computerization occurred, the "office-machine age" was launched during the World War I period with the development of central typing pools.

Mechanical Accounting and Calculating

Unlike the typewriter, the adding machine replaced mental, rather than physical, clerical activities. Adding machines assisted clerks in processing the mass of numerical data required by modern business. Machines eliminated tedious calculations, saving time and improving the accuracy of the results. While bookkeeping and accounting clerks no doubt welcomed this assistance, it must be weighed against the reduction of their more challenging and satisfying "brain work." To the extent that adding and calculating machines embodied many of the skills previously possessed by the book-keeper, they contributed to a reduction of skill requirements. The erosion of craft elements in office work was reflected in the rise of a new stratum of female clerks. "The very word 'clerk,'" one writer has concluded, "came to have almost the opposite connotation from that which it had its origin."[60]

The Burrough's Adding Machine Company was a pioneer in the field of mechanical calculating. William S. Burroughs, a bank clerk, set out to invent a machine that would expunge the drudgery from his job and provide greater precision in calculations.[61] His adding machine was marketed in the U.S. in 1883, with subtraction, multiplication, and division functions incorporated soon after. Around 1900, advertisements for adding machines began to appear regularly in Canadian business publications. Factory engineers soon claimed that tabulating machines were indispensable in cost accounting, allowing the same set of figures to be analysed in different ways.[62] Organizations having to process vast quantities of numerical data – the governments, banks, insurance firms, and utilities – were quick to make extensive use of the machines. Sun Life Assurance Company, for example, purchased its first adding machine in the late 1880s and, by the early 1900s, had a whole battery of the machines in almost constant use.[63] One description of the firm's actuarial department asserted that the machines "seem capable of thinking."[64] By the 1920s, the basic technology was highly perfected, and many of the machines acquired during these years were used well into the 1950s by Sun Life.

H.A. Rhee argues that more advanced bookkeeping and accounting machines detracted from the trend toward rationalized offices by accentuating departmentalism.[65] However, evidence indicates that management was usually able to counter any negative effects by designing mechanized accounting and record-keeping systems with the goals of greater integration and co-ordination foremost in mind. For example, Consumers' Gas Company of Toronto updated its customer-billing methods by carefully installing accounting machines within an integrated organizational structure.[66] Sun Life's 1922 mechanization of all bookkeeping records was assisted by Burroughs experts who designed a set of work procedures that would ensure overall co-ordination.[67] Burroughs also collaborated with American Telephone & Telegraph to develop a mechanized billing system to achieve reduced costs, greater accuracy, and better supervision of clerical work. The system was adopted by Bell Telephone's Revenue Accounting Centre in Montreal in 1928, greatly simplifying billing procedures. Eight specially designed billing machines and three statement machines – each only requiring a two-week training course for operators – effortlessly handled 240,000 accounts. The machines calculated all charges and credits, as well as the amount payable, printing this information on each customer's bill and three stubs.[68] Adding and calculating machines clearly facilitated a more rationalized form of office organization.

The mechanization of accounting and bookkeeping did, however, produce organizational strains through their tendency to enlarge administrative staff. As the International Labour Organization noted:

The number of office employees thus increases with mechanization. The reason is simple enough: office machines make it possible to carry out profitably a whole series of operations which would be too expensive if they had to be done by hand. The growth of large administrative departments and the extension and concentration of undertakings have made it easier to install office machinery on a large scale and to increase supervisor and statistical work to an enormous extent, for the machine reduces the cost of each item to a minute degree.[69]

Somewhat paradoxically, machine-induced clerical growth indirectly helped rationalize the office. In the first place, adding machines created a specialized division of labour in accounting procedures. Fragmented tasks demanded less skill and responsibility on the part of the worker. This provided management with more direction over the planning and execution of the work. An example of how the growing number of machine-related jobs were routinized is found in the federal government. A multi-grade classification was implemented for office-machine operators. According to the 1930 job description of a Grade Three Office Appliance Operator, the worker was "to operate, adjust, and maintain in good running condition office appliances requiring a high degree of specialization."[70] It thus appears that machines afforded management tighter regulation of clerical work, thereby tempering the inefficiencies inherent in larger staffs.

By the 1920s it was rare to find a large office without mechanized systems of accounting and record-keeping. The most visible changes often occurred in the centralized accounting departments where rows of routine clerks mechanically transformed mountains of statistics into clear measures of productivity, costs, and profits. Yet, we must be careful not to idealize the pre-1900 office, where low-ranking clerks also performed in monotonous and unrewarding tasks. Of course, machines created many new "female" jobs in which low skill requirements, repetition, and regimentation were the norm. But the extent of this machine-related work can be too easily inflated. Many adding and calculating machines were simply adapted to existing clerical procedures, used in an auxiliary capacity by clerks. Not until the introduction of Hollerith machines did mechanization trigger fundamental changes in the clerical labour process.

Toward the Automated Office: Hollerith Machines

The first wave of office technology – typewriters and adding machines – were essentially single purpose. Addressographs fell into this category, even though they constituted a more advanced form of machine production. The addressograph clerk merely fed hundreds of name plates – for billings, payrolls, shareholder notices, policy renewals, and other purposes – into the machine and let it do the rest. The quest for faster, more efficient methods of machine production sparked the development of complex multi-function machines, signifying a second stage in office technology. Two or more operations were performed continuously and often several machines were linked together. Some of the more common multi-purpose machines found in offices during the 1920s were multi-register bookkeeping machines, combination cheque-writing and adding machines, combination cheque-sorting, adding, and listing machines (which combined addressing and statistical analysis), and Hollerith punch-card equipment. The Hollerith system greatly accelerated the trend toward linking several multi-purpose machines in sequence, bridging the technological gap between mechanization and automation. Punch-card machinery thus represented the third and final stage of office mechanization.

One of the few studies of office automation in Canada concisely summarizes the central thrust of Hollerith technology in the office:

Of all the types of mechanization introduced into the office in the period between the two wars, the most dramatic innovation was the punch card and its accompanying battery of keypunch machines and verifiers, sorters, collators, reproducing punches, and mechanical tabulators. The punch card concept with its advantages of standardization, increased output, and improved quality control over clerical work – especially in accounting-type operations – caught on rapidly and the mechanical accounting or tabulating department is now a familiar feature of most larger Canadian offices. This is the aspect of the modern office that commentators are usually thinking about when they observe that the office is becoming more and more like a factory.[71]

The revolutionary aspect of the Hollerith was its use of a standardized punch card on which a vast assortment of data could be recorded. The card was processed by a series of collating, sorting, tabulating, and printing machines. The concept of controlling machines by data cards – a basic principle in computers – was derived from the factory. The relationship between the office worker and a Hollerith machine resembled machine-paced production in, for example, textile factories.[72] While relatively few in number, operators of key punches, tabulators, and other punch-card equipment emerged as the machine-minders of the modern office.[73]

Dr Herman Hollerith, a statistician working on the 1880 U.S. Census, realized that it would take an army of clerks years to analyse its results. By 1887, he had developed a mechanical means of recording, tabulating, and analysing this vast quantity of data utilizing standardized punch cards. The machines were soon put to work analysing vital population statistics for several cities, and the U.S. government adopted Hollerith's system for use in the 1890 Census. Word of the machine's potential for lightning-fast processing of huge quantities of data opened up a large market. In 1896, Hollerith incorporated the Tabulating Machine Company to manufacture the equipment. A loose alliance with two other small business-machine firms created the Computing-Tabulating-Recording Company, which later evolved into the International Business Machine Corporation (IBM).[74]

The engineering and marketing capabilities of IBM made Hollerith's name synonymous with electric accounting systems. The company had little difficulty convincing business and government that "Electric Tabulating Machines *prevent* the waste of motions, minutes, and material and enable fewer people to do more work in less time."[75] The basic IBM system used punch cards, a gang punch, a sorter, a verifier, and a tabulating machine. The feature that had the most dramatic repercussions for the clerical work process was the integration of several machines into a semi-automatic data-analysis system. The only significant innovation on the basic system was the marketing in 1920 of tabulating machines that printed results. The mechanical printer culminated the progress of pre-computer office technology, eliminating the last remnant of manual clerical labour in mechanical data processing. According to IBM promotional literature:

Prior to the introduction of [the mechanical printer], the part played by the mechanism in tabulating ended with the appearance of totals on the counters; they had to be transcribed to the record sheets by hand, which of course brought in human fallibility, manifesting itself sometimes in illegible entries and sometimes in outright errors, besides limiting the speed of the operation to the speed attainable in writing down the correct figures in the correct columns. The new device thus carried forward the principle of speed, economy, and precision obtainable only by purely mechanical operation, through the final stage of the accounting process.[76]

Some of the early, integrated data-processing units were quite sophisticated. Hollerith departments in the 1920s used a variety of automatic and semi-automatic machines. Besides the basic components of the punch-card system, IBM marketed an array of special-purpose equipment: accounting machines, which automatically printed reports from tabulating cards at a rate of 75–150 per minute; alphabetic accounting machines, which printed names, addresses, descriptions, and other information, eliminating the use of codes; card-counting printers; direct-subtraction machines; automatic-multiplying punches; automatic-checking machines; invoice tabulators; continuous-form bill-feed machines; and automatic bill-feed tabulators, useful for compiling production statistics and piecework rates.[77] In various combinations, these machines could handle almost any information-processing need in business or government.

Hollerith granted a Canadian licence to operate the Canadian Tabulating Machine Company in 1910, supplying the machines at cost in return for 20 per cent of the revenues. The new firm's first order was from the Toronto Library Bureau, and the machines were installed in December 1910. Business took off, and by 1916 there were over 41 customers across the country with annual revenues surpassing $60,000.[78] IBM was incorporated in Canada during 1917. Two years later, the company's Toronto plant was manufacturing punch cards and assembling accounting machines for the Canadian market. That same year, sales topped $1 million, and new models were being continually introduced. By 1937, the Canadian factory was producing sixteen types of machines for the domestic market.[79] The appendix lists organizations that installed Hollerith systems between 1910 and 1936. Among the 105 customers were some of the largest corporations and government departments. The list probably underestimates the number of installations, as IBM sales records for this period are incomplete. Even so, we must conclude that Hollerith technology precipitated a minor revolution in accounting, bookkeeping, record-keeping, and numerous other clerical procedures in the Canadian office.

Over 20 per cent of the firms listed in the appendix are insurance companies. Hollerith methods were especially suited to this industry because of the mountains of uniform statistics required. When Manufacturers Life Insurance Company introduced Holleriths in 1920, an employee observed that the machines "revolutionized the bookkeeping operations to quite an extent."[80] Sun Life installed its first Hollerith in 1917, and by 1931 was IBM's largest Canadian customer. The company's extensive use of the machines led to the creation of a centralized Hollerith Service Department in 1935. Hollerith systems were discussed at the 1924 founding convention of the Life

Office Management Association (LOMA), an organization dedicated to achieving more efficient clerical systems in insurance offices on both sides of the border. It was reported that, despite their high initial costs, Hollerith machines could take over all office record-keeping.[81] Managers also noted that female Hollerith operators were cheaper to hire and more easily trained than general clerks. A survey by LOMA in 1925 indicated that the use of punch-card equipment was sharply on the increase. Forty-five of the eighty insurance companies responding indicated that Holleriths had been introduced with very satisfactory results.[82]

In 1914, the Canadian Pacific Railway also installed the machines in the Calgary office of its Department of Natural Resources as part of a general reorganization of land-sale accounting methods by an American efficiency expert. The railway's largest office installed fifteen Holleriths into a sound-proofed room in the 1930s.[83] More of the machines were subsequently introduced into two other large departments. Commenting on the Holleriths' "almost invisible" margin of error, the staff bulletin heralded their introduction with these words: "To say that these machines are 'human' in skill and intelligence is grossly to understate the case; they are actually superhuman, performing prodigies of involved arithmetic, sortation and compilation of records."[84] The Bell Telephone Company had similar Hollerith operations. For example, the plant accounting department employed eight women on key-punch machines by the early 1920s.[85] The women recorded plant expense data on cards, which were then sorted and analysed by other machines. But it was the federal government that led the way in merging the new technology with scientific management. The post office's money-order division introduced a bonus system that tied the wages of key-punch operators to their productivity.[86]

Holleriths were responsible for the first automated clerical routines, thereby launching a new era in the office. The machines' greatest impact was on working conditions in the departments where they were located. Computerization would broaden this rationalizing trend to encompass other departments. Still, the impact of punch-card equipment should not be underestimated. Information processing became a highly centralized operation in which clerical tasks were carefully paced and planned according to the dictates of the machines. Each mechanical step – coding, key punching, sorting, collating, computing, storing, and so on – became a specialized clerical function.[87] As well, sweeping reforms in office administration were facilitated by Hollerith machines. Managers were able to achieve greater control over organizational operations by having precise information at their fingertips. In short, Hollerith machines were "wizards at producing facts ... [and] disclosed to management the value of obtaining essential statistics accurately and on time."[88] The first computer in Canada was an IBM 650 installed by Manufacturers Life in 1956. This signalled the beginning of the electronic phase of automatic data processing, a development that emerged directly from the solid foundations laid decades earlier by Hollerith machines.

FEMINIZATION AND
DEGRADATION

At the forefront of any discussion of technology is its impact on the nature of work. There can be little doubt that numerous clerical jobs lost their skill requirements, task variety, and worker autonomy as office technology progressed from the typewriter to electronic data-processing systems. Nineteenth-century office routines are often portrayed as craft-like work. The traditional male bookkeeper was an experienced generalist who at any given moment could report to his boss on the state of the business. But with industrial expansion and increasingly complex business dealings, the rise of the large-scale office bureaucracy after 1900 wrought fundamental changes in the division of administrative labour. The mounting volume of routine work induced employers to hire women largely because they could be paid much less than men. As the scope of administration widened, the focus of individual clerical tasks narrowed. By the 1920s, the generalist male bookkeeper had become a relic of the past in most large offices, succeeded by teams of female functionaries monotonously processing financial data with the aid of machines.

Observing these changes, a number of analysts conclude that a revolution had occurred in the areas of technology, organization, and management. Elyce Rotella claims, for example, that by 1930, American offices resembled "factories with specialized labour and continuous work processes. A variety of business machines replaced the pen and ledgerbook."[89] Mechanical innovations were often complemented by bureaucratic office organizations and management cost-reduction and efficiency programs. According to Jon Shepard, the result was a "greatly accelerated ... trend toward functional specialization. Many more special purpose machine-operating jobs evolved, placing employees filling these jobs in a relationship to technology similar to the mass-production factory workers."[90] And as the International Labour Organization aptly observed, office technology at its most effective level incorporated "a strictly rationalized system of work organization, without which the machine would be useless."[91]

Harry Braverman is perhaps the best-known proponent of the thesis that the office has developed a more factory-like environment over the course of this century.[92] According to Braverman, technology and Taylorism were the scissor-like cutting edges of work rationalization. Managers in the factory, then the office, applied techniques that fragmented, deskilled, and universally degraded labour in order to achieve greater operating efficiency and extend their control over the labour process. This destruction of the craft basis of the office was a by-product of the rise of corporate capitalism. In Braverman's view, managerial functions related to appropriation and control became discrete labour processes, which in turn were delegated to an army of proletarian clerks. The administrative division of labour grew more specialized as tasks were mechanized and reorganized according to scientific management principles. The result of these changes, argues Braverman, is that the office came to resemble a factory in which "the productive process of society disappears into a stream of paper ... which is processed in a continuous flow like that of the cannery, the meatpacking line, the car assembly conveyor, by workers organized in much the same way."[93]

However compelling Braverman's thesis may at first appear, its broad assertions about the homogenous degradation of clerical work requires qualification. As Stephen Wood points out, a "crude" deskilling thesis that posits workplace rationalization as a sweeping trend within modern capitalism must be replaced by more subtle analysis based on careful empirical documentation.[94] It is questionable, for example, whether white-collar and blue-collar work can in fact converge. Paper processing is a considerably less tangible activity than manufacturing, often lacking a visible product. The less quantifiable the workers' output, the more difficult it is for management to strictly regulate the labour process. Even a highly automated office cannot be totally equated with a factory. Certainly there remain significant differences in the minds of the clerical workers, who perceive their cleaner jobs, more fashionable work attire, and scope (albeit limited) for making work-related decisions as the basis of higher social status.[95] And historical comparisons of white- and blue-collar workers show that technology has a less pervasive influence on the former simply because the order and pace of task execution and freedom of worker movement is more difficult to control in the office.[96]

The degradation thesis also implies that the craft ideal was the hallmark of the office around the turn of the century. When C. Wright Mills talked of "the ideal of craftsmanship," he had in mind workers who are fairly autonomous, can see a job through from beginning to end, and are able to further develop their skills.[97] Yet in reality, considerable drudgery was associated with traditional male clerking, as was the case, for that matter, with most other nineteenth-century crafts. For example, the lowest and largest class of Canadian federal civil-service clerks performed tasks every bit as tedious and unrewarding as those executed by today's female functionaries. In the early 1880s, these petty bureaucrats spent their days "checking, comparing, copying, compiling and transcribing Accounts and Documents. This, so far as we can ascertain, comprises four-fifths of the whole work to be done, and requires for its performance no special attainments beyond what can be acquired in the Common Schools."[98] In work situations such as this, the introduction of machines may have provided welcome relief from monotonous work. But more to the point, an essential difference between the old and the new office is that clerical positions in the former provided men a stepping-stone into management or entrepreneurship, whereas the latter gave rise to occupational ghettos that trapped women in menial, dead-end jobs.

With respect to the pervasive effects of work rationalization suggested by Braverman, typing provides good counter-evidence of how mechanization did not necessarily signal a transition to factory-like working conditions. Typing is the oldest of the mechanized office jobs and as such, one might expect it to be among the most highly rationalized. However, there are striking contrasts within the typing/stenography occupational group. When correspondence and recording work was reorganized into a central typing pool (using numerous typewriters and dictation machines), conditions indeed resembled a paper-generating assembly line. But the pool typists occupied the bottom rung of the machine-based hierarchy. At the top were the private stenographers, a coveted position that offered working women relative economic and social rewards quite similar to the traditional female profes- sions of teaching, nursing, and social work.[99] The modern secretary occupies a paradoxical role: despite her use of the most advanced typewriter technology within a bureaucratic organization, her working conditions are shaped by informal, particularistic criteria. As Rosabeth Moss Kanter has shown, this small but privileged group derives status indirectly from its male bosses.[100] Despite being paternalistic and often arbitrary in nature, the interpersonal relations governing much secretarial work may temper the more routinizing aspects of mechanization or bureaucracy.

Recent studies of the impact of automation on female clerks also caution against talking about a uniform downgrading effect. In a recent study, Feldberg and Glenn discovered that office automation had an uneven impact on various segments of the office work force and, moreover, had different effects at the aggregate, organizational, and work-process levels.[101] They found little evidence of an overall trend toward a more degraded and deskilled type of work. Often contradictory forces were present, with some women obtaining access to more rewarding jobs while others experienced negative effects. Likewise, one case study found that while the change-over from copy to video typing had a routinizing, fragmenting, and depersonalizing impact, the new word-processing equipment provided several benefits for typists: increased pay and promotion opportunities, greater control over quality, and some degree of skill upgrading.[102] Admittedly, these findings are challenged by Heather Menzie's Canadian research, which perhaps is indicative of the controversy surrounding this particular topic.[103] Nonetheless, one critical point must be borne in mind: it is quite possible that many of the negative aspects of video display terminal (VDT) work are not a direct outcome of the new word-processing technology per se. Rather, they may result from strategic decisions by management to reorganize work around VDT equipment in the interest of higher productivity. Technology thus serves as a tool used by management in its profit-motivated drive to control the labour process.

TABLE 1

Female Office-Machine Operators, Stenographers, and Typists, Canada, 1891–1971

	Office-machine operators*			Stenographers and typists		
	Total number of females employed	Females as a percentage of occupational group	Female office-machine operators as a percentage of total female clerical	Total number of females employed	Females as a percentage of occupational group	Female stenographers and typists as a percentage of total female clerical
1891	–	–	–	851	64.5	18.1
1911	–	–	–	9,754	85.9	28.9
1931	1,503	86.3	1.3	64,993	94.8	55.6
1951	9,764	88.6	3.0	133,485	96.4	41.5
1971	37,980	73.1	4.2	326,895	96.8	34.8

*The job title of office-machine operator first appeared in the 1921 Census, although separate data for this occupation were not published until the 1931 Census.

Source:

1891 Census of Canada, vol. II, table XII.

1911 Census of Canada, vol. VI, table III.

1931 Census of Canada, vol. 7, table 40.

1951 Census of Canada, vol. 4, table 11.

1971 Census of Canada, vol. III (part 2), table 2.

There is a final qualification regarding the applicability of the work-degradation thesis to the office. Most arguments about office work becoming more factory-like rest on the often untested assumption that by 1930, when the foundations of the modern office were in place, most clerks were tied to machines. Our evidence above clearly depicts the sometimes pervasive influence of office machines, especially when integrated into broad managerial strategies to rationalize and regulate the flow of paperwork. However, we must also recognize the tendency in the past to overstate the diffusion and impact of office technology. Grace Coyle, for instance, describes how the American office had evolved up to 1929: "Within the last decade mechanical devices have become as universal and as essential to almost every detail of office work as [they are] in the factory ... In every corner human labour is being replaced by mechanical devices or is being used to tend machines which seem almost human in their capacities."[104]

Table 1 documents the extent to which clerks were tied to typewriters and office machines in the early twentieth-century Canadian office. It gives an accurate picture of the number of workers whose jobs were forged directly by technology. The much greater indirect use of machines, assisting in performing other clerical tasks, is difficult to determine. A major observation deduced from table 1 is that a very small number of female clerks, even in

1971, could be classified as full-time machine-operators. The occupational category of office-machine operator first appeared in the 1921 Census, but there were too few workers to warrant publication of separate data for this group until 1931.[105] By then 1,503 women – composing 86.3 per cent of the total employees in this category – operated office machines exclusively in a distinctive female job ghetto. The situation with stenography and typing occupations is somewhat different. These jobs are a much larger share of the total female clerical work force, constituting 34.8 per cent by 1971, compared to only 4.2 per cent for office-machine operators in the same year. These jobs were defined as "women's work." The extensive use of the typewriter is evident from the rapid increase in the number of women employed in stenography and typing, from 851 in 1891 to 64,993 by 1931. (There were no stenographers listed in the 1871 Census and only 72 reported in the 1881 Census.)[106] Furthermore, the use of office mechanization varied considerably among organizations and industries, depending on the amount and type of paperwork required. Banks, insurance companies, and firms with large accounts receivable tended to develop more extensive office operations. But the relative number of office-equipment operators did not grow in leaps and bounds. For example, by 1953 the Bank of Nova Scotia employed a total of 2,275 women clerks, of whom 200 (9 per cent) were office-machine operators and 481 (21 per cent) were stenographers and typists.[107]

In short, empirical evidence does not negate the degradation thesis as it applies to the office; rather, it systematically reveals the limitations of such an argument. Mills, in discussing the fusion of technology and work reorganization, asserted: "as we compare the personnel of the new office with that of the old, it is the mass of clerical machine operatives that immediately strikes us. They are the most factory-like operatives in the white-collar world."[108] Far from denying the existence of factory-like conditions in the emerging modern office, we can bring this image more sharply into focus. Specifically, office-machine operators constituted only a fraction of the entire Canadian female clerical labour force. Now, conversely, a sizeable proportion of clerks continue to perform their tasks in a more traditional manner, especially in smaller offices. This latter point suggests that office-machine operators and pool typists were disproportionately concentrated in the largest corporate and government offices. Such organizations were at the leading edge of the administrative revolution. It is useful to view the small, traditional office and the huge, modern bureaucracy as polar ends of a continuum along which various technological, organizational, and managerial innovations in the realm of administration can be placed over time. Thus, even though the machine-related jobs that gave rise to the most monotonous, restrictive, and unrewarding employment conditions were relatively few in number, a much larger number of clerical jobs were partially affected by the broad thrust of workplace rationalization. Whether it be the intensification of work resulting from the adoption of efficiency measures in the front office of a small manufacturer, or the streamlining of a major financial institution's office routines following the introduction of Hollerith equipment, the rationalizing effects of the administrative revolution often were spread through a variety of indirect channels.

My discussion may be summarized by highlighting its three interrelated themes: mechanization, feminization and managerial control. Adopting a broad perspective on the trend toward stricter controls over office operations, I have noted that while the more elusive nature of clerical work militated against full-blown rationalization as in the factory, scientific-management reforms did influence the development of the modern office. More precisely, it was the combination of technology and modern management, when applied to the growing mountain of facts and figures required by corporate capitalism, that underlay the shift to a female labour supply. In short, mechanization and feminization went hand in hand. By the 1930s, women formed a new subordinate class of clerical functionaries, relegated to the most routinized and mechanized tasks – a trend that still persists today. The complex interplay among machines, managerial strategies, and the recruitment of female clerks documented here gives a picture of the modern office during its emergent stage that differs from the picture portrayed by Braverman and other advocates of the office-as-factory thesis. I have shown how the most "degraded" clerical jobs resulted when machines were organized into rationalized production units according to scientific-management principles. Only in corners of the office best exemplified by the typing pool and the Hollerith department could one find anything resembling factory-like conditions. This conclusion must be further tempered by the knowledge that pool typists and Hollerith operators composed a minority of clerical workers. A more substantial proportion of clerks experienced elements of factory-style routinization through the piece-meal diffusion of the administration revolution.

Having rejected a blanket degradation thesis in favour of a more limited and empirically grounded approach to the deterioration of office working conditions, we are left wondering how clerks reacted to the changes that occurred. Did they actively resist new technologies and more restrictive forms of work organization, or did they quietly succumb?[109] Considerably more research is required before a definitive answer can be offered, but there is a direction this inquiry might fruitfully take.

For several reasons, there was a marked absence of resistance to transformations in the early twentieth-century office among male clerks. A primary reason would be the opportunity for mobility into management. As offices grew, females entered the burgeoning lower ranks and, simultaneously, a good proportion of the male clerks were elevated into the expanding supervisory corps. A second factor, relating to the management-training function of clerical positions, was that prior to the MBA programs of today, many males received their business training as clerks. A third factor concerns the ideology of individualism, which, of course, was reinforced by tangible evidence of promotion into management. Thus, a careerist orientation founded on individualism acted as a powerful deterent to organized resistance. Mills, discussing the pervasiveness of white-collar individualism, argues that these employees "usually remain psychologically the little individual scrambling to get to the top."[110]

These arguments hold little sway, however, when applied to female clerks. To be sure, the anti-union stance of Canadian employers during the period under investigation was a major impediment to collective responses on the part of any group of employees. However, since female clerks experienced the full weight of mechanization, one might hypothesize that they would, therefore, be most likely to agitate for improvements. But the combined effect of prevailing sex-role norms and poor working conditions undermined the potential for such collective responses.[111]

To this day, the monotonous and unrewarding nature of female clerical job ghettos fosters a type of work behaviour unconducive to collective action. Women facing these poor conditions typically adapt by avoiding any lasting job commitment, reacting apathetically to work problems, or quitting. This behaviour was strongly reinforced, well into the post–World War II period, by ideological constraints on women's economic role. The dominant expectation was that working was a prelude to marriage. In the early part of the century, about 90 per cent of the paid female workers were single.[112] Mary Vipond reports that during the 1920s, young women resolved the conflicting pressures to enter the labour force, on the one hand, and to marry and raise a family, on the other, by working until about age 25 and then retreating into the matrimonial home.[113] Employers undoubtedly benefited from the depressing effect this constant turnover had on wage levels. This ideology was given clear expression by a female bank employee in 1916: "When the opportunity offers, the most successful banking woman amongst us will cheerfully retire to her own hearthstone, preferring the love of a husband and little children to thousands a year and a seat in the council of the mighty."[114] As if these normative strictures were not enough, numerous employers formally adopted policies barring the employment of married women.[115] Thus, it was the interaction of structural factors such as rapid female labour turnover, a large reserve pool from which new workers could be recruited to replace would-be strikers, and constraints on women with family responsibilities, which make attending meetings difficult – all buttressed by prevailing gender-role stereotypes – that chronically undermined the unionization potential of female office workers.

Even today, the level of unionization among Canadian clerks is low, especially in the private sector.[116] Historically, union recruitment drives have bypassed those industries in which white-collar workers are most heavily concentrated. Any inroads have been made almost solely in the public sector. During the 1900 to 1930 period, the available evidence reveals little union activity among clerical employees. Male bank employees did launch weak organizing drives during, before, and after World War I, only to be swiftly crushed by management.[117] Federal civil-service clerks had formed associations by the end of the war, and some factions even pushed for union affiliation. But full-fledged collective bargaining would not be achieved until the late 1960s.[118] The railway clerks appear to have been the only office workers to display solid trade unionism. For example, the CPR clerks struck in 1912, tying up the railway's western lines.[119] Any form of collective action to emerge during this early period invariably was a response to poor wages. The major exception here would be the vocal protests of the civil-service associations against the reorganization of the federal bureaucracy by American efficiency experts after World War I.[120] However, the most vigorous opposition was directed at the new salary scales – based on a pre-war cost of living index – that ignored the ravaging effects of post-war inflation.

The World War II era also led to agitation for collective-bargaining rights among scattered groups of white-collar employees.[121] Spearheading these organizing drives among banking, office, and retail workers were the Office Employees' International Union and the Canadian Congress of Labour's Office and Professional Workers' Organizing Committees. Failure of the two most concerted campaigns – among Quebec and Ontario bank employees in the early 1940s and in Eaton's Toronto department store between 1948 and 1952 – were clearly foreboding: unions have yet to gain more than a toehold in banking, and Eaton's clerks remained unorganized until the 1984/85 efforts to unionize. Only in the public sector can significant union-membership gains be found among clerical and other white-collar workers in recent years.

Historical evidence indicates that skilled manual workers often registered their discontent over their employer's work-rationalization measures by striking.[122] And there is some suggestion that the recent wave of office automation may have precipitated union organization in protest against deskilling and routinization.[123] In short, we should not dismiss the connection between the impact of technology on jobs and worker resistance to such changes. Yet, in the case of the early office technologies – and, indeed, in the present onslaught of microtechnology – the question remains open. Of central importance is the form resistance may take among clerks. Although manifest signs of collective action were hard to detect during the early twentieth-century administrative revolution, future research may well reveal more subtle and covert modes of resistance among those most affected by the march of office rationalization.

APPENDIX

MAJOR CANADIAN ORGANIZATIONS PURCHASING HOLLERITH
EQUIPMENT FROM INTERNATIONAL BUSINESS MACHINES CO.
LTD AND ITS PREDECESSOR, THE TABULATING MACHINE CO.,
1910–1936*

Year	Organization	Year	Organization
1910	Library Bureau of Toronto	1921	Dominion Steel and Coal Co.
	British American Assurance Co.		Canada Life
1911	Royal Insurance	1922	Canadian General Electric
	Government of Canada (1911 Census)		Great West Life
1912	Hollinger Consolidating Mining	1923	Metropolitan Stores
	Liverpool, London and Globe Insurance		Tuckett Tobacco Co.
	Steel Company of Canada	1924	Canadian National Railways
	Toronto Hydro		General Motors
1913	Canadian Pacific Railway		Imperial Life
	Canadian Car and Foundry		J.E. Clement
	Pilkington Bros Glass	1925	Abitibi Power and Paper Co.
	Library Bureau of Montreal		Canadian Pacific Railway, Department of Natural Resources
1914	Government of Canada, Department of Public Health		Canadian Pacific Express
	Government of Canada (war registration)		Goodyear Rubber
		1926	B.F. Goodrich Co.
1915	Dominion Bureau of Statistics		Mercury Mills
	Maritime Telephone and Telegraph		Mill Owners
1916	Ontario Workmen's Compensation Board		North American Life
	Canada Packers		Provident Adjustment and Investment Co.
	Winnipeg Hydro		Western Assurance
1917	Sun Life Assurance	1927	Eaton's
	Ford Motor Co.		Canadian Industries Ltd.
	Patrick Burns		Dominion Life
1918	Confederation Life Assurance		Eagle Star Insurance
	Government of Canada (pensions)		Employers' Liability
	Independent Order of Foresters		Sieberling Rubber
	London Life	1928	Britannia
1919	Canadian Kodak		Canadian Canners
	London Lancashire Insurance		Canadian General Electric
	Norwich Union Fire Insurance		Dominion of Canada General Insurance
1920	Manufacturers Life		Economical Mutual Insurance
	Mutual Life		General Steelwares

Year	Organization	Year	Organization
	General Accident Insurance	1934	Hiram Walkers
	Imperial Tobacco		Labatt's Brewery
	Link Belt		Toronto Transportation Commission
	RCA Victor	1935	Bery Moore
1929	Canadian Car		Canadian Cellucotton
	Hudson Bay Mining		Crown Life Insurance
	Wabasso		City of Montreal (payroll)
1930	Canadian Bank of Commerce		British Columbia, Department of
1931	Canada Sugar		Vital Statistics
	Chrysler Corp.		Quebec Department of Health
	Lake Shore Mines		Winnipeg Grain Commission
	Quebec Power Commission	1936	Appleford
	Shawinigan Water and Power Co.		Canadian Wire and Cable
	Rock City Tobacco		City of Montreal Association
1932	British Columbia Electric		City of Toronto Welfare Department
	The Montreal Gazette		City of Winnipeg Relief Department
	Sanford Evans		Industrial Acceptance Corp.
1933	Canadian General Rubber		McIntyre Mines
	Government of Canada, Department of Finance		Wrigley
	Quebec Workmen's Compensation Board		City of Montreal, Department of Relief
	Gutta Percha Rubber Co.		Government of Canada, Department of Trade and Commerce
	Government of Canada, Department of National Revenue		

*This list probably does not represent a complete sales record for the period. IBM's Canadian operation was established in 1917.

Source: Compiled from various sales records, International Business Machines Co. Ltd, Archives, Toronto.

NOTES

This is a revised version of a paper presented at the 10th World Congress of Sociology, Mexico City, August 1982. An SSHRC doctoral fellowship provided financial support for much of the research reported. I would also like to acknowledge the typing services of Val Caskey.

1 For an overview of the impact of the new microchip technology see J. Forester, ed., *The Microelectronics Revolution: The Complete Guide to New Technology and Its Impact on Society* (Oxford 1980); for Canada, see Heather Menzies,

Women and the Chip: Case Studies of the Effects of Informatics on Employment in Canada (Montreal 1981).

2 For a detailed discussion of the administrative revolution, see Graham S. Lowe, "The Administrative Revolution in the Canadian Office: An Overview," in K. Lundy and B. Warme, eds, *Work in the Canadian Context* (Toronto 1981).

3 The preceding data, based on the decennial censuses, are from Lowe, "Women, Work and the Office: The Feminization of Clerical Occupations in Canada, 1901–31," *Canadian Journal of Sociology* 5 (1980): 354–65.

4 Expressed as the number of office and supervisory employees per 100 production workers, the administration/production (A/P) ratio rose from 10.1 in 1905 to 15.8 in 1925, and reached 21.4 by 1935. While the last figure reflects the sharp decline in blue-collar employment during the depression, it should be noted that the ratio remained at this level until 1950 (computed from M.C. Urquhart and K.A.H. Buckley, eds, *Historical Statistics of Canada* [Toronto 1965], 463). The classic statement of the tendency for the A/P ratio to grow as managerial control functions proliferate is found in Seymour Melman, "The Rise of Administrative Overhead in the Manufacturing Industries of the United States, 1899–1947," *Oxford Economic Papers*, new series 3 (1951): 62–112.

5 Paul Craven, *An "Impartial Umpire": Industrial Relations and the Canadian State 1900–1911* (Toronto 1980), 375–80.

6 Meredith G. Rountree, *The Railway Worker: A Study of the Employment and Unemployment Problems of the Canadian Railways* (Toronto 1936), 153.

7 Sun Life Assurance Co. Archives, Montreal, "Number on Staff," n.d.

8 Bank of Nova Scotia Archives, Toronto, "Summary of Work Done, 1876–1927," n.d.

9 Canada, Dominion Bureau of Statistics, *Statistics of the Civil Service of Canada* (Ottawa 1926 and 1938), 16 and 12, respectively.

10 Robert H. Parker, *Management Accounting: An Historical Perspective* (London 1969), 19–20.

11 Daniel Nelson, *Frederick W. Taylor and the Rise of Scientific Management* (Madison, Wisc. 1980), 13.

12 Paul Craven argues that scientific management was primarily concerned with cost-accounting techniques (*Impartial Umpire*, 96).

13 John P. Jordan and Gould L. Harris, *Cost Accounting: Principles and Practice* (New York 1925), 19.

14 Kenneth Falconer, "Practical Value of Cost Accounting," *Industrial Canada* (August 1903): 26.

15 H.L.C. Hall, "Economy in Manufacturing," *Industrial Canada* (February 1906): 430–1.

16 *Monetary Times* (19 December 1908), 1010.

17 *Monetary Times* (24 September 1920), 10.

18 *Monetary Times* (6 October 1916), 9.

19 *Monetary Times* (26 September 1919), 30.

20 Hall, "Economy in Manufacturing."

21 E.W. King, "Administrative Expense," *Monetary Times* (1 January 1925), 31.

22 For example, J.N. Milner advised managers that cost-accounting procedures could be simplified by using job and time cards processed by Hollerith machinery. See his "Keeping Track of Time and Cost Records," *Industrial Canada* (December 1920): 101–3.

23 E. Palm, "Uniform System of Accounting for Canada," *Proceedings*, Second Canadian Telephone Convention (1922), 50–68.

24 W.H. Leffingwell, "The Present State of the Art of Office Management," *Proceedings*, Life Office Management Association (hereafter LOMA) (1926), 27.

25 Leffingwell's recommendations, made in 1925, are cited in I.O. Royse et al., *Significant Developments in Office Management*, American Management Association, Office Management Series no. 78 (New York 1937), 13.

26 See Lee Galloway, *Office Management: Its Principles and Practice* (New York 1918), and *Organizing the Stenographic Department* (New York 1924). The latter is essentially a reprint of part IV of the 1918 book.

27 Galloway, *Office Management*, 75.

28 Galloway, *Organizing the Stenographic Department*.

29 Galloway, *Office Management*, 50.

30 Harold W. Nance and Robert E. Nolan, *Office Work Measurement* (New York 1971), 1.

31 Ibid., 16.

32 Ibid., 3.

33 C. Wright Mills, *White Collar: The American Middle Classes* (New York 1956), 193. See Margery W. Davis, *Woman's Place Is at the Typewriter* (Philadelphia 1982), ch. 6, for an overview of the introduction of scientific management into U.S. offices prior to 1930.

34 Nelson, *Frederick W. Taylor*, 149.

35 For a description of Gantt's plan to reorganize locomotive repair work, see "Piece Work Price Setting at the C.P.R. Angus Shops," *The Railway and Marine World* (January 1912): 1–3. General overviews of the various scientific-management schemes used in early twentieth-century Canadian shops and factories are provided in Bryan Palmer, *A Culture in Conflict: Skilled Workers and Industrial Capitalism in Hamilton, Ontario, 1860–1914* (Montreal 1979), 216–22; and Craven, *Impartial Umpire*, ch. 4.

36 This is described in J.E. Hodgetts, William McCloskey, Reginald Whitaker, and V. Seymour Wilson, *The Biography of an Institution: The Civil Service Commission of Canada, 1908–1967* (Montreal 1972), chs 3 and 4.

37 Provincial Archives of Ontario (hereafter PAO), Civil Service Commission, "Draft Regulations Regarding Employees in the Public Service, 30 August 1920."

38 *Industrial Canada* (April 1920): 108.

39 Wallace Clark, "Intelligent Revision of Office Methods," *Industrial Canada* (August 1923): 91–4.

40 Harry Braverman, *Labor and Monopoly Capital* (New York 1974), 79–82. According to Braverman, Babbage translated Adam Smith's famous example of pin making into a basic axiom of modern business: by fragmenting the labour process, and thereby downgrading skill requirements, labour costs can be reduced.

41 International Business Machines Corp. (hereafter IBM), *Machine Methods of Accounting* (New York 1936), 1; pamphlet in IBM Archives, Toronto.

42 Charles Perrow, *Complex Organizations: A Critical Essay*, 2nd ed. (Glenview, Ill. 1979), 23.

43 This typology is derived from the four-stage model used by Jon M. Shepard, *Automation and Alienation: A Study of Office and Factory Workers* (Cambridge, Mass. 1971), 63.

44 Ibid., 63.

45 *Monetary Times* (20 September 1901), 376.

46 *Monetary Times* (18 August 1905), 204.

47 *Industrial Canada* (October 1906): 329.

48 *Industrial Canada* (December 1909): 530.

49 *Monetary Times* (21 February 1919), 50.

50 Cited by Bruce Bliven, Jr, *The Wonderful Writing Machine* (New York 1954), 15.

51 PAO, "Statement Presented to the Government of Ontario, 1920" by the Ontario Civil Service Association.

52 Cited in Bliven, *The Wonderful Writing Machine*, 3.

53 International Labour Office, "The Use of Office Machinery and Its Influence on Conditions of Work for Staff," *International Labour Review* 36 (1937): 491.

54 W.H. Leffingwell and Edwin M. Robinson, *Textbook of Office Management*, 2nd ed. (New York 1943), 25.

55 Sun Life Archives, Montreal, "Personnel Files, number 2, data for 1 December 1939."

56 Canadian Pacific Staff Bulletin (1 December 1935), 5.

57 For details, see International Labour Office, "The Effects of Mechanization and Automation on Offices: III," *International Labour Review* 81 (1960): 350–69.

58 Leffingwell, "The Office through a Microscope," *National Efficiency Quarterly* 1 (1918): 91.

59 Mills, *White Collar*, 195.

60 H.A. Rhee, *Office Automation in Social Perspective* (Oxford 1968), 44. See also 44–7, for a good summary of the developments of adding and calculating machines.

61 Burroughs Adding Machine Co., *A Better Day's Work* (Detroit 1908), ch. VI.

62 Parker, *Management Accounting*, 24.

63 Sun Life Archives, Montreal, "T.B. Macaulay to Mr. Tate," n.d., letterbook no. 31, letter no. 1,437.

64 Montreal *Standard*, 14 October 1911.

65 Rhee, *Office Automation*, 47.

66 *Intercolonial Gas Journal of Canada* (1 November 1912), 416–17.

67 Sun Life employee magazine, *Sun Dial* (August 1927): 16.

68 Bell Telephone Co. employee magazine, *Blue Bell* (November 1928): 25–6.

69 International Labour Office, "Office Machinery," 515.

70 Gilbert Jackson, *The Civil Service of Canada in 1930: Position, Salary Scales and Number of Appointments for Each Department*, vol. 3, prepared for the Royal Commission on Technical and Professional Service, 1929–1930 (mimeo, n.d.), 90.

71 John C. McDonald, *Impact and Implications of Office Automation*, Occasional Paper no. 1, Economics and Research Branch, Department of Labour (Ottawa 1964), 3–4.

72 According to one report, "the speed at which [office machines such as Holleriths] function imposes a rapid work rhythm comparable to assembly-line production" (International Labour Office, "Effects of mechanization and automation, III," 351). A more accurate comparison would be with the type of worker/machine relationship found in machine production, such as in the textile industry (see Robert Blauner, *Alienation and Freedom* [Chicago 1964], ch. 4).

73 Ida R. Hoos, *Automation in the Office* (Washington 1961), 67.

74 This brief historical sketch is based largely on the following: IBM Corp, *Machine Methods of Accounting* (New York 1936); pamphlet in IBM Archives, Toronto.

75 IBM Archives, Toronto, "Antique Machines File," 1916 sales brochure.

76 IBM Corp, *Machine Methods of Accounting* (New York and Toronto 1936), 8; pamphlet in IBM Archives, Toronto.

77 Ibid., 7.

78 IBM Archives, Toronto, Canadian chronology file, "Personal observations and comments concerning history and development of IBM, as customer, salesman and executive," by Walter D. Jones (August 1944), 25.

79 These included six types of key punches, two verifiers, three tabulators, and sorting, reproducing, collating, interpreting, and bank-proof machines.

80 Manufacturers Life Insurance Co. Archives, Toronto, transcript of interview with G.L. Holmes by N.T. Sheppard, 19 January 1977.

81 LOMA, *Proceedings* (1924), 22. In 1931, LOMA held a conference on the use of punch cards in insurance head offices (see LOMA, Special Conferences, *Proceedings*, 115–296).

82 LOMA, "Use of tabulating punch cards in connection with home office operations," Questionnaire Summary, *Special Report*, no. 5 (5 October 1925), 1.

83 *Canadian Pacific Staff Bulletin* (1 April 1936), 3. Six card punches, three sorters, one non-printing tabulator, and two summary printers hooked up to two tabulators processed 710,000 punch cards daily.

84 Ibid., 3.

85 *Blue Bell* (March 1923): 8.

86 Canada, *16th Annual Report of the Civil Service Commission*, Sessional Paper no. 24 (1925), vi.

87 Rhee, *Office Automation*, 49.

88 Royse et al., *Significant Developments in Office Management*, 31.

89 Elyce J. Rotella, "The Transformation of the American Office: Changes in Employment and Technology," *Journal of Economic History* 41 (1981): 53.

90 Shepard, *Automation and Alienation*, 63.

91 International Labour Office, "Effects of Mechanization and Automation in Offices: I," *International Labour Review* 81 (1960): 161. For an update of this argument, see Mike Cooley, "Computerization – Taylor's Latest Disguise," *Economic and Industrial Democracy* I (1980): 523–39.

92 See Braverman, *Labor and Monopoly Capital*, especially ch. 15 on clerical workers.

93 Ibid., 301.

94 Stephen Wood, "Introduction," in Wood, ed., *The Degradation of Work?* (London 1982), 18. Also see Andrew Zimbalist, ed., *Case Studies on the Labor Process* (New York 1979), especially the editor's introduction.

95 Mary K. Benet, *Secretary: Enquiry into the Female Ghetto* (London 1972), 140–1.

96 Jurgen Kocka, *White Collar Workers in America 1890–1940* (Beverly Hills, Calif. 1980), 12.

97 Mills, *White Collar*, 220.

98 Canada, *First Report of the Civil Service Commission*, sessional paper no. 113 (1881), 28.

99 During the 1910s and 1920s, stenographers could command salaries at least on a par with nurses and teachers. In one bank, stenographers were the highest paid clerical group of either sex between 1911 and 1926 (see Lowe, "Women, Work and the Office," 377).

100 See Rosabeth Moss Kanter's excellent analysis of the secretarial role in her *Men and Women of the Corporation* (New York 1977), ch. 4.

101 Roslyn L. Feldberg and Evelyn Nakano Glenn, "Technology and Work Degradation: Re-examining the Impacts of Office Automation," unpublished MS, Boston University 1980.

102 David A. Buchanan and David Boddy, "Advanced Technology and the Quality of Working Life: the Effects of Word Processing Technology on Video Typists," *Journal of Occupational Psychology* 55 (1982): 1–11.

103 Menzies, *Women and the Chip*.

104 Grace L. Coyle, "Women in the Clerical Occupations," *Annals of the American Academy of Political and Social Science* 143 (1929): 182.

105 For the specific occupational titles within the clerical category, see Canada, *Classified Index of Occupations*, 1921 Census.

106 Canada, 1881 Census, vol. III, table XIV.

107 Employee magazine published by the Bank of Nova Scotia, *The Nova Scotian* (Spring–Summer 1953): 2.

108 Mills, *White Collar*, 206.

109 Despite the obvious implications of his work-degradation thesis for worker resistance, Braverman does not consider this issue in *Labor and Monopoly Capital*.

110 Mills, *White Collar*, 309.

111 See Julie White, *Women and Unions* (Ottawa 1980).

112 Mary Vipond, "The Image of Women in Mass Circulation Magazines in the 1920s," in S.M. Trofimenkoff and A. Prentice, eds, *The Neglected Majority* (Toronto 1977), 117.

113 Ibid., 118.

114 E.G. Gowdy, "Women in the Banking World," *Journal of the Canadian Bankers' Association* (July 1916): 320.

115 For example, the standard contract in 1932 for Ontario female teachers prohibited them from marrying (see John Crispo, *The Canadian Industrial Relations System* [Toronto 1978], 112–13).

116 While no exact information on the occupational breakdown of union membership is available, the level of white-collar unionization was estimated to be at 15 per cent, compared with 60 per cent for manual workers, in 1969. Only about 8 per cent of the white-collar union members were in the private sector at that time. These figures do not, of course, reflect the upsurge of white-collar unionism in the 1970s, especially in the public sector. These estimates are cited by George S. Bain, *Union Growth and Public Policy in Canada* (Ottawa 1978), 12.

117 For details, see Lowe, *Bank Unionization in Canada: A Preliminary Analysis* (Toronto 1980), ch. II.

118 For a discussion of employee organization in the federal civil service, see Hodgetts et al., *Biography of an Institution*, ch. 8; and Anthony Thompson, "The Large and Generous View: The Debate on Labour Affiliation in the Canadian Civil Service, 1918–1928," *Labour/Le Travailleur* 2 (1977): 108–36.

119 Documentation is found in the CPR Archives, Montreal, "Shaughnessy Letter-books," correspondence for November 1912 to January 1913. These clerks soon after joined with other railway clerks to form the Canadian Brotherhood of Railway Employees.

120 See Hodgetts et al., *Biography of an Institution*, 68–83.

121 See Rick Salutin, *Kent Rowley: The Organizer* (Toronto 1980), 15–17; Eileen Sufrin, *The Eaton Drive* (Toronto 1982); Lowe, *Bank Unionization in Canada: A Preliminary Analysis*, 27–31.

122 See Craig Heron and Bryan Palmer, "Through the Prism of the Strike: Industrial Conflict in Southern Ontario, 1901–1914," *Canadian Historical Review* 58 (1977): 423–58. The virtual absence of overt conflict in the white-collar sector makes it difficult to use their methodology to analyse the reactions of clerks to changes in the administrative labour process.

123 See, for example, Rosemary Crompton, "Trade Unionism and the Insurance Clerk," *Sociology* 13 (1979): 402–26.

CRAIG HERON AND ROBERT STOREY

Work and Struggle in the Canadian Steel Industry, 1900–1950

Until quite recently, a steel plant was a vast, terrifying inferno. The heat was scorching, the air thick and choking, and the noise overpowering. Blinding flashes and showers of sparks would explode in the gloom of smoke and dust beneath towering hulks of machinery. Deafening roars, wailing sirens, and clattering bells heightened the atmosphere of tension and danger. Out of this eerie world of fire-breathing machines and toiling men flowed a vital commodity for modern industrial society – primary steel.

Canadian steelworkers participate in a labour process that we have come to know as mass production – a large-scale, high-speed, continuous, and technologically sophisticated system of production. In Canada, researchers and writers have seldom asked how industries like steel (or auto or any of a number of others) evolved to this stage of development. This paper attempts to begin to fill that gap in our understanding of Canadian industrial life. It will carry the reader from the formative years of the modern, mass-production steel industry at the turn of the century to the early 1950s, when steel-plant work relations reached a new stability. We begin by outlining the economic structure of the industry and then consider the nature and impact of technological change and managerial labour policies; we discuss the responses of the steelworkers themselves to this new work world, and finally, the consolidation of industrial unionism in the 1940s.

The story that unfolds suggests some of the main dynamics of the mass-production labour process in Canada. New machines and new managerial policies provided a substantial increase in the power of owners and managers to control the workplace and thus to boost productivity. Resistance to that unbridled control arose from the workers, whose role in the steel-making process gave them some independence on the shop floor. These men led an ultimately successful effort to give steelworkers some power to negotiate the terms of their employment and to impose new standards of fairness on steel-plant administration. Yet they neither demanded nor won any fundamental change in the essential shape of the labour process that had been created in the early years of the twentieth century: the technology, the work routines, and the power to control the process.

THE ANATOMY OF AN INDUSTRY

In 1896 the manager of Nova Scotia's Londonderry Iron Company raised few eyebrows among his fellow industrialists when he lamented that "there is only one country under the sun with 15,000 miles of railway that does not manufacture a single steel rail, and that country is Canada."[1] Canadian businessmen could only nod soberly in agreement that the history of iron and steel production in the country up to that point had been a tale of failures and disappointments. Why?

Three problems had plagued would-be ironmasters in Canada – problems that would persist well into the twentieth century.[2] First, Canada lacked large, known supplies of good-quality iron ore, and only in Nova Scotia was coal easily accessible. Second, foreign competition was crippling. The small Canadian market had not permitted the economies of scale and technological innovations of the British and American producers. And third, tariff protection was inadequate to meet this competition. The numerous consumers of primary iron and steel – particularly railways, agricultural implement firms, foundries, and independent rolling mills – did not believe that the small, inefficient primary industry in Canada could provide cheap-enough metal and convinced the Canadian state that the tariff system should have major loopholes to allow in various primary and semi-finished steel products. Canadian steel producers, especially in Sydney and Sault Ste Marie, were still agitating for more effective tariff protection as late as the 1920s, when Canada's primary producers supplied only half of all primary iron and steel products consumed in the country.[3]

Clearly the economic and political climate was far from favourable for a large, successful steel industry in Canada. There were some major structural constraints that would inhibit development and provide chronic instability for any steel-makers who undertook production in this context. Under these circumstances, the Canadian steel industry developed along two separate paths in the late nineteenth and early twentieth centuries. The first, pioneered by the Nova Scotia Steel Company at Trenton, NS, in the 1880s, involved slow, cautious growth with diversified markets and close integration with the finishing industries. The most successful example of this development path began as the Hamilton Blast Furnace Company in 1895, and after a series of mergers with a string of finishing plants, became the Steel Company of Canada (Stelco) in 1910.[4]

The second path was more dramatic and posed more risks. At the turn of the century, two free-wheeling American entrepreneurs launched widely hailed steel-production projects at Sydney in Nova Scotia and Sault Ste Marie in northern Ontario. H.M. Whitney organized the Dominion Iron and Steel Company (Dosco) in 1899, and Francis Clergue created the Algoma Steel Company in 1901. Both firms opened highly specialized facilities capable of turning out a large-enough volume to keep costs competitive with the Americans, and both looked to the new Canadian railways for their principal market, especially for steel rails. Both were also in serious trouble by the 1920s when their over-specialization and distance from markets in the industrial heartland of southern Ontario forced them to curtail production drastically. Nova Scotia Steel was dragged down at the same time, when it merged with Dosco into Cape Breton's new corporate monster, the British Empire Steel Corporation (Besco), after World War I.[5] Of the three major steel producers, only Stelco consistently turned a profit, not only in the 1920s but in each year of the 1930s depression.

World War II saved most of the teetering Canadian steel industry. The renewed demand for steel products in munition plants helped, but equally important was the active intervention of the Canadian state. A steel controller in C.D. Howe's Department of Munitions and Supply presided over a revitalization of steel-making facilities. An essential component of this resurgence was the provision, for the first time, of generous depreciation allowances that encouraged rapid expansion and modernization of their facilities. The major Ontario producers emerged into the post-war world as efficient, diversified, integrated industrial complexes capable of surviving in a continental market. The Sydney operations, however, continued their steady decline into marginality in Canadian steel production.[6]

The structure of the Canadian steel industry, then, would have major implications for the country's steelworkers. They had to confront three large, powerful corporations that controlled all primary steel production.[7] The workers were grouped in three major centres, each hundreds of miles from the others. Small and unsteady orders for steel, along with over-specialization, created an uneven demand for labour and fear among workers for the existence of their jobs. But, probably most important, these workers would find that their employers all recognized the need for cutting costs to match American standards of productivity if their products were going to find a market. The results for the labour process in Canada's steel plants were profound.

MACHINES AND MEN

In 1924 a business journalist emerged from a Canadian steel plant marvelling at what "a gigantic automaton" it was. On his tour he had found huge mechanical devices for handling and treating the iron on its progress through to rolled steel, and the workers he encountered seemed to be overwhelmingly machine-operators: "The labor in every branch of the industry consists mainly in the supervision and maintenance of machinery," he wrote.[8] The labour process this writer observed was, in fact, the recognizably modern mass-production system of steel making, which would see few significant changes in the next quarter century.

The mechanization of the Canadian steel industry had been a fairly abrupt process beginning at the turn of the century, and leaving behind the slow, labour-intensive methods of the scattered nineteenth-century producers. In part, Canadian steelmasters simply installed the most advanced technology available, virtually all of it American.[9] They were thus able to incorporate into their production processes many years of experimentation by American manufacturers aimed at reducing costs through eliminating as much self-directed manual labour as possible and using their control over the new machinery to intensify the work in the mills.[10] At the same time, in response to local experience turning out steel and managing steelworkers, Canadian companies continued to innovate with production techniques of their own. As a result, each of the three main stages of steel production – the blast-furnace, steel-making, and rolling-mill departments – was transformed in the late nineteenth and early twentieth centuries.

The blast-furnace had been at the core of the typical early Canadian ironworks. A small, perhaps thirty-foot stone stack would be built beside a hill, and wheelbarrows full of raw materials for the furnace would be trundled from the hilltop, across a ramp, and into the top of the furnace. Along with iron ore and limestone, quantities of charcoal, prepared by simply burning a large pile of local trees, would be dumped in. The "blast" of air blown into the bottom of the furnace would normally be powered by a simple waterwheel. The molten iron that flowed out at the bottom of these primitive furnaces would most often be directed along channels in the sandy floor of the casting house to form blocks of iron known as "pigs." Once cooled, these pigs were separated by brawny men with sledge-hammers and piled up by hand. These methods could produce no more than 5–10 tons of iron per day, and numerous labourers were required to run to and fro around the furnace with their barrows, shovels, and hammers.[11]

The typical blast-furnace of the 1890s had changed remarkably little. It had a larger capacity, steam had replaced waterpower, and in the newer operations, elevators carried the wheelbarrows of raw material up the side of the furnace. But the brigades of shovellers and "barrow-men" still hauled the material from piles by the railway tracks into and out of the elevators. At the base of the furnace, labourers still scampered about in the smokey heat and deafening noise to direct the molten iron into the beds of pigs. By this point, many firms were abandoning charcoal in favour of coke, and several companies had developed coke ovens for preparing coal for use in the furnace. These so-called bee-hive ovens required men to shovel coal into a small car, shove it in and out of ovens, hose it down, and fork the still-warm coke into wheelbarrows.[12]

The opening of the Dosco plant in 1901 unveiled much more sophisticated techniques of blast-furnace work that eliminated a large amount of brute labour, and that most other Canadian steel plants promptly adopted.[13] Workers now ran new electrically powered machines for hoisting coal and ore out of ships, for scooping them up from the stockyard and transporting them to the furnace, and for carrying them up and dropping them into the top of the furnace without any manual assistance. Crane operators now caught the molten pig iron in huge ladles and swept it away for use immediately in the steel-making departments, or else emptied the hot metal into new "pig-casting machines" – conveyor belts of metal moulds, which eliminated the old work in sand on the casting-house floor. The new coke ovens built at Canadian steel plants after 1900 were similarly mechanized, so that conveying vehicles and belts moved the coal speedily through its stages of preparation into coke.[14] Gone from all this work were most of the shovels, wheelbarrows, and small armies of brawny labourers, and in their place were a few handfuls of men who manipulated gears.[15]

In the nineteenth century, most Canadian ironmasters had sold the pig iron produced in their furnaces either to foundries, which would turn it into "cast iron" goods, or to forges and rolling mills, where the iron would be reheated and shaped into usable "wrought iron" products. The earliest method of producing wrought-iron goods had involved heating the iron in forges and hammering out the impurities – the work of the all-round blacksmith. In the last quarter of the nineteenth century, however, the more common procedure was "puddling" the pig iron – that is, while heating it in a special furnace, to stir the iron to separate out the dross, to form it into pasty balls of iron, and to put the balls through a "squeezer" to extract the last impurities. The iron could then be sent through the rolling mills to produce bars and other shapes. The slow, painstaking labour of the iron puddler, a highly skilled craftsman, made this a costly process, and, while iron enterprises at Londonderry and Hamilton employed these men from time to time, most rolling mills in the country preferred working with scrap iron, which was cheaper and did not require this purification process. The iron puddler who was so important in the American and British industries was, therefore, comparatively less so in Canada.[16]

In any case, by the 1890s, wrought iron was no longer the wave of the future. Puddling would not be challenged and transformed; it would simply be bypassed. Experiments in Britain and Germany in the 1870s had brought about a new, tougher, more-resilient type of iron, with a lower carbon content that was soon known as steel. The processes developed in Britain and the United States for producing steel from pig iron avoided the labour-intensive routines of puddling. The first and initially most popular was the Bessemer process: in a huge pear-shaped converter, air was blown through the molten iron to oxidize or burn out the impurities; the vessel would then be tilted to drain out the steel thus formed. The Bessemer method, however, required a high quality of ore, which was becoming scarce in North America by the turn of the century. Francis Clergue installed Bessemer converters at Algoma Steel in 1902, to use the ores of the corporation's nearby Helen Mine, but unending problems with the process forced the firm to abandon these converters completely in 1916.[17]

By 1900, in fact, the increasingly more common method of steel making in North America was "open-hearth" production.[18] Molten pig iron and a quantity of scrap metal would be exposed to the intense heat of a gas flame in special furnaces to draw out the last impurities in the iron, and, once small quantities of ferro-alloys had been shovelled in to adjust the chemical composition for hardness, the molten steel could be tapped from the back of the furnace in a thunderous explosion of liquid fire – perhaps the most dramatic spectacle in a steel plant. The first open-hearth installation in Canada was a small operation at the Trenton works of Nova Scotia Steel in 1883. The chemical process within these large new furnaces had replaced the puddler's craft, but human muscle was still straining to produce the steel. The furnaces were charged by hand, according to old-timers:

The crew of four helpers charged their furnace, then pushed buggies to outdoor scrap and ore piles, loaded up the buggies by hand, then pushed them back to the furnace, to be ready for the next charging. They helped the ladleman push the molten ladle of steel suspended from a swinging arm over the ingot mould. Rain or shine, snow or frost, the buggies were loaded outdoors. Indoors, the temperature near the furnaces was between one hundred and one hundred and thirty degrees F., depending upon the season.[19]

The open-hearth departments, which opened in the main steel-making centres between 1900 and 1907, incorporated numerous "labour-saving devices," which eliminated much of this manual labour.[20] Skilled furnace-tenders, known as "melters," still had to use considerable discretion in determining the quality and timing of the brew, and at regular intervals melters' helpers had to face the gates of hell with shovels full of chemicals[21]; but machinery had replaced most other manual labour. Men now drove small vehicles mounted on railway tracks for thrusting iron and scrap into the furnaces. Others used powerful electric cranes to pick up ladles of molten steel and to fill ingot moulds sitting upright on railway cars. Other operators handled specially designed "stripping cranes" to slip off the moulds, while another crane carried them off to the "soaking pits," where they were heated to a uniform temperature for their trip through the mills. A few key workers were still responsible for quality control, but, in contrast to the arduous, manual work of the old puddlers, many more men in the open-hearth department were operating or helping to maintain machinery, which handled the tasks of large-scale steel production quickly and smoothly.

The final phase of steel production took place in the rolling-mill plants, where the ingots passed back and forth between sets of massive rolls (like an old-fashioned wringer washing machine) to produce smaller shapes, from rails to structural steel to wire rods. The first rolling mills had appeared in Canada between the 1850s and 1880s to meet the needs of, first, the railway industry and eventually a wide range of metal-working enterprises. By the turn of the century, there were numerous independent firms still running on the older technology of that era.[22] Most continued to produce relatively small quantities of varied products for the small Canadian market and consequently could not afford the expensive investment in highly specialized, highly mechanized rolling-mill equipment. In 1910 a supervisor at Stelco, which brought a number of these older operations into its merger that year, told a parliamentary committee: "We consider we would have a very good order if we ran a day on it."[23] As a result, many Canadian rolling-mill operations still needed the muscle and the savvy of the "heaters" and "rollers" – the men who used simple tongs to snatch the hot bars from reheating furnaces and thrust them into the successive sets of rolls, working at their own pace and judging the quality of the product themselves. "We knew when we were handling that steel what its potentials were, what we could and couldn't do with it," one rolling-mill worker explained many years later. "We had to do it all with our eyes and judgment, mainly judgment. There were no gauges like today."[24]

Besides these older, hand-operated mills, however, each of the big three firms opened specialized rolling-mill facilities before World War 1 that transformed the traditional labour process. In these operations, a crane operator would fetch a reheated ingot from the soaking pit and place it on a bed of rollers. From here men perched high up in "pulpits" controlled the complex machinery by pulling levers and pressing buttons, sending the hot steel block back and forth through the rolls. Each time through, the flip of one lever would raise or lower the large table on which the ingot rested, while another would activate mechanical arms called "manipulators" for turning it over. The "bloom" that emerged from this process would then be sent along more automatic conveyors to giant shears, where men cut it into appropriate lengths, and then on to smaller sets of rolls. As the *Canadian Foundryman* noted after surveying Stelco's new continuous, electrically driven operation in 1913: "Modern rolling mills are really automatic machines on a large scale, one machine sometimes covering an acre or more of ground, and operated by a few men almost entirely without hard muscular labour." The efforts to modernize the older, smaller rolling-mill plants, which in some cases would last until the 1930s, aimed at achieving the same level of mechanization.[25]

The techniques of steel making in Canada thus changed quickly and dramatically after 1900. Much of the old craft knowledge of preparing and shaping metal had been embodied in large, complex, new machinery. Perhaps even more important, powerful, fast-paced lifting and conveying devices were performing feats of superhuman strength in moving raw materials and finished steel through the plants. The unprecedented speed and reliability of these machines was pushing up the pace of production and closely integrating all the stages in the process. Wherever possible, machines had replaced men.

The object of all this mechanization was not to save sweat, but to cut production costs. As the directors of Algoma Steel boasted in 1902: "The arrangement of the plant is such that the material can be handled at a minimum labor cost, and an unusually large output per man is thus obtainable." Twenty years later, a business journalist found this claim true for the whole industry: "The products could not be turned out at anything even approaching their present low price if human labour had to be utilized to do what is now done by mechanism." Federal government statistics also sustain these claims of higher productivity: in 1901 some 4,110 workers were needed to produce the country's 245,000 long tons of pig iron and 26,000 tons of steel; by 1929, the number of workers had risen to 10,500, but they were turning out 1.1 million tons of pig iron and 1.3 million tons of steel.[26] Machines could work faster, more reliably, and with fewer interruptions from human frailty or wilfulness. Human foibles had confronted the steelmasters in the form of occasional labour shortages and frequent unruliness – both strikes (as we will see) and labour turnover. "Workmen find it bad enough to be forced to handle frozen pig and scrap iron in the winter," the *Canadian Foundryman* noted, "but when the sun comes beating down the men become inefficient and discontented. Many of them leave."[27] Machines in a steel plant that eliminated such men, therefore, embodied more effective managerial control over production.

Journalistic enthusiasm for the new technology could also mask the hazards of the new work environment. The vast new steel plants became fiercely hot, smokey, deafeningly noisy caverns filled with massive, towering machinery that dwarfed the workmen toiling below. Brilliant, fiery flashes from the mouths of furnaces or showers of sparks from cauldrons of molten metal penetrated the gloom and seared the flesh of any nearby workers. If the men were not scampering out of the way of ladles, moulds, and great hunks of glowing steel which soared through the air at the end of giant cranes, they were dodging locomotives or charging machines whose tracks criss-crossed the plants. Dirt and danger remained hallmarks of the work experience in the steel industry.

The labour requirements of Canadian steel plants changed as rapidly as the technology. The observation of a Nova Scotia royal commission in 1910 that Dosco's work force had been "enormously reduced" in order to "eliminate needless cost wherever possible" reflected the trend in the industry.[28] Yet "labour-saving devices" by no means displaced all manual labour. Mishaps, delays, and clean-up and maintenance functions still demanded both skill and brute labour; so, too, did the crucial judgments of the men at the furnace doors and on some of the old rolling mills. As Stelco's open-hearth superintendent explained in 1910: "You cannot go and round up the skilled men and pick them up on the street corner. Take our melters, rollers and first helpers, they are skilled men and the next man to one of these cannot take his place. The second helper or third helper cannot take the place of the first helper and the same with the men at the ladles."[29] Over the long term, however, the jobs eliminated were the most skilled (notably the work of the puddlers) and the least skilled. In 1923, for example, a royal commission on industrial unrest in the Sydney steel industry learned that only about 20 per cent of Dosco's total staff was "common labour."[30] On the whole, the new technology had replaced the old nineteenth-century dichotomy between craftsman and labourer with more homogeneity among the steelworking occupations, a large percentage of which now involved machine operation.

The term for this new body of workers, which became current in the early twentieth century, was "semi-skilled," but the phrase disguised how little skill was required in most jobs and how easily these workers could be replaced. In an address to the American Iron and Steel Institute in 1919, Stelco's president proudly announced that in four-and-a-half years of operating the company's new electrically driven blooming mill, less than an hour and a half had been necessary for "breaking in new men to operate the motor for the mill."[31] For a former labourer, the most significant changes in the shift to semi-skilled work in a steel plant were the move from the periphery to the centre of the production processes and an increased responsibility for the machinery and for output. He was not as indispensable as the old craftsman, but his employer would soon grow reliant on the regularity, stability, and experience of these new mass-production workers.

Labour economist Richard Edwards has applied the term "technical control" to managerial systems in which "the entire production process of the plant or large segments of it are based on a technology that paces and directs the labor process."[32] The term is only partially applicable to the Canadian steel industry. While machines in a steel plant could replace slow-moving, obstreperous, unreliable labourers and independent-minded craftsmen, they did not necessarily discipline the workers who remained. The chemical processes in the furnace played an autonomous role in setting work rhythms, as did the close integration of processes that demanded speedy movement of molten metal about the plant. Yet few steelworkers fit Charlie Chaplin's stereotype of the assembly-line worker feverishly struggling to keep up with the relentless pace of self-propelled machinery. Most of the individual machines, whether hoists, cranes, conveying vehicles, charging devices, or even furnaces, had to be activated by workers making their own judgments about timing and pacing. Under these circumstances, new technology was not enough: owners and managers of Canada's steel plants recognized the need for new policies for managing their workers – policies designed to extract from them the maximum effort in their hours on the job, with a minimum of resistance.

MANAGERS AND MEN

In the nineteenth century, ironmasters had most often left direct supervision of the work process to their most skilled workers. Subcontracting the work to these men had been common in the British and American industries[33] and in the early years at Londonderry, but such practices seem to have largely disappeared in Canada by the late 1880s.[34] Skilled workers nonetheless still had responsibility for directing the work of their less-skilled workmates. Ironmasters indirectly disciplined these skilled work leaders by tying their earnings to the company's economic fortunes: they were paid on a tonnage basis and on a sliding scale that reflected the selling price of iron products. A unionist in a small rolling-mill department at the Hamilton steel plant described this system still in use in 1910: "Our scale is what is called the sliding scale, and our officials examine the books of the Iron and Steel Company every six months – every sixty days I should say – and if the selling price of iron and steel has gone up we will say one point, why we get a two per cent advance. If it goes down one point, we get a two per cent reduction."[35] The historic defeat of the skilled workers' union in the brutal Homestead strike of 1892 sounded the death knell for these practices and, combined with ongoing technological innovations, allowed the major American steel companies to break the connection between corporate earnings and skilled workers' pay. Henceforth the pattern – soon copied in Canada – was to establish wage scales from the base rate for unskilled labour.[36]

After 1900, new Canadian steel-making corporations were too obsessed with cutting costs to tolerate an indirect form of management. Productivity, they believed, would rise only if managers exercised a centralized control over the labour process. Although there is no evidence of simon-pure scientific managers in Canadian steel plants,[37] the companies' owners and managers showed the characteristic mania for "efficiency" that swept through industrial Canada in the early twentieth century: meticulous calculation and minimizing of costs, careful planning and scheduling in the front office, centralized job redesign, and so on.[38] It would be a mistake, however, to expect to find many white-collared men with stop watches roaming about amidst the smoke and din. The steel companies' management of their work force was less genteel than all that. Their labour policies in the early twentieth century were reminiscent of the techniques of the pioneers in Britain's Industrial Revolution a century earlier: new machines, a new work force, long hours, and a rigid discipline based on the carrot and the stick. In this case, the new industrial recruits were migrant labourers from the villages of southern and eastern Europe and the outports of Atlantic Canada. The workplace discipline came from both rigid, authoritarian direction of the workers and the incentives of piecework and welfare capitalism.

Canadian iron and steel producers who pondered the weakness of their industry in the 1890s recognized that their chief competitors south of the border had reduced their labour costs by hiring European immigrants and American blacks. As John F. Stairs of Nova Scotia Steel told a gathering of iron men in 1897: "If we in Nova Scotia were able to compete in wages with those in Alabama we could make iron as cheap as they do."[39] By the early 1900s each of the major corporations in the industry was trying to "compete in wages" with the Americans by recruiting from new pools of cheaper labour. Both Dosco and Algoma found the large number of Italians hired to build their new plants or nearby railways could be profitably shifted into manufacturing jobs. Each of these firms also actively recruited European migrants in Europe and the United States through special employment agencies.[40] Similarly, the Hamilton Steel and Iron Company, Stelco's predecessor, imported a trainload of Italians to help break a turn-of-the-century strike and encouraged these newcomers to set up shacks on the company's lakefront property.[41] Nova Scotia Steel was the only large steel firm that shunned this "foreign" labour force, but, like Dosco, it employed migrant labour from the outports of Newfoundland.[42] Eventually, once a decided preference for certain ethnic groups was known, intermediaries in the immigrant communities, usually labour agents of some kind, would keep up the flow of new workers into the plants.[43] In the pre-war decade, therefore, the steelworking labour force became a multicultural patchwork, including Italians, Poles, Hungarians, Ukrainians, southern blacks, and Anglo-Celtic Newfoundlanders, Canadians, and Americans.

This new work force had several advantages for the steelmasters. In the first place, large numbers of these workers were transients, migrating from distant villages or outports in search of cash to help their peasant families back home cope with worsening underemployment, overpopulation, and agricultural depression. They tended to come alone and to board in tightly packed little ethnic ghettoes near the steel plants.[44] Their economical life-style allowed them to save much of their earnings, but also to work for unusually low wages. "The Italian will board himself and thrive upon a dollar a week, on which men of any other nationality would starve," the Sault *Star* complained in 1903.[45] These migrant labourers who were only expecting to work for a short spell in a steel plant were, therefore, cheap labour for the companies. "It would be a very serious matter to do away with foreign labour," a Stelco official warned in 1919 during heated debates about deporting the "aliens." "If we expect returned soldiers to do the rough, rugged work, many of us would be out of business because we could not produce at anything like low enough cost."[46]

The transiency and inexperience of this new work force had a second advantage for the steel companies. Since they had no long-term commitment to their jobs in the steel plants and seldom stayed more than a few years at the most,[47] their bosses could intensify the labour process to extract the maximum from their labour power in a working day. One technique was the twelve-hour day (eleven on the day shift, thirteen at night) in the continuous production departments: blast-furnace, open hearth, and, quite often, the larger rolling mills. The companies repeatedly resisted efforts to introduce the eight-hour day, and they won support from a Nova Scotia Commission on Hours of Labour in 1910. "No one can deny," the commissioners reported, "that a day of twelve hours' manual labor, or of twelve or ten hours of attendance on ovens, furnaces, and machines, amid the conditions of such an industry, is long, and leaves the man little time, inclination or energy for other interests"; but "as the business stands at present, the men cannot live on 8 hours pay, and the Company cannot afford 12 hours pay for 8 hours work." Not surprisingly, the commission found the heaviest concentration of Europeans and New-foundlanders in departments on twelve-hour shifts, especially around the coke ovens and blast- and open-hearth furnaces.[48] Probably only these "sojourners" could tolerate such exhausting work.

The twelve-hour day and seven-day work week also had a disciplinary power, which Stelco's steel-plant superintendent explained to a parliamentary committee on the eight-hour day in 1910. In describing the long night shift, he noted that the men did nothing but work and sleep: "They prefer to work at night and then go home, go to bed right away and sleep all day. They get up at five or half-past five and go to the plant." This endless cycle of work made the men easier to manage. "We get better results from our men where we have them work 11 and 13 hours," the official stressed repeatedly in his testimony; moreover, "the best men we have and from whom we get the best results are the men who stay at work at least 325, 330, or 340 days a year." Shortening the work week, especially by shutting down on Sundays or holidays, created "constant trouble" and "dissipation": "It seems to give them too much time off; too much chance of spending money or to get around." Evidently the long hours in the steel industry gave the companies control over the whole lives of their workers. These hours would last until 1930 in Hamilton, and 1935 in Sydney and Sault Ste Marie.[49]

Steel company managers also wanted to provide incentives to drive the workers harder during their long hours on the job. In the decade before the war, superintendents and foremen were under steady pressure to increase the daily output beyond the rated capacity of the steel-making facilities. In April 1906, for example, Algoma proudly announced that its rail mill had set a new record: 859 tons of rails had been turned out in 24 hours, on equipment built to produce 500 tons per day, and Dosco's previous record had been smashed by 50 tons. By September, the daily output had passed 1,000 tons, and seven years later reached 1,400. Both these plants continued to report "record months" in all departments.[50]

In part, this increased output came from close supervision by foremen whose tyrannical rule was notorious. A Stelco executive admitted in 1919 that "we have more trouble through workmen and foremen than anywhere else," and until the 1940s workers had to learn to curry the favour of foremen with money, food, liquor, and occasionally even the sexual services of their wives.[51] An important figure in this system of control was the ethnic "straw boss" who imposed managerial discipline on small groups of workers of the same nationality. At the same time, however, managers were making full use of piecework to stimulate the individual worker's effort. Payment by tonnage rates had begun in the late nineteenth century and was well established throughout the industry by World War I. In 1923, Stelco's blast-furnace superintendent described "good incentive wages" as one of the keystones of the firm's industrial relations policies.[52] The federal government's statistics on average annual wages suggest that the long hours on piecework did pay off for those who held onto their jobs: as table 1 indicates, steelworkers' annual earnings were always well above the average manufacturing wage, and even above the earnings of the largely skilled workers in printing; among mass-production workers, only workers in the auto and pulp and paper industries did better (like steel, both these industries had virtually no women workers whose low wages would drag down the average figure).

In this context, the new immigrants' desire for quick money was a boon to employers who were undertaking to intensify production in their plants. Two American scholars, for example, noted in 1918 how migrant Polish peasants in Europe had already adjusted their work rhythms in order to earn as much and as fast as possible:

The peasant begins to search, not only for the best possible remuneration for a given amount of work, but for the opportunity to do as much work as possible. No efforts are spared, no sacrifice is too great, when the absolute amount of income can be increased. The peasant at this stage is therefore so eager to get piece-work ... They take the hardship and bad treatment into account, but accept them as an inevitable condition of higher income. When they come back [home], they take an absolute rest for two or three months and are not to be moved to do the slightest work.[53]

One unfortunate by-product of the speedup that was possible in this situation was a deplorably high accident rate. Industrial accidents were not reported with any consistency before 1910, but in Ontario, in 1912, at least 388 Algoma employees and 113 at Stelco suffered occupational injuries requiring at least a week off work. Four years later, the last detailed statistics available included 473 and 488 victims respectively, amounting to almost one worker in six at Stelco and involving four deaths at the two plants. The same year,

TABLE 1
Average Annual Wages in Selected Canadian Manufacturing Industries, 1917–50

Year	All manufacturing	Agricultural implements	Automobiles	Electrical parts	Printing & publishing	Pulp & paper	Steel
1917	$759	$838	$970	$736	$776	$865	$1,217
1918	878	934	1,191	856	775	1,020	1,371
1919	938	1,047	1,397	884	989	1,230	1,246
1920	1,109	–	–	–	–	–	–
1921	1,002	1,193	1,458	1,091	1,238	1,251	1,441
1922	939	1,004	1,400	948	1,135	1,145	1,259
1923	959	1,043	1,500	957	1,233	1,185	1,746
1924	972	1,086	1,387	1,012	1,343	1,247	1,262
1925	971	1,101	1,577	992	1,305	1,267	1,325
1926	1,003	1,178	1,535	1,061	1,365	1,302	1,382
1927	997	1,147	1,581	1,070	1,333	1,265	1,529
1928	1,024	1,158	1,697	1,080	1,397	1,282	1,650
1929	1,045	1,188	1,530	1,121	1,465	1,340	1,598
1930	1,001	1,145	1,422	999	1,459	1,221	1,449
1931	957	–	1,133	970	1,457	1,146	1,252
1932	852	859	1,063	846	1,364	984	1,117
1933	785	806	809	746	1,243	956	1,049
1934	837	859	1,191	750	1,254	1,098	1,135
1935	874	962	1,321	906	1,275	1,143	1,247
1936	896	996	1,286	924	1,316	1,201	1,144
1937	965	1,051	1,371	996	1,338	1,344	1,333
1938	956	1,088	1,263	976	1,334	1,192	1,284
1939	975	1,028	1,263	982	1,334	1,271	1,373
1940	1,084	1,199	1,781	1,123	1,397	1,475	1,566
1941	1,220	1,331	1,963	1,280	1,444	1,855	1,855
1942	1,383	1,516	2,135	1,443	1,505	1,701	1,797
1943	1,525	1,718	2,351	1,518	1,575	1,787	1,883
1944	1,564	1,762	2,347	1,548	1,657	1,858	1,930
1945	1,538	1,739	2,365	1,576	1,705	1,873	1,907
1946	1,516	1,735	1,887	1,523	1,775	2,113	1,998
1947	1,713	1,898	2,337	1,817	1,975	2,443	2,149
1948	1,960	2,306	2,639	2,125	2,440	2,764	2,561
1949	2,067	2,506	2,660	2,212	2,255	2,851	2,757
1950	2,183	2,574	3,045	2,336	2,621	3,051	2,841

Source: *Canada Year Book* (Ottawa), 1917–50.

Nova Scotia's factories' inspector reported 345 injuries at Dosco, 9 of them
fatal. In 1917 he commented on the connection between transiency and
accidents:

Most of the accidents are due to inexperience, and happen mostly to unskilled
labourers about the large plants. Large numbers are injured by material of all kinds

falling on their hands or feet, by being jammed between objects, by falling or tripping, and in many other ways, which can only be avoided by experience or when workmen get to know the dangers and mishaps liable to occur while they are at their work.[54]

There was one final bonus for the steel companies who hired these "birds of passage" – the cultural gulf that set them apart from the rest of the city's working class and inhibited class-conscious activity. These were men from peasant or outport backgrounds whose ties were usually stronger with family and village across the water than with fellow workers a few blocks away. The presence of so many Europeans, moreover, deeply troubled the native-born and American workers, who charged that these "foreigners" had been "brought over to lower the standard of living."[55] There were a few incidents (surprisingly few, actually) of open conflict between these two distinct groups of workers before World War I, such as a 1912 strike precipitated by the introduction of two Poles into Stelco's wire-drawing department.[56] The war, however, ignited some vigorous nativist sentiments, often based on resentment of the better jobs the "foreigners" had acquired in the wartime prosperity and the higher earnings they were stashing away. By 1919, Anglo-Canadian workers in the three major steel centres were agitating for exclusion of "aliens" from "white" jobs. "The Government should be told now and told plainly," a Nova Scotia labour paper argued early that year, "that restrictions should be placed on all cheap European labor, especially should this apply to Germans, Austrians, Hungarians, and Russians"; and another voice of labour in the same steel towns insisted a few months later: "Cheap alien labour must not be allowed to encroach on the hours and wages of good Anglo-Saxon wage-earners." In Hamilton in February 1919, a boisterous crowd of 10,000, in which "returned soldiers and working men seemed to predominate," demanded the deportation of "enemy aliens and other undesirables."[57]

As important as these thundering denunciations were, it should be borne in mind that there were no race riots comparable to those in British Columbia or the United States at the time. Ultimately, it was not so much the open conflict between ethnic groups under one factory roof as their completely separate social worlds. An Italian blast-furnace worker would return to his boarding house, or perhaps later to his own home, in a continental European enclave where he enjoyed the support of his own community institutions distinct from those of the English-speaking workers. A common working-class community developed only with great difficulty in these circumstances.

A Hamilton newspaper had early on observed how advantageous this ethnic segmentation of the steel-making work force could be. In the wake of a large strike at the Hamilton Steel and Iron Company in 1910, it noted how the transiency and the strangeness of so many of the city's steelworkers left the public "comparatively indifferent to their claims." The "great manufacturing corporations" thus reaped a twofold benefit: "They get work done at a cost less than the cost of getting it done by English-speaking workmen, and they prevent the enlistment of public opinion on the side of the workers when troubles arise with their foreign employees."[58] For these companies the interests of the migrant labourers in quick cash earnings meshed well with corporate strategies aimed at intensifying production and increasing productivity.

Modern theorists of "segmentation" in the working class have focused on the narrowing of the job hierarchy and concluded that homogenization was the main theme in the development of the labour force between 1870 and World War II, at which point segmentation began to emerge between core and peripheral sectors of the labour market.[59] This perspective misses the crucial divisions within mass-production industries along ethnic lines, which in Canada date from the turn of the century. Until the 1940s, ethnic fragmentation was a persistent counterpoint to occupational homogeneity.[60]

Intensive use of migrant workers unfamiliar with the industry's traditional work routines would bring results only with that part of the work force that could be easily replaced. But, as we have seen, technological and managerial innovations in the steel industry had not completely eliminated the need for skill and experience; in fact, they may have heightened the importance of permanently employed, experienced, responsible steelworkers. In the nineteenth century, Canadian ironmasters had generally imported their skilled labour, often from Britain, and all the new steel corporations in the early twentieth century had similarly turned to the United States and, to a lesser extent, to Europe for their first skilled workers.[61] The services of these men could not be treated as cavalierly as those of the thousands of unskilled labourers who flocked to the factory gates looking for work. Policies had to be developed that tied these workers to their employers without at the same time granting them too much autonomous shop-floor control (to prevent the re-emergence of the kinds of independent craftsmanship that had characterized nineteenth-century iron work). The key seemed to be ensuring worker dependence on the company.

One set of employment policies that helped immensely to heighten the dependency of the more skilled workers on their employers was internal recruitment. After the initial importation of skilled men, Canada's steel companies apparently made every effort to hire replacements from within their own work forces. Like its American counterparts, Nova Scotia Steel had first used a policy of training local residents for as many jobs as possible and drawing them up "job ladders" into more-skilled, higher-paying jobs. Presiding over this process of job placement were the foremen, who were able to develop powerful systems of patronage in the plants. Not only did this kind of promotion system encourage men to stay in their jobs (and to curry favour) in the hopes of advancement, it also left them with skills that were seldom easily transported to other industries, or even to other Canadian steel plants, which were hundreds of miles away. This dependent status contrasted with that of the older-style craftsman, like a moulder or pattern-maker, whose skills were learned within independent craft traditions and controlled by craft unions.[62]

At the same time, the Canadian steel companies all sponsored welfare programs, which would encourage their more valuable employees to identify their long-term economic security with the company. Employees' benefit societies in each of the firms provided insurance against sickness and death, and pension, stock-subscription, and group-insurance plans were gradually added. So, too, were some limited, long-overdue safety programs. The range of welfare programs increased whenever industrial conflict intensified in the steel plants and the spectre of trade unionism appeared, notably after World War I and in the later 1930s.[63] The most elaborate, and ultimately the most successful plan, introduced at the Dominion Foundries and Steel (Dofasco) plant in Hamilton in 1937, showered steelworkers and their families with recreational activities and, more important, incorporated them into a much publicized profit-sharing scheme.[64] Dosco and Stelco also cast the illusion of industrial democracy over their plants in 1923 and 1935 respectively, by organizing "industrial councils" of equal numbers of workers and management staff, with limited powers to recommend changes in working conditions (though seldom in hours or wages).[65] In 1943, Stelco took the further step of sponsoring a company union – a move Algoma was originally contemplating before it recognized an independent union in 1935.[66] The steel companies were invariably pushed into these welfare-capitalist measures by restlessness among their more stable employees. In 1919, Stelco's vice-president explained to a royal commission that they were not acts of philanthropy toward the firm's employees but were intended "to give them a direct interest in the business and promote continuity of employment," since "continuous and contented service is an asset to any company."[67]

Maintaining an internal labour market and spinning a web of welfare capitalism over the workers were techniques for ensuring a stable, dependent work force that the American steelmasters had also developed. But there was a third force in Canada that tightened the bonds between these steelworkers and their employers: the chronic instability of much of the Canadian industry. The stable core of steelworkers who clung desperately to their jobs in the 1920s and 1930s occasionally joined company delegations to Ottawa to beg for better tariff protection or for government spending to stimulate the industry. The federal Advisory Board on Tariffs and Taxation heard particularly earnest pleas from Algoma's steelworkers requesting some state intervention to overcome the pattern of sporadic employment. Appealing to the same spirit, Algoma circulated a handbill in its plant in 1937: "Don't fight this Company but with it, come to Ottawa with us and get a

100,000 ton rail order."[68] Clearly the dependence of these steelworkers on their employer went beyond social mobility and a modicum of social security, to the very existence of their jobs.

The Canadian steel companies did not fashion this whole set of labour policies according to any industrial engineer's master plan. Most of the key practices were borrowed from the United States and implemented by managers with American experience, but there was plenty of experimentation in local contexts, particularly in the first twenty years. The pool of cheap, inexperienced, migrant labour provided the flexibility necessary for extracting unprecedented levels of productivity from the steelworkers. Out of the somewhat chaotic early years came distinctive patterns of managing men in the steel plants. Management emerged securely in the saddle of production, with the tyranny of the foreman as the spur and the cultivated self-interest of wage-incentive plans and internal promotion as the bit. Centrally important was a relentless effort to eliminate as far as possible the autonomy of workers on the job and to heighten their dependence on their employer. Despite the modest gestures of welfarism, the managerial style was ruthlessly authoritarian, and supervisors ruled their industrial domains with iron fists, supplementing their gruff commands and arbitrary patronage systems with spies, blacklisting, and company police.[69] Mechanization had facilitated predictability and speedups, but these shop-floor despots guaranteed to Canada's steelmasters that their workers' labour-power would be used to the fullest. Not surprisingly, most steelworkers eventually toiled in an atmosphere of fear – fear of injury in the heat, dust, and noise of fire-breathing machines and fear of losing their jobs for insubordination. Ultimately that fear was mixed with a deep resentment.

RESISTANCE

The response of Canada's steelworkers to their work environment followed two paths in the twentieth century. Before World War II, the predominant response was individualized and took two forms: initially, casual, short-term attachment to jobs; and, then, by the 1920s, integration into the web of longer-term dependency on employers. Yet groups of workers in the industry regularly challenged that pattern with forms of collective resistance. In the early years, before World War I, that resistance surged up in the apparently spontaneous strikes of migrant labourers. By the end of the war, more-formal trade unionism had become the vehicle of worker protest. Only in the course of the next world war, however, did that challenge to the relationship of dependency finally succeed.

The first generation of twentieth-century steelworkers in Canada had come of age by the 1920s. It had taken roughly twenty years for that work force to develop any cohesion and self-consciousness. In the two preceding decades, a large proportion of the new steelworkers seemed to be just passing through. These workers had no steady attachment to the industry and seemed to see their jobs as a short, if unpleasant, episode in a personal or family-oriented strategy for survival. As in so many other mass-production industries, they changed jobs frequently, partly as a result of the economic instability of the manufacturers and partly as means of dealing with intolerable working conditions.

"Floating" between jobs was a much discussed phenomenon in Canadian industrial life of the early twentieth century, one that had attracted the label of "labour turnover" by 1920.[70] This behaviour became a serious problem for managers only when the reserve army of labour dried up, especially during World War I. At that juncture, the companies faced wartime labour shortages and declining productivity. Without the whip of poverty to discipline them, workers quit or took days off, confident of their ability to find work again soon. Dosco's general manager reported in 1916: "The foreigners in our employ, particularly the Austrians, realizing the scarcity of labour, are not doing a fair day's work. It is extremely difficult to keep them in hand." The next winter, Algoma's president reckoned the "efficiency" of the company's work force at about 60 per cent. In 1918, a federal board of conciliation was appalled to discover this attitude in Algoma's coke-oven and open-hearth departments:

In these basic departments there are nearly twelve hundred (1200) Austrians employed (alien enemies); they almost entirely run the coking ovens; they have been hard to control; they receive such good pay that they do not require to work all the time, so they knock off whenever they like, and do not come back until their money is spent, or they are good and ready. On occasion the company has been obliged to round these men up with the police in order to get men enough to operate this department, so as the mills could be kept going.

An official at Dosco told a royal commission in 1919 that labour turnover during the war was well above 20 per cent – "forty and fifty and maybe a hundred."[71]

Drifting between jobs, however, had become less common by 1930. In the first place, it proved to be a less successful strategy for survival in a period of depression, since there might be no job to move on to. Second, the flow of transatlantic migration was curtailed by the Canadian government between 1920 and 1925 and again for more than a decade in the 1930s. The footloose proletariat of the pre-war years that planned only brief work tours of North America was gradually disappearing. The European migrant community shrank most noticeably in Sydney, from 8 per cent in 1911 to 5.2 per cent in 1931. Those who remained were more settled: in 1927 a delegation of Algoma steelworkers informed the federal tariff board that only one-third of their ranks were "of foreign extraction," and two-thirds of those were naturalized citizens. It should not be surprising, therefore, that Stelco was able to report in 1935 that 88 per cent of its employees had been with the company at least five years.[72] Third, many of these former migrants were beginning to work their way into the semi-skilled jobs in steel making. The labour shortages of World War I seem to have opened up new opportunities that continued in the post-war world. These three new patterns of employment experience were producing a more stable work force, much more fully integrated into the structures of control that the companies had developed. Any working-class challenge to that control would have to reckon with deeply ingrained habits of fearful deference.

Steelworkers had, nonetheless, challenged their employers almost from the beginning. Surprisingly, the most consistent source of opposition arose from the supposedly docile continental European labourers. Each of the three companies discovered that these workers were capable of launching surprise strikes, using the ethnic solidarities cultivated in their close-knit little ghettos and on the job. These actions were often well timed to catch the companies in temporary labour shortages. One of the most dramatic of these incidents occurred in Hamilton in 1910, when the entire steel-making operations were shut down for two days by some 1,000 European workers. The strike spread alarm through much of the city's Anglo-Celtic population and made Stelco aware of the potential power of these groups of workers.[73] Despite their lack of permanent organization, these strikers always framed clear demands directed against unacceptable employment policies, especially low wages. For if the object of "sojourning" in North America was to accumulate as much cash as quickly as possible, it made sense to press for higher wages, just as it did on the many other work sites in Canada where immigrant workers seemed so rebellious.[74] In fact, it was the impermanence of their employment in the steel plants and the strength of their ethnic bonds that gave them a minimal autonomy from the steelmasters not shared by their Anglo-Celtic workmates.

That form of resistance declined, however, as the steel companies used machines to reduce their reliance on unskilled labourers and as the work force began to stabilize after World War I. Henceforth, steelworkers who wanted to stand up to their employers were more likely to be the more skilled workers turning to some brand of trade unionism, although workers were not successful in forcing recognition of their unions in the industry until 1946. The half century of struggle that culminated in that victory followed an uneven pattern, in which unionizing efforts were restricted to three distinct periods, each more intense than the last: 1901–4, 1917–23, and 1935–46.

The first union organization in the twentieth-century industry appeared in the new Dosco plant in 1901–2, in the form of two lodges of the Provincial Workmen's Association (PWA). The PWA had represented Nova Scotia miners for nearly twenty-five years, and at the turn of the century had widened its membership base to include many other occupations. In 1904, the PWA lodges in Sydney launched a long, bitter strike against the company that shattered the steelworkers' organization and led to extensive blacklisting.[75] No further unionization was seen in the Canadian steel industry until the war. This time, the workers used the vehicle of the Amalgamated Association of Iron, Steel, and Tin Workers. An erstwhile craft union, this association had formally opened its ranks to the unskilled but still drew the bulk of its membership from the technologically backward nooks and crannies of the American steel industry, particularly the older rolling mills. Its first Canadian lodge was organized in Gananoque in 1914, but the great burst of organization in Canada began in 1917, leading to 13 lodges from Sydney to Red Deer, Alberta, with perhaps 8,000 members.[76]

Overwhelmingly, this was a union of rolling-mill men in the older, hand-operated mills, who, as we have seen, often still exercised considerable skill in handling iron and steel between the rolls. Steelworkers in Sydney, Sault Ste Marie, and Gananoque made significant efforts to create all-inclusive industrial unions, but the international's official policy by 1919 was to subdivide the membership into smaller lodges based on occupational and skill groups. At Algoma and Stelco this quasi craft-unionist policy seriously weakened the local lodges. The Amalgamated Association's move away from craft unionism was ultimately only half-hearted, and a prominent Canadian member later reflected that "the division of the mills by crafts was its outstanding weakness."[77] A few of the association's lodges won temporary informal bargaining rights at the end of World War I, but virtually all of them collapsed in the depression of the early 1920s, in the face of aggressive employer hostility. The Sydney steelworkers fought the longest, most brutal battle in 1923, with the help of Cape Breton's militant coal miners, who struck in sympathy when federal troops violently attacked the striking steelworkers. The strike was broken, and, as in important sectors of the American steel industry after the historic 1919 strike, Besco established an industrial council as its pale alternative to trade unionism.[78]

The next attempts at organization began in the mid 1930s when independent steelworkers' unions appeared in Hamilton, Sault Ste Marie, Sydney, and Trenton. In 1936, the Steel Workers' Organizing Committee (SWOC) emerged in the United States, and the locals in Sydney, Trenton, and Hamilton resolved quickly in favour of affiliation. Algoma's workers waited until 1940, when a new leadership had emerged in the local, and when SWOC's Canadian national office had been purged of its communists. In their rush to affiliate, these Canadian steelworkers were responding to the almost magic appeal of the Congress of Industrial Organizations (CIO), of which SWOC was one of the first and most significant members. Yet the early successes of the American steelworkers were not matched in Canada: after the first wave of enthusiasm and rising membership levels, the Canadian steel companies fought back, and the struggle for collective representation became bitter and protracted. Indeed, despite the strength of the union in Sydney and the imminent affiliation of the Algoma local, SWOC, and Canadian steelworkers, were on the defensive by the end of the 1930s.[79]

The union's basic weakness in Canada lay in Stelco's Hamilton plant – the industry's trend-setter. There the local union members, the core of whom were the more skilled workers of the sheet mill, had been unable to build a successful union in the face of workers' fear, loyalism, and apathy, and in competition with a works council, started in 1935. In the context of new wartime labour shortages, however, the balance of forces at Stelco gradually shifted to the workers. The victory of eight of the eleven union candidates for the works council in 1942 emboldened Local 1005 to demand company recognition of the union – a demand raised in the midst of strikes by Algoma, Sydney, and Trenton steelworkers against company refusals to meet wage demands that government regulations forbade. Industrial relations within the industry had reached crisis proportions. In response to this and similar situations in other industries, the Mackenzie King Cabinet enacted an order in council, PC 1003, which established state-supervised union certification and collective bargaining.[80]

Events now moved quickly at Stelco. Local 1005 was certified in 1944, and the first contract was signed in February 1945. As both sides were aware, however, this was a paper agreement: the real confrontation would take place once the government's intervention into the field of industrial relations ended after the war. The Canadian steel companies were eager to return to the pre-war days of unfettered managerial control. Stelco became the main battleground for the industry. As the strike deadline approached, and the Algoma and Sydney plants seemed certain to be completely shut down by the overwhelming strength of the unions there, Stelco answered demands for union security (the "checkoff"), wage increases, seniority, and grievance procedures with a proclaimed determination to keep its Hamilton plant open during any strike. The workers themselves squared off along pro-union and pro-company lines. At the forefront of the strikers' ranks were the eastern and southern European workers, who were the most vulnerable to the capricious powers of supervisors and who were keenly interested in establishing the forms of security that union recognition promised. The steelworkers drew support from Hamilton rubber and electrical workers, themselves on strike and highly aware that the outcome of their conflicts depended on the fate of the Stelco strikers. Indeed, it was the support of these workers – and of the Hamilton working class generally – that sustained the picket lines at Stelco, perhaps the critical determinant in the ultimate victory of the strikers. After 81 days, Stelco and Local 1005 reached an agreement, and settlements at Sydney and Sault Ste Marie followed quickly. Stelco workers had established their union and had helped to set industrial relations in Canada on a completely new footing.[81]

Three features of this record of unionizing in the Canadian steel industry should be emphasized. The first is the social complexion of union enthusiasts. The initiative in each wave of organizing unquestionably came from some of the most skilled steelworkers, notably the rolling-mill hands, whose small edge of functional autonomy on the job gave them the pride, confidence, and leverage to challenge the companies' authoritarian rule.[82] In some cases in the SWOC era, these union militants had the additional leaven of radical politics sprinkled through their leadership, both communist and social democratic.[83] It was evident, moreover, that union success would be greater where steelworkers could draw on a vibrant, independent working-class community outside the steel plants. In Cape Breton the coal miners' advice and solidarity helped Sydney steelworkers in each wave of organizing. Hamilton, however, provided the striking contrast of a city of huge factories where traditions of workplace solidarity had largely been shattered by the 1920s.[84] In both wartime upsurges of union organizing, Hamilton lagged far behind the other major centres.

In fact, the importance of the tough-minded militants operating from a sphere of relative shop-floor independence and radical commitment should not blind us to the limited support they could count on. Thousands of workers were reluctant or unwilling to step outside the structures of dependence, deference, and loyalism to the firm. Nowhere was this more evident than in Hamilton, where more than 1,000 steelworkers stayed inside the plant during the 81-day strike of 1946 and organized themselves into the "Loyal Order of Scabs." These were predominantly men with long service to the company who saw their lifetime security tied to their employer. The more permanent monument to this working-class loyalism was next door at Dofasco, where prompt moves by the company in 1937 to break up an incipient union local and to launch an imaginative program of welfare capitalism solidified this alternative to the unionized workplace – the so-called "Dofasco Way."[85]

Second, the context of these unionizing efforts was crucial. Some crisis was necessary to overturn the stability and legitimacy of the steel companies' control over their work processes. In Cape Breton, the arrogance of outside corporate manipulations, especially in the 1920s, created a rupture. But more than any other factor, the two world wars disrupted established notions about the distribution of power and wealth and provided the catalyst for union growth. The labour shortages during both wars gave workers greater independence from the discipline of poverty, and the pressure to turn out munitions strengthened their hand with employers. During World War II, moreover, federal regulations froze essential workers in their jobs and effectively prevented employers from firing them in the traditional arbitrary fashion.[86]

Third, and even more important, was the wartime political climate. During both wars, Canadian workers were urged to sacrifice personal goals in the struggle for democracy. Unionists quickly transformed this rhetoric into demands for *industrial* democracy. In 1918, the Sydney steelworkers' newspaper attacked Dosco for its "attitude of stubbornness, of tyranny, of Steel-gloved Kaiserism"; it insisted that "the people of Cape Breton have suffered too dearly on the fields of Flanders and at home to be ruled by an autocracy."[87] A quarter of a century later, a Hamilton union bulletin declared that "every individual must decide whether he is for democracy or dictatorship – whether he supports 'der feuher' policy of having the bosses say how workers may present their case."[88] The strength of that sentiment ultimately pushed the Canadian state into a new activist role in industrial relations. The wartime political environment also generated the demand for social security, raised by workers during both wars. It was not until 1943–4 that the federal government began to act on questions of family allowances, contributory health insurance, and a contributory old-age pension scheme, promising as well to create a new Department of National Health and Welfare.[89] Organizers for the new industrial unions who took up Canadian workers' demands for these measures made the connections between industrial democracy and social security, and, by inaugurating the welfare state in Canada, Mackenzie King hoped to sap the new-found strength of the Co-operative Commonwealth Federation (CCF), as well as short-circuiting the alarming growth in industrial conflict. In general, this wartime experience not only demonstrates the impact of workplace relations on the political climate; it points as well to the ways in which workplace relations can themselves be profoundly influenced by the changing nature of politics and political behaviour.[90]

Finally, it is important to note the goals of industrial unionism in the Canadian steel industry. Neither the Amalgamated Association nor the United Steelworkers ever questioned the employers' right to control work routines in their plant. In part, these unions sought instead to reduce workers' contact with the job – through demands for an eight-hour day in the early years and for a forty-hour week and regular vacations in the 1940s. But even more important for these steelworkers was an industrial administration that was inherently *fair* and which assured a level of economic *security* for steelworkers. The means to those ends was a further bureaucratization of workplace relations – in effect, the creation of a "rule of law" within the steel plants.[91] The rules and regulations for hiring, promotion, wage payment, and settlement of grievances were to be clearly specified in a binding contract. Not surprisingly, one of the key provisions in the Algoma steelworkers' first contract in 1936 was a system of promotion based on seniority, which promised an end to nepotism, favouritism, and other forms of arbitrary supervision.[92] Seniority, grievance procedures, and union security were likewise at the heart of the great 1946 upheaval. A similar desire to inject new standards of equity was reflected in the union's drive, begun during the war, to standardize wage rates across the industry. In the early 1950s, successful efforts to rationalize the myriad of unequal distinctions along the "job ladders" involved an extensive program of job evaluation and classification jointly by unions and management, known as the "Co-operative Wage Study." The union went so far as to develop its own industrial-engineering department! As a result, according to the most thorough student of the program, "the rate for a particular job no longer depends upon such intangible factors as the personality of the worker or the whim of the foreman, but upon the job itself."[93]

For these steelworkers, the central concern lay in minimizing competition between themselves in the workplace, to avoid a return to the often degrading practices of the preceding decades. Their success altered one important element in the traditional administration of the steel-making work process – the unchecked authoritarianism of front-line supervisors, those ruthless, much despised "drivers" on the shop floor. Yet the "rule of law" within the industry did not mean any serious erosion of managerial power in the workplace; it affected only the *way* in which that power was wielded. In the words of Stelco's historian, William Kilbourn, the company avoided an "abdication of a certain basic responsibility of management for determining work rules ... Sound seniority provisions ... were thus prevented from becoming mere rigid ritual codes for the consecration of inefficiency."[94] In the late nineteenth century, those "rigid ritual codes" had been the work-place customs and regulations of the skilled craftsmen and their union. The consolidation of industrial unionism in the steel industry in the 1940s had clearly not brought back those mechanisms of workplace control. Moreover, steel companies, which had vigorously resisted collective bargaining and even, in some cases, the Co-operative Wage Study, learned the value of the new bureaucratized work relations. State legislation had not only bound the employers to recognize their employees' union, but also confined workers to the rigid channels of legally enforceable contracts and grievance procedures. Disruptions to the flow of production could be minimized when the union officials became the policemen of work relations. The steelmasters' long-standing concerns with predictability thus had a new solution.

For Canada's steelworkers, then, the victories of the 1940s had ensured formal negotiations over the price of their labour power, more consistency and equity in management labour policies, and a minimum level of job security. But their new power to influence the administration of the steel plants did not confront the deepest source of tension in their workplace – the relentless efforts of owners and managers to cheapen the cost of production by intensifying the use of the workers' labour-power. Those initiatives were outside the realm of collective bargaining, and the new bureaucratized structures of the Canadian industrial-relations system made resistance to them more difficult and more likely to find expression in absenteeism, sabotage, or wildcat strikes.[95] Industrial unionism brought undeniable benefits to workers like these, but it fell short of its potential.

The primary steel industry that emerged in Canada at the turn of the century made a radical break with the past. In contrast to the small, widely scattered ironworks of the nineteenth century, a handful of large corporations integrated all stages of primary steel making within large new production facilities at Sydney, Hamilton, and Sault Ste Marie. Inside these mammoth mills, the companies also introduced major changes in the way that steel and iron had previously been produced in Canada. A visitor to the plants would have been struck by the elaborate new machinery, which reduced or eliminated the firms' reliance on both highly skilled craftsmen and unskilled labourers. The same visitor might also have noticed the babble of strange tongues among the workers in the plants, since the companies had learned to make full use of inexperienced, tractable, transient labour from continental Europe, in order to extract the maximum from the new equipment and to push up productivity. Twelve-hour days, harsh, autocratic supervision, and high accident rates were the results. Mass production in the steel industry was born.

As the new work routines became firmly established, a new work force emerged – for the first time known as "steelworkers." Their "semi-skilled" jobs generally had low skill requirements, and only the long hours and incentive wages assured them a steady income. These men found themselves enmeshed in a relationship of almost inescapable dependency on their employers: few of them had portable skills, and most relied on promotion within the firm for any modest improvement in status and earnings; they were at the mercy of departmental despots for any promotion or even for keeping their jobs; and many had their long-term economic security tied to company welfare programs. The strands of this web of dependency were primarily deference and fear.

The first challenges to these work relations arose from those with a modicum of independence – the European labourers – who had no permanent commitment to the industry and whose ethnic enclaves in the steel towns provided the collective resources for successful resistance, and also from small groups of workers, especially in the rolling mills, whose jobs still demanded some skill and allowed some workplace autonomy. The footloose Europeans declined in importance as the steel work force stabilized, but the more skilled workers led the efforts to establish industrial unionism for all steelworkers. The companies' policies to promote a stable work force ultimately backfired when these more settled workers began to assert their own rights within the industry. The victory of the United Steelworkers of America by 1946 brought a significant shift in the administration of the steel-making labour process – from autocracy to bureaucracy. Henceforth, work relations were governed by a negotiated "rule of law," which would guarantee equitable treatment on the shop floor, job security, and, if possible, a decent wage. The labour movement's old adage of "a fair day's work for a fair day's wage" had finally won some acceptance in the industry. What did not change fundamentally, however, was the actual organization and execution of work. The early twentieth-century transformation of the labour process survived intact, and the steel companies could continue to use their highly mechanized, speeded-up system of production to maintain and increase productivity.

NOTES

1 *Canadian Mining Review* (hereafter CMR) 16, no. 2 (February 1897): 51. The contrast was quite clearly with the United States, where more than half the steel production was in the form of rails; Bernard Elbaum and Frank Wilkinson, "Industrial Relations and Uneven Development: A Comparative Study of the American and British Steel Industries," *Cambridge Journal of Economics*, no. 3 (1979): 279.

2 The history of the Canadian iron and steel industry can be traced in the following: James M. Cameron, *Industrial History of the New Glasgow District* (New Glasgow n.d.); W.J.A. Donald, *The Canadian Iron and Steel Industry: A Study in the Economic History of a Protected Industry* (Boston 1915); Donald Eldon, "American Influence in the Canadian Iron and Steel Industry" (PH D dissertation, Harvard University 1952); William Kilbourn, *The Elements Combined: A History of the Steel Company of Canada* (Toronto 1960); L.D. McCann, "The Mercantile-Industrial Transition in the Metal Towns of Pictou County, 1857–1931," *Acadiensis* 10, no. 2 (Spring 1981): 29–64; Edward J. McCracken, "The Steel Industry of Nova Scotia" (MA thesis, McGill University 1932); Duncan L. McDowall, "Steel at the Sault: Sir James Dunn and the Algoma Steel Corporation, 1906–1956" (PH D dissertation, Carleton University 1978); Tom Traves, *The State and Enterprise: Canadian Manufacturers and the Federal Government, 1917–1931* (Toronto 1979), 121–54.

3 This situation helps to explain why there were no significant American branch plants in the Canadian primary steel industry – there was no substantial tariff wall behind which to set up production facilities. The United States Steel Corporation secured lands at Ojibway in southwestern Ontario and announced elaborate plans for a branch plant in 1912 and then again in 1920. But much more modest facilities opened in 1927, only to close five years later. In 1938, Dosco bought out U.S. Steel's handful of Canadian subsidiaries, which were mostly in the finishing branches of steel production (Eldon, "American Influence," 163–4).

4 McCann, "Mercantile-Industrial Transition," 29–64; Kilbourn, *Elements Combined*, 51–96.

5 Don Macgillivray, "Henry Melville Whitney Comes to Cape Breton: The Saga of the Guilded Age Entrepreneur," *Acadiensis* 9, no. 1 (Autumn 1979): 44–70; David Frank, "The Cape Breton Coal Industry and the Rise and Fall of the British Empire Steel Corporation," ibid., 7, no. 2 (Autumn 1977): 3–34; McCracken, "Steel Industry," 96–127, 180–232; McDowall, "Steel at the Sault," 26–150; Margaret Van Emery, "Francis Hector Clergue and Rise of Sault Ste. Marie as an Industrial Centre," *Ontario History* 56, no. 3 (September 1964): 191–202. Several similar, though more limited, entrepreneurial ventures were undertaken in Ontario at the turn of the century, principally by American capitalists – at Midland, Collingwood, Deseronto, and Port Arthur – but most had given up the ghost by World War 1.

6 McDowall, "Steel at the Sault," 306–67; Kilbourn, *Elements Combined*, 159–81; Robert H. Storey, "Workers, Unions, and Steel: The Shaping of the Hamilton Working Class, 1935–1948" (PH D dissertation, University of Toronto 1981), 302–8; Steel Research Group, "Report on Sydney Steel," *Canadian Dimension* 14, nos 4–5 (February–March 1980): 33–52.

7 Alongside the big three stood a few smaller, more specialized companies – older rolling mills like the Manitoba Rolling Mills, and steel foundries like Dominion Foundries and Steel (Dofasco) and Canadian Steel Foundries in Montreal. Some of these firms had modest facilities for producing steel from pig iron, but none had blast furnaces before 1950.

8 A.R.R. Jones, "A Gigantic Automaton," *Iron and Steel of Canada* (hereafter ISC) 7, no. 4 (April 1924): 61.

9 Eldon, "American Influence," 294–328.

10 David Brody, *Steelworkers in America: The Nonunion Era* (New York 1960), 1–26.

11 B.J. Harrington, "Notes on the Iron Ores of Canada and Their Development," Canada, Geological Survey, *Report of Progress* (Montreal 1873–4), 242–59; Henry How, *The Mineralogy of Nova Scotia: A Report to the Provincial Government* (Halifax 1869), 84–95; Nova Scotia, Department of Mines, *Report* (Halifax 1877), 45–6; Michel Gaumond, *Les forges de Saint-Maurice* (Québec 1969), 11–13; Dollard Dubé, *Les vieilles forges il y a 60 ans* (Trois-Rivières 1933), 21–51; J.A. Bannister, "The Houghton Iron Works," Ontario Historical Society, *Papers and Records* 26, (1944): 80–1; W.J. Patterson, "The Long Point Furnace," ibid., 73–6; E.A. Owen, *Pioneer Sketches of Long Point Settlement* (Toronto 1898), 452–7; Elijah Leonard, *A Memoir* (London, n.d.); T.J. Drummond, "Charcoal and Its Bearing on the Utilization of Our Forests," *Canadian Engineer* (hereafter CE) 2, no. 10 (February 1895): 288–9 and no. 11 (March 1895), 310–12; John Birkinbine, "The Old and New Industry Compared," CMR 21, no. 4 (April 1902): 90–2.

12 *Canadian Mining Manual* (hereafter CMM), 1897, 58–111 and 1900, 65–7; Nova Scotia, Department of Mines, *Annual Report*, 1893, 38–42; Ontario, Bureau of Mines, *Annual Report* (hereafter OBMAR) (Toronto), 1902, 27–30 and 1908, 314;

CMR 15, no. 2 (February 1896): 39; CE 3, no. 7 (January 1896): 248–9; Hamilton *Spectator*, 10 February 1896; *Stelco Flashes* 14, no. 6 (June 1950): 6; Jones, "Gigantic Automaton," 63–4; Charles Reitell, *Machinery and Its Benefits to Labor in the Crude Iron and Steel Industries* (Menasha, Wisc. 1917), 8–21.

13 The Dosco blast-furnace operations are described in CMR 20, no. 10 (October 1901): 240, CMM, 1901, 129–30; Canada, Department of Mines, Mines Branch, *Report on the Mining and Metallurgical Industries of Canada, 1907–8* (hereafter RMMIC) (Ottawa 1908), 528–300. For descriptions of the new blast furnace equipment introduced at Collingwood in 1902, Sydney Mines in 1904, Sault Ste Marie in 1905, and Hamilton in 1907, see ibid., 325–6; 546; OBMAR, 1902, 2 and 1908, 291–7, 301–4; E.G. Brock, "Making Pig Iron at Hamilton," *Canadian Foundryman* (hereafter CF) 19, no. 2 (February 1928): 7–10.

14 CMR 21, no. 7 (July 1902): 195; F.E. Lucas, "By-Product Coke Manufacture at Sydney," *Canadian Mining Journal* (hereafter CMJ) 32, no. 18 (15 September 1912): 641–3; C.E. Wallin, "The Dominion Iron and Steel Coke Plant at Sydney, N.S.," ISC (December 1919): 291–7; W.S. Wilson and A.P. Theurkauf, "What the Eyes Behold at Sydney Steel Plant," ibid. (November 1927): 333–4; W.J. Dick, "By-Product Coke Ovens at the Algoma Steel Company, Sault Ste. Marie, Ont.," CMJ 35, no. 13 (15 July 1914): 487; William Seymour, "By-Product Coke Plant of the Algoma Steel Corporation at Sault Ste. Marie, Ont.," ISC (November 1919): 262–8; J.F. Slee, "The By-Product Coke Plant of the Steel Company of Canada at Hamilton, Ontario," ibid. (February 1929): 40.

15 Harry Jerome calculated that the greatest "labour-saving" innovations in the American steel industry were in blast-furnace work. See *Mechanization in Industry* (New York 1934), 58–66.

16 Peter Temin, *Iron and Steel in Nineteenth-Century America: An Economic Inquiry* (Cambridge 1964), 14–18; James J. Davis, *The Iron Puddler: My Life in the Rolling Mills and What Came of It* (Indianapolis 1922), 85–113; Donald, *Canadian Iron and Steel*, 99–101; Elbaum and Wilkinson, "Industrial Relations."

17 Temin, *Iron and Steel*, 125–38; Sault *Star*, 20 February 1902; Public Archives of Canada (hereafter PAC), RG 36/17 (Fielding Tariff Inquiry Commission, 1898–1906), vol. 5, 858–60; MG 31, B 3 (C.H. Speer, "Algoma Steel Corporation"), 86; McDowall, "Steel at the Sault," 74, 88; Eldon, "American Influence," 127.

18 Temin, *Iron and Steel*, 138–45.

19 Cameron, *New Glasgow*, V-2.

20 RMMIC, 327, 337–8, 530–1, 548–9; OBMAR, 1902, 24 and 1908, 304–7.

21 Jones, "Gigantic Automaton," 100–3; Charles Rumford Walker, *Steel: The Diary of a Furnace Worker* (Boston 1922), 21–6, 46–7, 52–3. The companies eventually developed laboratory staff who took full responsibility for testing the steel.

22 Kilbourn, *Elements Combined*, 3–50; Donald, *Canadian Iron and Steel*, 60–63; PAC, RG 87 (Mineral Resources Branch), vol. 18, F. 81.

23 Canada, House of Commons, *Journals*, vol. 45 (1909–10), appendix, part III

("Proceedings of the Special Committee on the Bill No. 21, 'An Act Respecting Hours of Labour on Public Works' ... December 9, 1909–May 3, 1910") (hereafter "Eight-Hour Committee"), 183. See also the testimony of Stelco president Robert Hobson in 1919: PAC, RG 36/8 (Tariff Commission, 1920), vol. 8, F. 21 (Hamilton), 3777.

24 Quoted in Wayne Roberts, ed., *Baptism of a Union: Stelco Strike of 1946* (Hamilton 1981), 16. See also John Fitch, *The Steel Workers* (New York 1910), 51.

25 Sault *Star*, 10 April 1902; OBMAR, 1908, 299; C.H. Speer, "The New Merchant Mills of Algoma Steel," ISC (March 1930): 53–7; CF 4, no. 9 (September 1913): 142–4; CMJ 24, no. 5 (1 August 1913): 489; *Stelco Flashes* 14, no. 6 (June 1950); C. Ochiltree Macdonald, *The Coal and Iron Industries of Nova Scotia* (Halifax 1909), 84–9; CE 13, no. 2 (February 1906): 38–43; 25 (31 July 1913): 251–2, and (4 September 1913): 416–18; ISC 3, no. 5 (May 1920): 113–19; Wilson and Theurkauf, "Sydney Steel Plant," 337–40; Cameron, *New Glasgow*, VI–V40.

26 Sault *Star*, 6 October 1902; Jones, "Gigantic Automaton," 118; *Canada Year Book* (Ottawa 1908), 138; Canada, Dominion Bureau of Statistics, *Iron and Steel and Their Products* (Ottawa 1929), 18 and (1930), 68, 73.

27 F.H. Bell, "Lifting and Conveying Material in the Foundry," CF 12, no. 3 (March 1921): 19.

28 Nova Scotia, Commission on Hours of Labor (hereafter CHLR), *Report* (Halifax 1910), 66.

29 "Eight-Hour Committee," 166.

30 University of British Columbia Library, Special Collections, James Robertson Papers, box 5, F. 1, handwritten memorandum, 3.

31 American Iron and Steel Institute, *Yearbook* (New York 1919), 414. A special report on the American steel industry also noted this change in the labour force: "The semi-skilled among the production force consist for the most part of workmen who have been taught to perform relatively complex functions, such as the operation of cranes and other mechanical appliances, but who possess little or no general mechanical or metallurgical knowledge" (United States, Bureau of Labor, *Report of Employment in the Iron and Steel Industry* 4 vols [Washington 1911–13], III, 81).

32 Richard Edwards, *Contested Terrain: The Transformation of the Workplace in the Twentieth Century* (New York 1979), 113.

33 Elbaum and Wilkinson, "Industrial Relations," 283–93; David Montgomery, *Workers Control in America: Studies in the History of Work, Technology, and Labor Struggles* (New York 1979), 11–12; David A. McCabe, *The Standard Rate in American Trade Unions* (Baltimore 1912), 62–5; Katherine Stone, "The Origin of Job Structures in the Steel Industry," *Radical America* 7, no. 6 (November–December 1973): 20–5.

34 Canada, Royal Commission on the Relations of Capital and Labor, *Report* (hereafter RCRCLR): II, *Evidence – New Brunswick* (Ottawa 1889), 17–18, 107; III,

Evidence – Nova Scotia, 237–68, 388–407; IV, *Evidence – Ontario*, 760–4, 786–94; Cameron, *New Glasgow*, VI–VI6. This was evidently a transitional point: when asked if he paid his own helpers, a Londonderry puddler explained, "It comes out of the puddlers' wages but the company pay them" (RCRCLR, III, 247).

35 "Eight-Hour Committee," 188. See also RCRCLR, III, 237, 240, 242, 249, 257–9, 266, 268, 390, 394–5, 398 and IV, 760, 763, 786–7.

36 Brody, *Steelworkers*, 27–9; Robertson Papers, "Notes from Conversations with Officers of the Steel Company of Canada, Hamilton, Ont., Dec. 21/23," 1.

37 F.W. Taylor, the "father" of scientific management, conducted some of his most important experiments at the Midvale Steel Company and later at the Bethlehem Steel Company. See Daniel Nelson, *Frederick W. Taylor and the Rise of Scientific Management* (Madison, Wisc. 1980).

38 Kilbourn, *Elements Combined*, 84–5; Craig Heron and Bryan D. Palmer, "Through the Prism of the Strike: Industrial Conflict in Southern Ontario, 1901–14," *Canadian Historical Review* (hereafter CHR) 58, no. 4 (December 1977): 430–4; Graham S. Lowe, "The Rise of Modern Management in Canada," *Canadian Dimension* 14, no. 3 (December 1979): 32–8; Paul Craven, *"An Impartial Umpire" : Industrial Relations and the Canadian State, 1900–1911* (Toronto 1980), 90–110.

39 CMR 16, no. 2 (February 1897): 52; see also C.A. Meisner, "Notes on Some Comparisons between Southern and Nova Scotia Iron Methods," ibid., 16, no. 1 (January 1897): 12–15.

40 *Labour Gazette* (hereafter LG) 1, no. 8 (April 1901): 389; Labour Canada Library (Hull), Provincial Workmen's Association, Grand Council, minutes, III, September 1904, 442; Ronald F. Crawley, "Class Conflict and the Establishment of the Sydney Steel Industry, 1899–1904" (MA thesis, Dalhousie University 1980), 52–61; CHLR, 65–72; Emilia Kolcon-Lach, "Early Italian Settlement at Sault Ste. Marie, Ontario, 1898–1921" (MA thesis, University of Western Ontario 1979), 1–21; Livo Ducin, "Labour's Emergent Years and the 1903 Riots," in *50 Years of Labour in Algoma: Essays on Aspects of Algoma's Working-Class History* (Sault Ste Marie 1978), 5–6; Francis M. Heath, "Labour, the Community, and Pre-World War I Immigration Issue," in ibid., 41–2.

41 Craig Heron, "Hamilton Steelworkers and the Rise of Mass Production," Canadian Historical Association, *Historical Papers* (Ottawa 1982), 114.

42 CHLR, 65–72.

43 Public Archives of Nova Scotia, MG 1, no. 1191C (Thomas Cozzolino Autobiography); R.W. Ripley, "Industrialization and the Attraction of Immigrants to Cape Breton County, 1893–1914" (MA thesis, Queen's University 1980); *Labor News* (Hamilton), 30 October 1914; Robert F. Harney, "The Commerce of Migration," *Canadian Ethnic Studies* 9, no. 1 (1977): 42–53; and "Montreal's King of Italian Labour: A Case Study of Padronism," *Labour/Le Travailleur* 4 (1979): 57–84.

44 W. Craig Heron, "Working-Class Hamilton, 1895–1930" (PH D dissertation,

Dalhousie University 1981), 330–41; Kolcon-Lach, "Italians"; Ripley, *Industrialization.*"

45 Sault *Star*, 5 March 1903.

46 Hamilton *Spectator*, 15 February 1919.

47 Kolcon-Lach calculated that of 252 Italians listed on Algoma's employment rolls in 1905, only 25 were still there in 1910.

48 CHLR, 64–75.

49 Ibid., 168–9, 171, 174; LG 30, no. 1 (January 1930): 2; McCracken, "Steel Industry," 269–70; McDowall, "Steel at the Sault"; University College of Cape Breton, Beaton Institute, William G. Snow, "Sydney Steelworkers: Their Troubled Past and the Birth of Lodge 1064" (typescript 1979), 20.

50 LG 5, no. 11 (May 1905): 1174; LG 6, no. 17 (January 1906): 703, no. 11 (May 1906): 1225; no. 12 (June 1906): 1336; LG 7, no. 3 (September 1906): 258; no. 4 (October 1906): 367; no. 6 (December 1906): 945; no. 9 (March 1907): 939; LG 8, no. 1 (July 1907): 13; LG 9, no. 4 (October 1908): 359; LG 10, no. 6 (December 1909): 634; LG 11, no. 5 (November 1910): 534; *Canadian Machinery* 10, no. 7 (14 August 1913): 170; John Ferris, *Algoma's Industrial and Trade Union Development* (Sault Ste Marie n.d.), 40–5, 61.

51 Storey, "Workers, Unions, and Steel," 208–11; Roberts, *Baptism*, 11–15; Harry J. Waisglass, "A Case Study in Union-Management Co-operation" (MA thesis, University of Toronto 1948), 89–94; George MacEachern, "Organizing Sydney's Steelworkers in the 1930s," in Gloria Montero, ed., *We Stood Together: First-Hand Accounts of Dramatic Events in Canada's Labour Past* (Toronto 1979), 58.

52 CHLR, 70; Robertson Papers, "Conversations."

53 William I. Thomas and Florian Znaniecki, *The Polish Peasant in Europe and America*, 5 vols (New York 1918–20), I, 199. See also Montgomery, *Workers' Control*, 37.

54 Ontario, Inspectors of Factories, *Reports* (Toronto), 1912, 1916; Nova Scotia, Factories Inspector, *Reports* (Halifax), 1916, 32 and 1917, 6.

55 PAC, RG 33/95 (Royal Commission on Industrial Relations, "Evidence"; hereafter RCIRE), 3744.

56 PAC, RG 27 (Department of Labour), vol. 299, F. 3475.

57 *Labour Leader*, 25 January 1919; *Eastern Federationist*, 22 March 1919; Hamilton *Spectator*, 11 February 1919; see also *Amalgamated Journal*, 2 August 1917, 23; Kolcon-Lach, "Italians," 128–30.

58 Hamilton *Herald*, 4 April 1910.

59 David M. Gordon, Richard Edwards, and Michael Reich, *Segmented Work, Divided Workers: The Historical Transformation of Work in the United States* (New York 1982).

60 Probably the most pessimistic view of these ethnic divisions is presented in Gabriel Kolko, *Main Currents in Modern American History* (New York 1976), 67–99.

61 Cameron, *New Glasgow*, VI–V40; RCRCLR, III, 234–9, 241, 265, 268, 392, 407;

"Eight-Hour Committee," 188; Hamilton *Spectator*, 1 August 1901, 15 July 1926; Speer, "Algoma," 17–18, 23; Heath, "Immigration Issue," 39–56; Donald, *Canadian Iron and Steel*, 204; McCracken, "Steel Industry," 105; Crawley, "Class Conflict," 57; PAC, RG 36/8, vol. 6, F. 13.

62 Cameron, *New Glasgow*, V–V40; RCRCLR, III, 388, 391 and IV, 761, 821; Fitch, *Steel Workers*, 141–2; Stone, "Job Structures," 40–3; Brody, *Steelworkers*, 85–7. On the general phenomenon of "internal labour markets," see Michael Burawoy, *Manufacturing Consent: Changes in the Labor Process under Monopoly Capitalism* (Chicago 1979), 95–108; Edwards, *Contested Terrain*, 130–62. Elbaum and Wilkinson have correctly challenged Katherine Stone's suggestion that job ladders were purely the creation of the steel companies; they were instead demanded by the less skilled well before the end of the nineteenth century to ensure fairness in promotion. See "Industrial Relations," 292.

63 Heron, "Hamilton Steelworkers," 118–19; LG 6, no. 12 (June 1906): 1301; LG 7, no. 7 (January 1907): 783–4; no. 12 (June 1907); LG 9, no. 1 (July 1908): 70–1; no. 12 (June 1909): 1344; LG 11, no. 12 (June 1911): 1334–5; LG 12, no. 8 (February 1912): 725; no. 12 (June 1912): 1135; LG 18, no. 9 (September 1918): 696; LG 21, no. 3 (March 1921): 521–2; LG 22, no. 10 (October 1922): 1041–2; LG 23, no. 1 (January 1923): 5; LG 26, no. 3 (March 1926): 237–9; no. 11 (November 1926): 1106; LG 28, no. 2 (February 1928): 172–3; no. 9 (September 1928): 942–3; LG 29, no. 1 (January 1929): 45–6; LG 30, no. 7 (July 1930): 783; ISC (August 1920): 208; (August 1921): 198–200; (August 1922): 147; (September 1922): 168–9; (July 1924): 129; (January 1928): 24; (March 1928): 68, 88; Speer, "Algoma," 122–35; PAC, RG 36/8, vol. 6, F. 13, 1764–9.

64 Robert Storey, "Unionization versus Corporate Welfare: The 'Dofasco Way,'" *Labour/Le Travailleur* 12 (Autumn 1983): 7–42.

65 Storey, "Workers, Unions, and Steel," 190–3, 199–213; Canada, Commission to Inquire into the Industrial Unrest among the Steel Workers at Sydney, N.S. (hereafter CIIUR), *Report* (Ottawa 1924), 16–19; LG 26, no. 7 (July 1926): 665–6; McCracken, "Steel Industry," 261–4; MacEachern, "Organizing," 54–65.

66 Storey, "Workers, Unions, and Steel," 299, 336; "Early Union Reminiscing Reveals It Was Never Easy," *Algoma Steel News* 8, no. 3 (March 1977): 4.

67 RCIRE, III, 2289, 2299.

68 PAC, RG 36/11 (Advisory Board on Tariff and Taxation), vol. 1, F. 2–1, exhibit 10; F. 3–6, exhibit 16; McDowall, "Steel at the Sault," 293.

69 PAC, MG 30, A16 (Sir Joseph Flavelle Papers), vol. 2, F. 11 (Department of Labour), R. Hobson to J.W. Flavelle, 8 July 1916; Provincial Archives of Nova Scotia (PANS), MG 2 (Armstrong Papers), vol. 670, F. 5; PAC, RG 27, vol. 69, F. 222(7).

70 William Davenport, "As a Britisher Sees It," *Western Clarion*, 30 June 1906; Ontario, Commission on Unemployment, *Report* (Toronto 1916), 9; G.W. Austen, "Excessive Labor Turnover and its Remedies," *Industrial Canada* 21, no. 5 (May 1920): 74–5; "Cost of Labour Turnover," LG 20, no. 11 (November 1911):

1419; A.O. Dawson, "The Relations of Capital and Labour," *Social Welfare* 2, no. 7 (1 April 1920): 171–2; Paul F. Brissenden and Emil Frankel, *Labor Turnover in Industry: A Statistical Analysis* (New York 1922). On the transiency of workers in the period, see Edmund Bradwin, *The Bunkhouse Man* (Toronto 1972); A. Ross McCormack, *Reformers, Rebels and Revolutionaries: The Western Canadian Radical Movement, 1899–1919* (Toronto 1977), 98–117; John Herd Thompson, "Bringing in the Sheaves: The Harvest Excursionists, 1890–1919," CHR 59, no. 4 (December 1978): 467–89; Jack London, *The Road* (London 1967); G.H. Westerbury, *Misadventures of a Working Hobo in Canada* (Toronto 1930).

71 PAC, MG 26, H I(c) (Sir Robert Borden Papers), vol. 211, 118826 (D.H. McDougall to Mark Workman, 2 September 1916); vol. 216, 121857 (W.C. Franz to J.W. Flavelle, 20 January 1917); LG 28, no. 3 (March 1918): 180; RCIRE, 3843. See also PAC, MG 30, A 16, vol. 2, F. 11, Thomas Findley to T. Crothers, 31 March 1916.

72 Canada, *Census* (Ottawa), 1911, 447; 1931, 756; PAC, RG 36/11, vol. 8, F. 3–6; Steel Company of Canada, *The Twenty Fifth Milestone, 1910–1935: A Brief History of Stelco* (Hamilton 1935), 54.

73 Heron, "Hamilton Steelworkers," 122–4; see also Crawley, "Class Conflict," 70, 72–4; LG 4, no. 11 (May 1904): 1074.

74 See McCormack, *Reformers, Rebels, and Revolutionaries*, 98–117; Harney, "King of Italian Labour"; Jean Morrison, "Ethnicity and Violence: The Lakehead Freight Handlers before World War I," in Gregory S. Kealey and Peter Warrian, eds, *Essays in Canadian Working Class History* (Toronto 1976), 143–60; Stanley Scott, "A Profusion of Issues: Immigrant Labour, the World War, and the Cominco Strike of 1917," *Labour/Le Travailleur* 2 (1977): 54–78.

75 Provincial Workmen's Association (PWA), Grand Council, minutes, II, September 1901, 368; III, September 1904, 429–30; September 1905, 521; Crawley, "Class Conflict," 70–146; Paul MacEwan, *Miners and Steelworkers: Labour in Cape Breton* (Toronto 1976), 16–17, PAC, RG 27, vol. 69, F. 222(7).

76 *Amalgamated Journal*, 1914–23; Gordon Bishop, *Recollections of the Amalgamated* (n.p., n.d.), 4.

77 Bishop, *Recollections*, 5. See also Brody, *Steelworkers*, 255–8, and *Labor in Crisis: The Steel Strike of 1919* (Philadelphia 1965), 166–8.

78 *Amalgamated Journal*, 1917–23; Donald Macgillivray, "Industrial Unrest in Cape Breton, 1919–25" (MA thesis, University of New Brunswick 1971).

79 Storey, "Workers, Unions, and Steel," 179–244; MacEachern, "Organizing," 60–1; Waisglass, "Case Study," 57; Irving Martin Abella, *Nationalism, Communism, and Canadian Labour: The CIO, the Communist Party, and the Canadian Congress of Labour* (Toronto 1973), 55–60.

80 Storey, "Workers, Unions, and Steel," 297–370; MacEachern, "Organizing," 60–5; Ronald McDonald Adams, "The Development of the United Steel Workers of America in Canada, 1936–1951" (MA thesis, Queen's University 1952); Laurel Sefton McDowell, "The Formation of the Canadian Industrial Relations System

during World War Two," *Labour / Le Travailleur* 3 (1978): 175–96, and "The 1943 Steel Strike against Wartime Wage Controls," ibid., 10 (Autumn 1982): 65–85. In 1942 SWOC changed its name to the United Steelworkers of America and two years later had 50,000 members in 113 Canadian locals.

81 Storey, "Workers, Unions, and Steel," 370–418; Roberts, *Baptism*; Adams, "Development," 129–56; C.D. Martin, "The 1946 Steel Strike," in *50 Years of Labour in Algoma*, 101–16.

82 *Amalgamated Journal*, 1917–23; Storey, "Workers, Unions, and Steel"; Waite interview; Snow, "Sydney Steelworkers," 20.

83 Storey, "Workers, Unions, and Steel," 184–5, 189, 358–61; MacEachern, "Organizing," 159–60; Adams, "Development," 78; Abella, *Nationalism, Communism, and Canadian Labour*, 55–60.

84 Heron, "Working-Class Hamilton."

85 Storey, "Workers, Unions, and Steel."

86 Desmond Morton, *Canada and War: A Military and Political History* (Toronto 1981), 115.

87 *Canadian Labor Leader*, 12 October 1918.

88 Quoted in Storey, "Workers, Unions, and Steel," 336.

89 Dennis Guest, *The Emergence of Social Security in Canada* (Vancouver 1980), 101–38.

90 This experience undermines Michael Burawoy's contention that the work process is "relatively autonomous." See *Manufacturing Consent*, 123–57.

91 See David Brody, *Workers in Industrial America: Essays on the Twentieth Century Struggle* (New York 1980), 173–214. Burawoy uses the term "internal state" to describe the same phenomenon, though he emphasizes the conservatizing effect of the bureaucratic work relations. See *Manufacturing Consent*, 109–20.

92 Waite interview.

93 Ronald B. Bean, "Joint Union-Management Job Evaluation in the Canadian Steel Industry," *Relations industrielles/Industrial Relations* 17, no. 1 (April 1962): 115–26, and "The 'Cooperative Wage Study' and the Canadian Steelworkers," ibid., 19, no. 1 (January 1964): 55–70. See also C. Bryan Williams, "Collective Bargaining and Wage Equalization in Canada's Iron and Steel Industry, 1939–1964," ibid., 26, no. 2 (April 1971): 308–44.

94 Kilbourn, *Elements Combined*, 199–200.

95 See Maxwell Flood, *Wildcat Strike in Lake City* (Ottawa 1968).

IAN RADFORTH

Logging Pulpwood in Northern Ontario

Few jobs in Canada have a more secure place in our national folklore than that of the woodsworker. For many years the "Roistering Lumberjack" of the snowy northern woods was one of Hollywood's favourite characters in movies with a Canadian setting. School children today still learn about the heroic exploits of Paul Bunyan and his Ottawa Valley counterpart, Joe Montferrand.[1] Yet few jobs in Canada have moved further away from these popular stereotypes over the past three decades. A visit to the northern Ontario woods in the 1980s would reveal few axes wielded by brawny men. Today's loggers fell trees with chainsaws or gigantic, hydraulic-powered shears that cut down several jackpines like a pair of garden shears cutting as many blades of grass. Rather than shouting commands at horses pulling sleighs loaded with logs, woodsworkers now operate powerful diesel equipment capable of carrying heavy loads across muskeg and rock in summer as well as in winter. No longer do lumberjacks gather for Saturday-night buck dances in the camp cookery; most bushworkers spend weekends at home with their families.

This essay looks closely at the changing nature of work in Ontario's pulpwood logging industry, one of the most innovative sectors of North America's logging industry during the past thirty years.[2] I argue that although capital has always predominated, bushworkers have played a significant role in shaping the pace and nature of labour-process transformations in the industry. Before 1950, pulp and paper corporations found that in their logging operations, labour-intensive, seasonal methods, combined with piece-rate payment systems, were cheap and effective. For their part, bushworkers enjoyed considerable independence in performing their tough, dangerous jobs. After decades of struggle, bushworkers in the immediate post-World War II period succeeded in building a union that gave them some protection on the job and won substantial wage increases. By the early 1950s, the mounting costs of informal forms of worker protest, as well as trade-union pressure on wage rates, drove the corporations to adopt new, mechanized methods in a bid to remain competitive in post-war paper markets. Capital proved quite successful in reaching its objectives, although not all production snags have yet been eliminated. Woodsworkers continue to enjoy a considerable degree of independence in the new kinds of jobs they perform. Throughout the entire period, managers and workers in this primary-resource industry have had to confront the challenges and opportunities posed by the geography of the Canadian Shield, the changing weather and seasons of the north, and the characteristics of the coniferous forest itself.

This essay surveys briefly the origins of pulpwood logging in Ontario and the broad economic developments in the forest industry. It then scrutinizes labour processes in the period before 1950. Next follows a discussion of the rise of worker protest in the industry and management's reaction, particularly its mechanization program of the 1950s and 1960s. Finally, I outline workers' responses to mechanization, as well as the challenges they face today.

ONTARIO'S FOREST INDUSTRY

For nearly two centuries Ontario forests have been assaulted by armies of men who earned wages by felling trees and transporting timber. At the beginning of the nineteenth century, forests of towering white and red pines grew along the banks of Ottawa and upper St Lawrence rivers. Lumberjacks armed with axes felled these pines and hewed them into giant sticks of squared timber, which river drivers and raftsmen guided downstream to the port of Quebec. From there, timber ships sailed to markets in Britain where the wood was sawn into lumber for the construction and shipbuilding industries. Beginning in the mid-nineteenth century, timber from many parts of Ontario was also sawn into lumber in the province and transported by water and rail to markets in the United States.[3] While Ontario's forest industry continues to produce lumber today, an increasing proportion of the province's logging activity since 1900 has been undertaken to supply fibre for the manufacture of pulp and paper products.[4] During the third quarter of the nineteenth century, European and American discoveries made it possible to reduce drastically the cost of paper by manufacturing it from wood pulp – logs that have been ground or chemically treated to form a mash – rather than from rags, as had been the practice for centuries. Demand for this cheaper paper increased enormously in the late nineteenth century, largely as a result of the exponential growth of newspaper advertising in the United States.[5]

By the 1890s, investors were looking to Ontario forests as a source of pulpwood for paper making.[6] In the coniferous forest region stretching across much of northern Ontario grew vast stands of spruce, jackpine, and balsam fir. The long fibres of the black spruce were especially well suited to the manufacture of newsprint. The rivers rushing through the Canadian Shield to the Great Lakes provided a cheap form of log transportation, as well as an inexpensive source of hydro-electricity for mills. But it was a varied, rugged, and challenging landscape, broken by rocky outcroppings, spongy muskegs, and countless rivers and lakes. The audacious entrepreneur Francis Clergue was the first to exploit this forest resource in a manner that was soon to become the dominant Ontario pattern. In 1892, he acquired a long-term lease from the Ontario government for cutting rights to fifty square miles of crown forest. He was then able to raise the considerable capital necessary to build a pulp mill at Sault Ste Marie, Ontario, close to the forest resource and hydro-electric power. Pulp, and later newsprint, was shipped from this mill to u.s. markets south of the Sault.[7]

Following the passage in 1900 of Ontario regulations requiring the processing within the province of pulpwood cut on crown land, the removal in 1913 of the American tariff on newsprint, and rapidly rising prices for paper at the end of World War I, the Ontario industry expanded at a frantic pace, reaching a climax in the mid 1920s. By 1930, major pulp and paper companies held cutting rights to some 35.6 million acres of Ontario's crown timber. Mills had been constructed at such places as Iroquois Falls, Smooth Rock Falls, Kapuskasing, Espanola, Sturgeon Falls, the Sault, Port Arthur, Fort William, Fort Frances, and Kenora. The Canadian pulp and paper industry ranked as Canada's leading industry in terms of capital invested, labour employed, and export values, and Canada had won the lion's share of American newsprint markets.[8] Whereas in the lumber industry, capital requirements were comparatively low and family firms the norm, capital investments in pulp and paper were enormous and joint-stock corporations prevailed. The rapid expansion of the 1920s was undertaken by a handful of Canadian and American firms whose large debts had been underwritten on the assumption that mills could be run at close to full capacity. By 1928, it was clear that over-expansion had resulted in falling newsprint prices and reduced mill-operating ratios. Refinancing and consolidations followed, with Abitibi Power and Paper emerging as the provincial giant. Nevertheless, during the depression, more than one-half of Canada's newsprint manufacturing capacity passed into receivership or underwent drastic refinancing again. Further consolidations followed as the industry slowly recovered.[9]

Only after World War II did Ontario's pulp and paper industry begin growing significantly once again. Largely through expansion of existing mills, the province's pulp production has more than doubled since 1946. Today the industry is dominated by a few giant, integrated firms that conduct logging operations, manufacture pulp and paper products at some fourteen major mills, and produce lumber as well. Some of these firms, such as Boise Cascade, with mills at Kenora and Fort Frances, are branch plants of huge, diversified, u.s.-based multinational corporations. The provincial leader is the giant Abitibi-Price empire, itself one of the many holdings of Olympia-York Developments of Toronto, with total assets of more than $5 billion.

About one-fifth of Canada's logging activity and one-quarter of the country's paper production take place in Ontario.[10] This corporate structure and boom-bust-boom development pattern has had important consequences for bushworkers. But in order to understand the transformations in the logger's world of work, it is first necessary to look closely at the labour process in the period before 1950.

BUSHWORK

When pulp mills began to create a demand for Ontario logs, pulp and paper companies naturally turned to the readily available techniques and personnel of the much older lumber industry. Lumberjacks had long been developing skills, technologies, and organizational structures that were well suited to logging pine in the northern Ontario environment. During the first half of the twentieth century, pulp and paper corporations found these methods to be inexpensive and effective for logging pulpwood. Only minor adjustments were made in the pulpwood sector. Before 1950, logging operators took advantage of weather conditions to facilitate the transportation of logs from the stump to the mill. During the winter, timber was hauled across the snow to a river, where the spring thaw would later provide the high water for river drives. In this way, companies avoided large capital outlays for heavy equipment, roads, and railways. They relied, instead, on simple technology and large numbers of seasonal workers.

The demand for bush labour was heavily concentrated in the late fall and winter months. During the 1945–6 season, for instance, the number of jobs in Ontario pulpwood camps ranged from a low of 3,600 in April to a high of 10,000 in November.[11] Fortunately for the companies, large numbers of seasonal workers were available in winter as a result of the curtailing of agriculture, construction, and other industries. According to a 1942 study[12] of some 25,000 employment records cards, approximately 50 per cent of Ontario's woodsworkers came from farms. They were part of Canada's widespread agro-forest economy.[13] Some 20 per cent came from other industries, such as building and highway construction, where jobs were few in the winter months. Only about 30 per cent were "professional lumberjacks" who regarded logging as their chief or only occupation. About one-half of the logging labour force lived in Ontario; about one-quarter came in each year from Quebec, while the remainder came mainly from Manitoba and Saskatchewan. This pattern of hiring workers kept labour costs down. Wage rates were low due to the abundance of seasonal labour. Even in 1946, when there was little unemployment in Canada, the Department of Labour reported the wage rates in logging were lower than in all of Canada's leading industries.[14] In addition, training costs were minimal. Many bushworkers had first learned to cut and haul logs on their own farm woodlots, and others were taught by experienced men on the job.[15]

The decentralized organizational structure of pulpwood logging also mirrored the long-established patterns of the lumber industry. Like the biggest lumber firms, pulp and paper corporations often hired hundreds or even thousands of men who lived in 100-man camps scattered throughout the companies' timber limits. It was far cheaper to build camps within walking distance of the timber than to build access roads suitable for vehicular traffic. Consequently, camps were crude, temporary structures designed to last three seasons or so, until the timber within a radius of a couple of miles had been harvested. The different terrain and timber types also encouraged decentralization, so that practices could be easily modified to meet local conditions. Each camp fell under the direction of a camp boss who was in some instances an employee of the company and in others a "jobber" or subcontractor. In either case, the camp boss was responsible for the overall plan for harvesting in his area. Equally important, he was expected to be strong-willed and physically powerful so that he could maintain discipline in the camp. Each of the pulp and paper companies had a woodlands manager who, along with his small staff, worked in an office some distance from the camp, often in the mill town. Information flowed between the woodlands office and the camps via the "walking boss" who regularly moved among the various camps. As far as bushworkers were concerned, however, "the boss" was the camp boss whom they saw daily: he had the authority to hire and fire.[16]

Although the camp boss's word was final, the actual work performed by bushworkers allowed them considerable flexibility and independence on the job. Logging operations began each year in late August or September, after the worst of the fly and mosquito season was over, but early enough to allow cutters time to fell plenty of timber before the snow became deep and constricting. Harvesting white pines and hardwoods for the lumber market had demanded team work, since it took two men to drive a cross-cut saw through the big trees. Since pulpwood timber is soft and has a smaller average diameter, one man could fell on his own, using his axe for notching the tree and his bucksaw for felling. The camp boss, or a strip boss, assigned a strip of timber about 66 feet wide and 660 feet long to each cutter. Throughout the cutting season, each cutter toiled independently on his own strip each day, rarely seeing a fellow worker or even a supervisor. On the basis of his experience and skills, the cutter assessed the timber on his strip, determining the best direction and pattern to fell the trees in order to execute the subsequent steps rapidly and safely. After felling a few trees, he would remove the tops and branches and then "buck" the trees into four- or eight-foot logs. Toward the end of the day, he assembled his day's cut into neat piles ready to be measured by company employees known as "scalers."[17]

Cutting by hand was exhausting work. In order to minimize waste, trees had to be cut close to the ground and, therefore, fellers spent most of their days stooped over uncomfortably. Deep snow made felling all the more tiring, as cutters had to struggle through drifts. It took tremendous reserves of strength to pile eight-foot logs, an activity that a 1946 Ontario Royal Commission recommended be abandoned on "humanitarian grounds."[18] Cutting was also very dangerous. Fellers manipulated sharp cutting tools, often when standing on icy ground that prevented sure footings. Because each tree presented unique dangers, even the most experienced bushworkers needed to be constantly alert to a host of hazards, such as timber falling out of control and deadwood tumbling down from above. There was a grim humour, as well as a sense of bravado, in the colourful terminology bushworkers used to describe these various dangers: "widow-makers," "drunken sailors," "barberchairs," "foolcatchers," and "kickbacks."[19]

After the cutters had been at work for a few weeks, other men began "skidding," that is, dragging the logs with a horse and chain from the pile on the strip to skidways at the roadside. Here, too, the work was usually undertaken by an individual working on his own, using well-developed skills to control his horse and loads so that the logs would move smoothly and steadily out of the cutting area. In many operations, the men who did the skidding piled the logs at the skidways, but sometimes additional, strong young men performed the task that, according to surveys, most bushworkers regarded as the most exhausting.[20] Although logging was onerous, some men enjoyed bush life. Naturally, winter wages were the major incentive for working in the woods, and many men would probably have preferred steady indoor jobs had they been available. Some old-timers, however, say they preferred outdoor work in the woods to the confinement and discipline of factories and mills.[21] For men who enjoyed hunting, fishing, and other forms of wilderness recreation, woodswork probably did offer certain attractions. Perhaps, too, some men saw logging as a challenge, a test of their physical strength and stamina. In this way, logging may have had a machismo appeal.[22]

Logging work was made more varied by the ever-changing combinations of terrain and trees. Each cutting strip presented a unique situation that required adjustments on the part of workers. For decades, management had recognized regretfully that the work could never be fully controlled from above or routinized. In a 1912 *Canada Lumberman* article entitled "Scientific Management in Lumbering," Yale logging professor R.C. Bryant lamented:

It is doubtful if there is any close analogy between the workshop or factory with its specialized production, continuous operation without reference to climatic conditions; and the camp in the forest with its constantly changing crews, with climatic conditions which may hinder or prevent operations for a certain period, and where every acre logged and every tree felled may present a new problem.[23]

Judgment and flexibility were required. The best fellers carefully planned the cut, determining the direction trees should fall in order to economize on effort, facilitate subsequent steps, and ensure safety. Adjustments in felling procedures were needed to allow for bowed trunks, fire scars, uneven tops, and gusting winds. *Globe and Mail* journalist Arthur Cole described the skills of the cutters he saw at an Abitibi camp northeast of Iroquois Falls in 1947:

A real artist minimizes the heavy labour for himself by dropping the trees within inches of where he wants them. And that is no mean trick, any novice of the game will find. By dropping the tree mid-way across his skid-pile, the real artist can cut into lengths, strip the branches and pile neatly with little more than a twist of the wrists or the leverage afforded by a handy pike pole.[24]

A good teamster also had skills. He knew how to select the best location for trails in order to avoid zigzagging, rambling, and steep slopes. He sensed when to rest his horse and knew the appropriate load size given the ground conditions.[25] It took a considerable amount of experience – perhaps several seasons – before bushworkers acquired expertise.

Pulpwood cutting and skidding jobs had two characteristics commonly associated with skilled jobs: a significant amount of job autonomy and a fairly long period of job-learning time. Why, then, were woodsworkers widely regarded as "unskilled"? Part of the answer may lie in the outdoor nature of the work and the enormous amount of heavy lifting involved, characteristics shared with the pick-and-shovel work of unskilled labourers. More important was the logging labour market. Because so many men were available who knew the work, perhaps from farm woodlot experience, their skills were taken for granted. The skill content of logging went largely unrecognized and unrewarded because of attitudes shaped by the labour market. Furthermore, on account of the failure to unionize logging in the period before World War II, observers grouped woodsworkers with the unorganized and unskilled, rather than with unionized craftsmen.[26]

Nearly all workers who cut, skidded, and piled – and this amounted to most bushworkers – were paid on a piece-rate basis, their output being determined by measuring the volume of wood prepared. Companies preferred the piece-rate system because it reduced the problems of supervising a physically dispersed work force and it provided a strong incentive for workers to maximize their productivity. Piecework and a low capital/labour ratio made for a powerful managerial strategy, one that proved profitable for corporations in other industries as well.[27] Piecework, however, had a number of disadvantages for workers. The lure of higher incomes drove men to work hard and fast with few breaks. Given the heavy nature of the work, this put a severe strain on their physical well-being and exposed them to additional safety hazards.[28] Piecework also increased the chances of suffering from unfair practices of foremen and strongly encouraged workers to co-operate with, and even bribe, their strip bosses.[29] Since forest conditions are never uniform, bosses could assign the strips with the best timber and cleanest ground to their favourites, a factor that helps account for the fact that in Abitibi Power and Paper Company's Sault Division, 80 per cent of the 1950–1 harvest was cut by only 20 per cent of the crew.[30] Pieceworkers were also at the mercy of scalers who underestimated the volume of the cutters' piles of wood and marked good logs as "culls" for which bushworkers were not paid.

Yet, despite all these disadvantages, most bushworkers preferred piece-work to time work, mainly because they could make higher earnings in less time, a crucial consideration in an industry where an individual worked so few days in a year. One successful union organizer who signed up thousands of Ontario loggers in the early 1950s believes that if he had gone into the bush and said to the men that the union planned to take them off piecework and put them on a good, hourly wage, "they'd have killed me."[31] Many woodsworkers also liked the relative freedom from direct supervision. A bushworker could set his own pace, either working frantically during a short spell in the bush or more steadily for longer periods. Piecework, then, greatly enhanced the independence of bushworkers. It also encouraged them to compete among themselves for the highest cut of the day. Contractor Bill Plaunt recalls the tense competitiveness among his cutters when, at the end of each work day, they would line up at the camp office to report the size of their day's cut.[32] Each lumberjack wanted to report a total cut a bit larger than the rest. A bushworker's pride, his status among his peers, and even his manliness were tied up with his ability to turn in a respectable count.[33]

A similar spirit of competition prevailed in hauling. Workers knew that the success of a logging operation depended on getting the entire cut hauled to the dump site beside a river or railroad during the short mid-winter season when sleighs loaded with logs moved most easily along the iced logging roads.[34] Teams of men scrambled to load their sleighs to capacity in as little time as possible and then drove the horses or diesel haulers at top speeds so that their team's production would be highest at the day's end. Camp bosses naturally encouraged such competitiveness. One class-conscious Finn has recalled how these bosses would play off Finns against French Canadians by offering prizes to the highest producers. "The Finns were always suckers for a competition," says Felix Lukkarila. "Many of them were outstanding athletes in top shape" who drove themselves to achieve enormous production levels – "all for a pair of pants."[35] Although hauling was not done on a piecework basis, there were often bonuses for everyone in a camp at the end of the season if the haul had been completed by a specified date. Perhaps even more important was the proud woodsworker's satisfaction with a job well done. Old-timers often recall that in the isolated camp, men bragged about their prowess with women, but back in town, after a winter's work, they boasted about how fast they had got out their camp's cut.[36] All this boasting about physical capacities represented a distinctly masculine outlook that increased productivity – and ultimately employers' profits – at the same time as it expressed a commonality of experience and laid a basis for worker solidarity.[37]

When it came to boasting, there was no topping the river drivers. Each driver's skills were severely tested by the ubiquitous dangers of the drive.[38] Great agility and stamina were required to withstand gruelling twelve-hour days amid the jostling logs that hurtled downstream in the surge of frigid white water. Dynamiting log jams was a similarly treacherous hazard. Despite the dangers, however, companies were almost never short of manpower for the drive. "Professional" bushworkers needed spring and summer work. More-over, the hazards and the excitement had a strong appeal that was celebrated in the lusty old songs of the river drivers.[39] Here was a fine opportunity for self-reliant men to test their abilities in a life-and-death situation.

Thus, all these pulpwood logging activities were seasonal, outdoor tasks, greatly affected by nature and the weather. Dangers lurked everywhere. Yet, as pieceworkers in the bush, woodsworkers enjoyed a considerable degree of freedom from supervision. Woodswork fostered a sense of pride and independence and sometimes a keen competitiveness as well. What oppor-tunities were there for worker protest and the emergence of unions in an industry with these kinds of labour processes?

WORKER PROTEST

Until 1926 there was little union activity in the Ontario logging industry, and it would take another twenty years before a bushworkers' union would gain recognition from the pulp and paper companies. Nevertheless, worker protest was rarely, if ever, absent from the industry. Throughout the first half of the twentieth century, the most prevalent form of bushworker protest was "jumping," the woodsworker's habit of roaming from camp to camp in search of more appealing camp conditions and superior cutting "chances."[40] The decentralized organizational structure of the logging industry was partly responsible for widespread jumping. Even within a single district, there were often considerable differences among camps. Some offered clean bunkhouses with good, hearty meals; others had filthy shanties with bad grub. Some camp bosses were respected by their men; others were tyrants. Nature, too, played a role in encouraging jumping. Forest conditions are never uniform, and pieceworkers naturally preferred cutting strips where the trees were large and grew close together, and where the ground was "clean" – free of dense underbrush or muskeg.

Bushworkers also jumped for less concrete reasons. Moving to a new camp brought a change, if not a decided improvement. Boredom could be eased by finding new camp mates and working conditions. It was a way of letting off steam when tensions developed in the bunkhouse or when the boss was harassing someone. Jumping was also an expression of the bushworker's independence, an emphatic statement that he was not tied to one work site or committed to a single employer. During upswings in the business cycle, far more jumping took place than in bad times when jobs were few. Woods labour became especially unstable during both world wars, when many bushworkers enlisted in the armed forces and found jobs in urban centres. After World War II, the woods labour shortage persisted, and jumping became a major concern of woods managers. During the late 1940s, the average length of stay in a bush camp was just forty-three days. Some workers had as many as nine separate woods jobs in a season. One management study lamented: "If we hire 100 men, 13 of the original do not stay more than one week on the job, 50 of them do not complete one month's work."[41] Such high labour turnover rates added considerably to production costs by increasing administrative expenses, transportation charges, and feeding bills. When a worker jumped, he was not necessarily making a conscious protest. Yet the total effect of widespread jumping amounted to an expensive "problem" for the corporations.

Bushworkers also protested in a deliberate and collective way through their union activity. Ontario woodsworkers began organizing for the first time during World War I as part of the militant organizing drive of the Industrial Workers of the World ("Wobblies") who had been organizing West Coast loggers for some time.[42] Similarly, during the upsurge of militancy and radicalism that followed the war, organizers from the British Columbia-based Lumber Workers Industrial Union (LWIU) and from the One Big Union signed up members in Ontario.[43] But little was accomplished before internal disputes and the sharp recession beginning in 1921 virtually put an end to union activity in the Ontario bush. The breakthrough came in 1926. In that year Finnish immigrant members of the Communist Party of Canada and Finnish Wobblies co-operated in leading a large strike of pulpcutters in the Port Arthur district.[44] Although union recognition was not won, the union succeeded in gaining piece-rate increases and camp improvements. Thereafter, there was a continuing union presence in the Ontario pulpwood logging industry.

There are many reasons that help to explain why organizational progress was limited before 1926. Bushworkers were difficult to organize on account of the instability of the "unskilled" work force. Because of the abundance of workers willing to harvest pulpwood in the winters, bosses usually found it easy to replace union "agitators." With such high labour-turnover rates, a union organizer might sign up members at one camp, only to find that a month or two later the personnel had changed drastically or the camp had been closed for the season.[45] Bushworkers lacked permanent communities and the kinds of institutions and neighbourhoods that helped form the basis for union contacts in, for example, mining towns.[46] Moreover, for 70 per cent of bushworkers, logging was not their only occupation. They had little stake in the industry: a short strike for immediate improvements might make sense, but there was little appeal in long-term union membership or a long strike that could eliminate a winter's income.

Other factors related to the labour process also made unionization difficult. The scattered nature of the camps, the physical obstacles, and the ever-shifting forest frontier made it hard for organizers to make contact with employees, stay in touch with members, and organize effective picket lines.[47] Although most bushworkers worked for large corporations, the face-to-face relationship between camp bosses and their men meant that employer/employee relations resembled those of the small firm. Perhaps, too, piecework and the isolation of felling on a strip fostered a competitive and individualistic thrust among the work force that made solidarity elusive. Even the hazards of logging usually affected individuals alone, in contrast to mining where fears of accidents and disasters encouraged solidarity.[48] However, these same structural factors also provided opportunities for union growth. Camps brought together groups of men who shared similar working and living situations and a common camp culture. In the all-male environment of the bunkhouse, camp mates had the time and opportunity to discuss common grievances. Poor food, for instance, was often the catalyst for a strike threat. Union organizers could build on these camp-level grievances, pointing out that union action could bring improvements. Similarly, jumping helped to make workers aware that grievances were not unique to one camp, but were part of a much wider problem that had to be fought throughout the industry.[49]

During the late 1920s and 1930s, union organizers seized these opportunities in their struggle to build a union movement among Ontario bushworkers. In the forefront of the struggle were the "red" Finns, many of them political exiles from their homeland.[50] Through the strong networks of Finnish-Canadian cultural societies, co-operatives, and sports clubs throughout northern Ontario, they had been able to organize hundreds of Finnish bushworkers. Most of these immigrants were not necessarily "reds" at first, but they were swayed by the radical leaders with their influential halls and newspapers in the closely knit, Finnish immigrant community. Finnish pulpcutters became immersed in a radical culture, reading the daily Sudbury newspaper *Vapaus* ("Liberty") and the northern Ontario monthly magazine *Metsätyöläinen* ("The Lumber Worker").[51] One Finnish old-timer has recalled that in the bunkhouse "our entertainment was to argue over politics ... I was a White ... Sometimes there were Reds all around my bunk trying to convert me."[52] In 1930, an Abitibi company official told a meeting of woodlands managers that if one "red" Finn enters a company camp, "he will ruin your whole camp ... if he can get anyone to listen to him."[53]

Finnish organizers did find an attentive audience among a woods work force fed up with primitive camp conditions, the favouritism of some bosses, and low wages. Recent immigrants were particularly determined to maximize their earnings in order to get a good start and save money for a farm during the tough, early years in Canada. It was in the Sault Ste Marie and Thunder Bay districts, where most of the northern Europeans worked, that this Finnish radical culture led to union breakthroughs. There, Finnish organizers, such as Alf Hautamaki, Karl Salo, and A.T. Hill, along with some Swedes and others, helped build a remarkably militant union that fought some of the most bitter strikes in Ontario during the late 1920s and 1930s.[54] In these often violent battles, the union sometimes won better pay rates. But during the 1930s, the big companies refused to sign agreements with the Lumber Workers' Industrial Union of Canada or its successor, the Lumber and Sawmill Workers Union (popularly known as Lumber and Saw).[55]

Partly as a result of the frequent strikes in the logging industry, Ontario's Hepburn government introduced the Industrial Standards Act (ISA) in 1935, legislation aimed at reducing industrial conflict and stabilizing wages across this industry as well as others. Under the act, the minister of labour brought together employer and employee representatives in an industry to negotiate wage rates for the industry in their region. If the minister believed the representatives were genuinely representative, and if the meetings resulted in agreement on wage rates, then orders in council declared these minimum rates to be binding for all the industry's workers in that region for a one-year period. Although the act had little impact in most industries, wage agreements were reached in the logging sector. Employers were anxious to end work stoppages as well as the wage-cutting practices of some small operators, and the union was pleased to gain tacit recognition.[56] During World War II, the federal War Labour Relations Board encouraged management and union representatives to negotiate a whole range of contentious issues.[57] As a result of these instances of state intervention, an informal collective bargaining relationship developed between the Lumber and Saw and the major pulp and paper companies.

At the end of World War II, labour was "on the march" throughout Canada. Unions were determined to win improvements and rights long deferred by depression and war. Bushworkers were no exception. In November 1946, Ontario woodsworkers, in far larger numbers than ever before, fought a province-wide strike for union recognition and wage and camp improvements. After holding out for three weeks while the demand for paper boomed, Ontario's pulp and paper companies conceded defeat. They signed the first industry-wide agreement with the Lumber and Saw and granted most of its demands. The union victory was a triumph of rank and file militancy and effective leadership under Swedish-born union official Bruce Magnuson, a left-winger who was widely respected among bushworkers for his long years of dedication to the union and his knowledge of the forest industry and its workers.[58]

Immediately after the 1946 strike, the union began to campaign to educate members in the use of the grievance and seniority provisions in their new contracts. At long last Ontario's woodsworkers had some protection from the discriminatory actions of bosses and scalers. "Jumping" was no longer their only recourse, although turnover rates remained high for some time. In 1951 the union was severely disrupted when, in the midst of the McCarthy era, the Lumber and Saw's parent organization, the United Brotherhood of Carpenters and Joiners, ousted local leaders for their communist leanings.[59] Soon, however, the corporations were once again faced with a fiesty, albeit non-communist, organization that proved able to win significant wage gains. Effective leadership in the early 1950s was given by André Wellsby, a one-time mill office employee at Spruce Falls Power and Paper Company in Kapuskasking, and his brother-in-law Lothar Bode, a recent German immigrant who proved to be a superb organizer, fine researcher, and shrewd negotiator. To Bode goes the credit for designing and successfully negotiating a system of timber classification that provided for higher piece rates on poor timber strips. Timber classification reduced the arbitrary authority of bosses who had previously assigned the best timber to favourites. By the mid 1950s, the leadership had gone to a veteran pulpcutter with a thorough knowledge of bushwork, as well as collective bargaining and grievance procedures, Tulio Mior, who has remained in charge ever since.[60]

A key reason for the union's success in winning improved wages, piece rates, and conditions during the late 1940s and the 1950s, however, was not leadership, but rather the labour-shortage problem in the logging industry. The neat dovetailing of labour requirements among seasonal industries was breaking down. A 1950 study undertaken for the industry showed that the preceding dozen years had seen an average annual net migration away from Canadian farms of 50,000 people, a significant statistic – given that half Ontario's logging labour force was composed of agriculturalists.[61] In 1955, one analyst noted that "with higher farm incomes in recent years, the urgency of need for some supplementary winter work became weaker."[62] Furthermore, as Canadian workers in the post-war period became accustomed to more regular employment as well as better incomes and benefits, logging seemed less attractive. In addition, many former bushworkers had learned new skills in the armed forces during the war that enabled them to work at steady, well-paid jobs in urban centres.

Naturally, the corporations' difficulties in attracting workers to their camps was a tremendous advantage for union leaders, who, during the decade following World War II, were repeatedly able to win real wage gains. This had a snowballing effect. Because the Lumber and Saw became widely known as a union that could "deliver," it easily recruited members who stood willing to support their leaders' tough bargaining positions. And because of the better incomes and conditions, large numbers of post-war immigrants – men with families and some education – showed an interest in staying in the industry and therefore took a greater interest in the future of their union.[63] For many of these immigrants, the union was perhaps the only institution that welcomed them and offered them protection, relevant services, and a chance to participate in the new society. Whereas woodsworkers had hesitated to pay $3 initiation dues in 1951, by the mid 1950s they had agreed in a referendum to raise dues to $25. Of course, they now could better afford higher dues. Weekly earnings of eastern Canadian loggers rose from their 1941 level *below* Canada's eight major industries to a 1951 level *above* all major industries.[64] Stories are told of bachelor pulpcutters who, in the 1950s, gambled with Cadillacs in camp poker games!

By the early 1950s, then, it seemed that bushworkers and their union had gained a strong position. Management had to contend with high rates of labour turnover, a dwindling supply of workers, and an increasingly powerful union ready to take advantage of the labour-market situation. In short, labour had forced management onto the defensive.

MANAGEMENT'S MECHANIZATION STRATEGY

Most Ontario woodlands managers recognized that new departures would be necessary if their firms were to flourish in the booming, but highly competitive post-war marketplace. After the war, pulp and paper producers in the southern United States expanded production rapidly. In comparison to the Ontario industry, they enjoyed such advantages as cheaper labour, more accessible and faster-growing forests, and efficient new mills. They were quickly gaining a greater share of American markets that had previously been supplied by Ontario mills. Since labour costs represented more than half the total cost of pulpwood delivered at the mill, rapidly rising woods wage rates alarmed pulp and paper executives in Ontario.[65] If their costs were to continue spiralling upwards as a result of increased labour costs, then Ontario paper would be priced out of its American markets.

The Ontario logging industry responded to its dilemma with two strategies. First, Canadian pulp and paper companies sought to increase the labour supply. Executives pressured the Canadian government to recruit new immigrants to logging camps.[66] Much to the initial consternation of woods union officials, logging camps did provide a first home for thousands of new arrivals from Europe, though, from management's perspective, the labour pool was never big enough. At the same time, some innovative companies tried to lure more workers to their camps and avoid costly wildcat strikes by providing more attractive living conditions – bunkhouses with two-man rooms, recreation facilities, and sports programs.[67] However, as long as camps remained only temporary, companies could afford to spend little on such improvements. These measures succeeded in holding down costs only to a limited degree.

Management's second and more promising strategy was to lower costs and increase productivity by stabilizing the work force and developing new, mechanized logging systems. In fact, the two were closely related, since labour stability depended on finding year-round, mechanized methods that would reduce the industry's dependence on snow, ice, and spring thaws, and permit easier access to camps. The woodlands managers' chief rationale for mechanization was reducing costs. Labour-saving equipment, they believed, would raise workers' productivity and cut the woods labour force. This would ease the problem of attracting enough workers to the woods and reduce the costs of feeding and housing them. In this way, Ontario companies might remain competitive while still paying the higher wages and providing the better conditions necessary to attract labour. Advocates expected that the lighter jobs of mechanized operations would prove more appealing to workers. They also hoped that mechanized methods would permit better use of forest resources and improve forest regeneration.[68]

Finding cost-effective mechanical methods for Ontario's bush land had long frustrated logging engineers and woodlands managers. During a previous crisis period – the years of war-related labour shortage in 1917–20 – eastern Canadian woodlands managers had formed the Woodlands Section of the Canadian Pulp and Paper Association to pool information about production techniques and to examine new, mechanized methods. Throughout the next three decades, the section found ways to cut costs in the hauling and driving phases of logging by introducing track vehicles and trucks, but little progress was made in felling and skidding where it seemed that equipment developed for other industries could not be easily adapted to the North.[69] Ontario's small-diameter trees, mix of species, muskeg, swamps, rock, and rolling terrain prevented logging engineers, with relatively limited amounts of capital at their disposal, from finding effective alternatives to conventional methods as long as labour remained so cheap. Adapting the methods of the West Coast logging industry, where the extremely rugged terrain and huge timber of British Columbia's coastal forests had forced lumbermen to develop mechanized methods almost from the industry's start in the nineteenth century, had not proven very successful. Neither had deploying farm tractors, which were widely used in the less rugged logging regions of Europe and the southern United States.[70] After numerous disappointments, many woods managers had grown skeptical of new-fangled equipment, while top executives of the pulp and paper companies, almost all of whom had received their training in the mills, were far more reluctant to invest in new woods machinery than in mill equipment.[71]

Nevertheless, when faced with the acute problems of the post-World War II period, the Woodlands Section set about the task of mechanizing with renewed vigour. In 1948, the section set up various committees to promote mechanization, and that summer the first annual outdoor mechanical-hauling meeting was held, at which attention was drawn to the acute need for mechanization at the stump and in the skidding phase.[72] The following year, the Woodlands Section's senior logging expert and long-time advocate of mechanization, Alexander Koroleff, published his *Stability as a Factor in Efficient Forest Management*, which thoroughly documented the case for mechanization. About the same time, W.A.E. Pepler and B.J. McColl, talented forest engineers with the Woodlands Section, presented an imaginative report that called for a re-conceptualization of logging along the lines of tree-length and full-tree methods, so that more steps could be performed under more controlled conditions at central points. The report also suggested developing multi-operation processing equipment that would perform several functions such as bucking, limbing, and debarking.[73] Even more important was Pepler and McColl's equipment-development project begun in the early 1950s under the auspices of the Woodlands Mechanization Committee, using funds from a special assessment of participating companies.[74] This proved to be the most complete expression of inter-company co-operation in the mechanization field.

Ultimately, the Ontario region, driven by the highest wage costs and strongest woods union in eastern North America, became a leader in successfully developing mechanized pulpwood-logging methods. The big Ontario corporations, with their easier access to capital and large-scale operations directly under company control, had both the financial resources and the opportunity to benefit from new logging systems intended to permit "the application of quantity methods."[75] Well before the industry-sponsored programs began to bear fruit, however, external developments had brought a major technological advance to the industry. In the early 1950s, many Ontario bushworkers began abandoning axes and handsaws for gasoline-powered chainsaws. Although the first United States chainsaw patent had been issued in 1858, not until after World War II did the technologies of light metals and air-cooled engines enable several equipment manufacturers to offer practical chainsaws.[76] They found a lucrative market in the North, as some companies and many pieceworkers purchased the new saws to improve productivity. A poor cutter could almost double his daily output with the new tool.

Meanwhile, the available supplies of horses, teamsters, and their equipment declined rapidly as farming and transportation were mechanized. Pulp and paper companies were compelled to invest in finding a mechanical substitute that could perform in the backwoods with the agility of the horse and, in addition, skid logs throughout the year. In the mid 1950s, equipment manufacturers introduced four-wheel drive tractors such as the "Blue Ox." However, they manoeuvred poorly and caused spinal injuries to many operators.[77] The breakthrough came in the late 1950s, partly as a result of the Woodlands Section's equipment-development project, which pioneered the concepts for the "articulated wheeled skidder," a diesel-powered vehicle designed especially for skidding logs in the boreal forest region. The skidder's huge, low-pressure tires gave it the floatation required for travelling over some types of muskeg, while it could manoeuvre around obstacles and "duckwalk" across soft terrain because of its articulated steering. A hydraulic scoop at the front aided piling. One of the most successful of the new skidders was the "Timberjack," designed and manufactured by a Canadian firm in Woodstock, Ontario. Sales were brisk: the number of wheeled skidders of this type on eastern Canadian logging operations increased from 62 in 1960 to 2160 in 1965 and 3550 in 1969. Skidders and other new methods resulted in a 45 per cent increase in the amount of wood cut by production workers per man-hour between 1954–5 and 1964–5. This substantial improvement in productivity kept production costs down, despite rising wage rates.[78]

Skidders remained popular, but a revolutionary technological development, the mechanical harvester, hit many operations in the 1960s and 1970s. Harvesters were developed by several equipment manufacturers who were finally convinced that the pulp and paper companies were serious about investing capital in good machines. In other instances, pulp and paper companies sought to gain advantages over their competitors by secretly developing new machines on their own or in partnership with other pulp and paper firms.[78] The risks proved high, whatever the approach.

Numerous types of harvesting machines were built during the 1960s, but by the end of the decade, one of the most impressive was the Koehring Short-Wood Harvester, an expensive, 95,000 pound machine designed to fell, top, limb, buck, and accumulate eight-foot pulpwood.[80] Some are still in use in the North today. The machine utterly dwarfs its single operator. By controlling numerous levers, gadgets, and joysticks, the operator guides his harvester through the forest, using the machine's huge hydraulic shears to fell the trees, which are then automatically processed into logs and stored at the rear of the vehicle. As it turned out, however, the machine's "downtime" was too high. Automatic-processing components were not rugged enough to withstand the jolting of travel in the backwoods. When a single part broke down, the entire harvesting and processing system ground to a halt. Consequently, the trend recently has been to use harvesters that fell the trees, bunch a few together, and bring them to a roadside clearing. Further processing is performed there by equipment that need not be as ruggedly built. Under ideal conditions, the latest equipment can cut some 150–180 small trees per hour.[81]

The final phase in the logging cycle – transporting logs from the bush to the mill – was also mechanized during the 1950s and 1960s. Pulp and paper firms, lumber companies, and the provincial government poured huge amounts of capital into constructing some 11,000 miles of logging access roads.[82] As a result, the sleigh haul and river drive utterly vanished. Now, logs piled at roadside clearings in the bush are loaded onto trucks by means of power loaders and transported directly to the mill, railway, or port. Many roads can be kept open for most of the year, and so pulp and paper firms have a steadier flow of logs to the mills and the high cost of storing enormous supplies of pulpwood at the mill are eliminated.[83]

All these innovations were part of a conscious corporate strategy to cut production costs by deploying labour-saving technologies. These new techniques did not simply appear on the scene: they were developed and implemented by capital in response to product market competition, labour scarcity, and instability, as well as trade-union pressure on wage rates. The case of pulpwood logging in Ontario differs substantially from earlier developments in manufacturing where several studies have argued that mechanization was primarily an employer's attack on the craftsman's control over his work.[84] It remains to be seen whether, in seeking to gain control over rising costs, managers in the pulpwood-logging industry had also gained greater control over workers and their workplace.

MECHANIZED BUSHWORK

Each new technological development altered the logging labour process, though in different ways and to varying extents, depending on the specific case. The chainsaw brought relatively few changes. It simply replaced the axe and bucksaw without reorganizing the work. Pulpcutting remained a highly independent job, paid by the piece. Few experienced cutters found it hard to learn how to handle and maintain a chainsaw. Because of its productivity advantages, it was readily accepted by pieceworkers. Moreover, the chainsaw eliminated some of the backbreaking drudgery of felling by hand.[85]

From the worker's standpoint, the chainsaw's chief drawbacks were the increased health and safety hazards. Power saws could rip through flesh at a terrifying speed. It was only too easy for a cutter to saw through a tree so fast that he lost control and risked being crushed by the falling timber. The grizzly results are evident in 1950s statistics that show a sharply rising trend in disabling accidents involving power equipment.[86] Piecework increases the dangers, for loggers paid on an incentive basis take less time to check for hazards and to plan escape routes.[87] Today, logging still has the highest fatality rate of any Ontario industry.[88]

Equally alarming is the occupational disease known to loggers as "white finger," a condition that results from chainsaw vibration. It has been estimated that about one-quarter of Canada's loggers now suffer from this condition. It begins with a numbness in the fingers and can eventually result in permanent loss of the use of the hand.[89] Similarly, chainsaw users often suffered hearing damage before they began to use protective ear muffs. Yet, these health and safety hazards did little to deter cutters from using powersaws because they lightened the work and permitted increased earnings without fundamentally altering the job.

Unlike the chainsaw, the introduction of the wheeled skidder brought profound changes in the labour process. The kinds of skills required to operate and maintain skidders were quite different from those of the teamster and blacksmith. It took some mechanical aptitude and a little experience with diesel equipment to operate a skidder with even a modicum of success. A competent operator had to learn how to manoeuvre the machine in tight spots, dodge trees, rocks, and other obstacles, and avoid becoming mired in muskeg. It helped, too, if a skidder operator could perform basic repairs, thereby eliminating long waits for a mechanic that cut into piecework earnings.[90]

When managers first introduced skidders in the 1950s, they often hired men from outside the logging industry who had experience with diesel equipment. Similarly, camp blacksmiths frequently knew little about main-taining and repairing diesel equipment, and so skilled mechanics had to be lured to the bush. Increasingly in the 1960s, however, young men interested in logging jobs brought mechanical expertise acquired on mechanized farms and construction sites and in technical training courses. Because logging was comparatively late to mechanize, there were many workers already prepared for the new kinds of jobs. Old-timers with redundant skills tried to find jobs in pockets of the industry that were slower to mechanize, such as jobbers' camps or in some saw-log operations.[91]

Skidders brought other changes as well. The bushworker lost some of his independence. Teamwork was needed in the "cut-and-skid" system.[92] Since skidders could operate nearly year-round, cutting and skidding could be closely synchronized, ensuring a smooth and comparatively continuous flow of wood. Moreover, the wheeled skidder's ability to pull several full trees or tree-length logs at a time enabled management to introduce a further division of labour. Instead of fellers cutting the trees into short lengths at the stump, trees could be cut up and piled under more controlled conditions at the roadside. At first this was done by "bucker-pilers" – men using chainsaws and brute strength. A crew was composed of a cutter on his strip and a bucker-piler at the roadside. The skidder operator skidded for a few crews, the number depending on skidding distances as well as ground and weather conditions. He became the co-ordinator and pace-setter for his crews. In the 1960s, however, powerful mechanical slashers resembling portable sawmills and hydraulic loading equipment were brought to the roadside. Crews of skidder operators and cutters then struggled to keep pace with the powerful machines.

Whatever the approach, teamwork was the order of the day. Great Lakes Forest Products wood supervisor Don Harris maintained recently that for crews on piece rates, "piling ... is where it's won or lost. If you start fiddling around at the landing, piling, then you're wasting a lot of your skidding time. When you work together as a real team, just about every time you get to the cutter he's all set for you."[93]

That there was a partial erosion of the cutter's independence and control over the pace of his work is also evident from management debates about piece rates and training schemes. Some managers argued that incentive pay systems were no longer appropriate, since an individual's productivity was so greatly affected by other team members and the performance of the mechanical equipment itself. In addition, because the new equipment reduced the industry's dependence on fall and winter conditions, logging could be carried out throughout most of the year. There was no longer any point in encouraging loggers to work at a feverish pace for short periods of time.[94] Therefore, some companies eliminated piecework. On the other hand, piece rates and bonus systems were retained in some firms because experts insisted that some 40 per cent of the variation in productivity among machine-operators was due to skill and motivation.[95] Similarly, some companies saw advantages in introducing training programs for operators; others preferred the cheap, customary, on-the-job approach. There was, thus, no consensus about whether it was more advantageous for managers to intrude into the training field, an area hitherto controlled largely by workers themselves. Managers who continued to support incentive pay systems and the retention of informal training methods were indicating that the bushworker's independence and control over aspects of his job had not yet vanished.

Like skidders, harvesters also resulted in several important changes in the labour process. The working environment changed drastically. Since operators worked in enclosed cabs, they were no longer exposed to familiar logging hazards such as sharp cutting edges and falling trees. "Heaters in winter, fans in summer, portable air conditioning units, insecticides, lighting systems, etc. can, as far as the worker is concerned, turn night into day and winter into summer," enthused one observer in 1966.[96] In fact, however, health hazards and discomforts were still numerous. High noise levels, vibrations, and jolting frequently caused hearing and back problems. All too often, cabs were badly ventilated and overheated. As one manager admitted in 1981: "Machine operations improved many a job, but it never became a guarantee for a good working environment."[97]

Skill requirements changed just as drastically. A visitor to a harvester cockpit is likely to be intimidated by the numerous gauges, levers, pedals, and joysticks, to say nothing of the gargantuan proportions of the machine itself. Keen visual perception and dexterity are needed to operate these complicated machines,[98] although physical strength is no longer a requirement. Partly as a result of the new emphasis on dexterity rather than strength, some women have been hired recently to operate the big, new machines. Harvester operators require less knowledge of the forest since the same techniques can be used on all types of trees. In contrast, sophisticated skills are required of mechanics who maintain and repair the diesel engines, automatic transmissions, and hydraulic and electrical systems.[99] The introduction of harvesters reduced the independence of bushworkers. Because they are costly machines to purchase, operate, and maintain, woodlands departments soon became anxious to minimize machine downtime in order to ensure optimal output from their substantial capital investments. Harvester operators are more closely supervised because managers believe supervisors can pressure workers to maintain a fast pace, reduce operator abuse of equipment, and attend quickly to any production snags. In some operations, two supervisors were assigned to every four-to-six operators.[100]

In the case of harvesters, then, there has been a narrowing of the individual worker's responsibilities. No longer does he (or she) do as much planning or repair work. These jobs have been assigned to supervisors and mechanics. No longer is the worker isolated on a strip; instead supervisors keep a close watch over operations. Harvester operators more closely resemble the semi-skilled machine-operators of the twentieth-century factory than bushworkers have at any time in the past.

The introduction of truck transport has also drastically altered aspects of bush life. The competitiveness, liveliness, and headlong rush of hauling and river driving had been entirely swept away. In their place is the far less colourful, but steadier, work of driving trucks throughout the greater part of the year. Truck drivers enjoy a measure of independence because they spend most of their working hours on their own. But they are on the fringes of logging operations; they need to know little about logging itself and have little contact with camp workers. Many truck drivers are contractors or employees of trucking firms, and they usually live in town, travelling into the bush each morning along the access roads.[101] These roads have had profound effects on the lives of loggers. Since bush-camp workers can be bused from camp to their work sites, pulp and paper companies can afford to build more permanent camps – designed to last up to twenty years – that have much improved facilities and furnishings.[102] Collective agreements now contain clauses concerning colour TVs, air conditioning, and humidifiers. In many operations camps have been eliminated altogether. Employees commute daily or weekly by bus and car as many as 175 miles between their homes and logging sites. For these workers, life has been "normalized." They can own houses, marry, and live with their families. Those working in woodlands division depot garages located in the mill towns and cities, and those working in commuter camps, find that logging has become a way of life much more similar to that experienced by workers in most other industries.[103]

This trend has been encouraged by other factors as well. Because machines have lightened the work, far more men continue logging until they reach retirement age. Mechanization also drastically reduces the seasonality of forest work. Most jobs are nearly year-round, which reduced turnover and permits steadier incomes. Shift work, too, has been introduced. Now harvesters operate at night in the glare of brilliant floodlights. Furthermore, the industry now employs many mechanics and heavy-equipment operators, workers widely respected for their skills and in demand in other industries.

All these changes of the 1960s and 1970s have had a strong impact on the composition of the work force, which is now divided into two distinct parts.[104] One group works in woodlands-department garages in town and in commuter operations. With their more attractive jobs and seniority, this labour force is strikingly different from the traditional logging crew. Most are highly experienced, older workers who have families and homes in the area. The second group works in the dozens of remote camps. These tend to be younger, single men who are willing to forgo the conveniences and pleasures of urban life in order to save some money and learn a skill like welding or equipment operating. Among this latter group, turnover rates have remained high because so many quit to find jobs in more attractive locations. Not surprisingly, the skilled mechanic will usually avoid a job that requires him to fiddle for hours with a skidder's temperamental carburetor in howling arctic gales. Even amid the rising unemployment of the 1970s, manpower shortages in remote areas were common.[105] In contrast to the past, neither of these two distinct groups contains many recent immigrants or agriculturalists.

Thus, mechanization has drastically transformed labour processes in pulpwood logging. No simple deskilling model satisfactorily describes the trends in the industry.[106] The old-time bushworker with his unappreciated skills has disappeared. Today, loggers engage in a variety of jobs that demand different kinds of skills, have various levels of skill content, and permit workers different amounts of independence on the job.

WORKERS' RESPONSES
TO MECHANIZATION

Generally speaking, Ontario bushworkers and their union heartily welcomed the numerous changes brought about by the construction of access roads and by mechanization. The elimination of bull work, steadier jobs, and a closer integration with other types of work and with urban communities – these seemed obvious advantages of the new methods. Rather than simply deskilling the work, mechanization has altered the kinds of skills required and increased the demand for highly skilled mechanics. Prestige, too, is associated with operating the big, powerful harvesters – the "muscle cars" of the bush.[107]

The main attraction of the new methods was the higher and steadier incomes that accompanied innovations. Tough union bargaining during a period of labour scarcity ensured that some corporate savings resulting from productivity increases were passed on to workers. Bushworkers have always put a very high priority on maximizing their incomes. A large proportion of the logging labour force took bush jobs in remote locations only because of the industry's better wages and opportunities for saving money. (Daily board charges in logging camps in 1983 were still only $1.75!) Any new method that would permit making a bigger stake was heartily welcomed. Jake Hildebrand, a thirty-year veteran woodcutter, recently explained that even the first chainsaws, which still had many "bugs," were "quite a thing for us at the time ... You could do more, you could produce more and limb easier. Everybody was for it."[108]

In the late 1950s, the union hailed the benefits of mechanization, declaring that it was "rapidly making progress and show[ing] signs of improvement of productivity, lower costs, higher wages and better working and living conditions." The Lumber and Saw even claimed some of the credit for mechanization: "The union has done its part to bring about this change to mechanical operations. Even increasing wages slowly, put a prohibitive price tag on the old types of piecework operations." The union went so far as to complain that "far too little" was being done "about higher mechanization, experiment and research work with the result that a great deal of effort, time and money is wasted with inefficient logging methods."[109] In stressing the practical benefits of mechanization, union leaders were no doubt expressing the feelings of the bulk of the membership. Union officials also saw potential advantages for the union itself in the form of a smaller, but more stable, membership, with members more committed to the union as a result of their long-term commitment to their jobs.

Union membership did drop dramatically – from 16,000 in 1957 to some 7,000 in 1982, indicating the profound impact of mechanization and deseasonalization on employment.[110] Yet, the corporations were faced with little worker protest in response to the declining job opportunities. Men were choosing to move into other industries in any case. Moreover, the high turnover rates and regular seasonal lay-offs in the 1950s obviated the need for mass lay-offs.[111] No doubt, during the fifties, some men did suffer when they could not get their old jobs back again following the annual spring lay-off. But such former employees had no direct claim on their old jobs and no ready means to organize against their former employers. Because of the unusual fluidity of the logging labour market, managers enjoyed the opportunity to introduce labour-saving equipment with little risk of labour protest. Of course, union leaders were well aware that vigilance was required to prevent management from introducing harmful practices alongside the new equipment. Each new piece of equipment required setting new piece rates or wage categories. Usually new rates were set by mutual agreement reached after thirty-day trial periods, during which workers were paid on an hourly basis. Occasionally, wildcat strikes erupted when employees believed they were being short-changed, but these were few in number.[112]

From the woods manager's point of view, a far more disturbing problem was the tendency of harvester operators to quit their jobs. Despite efforts to reduce labour turnover, managers found that many woodsworkers continued "to move to greener pastures at more or less regular intervals."[113] This was especially true of workers in remote camps. In certain respects, mechanization had even increased the tendency of workers to quit their jobs, since the skills of operators and mechanics were needed in construction, mining, and other industries. This kind of informal protest cost the pulp and paper companies money. In order to make the expensive new equipment pay, it had to operate virtually continuously. When workers quit, machine downtime increased and the continual training of new employees added to costs. In 1971, G.K. Seed, logging development engineer at Great Lakes Paper, noted that "investment in woods equipment has reached such proportions that operations can't be stopped without serious loss. Further, the job has become so skill demanding that it is difficult to satisfy operational requirements through substitution. It is essential to minimize absenteeism."[114] Managers realized, however, that eliminating high turnover and absentee rates would be difficult in remote areas where workers were always in relatively short supply. Geographical isolation enabled bushworkers to continue with their traditional forms of protest. This acted as a constraint on managers. They found that harvesters were not as productive as they had hoped and that it was best to deploy skidders as well as harvesters. Inadvertently, bushworkers' behaviour had limited the freedom of management to deploy the labour-saving technology it might otherwise have preferred. As a result, workers had helped preserve jobs and kept open the choice between working with skidders or harvesters.

This instance of worker resistance to management's innovations has important implications. It indicates that pulp and paper managers did not enjoy uncontested control over the logging labour process. As David Noble has argued in another context: "The technology of production is ... twice determined by the social relations of production: first it is designed and deployed according to the ideology and social power of those who make such decisions; and second, its actual use in production is determined by the realities of the shop-floor struggles between classes."[115]

In the case of pulpwood logging, capital was responsible for the development and introduction of a new technology, but productivity fell short of managers' expectations because of a peculiar form of "shop-floor" struggle that was directly related to the environment of remote logging sites. There are parallels with developments in another resource-extraction industry, coal mining. Michael Yarrow has found that new technology recently introduced by United States coal operators has failed partly because of "technical and geographical factors" related to the miners' "unpredictable work environment."[116] It would be worth explaining whether these two examples are representative of a wider pattern in resource industries.

RECENT CHALLENGES

The power of bushworkers to shape management decisions should not be exaggerated. Recently, it has become clear that Ontario's loggers are once again on the defensive. One of the most serious threats to workers and their union today is owner-operating, the practice whereby loggers who own their own costly equipment work on a contract or piecework basis. The transition from hand technology to mechanized methods has greatly increased fixed capital costs.[117] Consequently, some corporations have attempted to shift to owner-operators – in effect, their employees – a large chunk of the burden of these costs, the accompanying bank interest and risk involved. According to some employers, owner-operating has other advantages as well: it reduces the high cost of employee benefits (reported in 1971 at 23 per cent of total logging labour costs),[118] and, because owner-operators have a very strong incentive to work incredibly hard and fast, the firm's competitive position is enhanced and employees' incomes rise dramatically.[119]

Although owner-operating is a widespread practice elsewhere in North America, it has not been nearly so prevalent in Ontario, largely because the union has strenuously opposed it.[120] A notable failure, however, has been the case of Boise Cascade Canada, Ltd, in the Kenora and Fort Frances area of northwestern Ontario. In 1959, the company used its leverage as the major employer in the district to win the right to introduce a limited number of independent contractors. And in 1978, Boise decided to expand their numbers by selling company machinery to its employees with the declared objective of reducing costs and improving the company's competitive position.[121] The union resisted Boise's move, arguing that the spread of owner-operating would be disastrous for employees and their union. Lumber and Saw officials pointed out that owner-operators responsible for maintaining their own equipment find that repairs can be expensive and time consuming, eating into the supposedly increased earnings as well as leisure time. A skidder, powersaw, truck, and other equipment costs more than $60,000, a huge outlay requiring bank loans and substantial collateral (probably the operator's house). The worker would need steady employment to maintain payments. Lay-offs or strikes could mean falling behind in payments and losing his equipment and even his home. Consequently, even though owner-operators might be union members, they would hesitate to strike. Lumber and Saw perceived the spread of owner-operating as an attack on union solidarity, pitting regular employees against owner-operators.[122]

Beginning in August 1978, the union waged a two-year strike against Boise Canada over this issue. Bitter and frequently violent confrontations arose among strikers, contractors, and millworkers who crossed picket lines.[123] In the end, Boise won. Its logging operations are now non-union, and much of the logging is done by owner-operators. It remains to be seen whether Boise will profit from the new system and, more important, whether other companies in Ontario will follow Boise's example. Unfortunately, just when the union needs all its strength to meet this challenge, it is under attack on another front. The Boise strike revealed the lack of solidarity between millworkers and their unions on the one hand, and woods employees and their union, on the other. The long-standing social gulf between skilled, settled mill employees and the less skilled, transient men of the camps remains, even though woodsworkers have become increasingly more skilled and sedentary. The Canadian Paperworkers' Union, which has recently gained strength in the mills, is now raiding Lumber and Saw. Greater bargaining strength might result from an all-inclusive pulp and paper union, as the Canadian Paperworkers maintain. In the short term, however, the raiding will seriously weaken the position of woodsworkers and the bargaining power of their union. Lumber and Saw is even more vulnerable to raiding now that, as part of the United Brotherhood of Carpenters and Joiners of America, it has withdrawn from the Canadian Labour Congress and joined the smaller Canadian Federation of Labour, an organization dominated by construction unions with little in common with the loggers.

To this list of loggers' current problems must be added the threat of further job losses. Lumber and Saw leader Tulio Mior has recently identified rapidly dwindling timber supplies as the biggest challenge loggers face today.[124] Recent forest-management agreements between the big pulp and paper corporations and the Ministry of Environment amount to "too little too late."[125] Moreover, current logging methods do much harm to the forest environment. The heavy new equipment has worsened forest regeneration prospects, because the deep ruts left by the huge tires utterly destroy drainage systems.[126] And as long as some companies continue to use incentive pay systems, bushworkers are, in fact, discouraged from taking the time required to ensure that young growth survives. Possibly, the growing awareness that we desperately need reforestation will hasten the abandonment of incentive pay schemes and companies will be forced to pay hourly rates high enough to retain workers even in remote areas. Perhaps, then, the logging labour process will change once again in the near future.

Labour processes in Ontario's pulpwood-logging industry have undergone a host of astonishing changes since 1950. The shouts of men and the snorting of horses have given way to the screams of chainsaws and the deafening roar of diesel engines. This paper has attempted to show that workers in this resource industry have done much to shape the pace and nature of technological change. Largely because of the pulp and paper companies' problems in attracting adequate numbers of steady workers to dangerous and remote logging jobs in the improved economic climate of post-war Canada, the Lumber and Saw was able to drive a hard bargain. The union forced pulp and paper companies to grant substantial wage concessions as well as better conditions, and union members won the right to insist on fairer treatment from their bosses. In response to union pressure on wage rates that threatened the corporations' competitiveness in American markets, Ontario pulp and paper firms led the way in finding labour-saving, mechanized logging methods that increased productivity. By and large, bushworkers and their union welcomed the new methods, which brought lighter, steadier, and more remunerative jobs requiring new kinds of more widely marketable skills. However, the union has steadfastly fought to ensure that members' interests have not been overly harmed by new corporate schemes to reorganize logging methods, most notably in the case of owner-operating, which the union now perceives as a very serious threat to bushworkers and their organization.

In recent years the bushworker's autonomy on the job has decreased somewhat. Yet, in the wilderness, pulp and paper corporations have been unable to enjoy as much control over the labour process and their employees as is now found in most factories and mills. Loggers retain at least some of the independence they have long enjoyed. Despite all the changes, bushwork continues to attract many hardy men who take pride in their ability to perform tough, dangerous jobs in a rugged northern environment. In this respect, at least, woodsworkers still resemble the lumberjack of popular mythology.

NOTES

This paper is an outgrowth of my York University PH D dissertation, "Bushworkers and Bosses: A Social History of the Logging Industry of Northern Ontario, 1900–1980" (York University 1985), the research for which has been supported by doctoral fellowships from the Social Sciences and Humanities Research Council of Canada and by a Labour Canada research grant. For comments on earlier drafts of this paper, I would like to thank the Labour Studies Research Group and especially the editors of this volume.

1 Pierre Berton, *Hollywood's Canada* (Toronto 1975), 80. On Paul Bunyan and Joe Montferrand, see Donald MacKay, *The Lumberjacks* (Toronto 1978), 35–40. On the image of the lumberjack, see Graeme Wynn, "'Deplorably Dark and Demoralized Lumberers'?: Rhetoric and Reality in Early Nineteenth-

Century New Brunswick," *Journal of Forest History* 24, no. 4 (October 1980): 168–87.

2 This paper focuses on the work performed by employees of the woodlands departments of the pulp and paper industry, the largest and most innovative sector of the logging industry. Somewhat different patterns developed among logger-contractors who worked independently on privately owned lands, and among lumberjacks who worked in the lumber industry.

3 MacKay, *Lumberjacks*; A.R.M. Lower, *Settlement and the Forest Frontier in Eastern Canada* (Toronto 1936), *The North American Assault on the Canadian Forest* (Toronto 1938), and *"Great Britain's Woodyard" : British America and the Timber Trade, 1763–1867* (Montreal 1973); Michael S. Cross, " 'The Dark Druidical Groves' " (PH D dissertation, Toronto 1968) and "The Lumber Community of Upper Canada, 1815–1867," *Ontario History* 52 (1960): 213–33; J.W. Hughson and C.J. Bond, *Hurling Down the Pine* (Old Chelsea 1964); T. Brennan, *Lumbering in the Ottawa Valley* (Ottawa 1974); J.E. Macdonald, *Shantymen and Sodbusters* (Sault Ste Marie 1966); Chris Curtis, "Shanty Life in the Kawarthas, Ontario, 1850–1855," *Material History Bulletin* 13 (Fall 1981): 39–50; R.S. Lambert and Paul Pross, *Renewing Nature's Wealth* (Toronto 1967).

4 Ministry of Natural Resources (hereafter MNR), *The Forest Industry in the Economy of Ontario* (Toronto 1981).

5 George Carruthers, *Paper in the Making* (Toronto 1947); H.V. Nelles, *The Politics of Development* (Toronto 1974), 81–2; Trevor Dick, "The Canadian Newsprint Industry, 1900–1930," *Journal of Economic History* 42 (September 1982): 661–3.

6 J.A. Guthrie, *The Newsprint Paper Industry* (Cambridge 1941), chs 1–3; Nathan Reich, *The Pulp and Paper Industry in Canada* (Toronto 1926); Dick, "Canadian Newsprint Industry," 659–64.

7 On Clergue, see Nelles, *Politics of Development*, 56–62, 82–5, 132–8.

8 Dick, "Canadian Newsprint Industry," 660–4; L.E. Ellis, *The Print Paper Pendulum* (New Brunswick, NJ 1960); Christopher Armstrong, *The Politics of Federalism* (Toronto 1981), 31–48.

9 Nelles, *Politics of Development*, 443–64; A.E. Safarian, *The Canadian Economy in the Great Depresion* (Toronto 1970), 201–4; Tom Traves, *The State and Enterprise* (Toronto 1979), ch. 3; Guthrie, *Newsprint Paper*, chs 5–8; Dick, "Canadian Newsprint Industry," 664–5.

10 MNR, *Forest Industry*, vii, 75; On the vulnerability of a forest-based export economy and of its workers, see Patricia Marchak, *Green Gold: the Forest Industry in British Columbia* (Vancouver 1983).

11 Public Archives of Canada (hereafter PAO), RG 18, B-109, 6, Canadian Pulp and Paper Association (CPPA), "A Brief for Presentation to the Ontario Royal Commission on Forestry by Canadian Pulp and Paper Association on behalf of the Pulp and Paper Industry of Ontario, December 1946," 9–10.

12 Pulpwood Committee, "Woods Labour Inventory Report," cited in ibid., 10–11.

13 On the history of the agro-forest economy, see Lower, *Settlement*; Normand Séguin, *La Conquête du Sol au 19e Siècle* (Sillery 1977) and "L'économie agro-forestière: genèse du developpement au Saguenay au 19e siècle," in Séguin, ed., *Agriculture et colonization au Québec* (Montréal 1980); Graeme Wynn, *Timber Colony* (Toronto 1981); Chad Gaffield, "Boom and Bust: the Demography and Economy of the Lower Ottawa Valley in the Nineteenth Century," *Historical Papers 1982*, 172–95.

14 Canada, Department of Labour, *Wage Rates and Hours of Labour in Canada* 38 (Ottawa 1955): 14–5.

15 C.D. Sewell, "Opening Remarks, Symposium on Manpower Requirements and Selection and Training," CPPA, Woodlands Section (WS), Index no. 2342 (1965), 1–2. (Henceforth, all Woodlands Section papers will be cited as WSI followed by the index number.)

16 CPPA, WS, *Organization and Administration of Woods Operations* (Montreal 1928).

17 On cutting techniques, see MacKay, *Lumberjacks*, ch. 5; CPPA, WS, *Pulpwood Cutting* (Montreal 1941) and *Woodcutter's Handbook* (Montreal 1942); A. Koroleff, "Pulpwood Cutting (Techniques and Equipment)," WSI 565 (1940).

18 Ontario, Royal Commission on Forestry, *Report* (Toronto 1947), 34–5.

19 Wayne Lennox, *Ya Can't Holler Timber With All That Racket!* (Cobalt 1979), 11–12; J.E. Rothery, "Safety in Woods Operations," WSI 71 (1933); E.R. Goulet, "Accidents Are Still with Us," WSI 940 (1942).

20 CPPA, WS, *Pulpwood Skidding with Horses and Sleighs* (Montreal 1943); Koroleff, "Land Transportation in Woods Operations," *Journal of Forestry* 31 (November 1933).

21 Arvi Tuumanen, veteran bushworker, interviewed by author, Sault Ste Marie, August 1980.

22 On the machismo appeal of logging today, see Geoffrey York, "Woodsylore: Macho Culture Helps Loggers Conquer Fear," *Globe and Mail*, 4 April 1983.

23 R.C. Bryant, "Scientific Management in Lumbering," *Canada Lumberman* February 1912; see also Edward A. Brainiff, "Scientific Management in the Lumber Business," *Forestry Quarterly* 10 (1912): 9–16.

24 *Globe and Mail*, 4 February 1947.

25 CPPA, WS, *Pulpwood Skidding*.

26 For a helpful theoretical discussion of the meaning of "skill," see Craig R. Littler, *The Development of the Labour Process in Capitalist Societies* (London 1982), ch. 2.

27 See, for instance, Louise Lamphere, "Fighting the Piece-Rate System: New Dimension of an Old Struggle in the Apparel Industry," in Andrew Zimbalist, ed., *Case Studies on the Labour Process* (New York 1979), 257–76; Wayne Lewchuk, "The British Motor Vehicle Industry, 1896–1982: The Roots of Decline," paper presented at the Anglo-American Conference on the Decline of the British Economy, Boston University, 1983.

28 C.R. Townsend, "New Developments and Trends in Logging Techniques," WSI 590 (1940).

29 Lothar Bode (former Lumber and Sawmill Workers Union business agent in northern Ontario), interviewed by author in Thunder Bay, July 1982.

30 Alexander Koroleff, *Stability as a Factor in Efficient Forest Management* (Montreal 1951), 71.

31 Bode interview.

32 Bill Plaunt, lumber company owner and pulp contractor, interviewed by author in Sudbury, July 1982.

33 For similar attitudes among loggers today, see Jamie Swift, *Cut and Run: The Assault on Canada's Forests* (Toronto 1983), 153.

34 CPPA, WS, *Pulpwood Hauling with Horses and Sleighs* (Montreal 1943); MacKay, *Lumberjacks*, ch. 7.

35 Multicultural History Society of Ontario (hereafter OHC/MHSO), Oral History Collection, Felix Lukkarila, taped interview by A.-M. Lahtinen, 1978, translation by Varpu Lindstrom-Best. On management's use of competitions, see T.B. Fraser, "Encouraging the Chopper," WSI 603 (1940); M.R. Wilson, "The Value of Sawing Contests in Labour Relations," WSI 965 (1948).

36 Plaunt interview.

37 For a stimulating discussion of masculinity at the workplace, see Paul Willis, "Shop Floor Culture, Masculinity and the Wage Form," in J. Clarke, C. Critchen, and R. Johnson, eds, *Working-Class Culture* (New York 1979).

38 CPPA, WS, *River Drive of Pulpwood* (Montreal 1946); MacKay, *Lumberjacks*, 120–43.

39 Edith Fowke, *Lumbering Songs of the North Woods* (Toronto 1970); William M. Doerflinger, comp., *Songs of the Sailor and Lumberman* (New York 1972).

40 Koroleff, *Stability*, 15–8; G.E. Lamothe, "Efficiency and Stability of Woods Labour in Eastern Canada," WSI 36 (1930); L.A. Nix, "Woods Labour," WSI 541 (1938); W.A.E. Pepler, "Labour Turnover in Our Pulpwood Camps," WSI 1013 (1949); M.S.M. Hamilton, "Study of Woods Labour Turnover," WSI 1287 (1953).

41 W.A.E. Pepler, "Woods Labour in Eastern Canada," cited in Koroleff, *Stability*, 15.

42 Thunder Bay Finnish Canadian Historical Society Archives, A.T. Hill, "Historic Basis and Development of the Lumber Workers' Organization and Struggles in Ontario"; Thunder Bay Historical Museum, A.T. Hill Collection 980.83.41, A.T. Hill, "Autobiography"; Donald Avery, *"Dangerous Foreigners"* (Toronto 1979), 118–24; Dorothy Steeves, *The Compassionate Rebel* (Vancouver 1960), ch. 4.

43 *The Worker/Le Travailleur* 1 May 1920–15 November 1920.

44 Public Archives of Canada (hereafter PAC), RG 27 (Department of Labour, Strikes and lockouts files), 337–76.

45 PAO, Communist Party of Canada records, 9C 759, organizers reports, *Metsä-työläinen*, 1928, no. 2; Tim Buck, "New Struggles and New Tasks for the Left Wing in Canada," 31 December 1929.

46 See, for example, Charles Allen Seager, "A Proletariat in Wild Rose Country: The Alberta Coal Miners 1905–1945" (PH D dissertation, York University 1981).

47 Buck, "New Struggles."

48 Seager, "Albert Coal Miners," 148–52; David Bercuson, *Fools and Wise Men* (Toronto 1978), 1–8; David Frank, "Class Conflict in the Coal Industry: Cape Breton 1922," in Gregory S. Kealey and Peter Warrian, eds, *Essays in Canadian Working Class History* (Toronto 1976), 167.

49 For a discussion of the importance of food in camps, see Joseph R. Conlin, "'Did you get enough of pie?: A Social History of Food in Logging Camps," *Journal of Forest History* (October 1979). On structural factors promoting unionization and militancy in the forest industry, see Clark Kerr and A. Siegel, "The Inter-Industry Propensity to Strike," in A. Kornhauser et al., eds, *Industrial Conflict* (New York 1954).

50 On Finnish-Canadian radicalism, see Edward W. Laine, "Finnish Canadian Radicalism and Canadian Politics: The First Forty Years 1900–40," in Jorgen Dahlie and Tissa Fernando, eds, *Ethnicity Power and Politics in Canada* (Toronto 1981), 94–112; "Finnish Issue," *Lakehead University Review* 9 (Spring 1976); Varpu Lindstrom-Best, "Finns in Ontario," special issue of *Polyphony* 3, no. 2 (Fall 1981).

51 Arja Pilli, *The Finnish Language Press in Canada*, 1901–1939 (Turku 1982).

52 MHSO/OHC 1977, Toivo Tienhara, interviewed by Lennard Sillanpaa, translated by Varpu Lindstrom-Best.

53 C.B. Davis, *Proceedings of the Annual Meeting of the Woodlands Section, 1930*. For company views of the union, see also Nix, *Woods Labour* revised ed. (Montreal 1939), 15.

54 Ian Radforth, "Finnish Lumber Workers in Ontario, 1919–46," *Polyphony* 3, no. 2 (Fall 1981): 23–34; Satu Repo, "Rosvall and Voutilainen: Two Union Men Who Never Died," *Labour/Le Travailleur* 8/9 (Autumn/Spring 1981–82): 279–302; Livo Ducin (pseud.), "Unrest in the Algoma Lumbercamps; the Bushworkers' Strikes of 1933–34," in John Ferris, ed., *50 Years of Labour in Algoma* (Sault Ste Marie 1978).

55 The Lumber Workers Industrial Union of Canada was formed in 1926 and affiliated with the Workers' Unity League in 1930. When the league was dissolved in 1935, former northern Ontario activists applied to the United Brotherhood of Carpenters and Joiners of America for charters to form locals of its affiliate, the Lumber and Sawmill Workers' Union.

56 The logging industry's experiences with the ISA can be traced in the files of the Ontario Deputy Minister of Labour, PAO, RG 7 II-4, vols 1–3. On the legislation in general, see H.A. Logan, *Trade Unions in Canada* (Toronto 1948), 220–1, 460–2.

57 See the files of the Ontario Regional Advisory Board, Department of Labour, PAC, RG 27 838-9.

58 MHSO, Magnuson Collection, Bruce Magnuson scrapbooks; PAC, RG 27, 451. On

labour relations in the mills, see Egil Schonning, "Union – Management Relations in the Pulp and Paper Industry of Ontario and Quebec, 1914–50" (PH D dissertation, Toronto 1955).

59 Magnuson scrapbooks.

60 Bode interview. In fact, there is no Canadian head of the union since there is no Canadian headquarters. The largest and dominant local is 2693, based in Thunder Bay.

61 David L. MacFarlane, cited in Koroleff, *Stability*, 52.

62 David L. MacFarlane, "The Labour Force Problems of the Eastern Canadian Woods Industry, 1955" (photocopy in author's possession).

63 Bode interview.

64 Koroleff, *Stability*, 2. His statistics are confirmed in Canada, Department of Labour, *Wage Rates and Hours of Labour in Canada*, 14–5.

65 Arthur S. Michell, "Mechanical Harvesting of Timber Crops," *Proceedings of the Royal Canadian Institute* v, no. 11 (1964): 12–13; W.S. Bromley, "U.S. Southern Forest Developments," WSI 2580 (1970).

66 See the records of the Ontario Regional Advisory Board, Department of Labour, PAC, RG 27 838-9.

67 See, for example, C.C. Wright, "Leisure Time Classes in Camps," *Woodlands Review* 38, no. 5 (May 1952); J.T. Walker, "Camp Construction Trends at Smooth Rock Falls," *Woodlands Review* 61, no. 3 (March 1960).

68 Koroleff, *Stability*; W.A.E. Pepler and B.J. McColl, "The Status of Mechanization," WSI 1011 (1949).

69 Koroleff, "Mechanization of Logging," *Pulp and Paper Magazine of Canada* 38, no. 1 (October 1937).

70 W.D. Bennett, "Cable Yarding Developments in Eastern Canada," WSI 1466 (1966); C.R. Silversides, "Use of Articulated Wheeled Tractors in Logging," *Unasylva* 20, no. 4 (1965); On BC, see Ken Bernsholn, *Cutting Up the North: The History of the Forest Industry in the Northern Interior* (North Vancouver 1981); G.W. Taylor, *Timber: History of the Forest Industry in B.C.* (Vancouver 1975). On mechanization in Newfoundland, see J.P. Curran, "The Process of Mechanization in the Forest Industries of Newfoundland" (MA thesis, Memorial University 1971).

71 Koroleff, "Economic Possibilities of Mechanized Logging," WSI B54 (1938); Swift, *Cut and Run*, 119, 126–30; Radforth, "Woodsworkers and Mechanization," 72–5.

72 "Report of the Mechanical Hauling Field Meeting," WSI 1116 (1950).

73 Pepler and McColl, "The Development of Mechanical Pulpwood Logging Methods for Eastern Canada," WSI 1325 (1953).

74 CPPA, *Annual Report* 1957, 17; C.R. Silversides, "Achievements and Failures," WSI 2619 (1972).

75 Pepler and McColl, "Developments of Mechanical Pulpwood Logging Methods," 1.

76 Jim Wardrop, "British Columbia's Experience with Early Chain Saws," *Material History Bulletin* 21 (Ottawa 1977); Ellis Lucia, "A Lesson from Nature: Joe Cox and His Revolutionary Saw Chain," *Journal of Forest History* 25, no. 3 (July 1981).

77 D.V. Miller, "Present Situation and Trends in Occupational Safety and Health," Food and Agricultural Organization of the United Nations (FAO), *Seminar on Occupational Health and Safety and Applied Ergonomics on Highly Mechanized Logging Operations* (Ottawa 1981), 69.

78 Gordon Godwin, "The Beginning of a Beginning," WSI 2479 (1968); Jean A. Benard, "Articulated Wheeled Skidders in Canada, 1961–66," *Woodlands Review* (November 1967); J.R. Hughes, "Logging Operations in Canada – Review and Forecast," WSI 2553; C.R. Silversides, interviewed by author, Prescott, June 1982.

79 Radforth, "Woodsworkers and Mechanization," 83–4.

80 W.R. Beatty, "The Koehring KHIIIB Harvester," WSI 2592 (1970).

81 Swift, *Cut and Run*, 139.

82 MNR, *Forest Industry*, 78.

83 A.S. Richards, "Economics and Technology in Pulpwood Transportation," WSI 2184 (1962); J.A. McNally, "Mechanized Logging and Road Requirements," in CPPA, *Report of Logging Field Meeting of the Woodlands Section* (1963).

84 See Bryan D. Palmer, *A Culture in Conflict* (Montreal 1979), ch. 3; Gregory S. Kealey, *Toronto Workers Respond to Industrial Capitalism, 1867–92* (Toronto 1980), chs 3–6; Craig Heron, "The Crisis of the Craftsmen: Hamilton's Metal Workers in the Early Twentieth Century," *Labour/Le Travailleur* 6 (1980); Wayne Roberts, "The Last Artisans: Toronto Printers 1896–1914," in Kealey and Warrian, eds, *Essays in Working Class History*, 125–42.

85 "Power Saw Training – Panel Discussion," WSI 132 (1953). For a vivid description of felling with a chainsaw, see Lennox, *Ya Can't Holler*, ch. 5.

86 D.W. Gray, "Accident Prevention on Mechanized Operations," *Woodlands Review* (January 1958).

87 Swift, *Cut and Run*, 152–4; Keith Mason, "The Effects of Piecework on Accident Rates in the Logging Industry," *Journal of Occupational Accidents* 1, no. 3 (1977) disagrees, but he has been challenged. See Charles E. Reasons, Lois L. Ross, Craig Patterson, *Assault on the Worker: Occupational Health and Safety in Canada* (Toronto 1981), 23–4.

88 Ontario's average annual fatality rates (1975–78) were logging: 0.597; mining: 0.546; construction 0.160; manufacturing: 0.038 (Joint Federal Provincial Inquiry Commission into Safety in Mining and Mining Plants in Ontario, *Towards Safe Production*, vol. 2 [Toronto 1981], 15). The most recent data are for 1981 when Ontario's fatality-frequency rates per million man-hours were forestry: 0.40; mining: 0.26; manufacturing: 0.02 (Ontario Advisory Council on Occupational Health and Safety, *Fifth Annual Report, 1982–83*, vol. 1 [Toronto

1838], 233). For Canadian data, see Labour Canada, Occupational Health and Safety Branch, *Fatalities in Canadian Industry, 1969–78* (Ottawa 1980).

89 Swift, *Cut and Run*, 154–6.

90 Radforth, "Woodsworkers and Mechanization," 90–1; Lennox, *Ya Can't Holler*, 28.

91 Plaunt interview; Duncan R. Campbell and Edward B. Power, *Manpower Implications of Prospective Technological Changes in the Eastern Canadian Pulpwood Logging Industry* (Ottawa 1966).

92 "Small Skidder Forum," WSI 2140 (1962).

93 Don Harris, interviewed by Jamie Swift, 1981; copy of transcript in author's possession.

94 Camille Legendre, "Improving Productivity: Expensive Hardware, Better Qualified Workers, How about the Organization?" WSI 2661 (1973).

95 W.D. Bennett, H.I. Winer, and A. Bartholomew, *A Measurement of Environmental Factors and Their Effect on the Productivity of Tree-Length Logging with Rubber-tired Skidders*, Pulp and Paper Research Institute of Canada, Report no. 22 (1965).

96 "Two-Shift Logging: A Symposium," WSI 2091 (1961).

97 S. Milling, "Training and Development Needs of Forest Workers in the 80s," *Pulp and Paper Canada* 82, no. 4 (April 1981).

98 P.L. Cottell et al., *Performance Variation among Logging-Machine Operators: Felling with Tree Shears*, Forest Engineering Research Institute of Canada, T.R. 4 (1976), 25. P.L. Cottell and R.J. Barth, "Factors Relating to Performance Variation," *Rélations industrielles/Industrial Relations* 32, no. 4 (February 1977): 566–85.

99 Mechanical Transport Branch, Industry, Trade and Commerce, *Mechanization in the Forest: Benefits and Opportunities* (Ottawa 1972). For discussions of "deskilling and reskilling" as "a two-way process," see Littler, *Development of the Labour Process*, 14–19; Richard Edwards, "Social Relations of Production at the Point of Production," *Insurgent Sociologist* 8, nos 2–3 (1979): 109–25.

100 G.K. Seed, "The Machine Resource – Current Options," WSI 2617 (1972).

101 Lennox, *Ya Can't Holler*, 39–42.

102 D. Burn, "Living Accommodation for Forest Workers in Remote Areas," in FAO, *Seminar*, 588–69.

103 W. Morrison, "Commuter-Camp Operations Result in Lower Wood Costs," WSI 2161 (1962); Gordon Kelly, "From City to Forest by Air," *Pulp and Paper Canada* 76, no. 9 (September 1975).

104 C.R. Silversides to author, 8 July 1982.

105 C.R. Day, "An Analysis of Woodlands Manpower," WSI 2633 (1973); D.M. Johnson, "The Manpower Situation," WSI 2622 (1972); C.A. Kearns, "Recruitment and Retention of Employees – Forestry and Mining," unpub. Canada Manpower study (1974); copy in author's possession.

106 Various case studies suggest the need for rethinking Harry Braverman's thesis in

Labour and Monopoly Capital (New York 1974). See especially Stephen Wood, ed., *The Degradation of Work?* (London 1982), and Zimbalist, ed., *Case Studies*.

107 Harris interview.

108 Jake Hildebrand, interviewed by Jamie Swift, 1981; copy of transcript in author's possession.

109 *Ontario's Bushworker*, 17 September 1956, 4 February 1957. Earlier communist leaders were equally supportive of mechanization; see *Ontario Timberworker* 1, 15 August 1948, 5 July 1950.

110 Tulio Mior, interviewed by author, August 1982. Unfortunately, Labour Canada's statistics lump Lumber and Saw members with the United Brotherhood of Carpenters and Joiners.

111 Campbell and Power, *Manpower Implications*, 108.

112 See, for example, *Ontario Bushworker* 18 February 1957.

113 Johnson, "Manpower Situation." Philip Cottell has argued that woodsworkers take pride in the portability of their skill and find job security in mobility itself. See his "Why Work in the Woods?" wsi 2662 (1974) and his *Occupational Choice and Employment Stability among Forest Workers* (New Haven 1974). Patricia Marchak maintains that the loggers' boasting about their ability to quit is only an image presented to the outside world and that high turnover is rooted in the instability of the industry itself; see her *Green Gold*, 116.

114 G.K. Seed, "The Machine Resource – Current Options," wsi 2617 (1972).

115 David F. Noble, "Social Choice in Machine Design: The Case of Automatically Controlled Machine Tools," in Zimbalist, ed., *Case Studies*, 19.

116 Michael Yarrow, "The Labour Process in Coal Mining: Struggle for Control," in ibid., 170–92. On mining in northern Ontario, see Wallace Clemment, *Hardrock Mining* (Toronto 1981).

117 Statistics Canada, *Net Capital Flows and Stocks, 1926–73* (Ottawa 1974), 121.

118 Johnson, "Manpower Situation."

119 Lumber and Sawmill Workers Union, Local 2693, "Review of the Strike of Woodlands Employees of Boise Cascade Canada, Ltd., 1978–79" (copy in author's possession).

120 Radforth, "Roots of the Loggers' Strike at Boise Cascade Canada, Ltd., 1978–80," paper presented to the North American Labour History Conference at Wayne State University 1982.

121 See statement of Boise Cascade Canada, Ltd, *Ontario Labour Relations Board Reports 1978* 0658-78-u, 670.

122 On other regions, see W.C. Osborn, *The Paper Plantation* (New York 1974). Legendre, "Le Developpement et les Organizations: Le Destin des Entrepreneurs Forèstiers," *Canadian Review of Sociology and Anthropology* 17 (1980). In Ontario the Lumber and Saw successfully battled owner-operating at Reed Paper in 1978. In 1963, however, "settlers" doing contract logging on private lands undermined a strike in the Great Clay Belt, formerly an agricultural district

with an unusually large number of "settlers" with their own woodlots. Bitter conflicts between pickets and contractors climaxed in tragedy when settlers armed with shotguns opened fire on strikers, killing three of them (see D.L. Stein, "Violence and Death Strike Ontario's North Country," *Maclean's Magazine*, 23 March 1963).

123 See Boise Cascade Canada statement, 670.
124 Mior interview.
125 Ontario New Democratic Party, *The Last Stand* (Toronto 1983).
126 J.F. Fowler, "Mechanical Logging and Its Impact on Forest Management," *Your Forests* 3, no. 3 (Winter 1970); C.R. Silversides, "Progress and Problems in the Mechanization of Forest Work in Relation to Modern Silvicultural Techniques," *Proceedings of the Seventh World Congress of Forestry* (Buenos Aires 1972); George Weetman, "Forest Mechanization and the Environment," in C.R. Silversides, ed., *Forest Harvesting, Mechanization and Automation* (Ottawa 1974); Swift, *Cut and Run*, 146–8.

J O H N   B E L L A M Y   F O S T E R

On the Waterfront:
Longshoring in Canada

The words, "On the Waterfront," for most people carry an air of mystery and suspense, vaguely evoking images of Marlon Brando and the New York harbour of the early 1950s.[1] But the sense of otherworldliness that clings to the longshore labour process goes far beyond its history of exploitation and violence, and arises instead out of the very nature of work relations. As one authority has put it, "the conditions of 'boom and bust' that determine the daily life of the world's ports have produced a labour jungle that few laymen have ever penetrated."[2] To a greater extent than in most industries, longshoring has been shaped not by managerial imperatives, but by the imperatives of the workers themselves. It has, therefore, been characterized by a pattern of development that sets it apart from all other workplace environments. What has been true in the past, however, may or may not be true in the future.

For about half a century now, the dominant interpretation of the path of development in the North American longshoring industry has been based on the West Coast experience, where (in ports like Vancouver, San Francisco, and Seattle) a strong hiring-hall system and a process of productivity bargaining evolved. On the East Coast and the St Lawrence, however, the hiring-hall system tended to be the exception rather than the rule. The development of a permanent, full-time work force ("decasualization") was much slower and workers' job control more limited. With the technological revolution in longshoring in the late 1960s, this relatively stable condition on both coasts began to break down. The advent of new technology resulted in widespread labour redundancy and greater differentiation within the work force. The labour process in the industry now seems to be following two distinct lines of evolution: one is represented by Vancouver, where the union managed to obtain a greater control over technological change than anywhere else in North America; the other by Montreal, where – through the introduction of computerized dispatch – management for the first time in

North America decasualized the work force on its own terms. This paper sketches the major developments in Canadian longshoring in the past twenty years and their impact on workers and unions in the industry, providing a basis for understanding the tensions on the waterfront in the 1980s.

ALONG THE SHORE

In its original form, longshoring is an excellent example of so-called casual labour. As British writer R.B. Oram has pointed out, "The first condition of dock work that one must accept is that on no two days is the number of men required the same." Longshoremen depend for their employment on the arrival of ships, and yet ships, "unlike trains do not run to time."[3] Demand for labour fluctuates widely and is relatively unpredictable. The labour pool, at the same time, must be sufficiently large to fill the needs of peak demand. Since the essence of economic efficiency in this sector lies in accelerating the turnaround time of ships, it is extremely difficult and even counterproductive to rely on a normal working day. Currently, as much as 40 per cent of all work in the Port of Vancouver may be done outside of 8:00–5:00 on weekdays. In the early sixties, over 50 per cent of total hours worked in Montreal and Quebec City were overtime.[4] In Canada's St Lawrence River ports, moreover, the industry traditionally closed down for several months during the winter. Since longshoring employment is irregular, it has been common for longshoremen in certain districts to spend part of their year employed in an entirely different occupation, like fishing.

Thus, the demand for labour on the waterfront is unstable and highly contingent on circumstances. However, the natural supply of waterfront labour tends toward a glut in the market, since the work itself is "unskilled," in the sense of being open to the common labourer.[5] The surge of labour brought in during peak periods became a labour surplus in times of normal or less-than-normal demand for labour. Given such a relationship between supply and demand, it is not surprising that shipping companies and stevedoring contractors were originally able to exploit labour through a "shape-up" system. In the early decades of this century, waterfront workers were required to show up at the docks, where management hand-picked the men they wanted on a daily basis. In Vancouver, longshoremen would indicate their desire for work by raising their cargo hooks. In such circumstances it was a simple matter to cut wages, introduce speedups, lay off employees at whim, and blacklist recalcitrant workers (not to mention the inevitable bribes and kickbacks).

The special character of the longshoring industry, however, lies not only in the fact that the labour market is "casual" in its natural form, but also in the enormous variety of operational circumstances that make worker co-operation necessary and close supervision difficult. These circumstances require a large number of standardized procedures where narrow efficiency with respect to a particular job is often sacrificed to overall flexibility in adapting to changing work conditions. Thus, working along the shore, while classified as "unskilled" work, traditionally required that longshoremen "innovate co-operatively" in response to the requirements of different ships and cargos.[6] A gang of longshoremen might work one ship, with a particular deck and hold configuration, and then move on a few hours later to an entirely different ship, carrying a very different cargo. Some longshoremen might find themselves working on or above the deck of a vessel, others might be stowing cargo in the hold, while still others would be manning the docks or working in the warehouses. For many years, the conventional way of moving cargo between dock and ship was the winch-operated sling, which could be used to lift all types of "break-bulk" cargo (general, individualized cargo, which is "broken out" of the hold, requiring labour-intensive handling). Hence, part of a crew (or gang) of longshoremen would be on the dock loading the sling, which would be guided to the hold by the winch-driver and hatch-tender, and then stowed within the hold by still another group of longshoremen.

The loading of a vessel required a "tight stow," making the most economical use of space by piling the cargo right up to the hatch-covers. In addition to his traditional hand tool, the cargo hook, the longshoreman employed all kinds of nets, slings, hooks, and ramps, as well as hand trucks, fork-lifts, gravity rollers, etc. At times the longshoreman "man-handled" or "belly-packed" cargo. The variability of the work obviously presented problems for the employers, making it difficult to impose the forms of managerial control that had evolved within the industrial core of the capitalist system.

Another circumstance that differentiates the longshoring industry from numerous other workplace environments is the strategic importance of dispatch procedures, which must quickly and efficiently allocate labour (gangs and fill-ins) along what often amounts to miles of waterfront, and to ships with differing labour demands (including skill requirements). Needless to say, it is in the area of dispatch that the real hiring takes place, and control over dispatch procedures is the key to job control within the industry. Viewed together, these three classic dilemmas of "casual labour," variability of work, and complex dispatch requirements have conditioned the course of class struggles on the waterfront. Out of this has arisen a deep-seated dialectical conflict between the shape-up, decasualization, and the struggle for job control.

THE STRUGGLE AGAINST THE SHAPE-UP: TWO PATHS OF EVOLUTION

The story of the West Coast longshoremen's struggle against the employers' use of the shape-up system as a means of exploiting "casual" workers has been well studied.[7] The thrust of that struggle was to "decasualize" the labour force by requiring employers to use the regularized, equitable procedures of a hiring hall. The most famous event in this long war was San Francisco's "Bloody Thursday" during the general strike of 1934, when the police fired on union members, killing 3 and wounding over 100. Through the 1934 strike, labour on the u.s. West Coast won the right to establish its own hiring halls to replace the shape-up system of hiring on the docks. Indeed, by 1937, the International Longshoremen's and Warehousemen's Union (ILWU) in the United States had laid the foundations for effective control of its work environment.[8] Union control of hiring and dispatch was followed by the development of a complex system of rules governing all aspects of the labour process in which the union for some time clearly had the upper hand.

The evolution of the labour process followed a somewhat similar pattern in Vancouver. Already in 1912, some twenty-two years before San Francisco longshoremen had won their hiring hall, the International Longshoremen's Association (ILA) in Vancouver had established a rudimentary form of hiring hall: a union hall with a blackboard listing newly arriving ships and their dock locations, but without any organized procedure for actually allocating work.[9] Although the Shipping Federation managed to smash the ILA in Vancouver in 1923 – with the help of an armed launch and the enlistment of a special force of 350 armed guards – it proved to be a Pyrrhic victory for two reasons. First, rather than abolishing the rudimentary hiring-hall system, management (for reasons that remain unclear) extended it, incorporating a system of "rotation dispatch," or the allocation of work opportunities according to a fixed rotational order, and thereby adding inadvertently to workers' job control.[10] Second, the company union that the employers established, known as the Vancouver District Waterfront Workers' Association, gradually turned into a genuine union and led the struggle in the famous "Battle of Ballentyne Pier" during the strike lockout of 1935, which resulted in 28 injuries after mounted police charged into a group of 1,000 longshoremen.[11] British Columbia's independent longshoremen's unions soon began to link up with the ILWU, and by 1944, all of the province's unionized dockworkers had joined. Undoubtedly much of the resilience of organized labour on the Vancouver waterfront was due to the unifying force of the hiring-hall system, which evolved steadily despite the various setbacks imposed on the union structures themselves.

A union-directed hiring hall, as we shall see in detail below, results in a level of control over the work force that is qualitatively different from the mere ability to open or close the doors of the labour market. As American writer Paul Hartman points out, it was the longshoremen's control of the hiring hall on the West Coast which was responsible for "establishing union hegemony in size, composition, flexibility and allegiance of the union work force."[12] It is no accident that within five years of management's concession (virtually forced upon it by the trade-union movement and the government) to allow labour to set up its own hiring halls on the u.s. West Coast, the employers lost almost all detailed control over the employment and deployment of labour. It is characteristic of the longshoring industry that the immediate supervisors or "walking bosses," and often some of the supervisory staff for the stevedoring contractors themselves, are union members. By the late 1940s, the only authority left to the employers on the u.s. Pacific coast in the area of hiring and dispatch was to request that a certain number of men be sent to them. Management was compelled to put to work any gang or labourer dispatched from the hiring hall.

One consequence of significant union control over the work force was that the union also obtained control over the hiring and dispatch of those longshoremen who remained either casual or semi-casual. It was soon discovered that in order for the union to institute a program of "decasualization," or full-time employment for union men, it was necessary to limit membership in the union to conform to normal or average availability of work, while at the same time ensuring the existence of a labour pool for periods of peak demand. The system that gradually evolved in most ports was a three-tier stratification of workers within the labour market. On the top, with the first pick of the jobs, were union members; below these were non-union members who were given a temporary status on a restricted list; the bottom tier was made up of those who remained entirely casual and could usually only expect intermittent employment.[13]

East Coast developments, with regard to the industry as a whole, were quite different. While the western ilwu has been famous for its left-wing leadership, the eastern ila has consistently been led by men with a more conservative point of view. Indeed, allegations of criminal misconduct (and Mafia connections) have been directed at the union leadership in both the u.s. and Canada throughout ila history. In spite of the fact that the shape-up is generally regarded as a form of hiring that lends itself to discrimination, labour strife, underemployment, inefficiency, and corruption, the ila at the Port of New York seemed little interested in changing this established work practice until the government, acting on recommendations of the New York State Crime Commission, legislated it away and established a form of state regulation in 1954. Thus, the New York harbour area was not "decasualized" until twenty years after the Pacific coast.[14]

In the Canadian ila ports (Saint John, Halifax, Quebec, and Montreal) the hiring and dispatch process remained largely within the constellation of the traditional shape-up until the government established a hiring hall in Halifax during World War ii, which was later taken over by the union, and until criminal misconduct and industrial strife prompted the federal government to bring the Quebec ports under a management-dominated system of computerized dispatch and formal job guarantees in the early 1970s. Meanwhile, Saint John has retained the shape-up as its root form of hiring and dispatch.[15]

It is crucial to understand that the "decasualization" process on the Canadian East Coast (and the St Lawrence) occurred for the most part *after* the technological revolution in cargo handling that began on the West Coast in the late 1960s had already created massive labour redundancy in the industry as a whole. Under these circumstances, the sudden "modernization" of the work process in Canadian ILA ports has strengthened managerial control, in contrast to that which had occurred decades before on the West Coast. Most analysts of the longshoring industry in North America have tended to focus on the West Coast experience, assuming (not entirely without reason) that, as far as labour relations were concerned, it presented a picture of the industry at its highest stage of development. The Quebec experience, where computerized dispatch was introduced apparently for the first time in North America, proves that this interpretation is not quite correct. It is now evident that there are two general lines of development in the industry. One is represented by the Vancouver case, where ILWU Local 500 managed to obtain a greater degree of control over technological change than in any other port in North America; the other is represented by Montreal where, as we will see, the new system of computerized dispatch has taken decasualization to its furthest conceivable length, overriding nearly all work-force control over the labour process. This latter tendency can be viewed as a process of creating a "standardized industrial work force" (the complete decasualization of the industry under managerial auspices). Thus decasualization is not, as traditionally assumed, synonymous with an improvement of working conditions on the waterfront. Instead, it is a contradictory process in which labour and management each attempt to seize control of the work process. Historically, the most important factor in this struggle has been the development (San Francisco, Vancouver, Halifax) or non-development (New York, Montreal, Quebec, Saint John) of a strong hiring-hall system.

THE CONTROL OF HIRING
AND DISPATCH

Analytically, it is useful to follow Paul Hartman's distinction between two types of job control: first, work-force control, and second, control over the production process.

The former includes regulation of entry of workers to the industry, control over the size of the work force, and designation of persons to be employed. The latter includes control over output methods, and pace of work. The two aspects of job control are often together, but not invariably so. The building trades and maritime unions exercise some control over both aspects. The printing trades, railroad unions, and musicians have attempted with varying success, to exercise control over the production process. Direct control over the work force is much less evident in their practice.[16]

The longshoring industry on the West Coast has long been the classic example of union work-force control. Indeed, in obtaining substantial control of the dispatch process, longshoremen regulated not only the employment, but also the deployment, of labour on a day-to-day basis. The power of the longshoring unions also extended into the control of the labour process in the usual sense. But this control of the actual work process has receded in the face of technological revolutions in cargo handling. The defence of traditional practices is strongest where the hiring-hall system has developed. Yet, it is above all else to protect their control of hiring and dispatch that longshoremen have fought: in this, they have generally refused to give way.

The importance of the hiring-hall system in governing work conditions on the waterfront can be readily illustrated, using the example of Vancouver. British Columbia longshoremen have the choice of being members of a permanent gang (of which there were some forty in Vancouver in the early 1960s) or to work as fill-ins (for either permanent or "scratch" gangs) dispatched from the hiring hall. Dispatch in the hiring hall is regulated by a number of "boards" attached to the wall. The "dock board" is reserved for those longshoremen who are no longer able to do heavy ship work because of old age or injury, and who are therefore assigned to somewhat easier work on the docks with a small discount in pay. The "wheat board" is for those longshoremen who have chosen to work only with wheat (not a preferred position). The "top-side board" is set up for senior union men who work as hatch-tenders and winch-drivers. The "machine board" is for the dispatch of men who drive the various machines (from the fork-lifts on up). The "union spareboard" is the most important board and is used to fill out the permanent gangs, or to make up "scratch gangs." At least half the men who are listed on the union spareboard have various skills or ratings for special jobs. Numbered boards are set up for the non-union men with preferred status. The so-called disk men have too little seniority to be listed on any of the boards and are general fill-ins, obligated to take undesirable jobs like wheat trimming (which involves spreading wheat in the holds and is extremely dusty – now more often done by machines). They rarely get dispatched to the relatively "cushy" jobs, and in fact, receive the very scraps of the trade.[17]

The various boards are arranged along the main wall on a sort of shutter with hinges, so that they can be swung into the dispatch office. Each man has one or more metal plates with his name and number on it set in a slot on whichever board he is associated with. His plate also has small coloured tags fastened to it, indicating whatever skills or special ratings he may have. When a dockworker wishes to "plug in," he simply turns his metal plate around so that the pink side shows. The dispatcher chooses the men according to a "fixed rotational order." The non-union "disk men" indicate their willingness to work by dropping their disks into the top of a tube. When these men are needed their disks are drawn from the bottom of the tube.

There are several dispatch periods during a day, corresponding to the number of shifts – which rose from two to three in 1970. Each of these periods is divided into three sections, which take into account the distance of the assigned docks from the hiring hall. Longshoremen are dispatched first to those docks furthest from the hiring hall, and so on. Consequently, it is commonplace for a longshoreman to "plug in" only just before the dispatch is due to take place to those docks (and ships) that he prefers. By choosing to plug in at a specific time, he is able to exert some control over where he will work. The ringing of a loud bell signals the beginning of each dispatch session, so that the hiring hall gets a last chance to plug in. The dispatcher then chooses the men as needed, according to the fixed rotational order established on the board. A coloured "button" is then attached to the slot of the last man chosen. The next dispatch will start at that point. Since the men also have certain ratings, there are distinct buttons, each representing a particular rating (e.g. the hatch button). The general principle of selection remains the same but only applies to those men with that rating. Consequently, the board invariably has a number of different buttons attached to it, indicating where the dispatch stopped last with respect to each individual rating.

Setting aside the difficult issue of hierarchy in the labour market, we can see that union longshoremen who are not members of a permanent gang have a great deal of freedom to choose when and where to work. The value of this right is enhanced by their knowledge of many of the details associated with any particular job. Thus they are able to select work according to a wide range of criteria. Blackboards set up in the union hall indicate which permanent gangs have been dispatched to a particular ship, the size of the gang, the machinery being used, the ship's name, the name of the dock itself, the starting time for the work, and sometimes the kind of cargo. Coupled with their detailed knowledge of particular gangs, ships, docks, and other details, longshoremen have a lot to consider in making their choice. In an excellent study, Stuart Philpott lists eight general "ends" that influence a longshoreman's day-to-day decisions on employment (or which determine whether or not he will choose to join a permanent gang): monetary reward, peer status, authority on the job, sociability opportunities (which vary according to whether one is in the hold, on the deck of the ship, on the dock, etc.), amount of physical effort involved, freedom of choice (which is less on a daily basis for those longshoremen who join a permanent gang), general working conditions, and length of job.

While designed somewhat differently in various ports, the hiring-hall system generally conforms to the classic pattern described above. Thus, in Halifax, the hall has a dispatch board with the names of all union members in alphabetical order and a hole beside each name. When a longshoreman enters the hall with the intention of working, he merely takes a nail and sticks it in the hole that lies alongside his name. Colours next to each name indicate the skills each man has. When a dispatch time arrives, the dispatcher begins with the name that comes immediately after the last man who was offered a job assignment. If a particular skill is required, and the next man on the board does not have the necessary rating, then the dispatcher goes down the board until he finds the first man who does. The fact that he does not have the skill needed, however, does not mean that a man is completely passed over. The dispatcher always goes back to the man who is next on the list and has not yet been offered a job for which he is suitably qualified. In contrast to Vancouver, however, one of the inequities of the system is that a skilled man will frequently have to take an unskilled job or lose his turn on the board. When there is a job for which no union member is available, non-union men with some seniority will be given first chance, while any additional men needed after this second pool has been exhausted will be selected from the "casuals" in the "bull pen."[18] It is interesting to note that although the Halifax collective agreement allows the Maritime Employers' Association to observe the operation of the union-operated dispatch system one day a week, the association had done so only once by 1981. According to one informant, when management first sent a man to observe, a union man kicked a chair out from under him. Whatever the truth of this statement, there is little doubt that the animosity directed against the employers' observers would be enormous.

It should be readily apparent that workers' job control of this calibre is a serious threat to managerial imperatives. In his *Principles of Scientific Management*, Frederick Winslow Taylor spent considerable space on the importance of breaking down the gang system and the possibilities opened up by managerial control of dispatch, in the context of labourers working for the Bethlehem Steel Company.[19] Given Taylor's general inclination to convey managerial imperatives in their baldest possible form, it is well worth quoting him at length:

A careful analysis has demonstrated the fact that when workmen are herded into gangs, each man in the gang becomes far less efficient than when his personal ambition is stimulated; that when men work in gangs, their individual efficiency falls almost invariably down to or below the level of the worst man in the gangs; and that they are pulled down instead of being elevated by being herded together. For this reason a general order had been issued in the Bethlehem Steel Works that not more than four men were to be allowed to work in a labour gang without a special permit, signed by the General Superintendent of the Works, this special permit to extend for one week only. It was arranged that as far as possible each labourer should be given a separate individual task.[20]

Taylor's comments here are mirrored in the current views of management on the waterfront where the gang system, while eroding, remains intact everywhere outside of Quebec. Earlier in his book, Taylor had described the elaborate dispatch system set up by the bosses in the labour office of the Bethlehem Steel Company, which had as its object the complete elimination of gangs. Thus, he explains how complex maps of the yard were developed, on the basis of which men were moved like pieces on a "chess board," backed up by telephone and messenger services.[21] Such methods (in more technically elaborate forms) have been universalized in industries where the deployment of labour to various locations is a problem, and where there is strong managerial control. Indeed, managerial control in the area of dispatch (where relevant) is the sine qua non for scientific management in general. Conversely, where a strong hiring-hall system has emerged, as in West Coast longshoring, employers have found it extremely difficult to undermine the gang structure of work organization and to create a "standard industrial work force" as a basis for scientific management.

Although shipowners, stevedoring contractors, and their negotiating representatives have understood this situation for some time, the means to actually develop effective managerial control of dispatch in the longshoring industry, while superseding the shape-up, have only recently become available. The difficulties that have faced management in this area have been a product of the variability of the work, the complex nature of the dispatch requirements, and the enormous degree of control traditionally exerted by the workers themselves. Of late, the big guns that management has brought to this battlefield consist of technological innovations in cargo handling that emerged during the 1960s, and the new system of computerized dispatch.

CONTROL OF THE ACTUAL LABOUR PROCESS

Through the gang system, and so-called restrictive work rules, longshoremen in all ports have managed to exercise some control over the labour process. Nevertheless, the greater the control over the work force, the greater were the possibilities for substantial control of the labour process itself. While longshoremen almost universally fought for and won certain stipulations as to gang size and maximum sling-load weights, for example, such provisions were most solidly entrenched in the practice of the ILWU. Many of these rules, of course, were simply make-work provisions. A full gang (sixteen men in the American ILWU) would be dispatched to each job, regardless of the size and type of ship and cargo. Sling loads were generally kept down to a level far below what was technically feasible, thereby stretching out the work. One of the most widespread forms of "featherbedding" in the ILWU was the "four on/four off" rule. Of the eight men in the hold, only four would be working at any given time, while the other four rested. A similar, though more corrupt, practice, known as the "spell 'o" system, developed in Montreal. Beginning as a brief interval of relief from physical toil, it gradually evolved into a form of paid absenteeism, with free and easy union timekeepers "looking the other way," even to the extent of allowing certain longshoremen to be paid for two different jobs in two different locations at the same time.[22] On the Pacific coast, certain "multiple handling" procedures were instituted which involved work that was altogether unnecessary. Paul Hartman quotes a "Los Angeles employer representative" concerning a procedure formerly common on the U.S. West Coast: "The present practice in this harbor area is to require that any outbound cargo prepalletized before arrival at the dock by persons other than longshoremen must be removed from the pallet boards by teamsters, placed on the dock and then reloaded on stevedore pallet boards by longshoremen. The same situation obtains in reverse on the discharge of palletized cargo from the ship."[23]

It would of course be wrong to imply that work rules designed to establish controls over the production process were constructed only for "featherbedding" and formed unnecessary restraints on productivity. Most of the requirements were formulated to ensure that longshoremen were not subject to arbitrary speedups and unsafe working conditions in what was (and is) an arduous and dangerous work environment. In certain cases, it was recognized by the workers that economic efficiency, narrowly conceived, was not synonymous with overall social efficiency. In an industry where exploitation of workers in an absolute sense had originally been second to none, the West Coast longshoremen had achieved a degree of control over their day-to-day work process that minimized insecurity and alienation.

THE TECHNOLOGICAL
REVOLUTION AND THE
LABOUR PROCESS, I

The technological revolution in cargo handling, which first began to make itself felt on a large scale in the early 1960s, immediately threatened to tear apart this fine fabric of union job control and labour privileges. The most important technical innovation to appear was the "container," a rectangular steel box that holds between 25 and 65 tons of freight, with bigger units on the way. First developed in the Seattle–Alaska trade, the container has made truly intermodal cargo transportation possible, since it is equally adaptable to rail, truck, air, and deep-sea transport. The actual cargo is "unseen and untouched," having been pre-stuffed at the factory or distribution centre and remaining sealed in the container in the ports; the container is handled by huge cranes. The advantages to shipping corporations are manifold: lower labour costs, faster turnaround, centralized cargo servicing, less chance of theft, and so on. Since labour alone has traditionally represented at least 60 per cent of the total cost of transportation (rail, truck, air, or deep water) to the consumer, containerization represents considerable savings in cost.[24]

The container itself, however, is far from the last word in mechanization. One form of operation, which requires radical changes in the design of a vessel, is the "roll-on/roll-off" (RO/RO) technique. In this form of loading and unloading, there is no hoist. Containers are wheeled on and off through the use of mobile vehicles carried aboard the specifically designed ship, across a series of ramps on docks and decks. The interior of the ship, as Herb Mills points out, comes to "resemble the flight and hanger decks of an aircraft carrier."[25] In fact, "a fully loaded deck aboard a RO/RO vessel can look like an industrial warehouse."[26] Perhaps even more threatening to the longshoreman's traditional occupation is the "lighter aboard ship" or LASH vessel, which carried up to 54 barges, each with almost 20,000 cubic feet of cargo capacity. These barges can be loaded or emptied of cargo much more easily than conventional vessels, usually at special "lighter stations." So far, however, these vessels have had limited use in North America.

Almost before this technological revolution had begun, however, the ILWU in the United States was already preparing to alter the structure of work relations on the waterfront. Shortly after the Korean War, an economic downturn in the shipping industry encouraged shipping companies to press for radical changes in the make-up of industrial relations, particularly in the Pacific ports, in order to make enhanced productivity possible. Their demands involved the elimination of so-called restrictive work rules and the introduction of more advanced mechanized methods into the industry. In 1954 Harry Bridges, the ILWU's famous radical president, promised to attempt to persuade the union membership to rationalize their work rules and adjust to the needs of mechanization and modernization.[27] It is clear that this change in approach, fostered by the ILWU leadership, was based on the notion that it was impossible to "beat the machine" and that the union must change its tactics to prevent an erosion of its hard-won position.

The result was the much publicized "Mechanization and Modernization" (M and M) agreement of 1961, which was extended to British Columbia in 1963, and which was designed to eliminate obstructions to mechanization and productivity growth, in exchange for a "share of the machine" and employment guarantees. The M and M agreement was to be "hailed by many as the biggest bribe ever made to labour." In essence, it provided that employers would supply $5 million each year (soon raised to $6.9 million) to be administered through a joint trustee fund for the purpose of maintaining longshoremen made redundant by the introduction of modern mechanical processes. In return, the union agreed to "tear up the book" and eliminate certain restrictive work practices that had emerged during the previous three decades.[28]

The principle was established that, barring a decline in tonnage going through west-coast ports of the U.S. and Canada, reduction of the work force would be confined to the amount of "natural attrition" – in other words, that the labour lost through retirement, death, or "voluntary quits" would not be replaced. Of the $5 million to be provided annually by the U.S. employers ($390,000 in BC), $3 million was considered to be equivalent to the workers' "share of the machine" and was used primarily for early retirement. According to the M and M agreement, each ILWU longshoreman in Canada was to be given a cash award of $7,200 (soon raised to $13,000) upon retirement. Early retirement at age 62 was encouraged by spreading out the lump sum in monthly payments over three years. Management was given the right to force compulsory retirement at age 62 "if available work opportunity was insufficient to meet the minimum guarantee" of employment – a guarantee of 1,820 hours had been agreed on, in principle, for BC but was never implemented – in which case, those retired would receive a higher monthly pension for several years.[29] The M and M agreement essentially ensured that current union members would not be laid off because of mechanization and modernization (or at least not without financial compensation), but only as a result of a decline in gross tonnage in the event of an economic downturn. Management accepted the agreement safe in the knowledge that, on the average, union members tended to be fairly advanced in age. Between 1960 and mid 1966, retirement and death reduced the numbers of workers in the U.S. Pacific-coast union by 25 per cent, and by 1971 the size of the total work force had dropped by nearly 50 per cent from its 1960 level.[30] In Vancouver-area locals, the effect of the M and M agreement was less dramatic, with the number of union members falling only by about 20 per cent from approximately 3,500 to about 2,800 between 1963 and 1979. This surprising stability in the size of the work force, in spite of the M and M buy-outs, is all the more significant when one recognizes that Vancouver longshoremen went so far as to allow the principle of "all the men necessary, no unnecessary men" to be adopted as part of the M and M agreement, with the basic gang size falling in a few years from 13 men to only 6 men.[31]

Quite logically, the main opposition to M and M came from some of the younger longshoremen who would not be retiring for some time. This discontent among the younger men was unfocused, however, and was less important in a union where old-timers made up the majority. The main burden of tightening the ranks in the labour market in response to the threat of labour redundancy fell on the shoulders of casuals and semi-casuals, rather than on union members. The work opportunities for non-union labour declined significantly.

British Columbia's longshoremen provided their own wrinkle in this process of adaptation to the new technology. Despite strong and continuing resistance from management, the ILWU Canadian area won a "stuffing and destuffing" clause in the collective agreement that extended their work jurisdiction beyond the docks themselves into a 50-mile radius of the surrounding region. Hammered out in the 1969–70 negotiations following a major strike on the Vancouver waterfront, the clause's underlying rationale was that the container was, in essence, a moveable part of the ship and hence lay within the jurisdiction of longshoremen, whether or not it rested on the ship itself. In all other North American ports, the stuffing and destuffing of containers is done by cheaper labour outside of the longshore work force.[32]

Obviously British Columbia shippers were less than pleased by this development, since they feared the competition of Seattle, the pre-eminent container port on the Pacific coast. In 1976, a year after another major strike, the issue was temporarily resolved, seemingly to the satisfaction of both labour and management, when a special report by a group of consultants concluded that the effect of the container clause on Vancouver's competitiveness was marginal.[33] In fact, for the most part, the big losers in the longshoremen's jurisdictional expansion were not so much the shippers (with the exception of a transportation giant like Canadian Pacific), as other transport firms and the teamsters. Over the last few years, however, Vancouver has continued to lose ground steadily to Seattle as a container port, and employers have renewed their attack on the container clause. The ILWU recently agreed to let the matter be referred to another independent investigation, but whatever the result, these longshoremen have provided a lesson in not lying down before the onslaught of the machine by devising a strategy that provides new forms of work maximization and job control. The radical tradition still has considerable force within the British Columbia ILWU and has encouraged it to seek out new and unconventional forms of resistance.

There were other issues associated with the transformation of the longshoring labour process, however – particularly the creation of a new work force of machine-operators and the computerization of dispatch procedures – that would test the mettle of the ILWU. Negotiations on greater management control of the work force began in the United States in 1966 and soon extended to Canada. The employers argued that the new, costly machinery required a skilled, stable work force organized on a standard industrial model, and demanded the right to hire these workers and assign them to work without reference to the hiring hall. It soon became apparent to an increasing number of longshoremen, however, that the "skill" required by the new technology was far less than previously supposed, and that efficient operation of such equipment actually required little in the way of formal training. Many men learned to operate this equipment when the regular force of machine-operators was too small for peak periods, but these men found themselves unable to get such work during periods when the container ports were operating at less than peak capacity. The "shape-up" seemed to be slipping back through the differentiation of the work force and the establishment of a "technological elite." A lengthy, bitter strike was fought over this issue in San Francisco in 1971–2, but only in 1978 were concessions won that established a procedure of limited rotation of the machine-operators through the hiring hall.[34]

True to much of its tradition, the ILWU in British Columbia has fought the creation of an industrialized work force in the high-technology sphere that would eventually split the workers by accelerating differentiation. Vancouver longshoremen are proud of the fact that, when RO/RO cargo vehicles and facilities first arrived in the port, they proved that their machine-operators could operate them after only one hour of formal training.[35] The union has pushed for the fullest extension of training, allowing even casuals to obtain machine ratings. Currently, some union men in Vancouver have as many as twelve ratings. Management, on the other hand, argues that the shortage of trained operators requires the imposition of more discipline, particularly the elimination of chronic absenteeism. At present, managerial logic seems destined to win out, though the battle will be a stiffer one than elsewhere.

A similar struggle over the effects of containerization took place in Halifax, the only East Coast port in Canada with a hiring-hall tradition. In 1970, Halterm Limited, the company operating the Halifax container terminal, successfully negotiated an agreement with ILA Local 269 that recognized the right of the former to employ a "basic work force" of machine-operators at the container terminal, outside the hiring hall. Furthermore, these men were to constitute a "flexible and interchangable" work force, devoid of any gang structure. The appropriate dispatch procedure for a basic work force, from management's standpoint, would be one that allowed it to skirt the hiring hall altogether, except in periods of peak activity. Under the 1970 agreement, however, Halterm failed to obtain this prerogative. The procedure arising from this agreement gave the union actual control over dispatch in this area. Halterm had the right to call the required number of men from its "basic work force" list, according to the principle of low man out. If there were any fill-ins or replacements required, however, Halterm was not allowed to continue to go down its list but instead had to turn to the union hiring hall for these men, with the single exception of crane operators.[36] The union provided these replacements and fill-ins from its general dispatch board according to normal dispatch procedures. According to the original agreement, Halterm could only call the remainder of its "basic work force" if the union could not provide adequate numbers of men to replace absentees. However, owing to the high rate of absenteeism among "basic work force" members, which management had no real way of controlling, reliance on men provided by the hiring hall was heavy.

This was the situation that the Maritime Employers' Association (MEA) inherited when it first appeared in Halifax in 1971 (it was organized in Montreal in 1968). The struggle that followed was bitter and drawn out. The association tried to win management control of dispatch through lockouts in 1973 and 1976, but it was facing a union with a strong hiring-hall system and a history of job control. Moreover, the ILA in Halifax was in a much stronger position than the ILWU had been in San Francisco, where the union had tried to resist the creation of a separate industrial work force in the container terminals after such provisions were already included in the collective agreement. The union's position was clear. Longshoremen were concerned about the possibility of a "class division" within their ranks, with Halterm employees having the opportunity to earn more than $30,000 per year, while regular longshoremen might only earn as little as $20,000. The creation of a "basic work force" threatened this tradition. More important, it threatened the hiring hall itself.

Matters became more explosive in 1976 when Judge Nathan Green escalated the conflict by proposing dispatch rules ensuring that for important tasks only the "basic work force" would be utilized at the container terminal, along with new dispatch rules designed to discipline those workers who refused work for which they were qualified, or who failed to plug into the dispatch board upon entering the hiring hall. Hence the original issue centring on the basic work force had, through government intervention, escalated into other areas, questioning the longshoremen's traditional right *not* to work. The union resisted and the MEA replied with a lockout.

The result was a partial deadlock – though one in which the union's position was decisively weakened. Management won the right, in binding arbitration, to call all members of its basic work force, going to the hiring hall only in the event that there were insufficient men available within the basic work force itself.[37] And longshoremen could no longer legitimately refuse jobs for which they were qualified. Hence, all of Judge Green's dispatch rules were formally enacted. But, in practice, management does not yet have the power to compel longshoremen to accept a particular job, or to work from one day (or year) to another. Any attempt to impose the dispatch rules in full would lead to a virtual war on the waterfront. Still, it is clear that the ILA in Halifax is now on the defensive. The position of Halifax longshoremen was doubly undermined by the fact that their counterparts in Saint John, where a hiring-hall system had never developed, accepted "the basic work force" concept without a murmur.

More threatening to union job control on the waterfront than the revolution in cargo handling itself is the appearance of a computerized dispatch system in Canada. In principle, there is nothing particularly complex about such a system. It simply means that a computer is utilized to make the day-to-day, hour-to-hour decisions about the allocation of work to longshoremen according to certain fixed principles. Up to 50 longshoremen can then call in at a given time to find out from the "talking computer" what their job assignments are. In contrast to the hiring-hall system, however, the computer provides the means for effective managerial control of the dispatch process, the first consequence of which is the elimination of the gang structure.

Given the advantages that longshoremen obtain from the hiring-hall system, it is not surprising that Vancouver longshoremen resisted the introduction of a computerized dispatch system in British Columbia, where it was first developed. What is perhaps more surprising is that the ILWU leadership originally entertained the possibility of a computerized dispatch system, in principle. The 1970 collective agreement actually included the provision of setting up a system of dispatch utilizing a computer. Theoretically, computerized dispatch could promote overall social efficiency, while maximizing the amount of choice open to the individual longshoreman. No doubt the acceptance of the principle of computerized dispatch by the union leadership was based on the rather naive notion that it would mean an all-round improvement in the quality of work. Yet, for management, the object of a computerized dispatch system was to break down the gang system and the hiring hall; in other words, it had as its immediate end the accumulation of power in the workplace. Rather than a means of unleashing human potential, the computer becomes a tool in management's war against the relative autonomy of the worker. This became readily apparent to Vancouver longshoremen as soon as the proposal moved from the abstract phase into a concrete project. While the employers demonstrated some willingness to consider the possibility of computerized dispatch that utilized the "low man out" system or even "button rotation," the union saw it, even then, as an assault on the hiring hall and the quality of work.[38]

The battle over the computer in the Vancouver region lasted for several years. Not long after they had formally agreed to the introduction of computer dispatch, the union began to use every means at its disposal to block any movement whatsoever in that direction. Thus it resorted to all kinds of stalling tactics, before finally refusing to deal with the matter at all. In general, the ILWU claimed that no computer dispatch system could be put into force unless the entire contract was renegotiated. This the employers refused to do, since it would allow the union to win concessions to offset such a system. In the face of concerted union resistance, the employers were in fact deeply divided. They considered the possibility of using court action and government intervention to force the union's hand. Yet, they were no doubt hindered by the fact that they were trying to introduce a system for which there was as yet no precedent in North America. In opposition to the recommendations of the president of the British Columbia MEA, the employers decided to unilaterally develop the computerized dispatch system and to try to cajole the union into going along with it in the end.[39]

The issue of computerized dispatch was the most important point of contention in the 1972 strike, which took place in the BC ports, and which was ended by federal back-to-work legislation. This issue was referred to a joint committee and eventual oblivion. The MEA gradually came to the recognition that they could not get to first base in this area at the present time and dropped the entire project, with the loss of countless dollars. The computer system that had been developed was later sold to Montreal where there was relatively little labour resistance (though even then, it had to be imposed on labour through government "mediation" and legislation). The response of the British Columbia longshoremen to computerized dispatch is indicative of the general response of labour on the West Coast waterfront to management's attempts to gain control of dispatch. The battle is far from over. It may be that in the long run the hiring-hall system is doomed. Still, it is probable that any concerted attempt by the employers and the state to destroy the hiring hall, where it is firmly entrenched, will create a class war on the waterfront the likes of which has not been seen since the 1930s.

THE TECHNOLOGICAL REVOLUTION AND THE LABOUR PROCESS, II

In contrast to the ports with hiring-hall traditions, the technological revolution in cargo handling found Saint John and the St Lawrence ports still operating within the constellation of the traditional shape-up, the sharp edges of which were somewhat blunted by the existence of elaborate gang systems. In Saint John, some 2,267 casuals (known as "highbooters"), hired on the wharf, worked during 1976. The elite of the work force, however, consists of 650 longshoremen who are usually members of permanent gangs and of whom only 500 are actually "active."[40] Without a hiring-hall system, Saint John longshoremen have accepted "the basic work force principle" at the container facilities with relative equanimity. The long-term trend of labour relations in the port is undoubtedly toward decasualization under managerial auspices. But the traditional system (probably the most backward and discriminatory in North America) did not come under an intensive attack from management in the 1970s and 1980s. One of the reasons for this delay was that the technological revolution did not have the effect of creating labour redundancy in the major Canadian Atlantic ports – both of which became key ports for container traffic. Thus, total cargo handled by Saint John and Halifax in the Canadian eastern traffic rose from 24 per cent in 1968 to approximately 49 per cent in 1975, while that of Montreal sank from 58 per cent to 39 per cent.[41] In more recent years, Montreal has made gains at the expense of the Maritime ports (particularly in container traffic).[42] If this reversal of the trend of the late 1960s and 1970s continues, the position of longshoremen in the Atlantic ports will be seriously destabilized.

This is what happened on the St Lawrence a decade and a half ago. Prior to 1967, the distribution of work among gangs in Montreal was uneven and depended on the amount of work available to the stevedoring company to which a particular gang was attached. Some gangs might obtain twice as much work as less fortunate gangs. Foremen were complete masters of their gangs, hiring and firing virtually at will, although they, too, were union members. Those longshoremen who were not members of a parent gang, or those who simply did not have work on a particular day, had no choice but to go fishing for work along the waterfront – a practice known as "La seine." Since the port of Montreal extended over an area of eleven miles, longshoremen would not always find the dockwork they sought, even when such work was available.[43]

As usual, in the longshoring industry, this situation was further complicated by the existence of a sizeable non-union labour force. In 1966, 3,851 non-union men worked on the Montreal docks, alongside only 3,049 union men. While the percentage of hours worked by non-union men still made up less than 10 per cent of the total hours worked on the waterfront, the number of hours accounted for by such labour had more than doubled since 1959, compared to an increase of less than 20 per cent in the hours worked by union longshoremen over the same period. Since only union members could belong to a permanent gang, non-union men were especially vulnerable to all of the discriminatory practices associated with the shape-up.

Although union job control in Montreal had never been consolidated and institutionalized to the same degree as on the West Coast, it had nonetheless reached formidable proportions through a long and continuous struggle. And if the longshoring work force did not demonstrate the same level of political acumen as their Pacific brethren, they were nonetheless extremely militant and a force to be reckoned with. In fact, it was the enormous militancy of the dockworkers themselves, initiating strike after strike in the turbulent 1960s (as the cargo-handling revolution brought a rise in labour redundancy) who forced the whole issue of work relations on the waterfront to a head. The result was a short-run victory for labour that led to long-term losses.

The new regime that initially emerged out of the 1967 report of the government-appointed arbitrator, Laurent Picard, was aimed at stabilizing the Montreal waterfront, but was nonetheless in many ways relatively favourable to labour. Despite strong management objections, it provided, in particular, a weekly work guarantee, which proved to be "the highest in North America."[44] This "job security plan," as it was called, guaranteed 40 hours of work per week over 37 weeks for each longshoreman in the union. There were some catches, however. First, any man who did not come in for work when called would have his guarantee reduced by the number of hours worked by his gang during that day. Second, any man who refused 20 per cent of the work offered to him during the "job security season" would immediately be removed from the security plan. Third, a man "discharged for cause" would cease to be eligible for job security. Fourth, the guarantee was tied to a production index that lowered the number of hours guaranteed for each drop in productivity. At the same time, while the gang system was not abolished, the size of the gang was reduced slightly from the existing standard of 19 men for loading and 21 for unloading to 17 for each. The longshoremen also gained certain rights with respect to the setting of official rest periods – an attempt to compensate for the elimination of the old "spell 'o'" system.[45]

Implementation of this new system required elimination of the last vestiges of the shape-up, to be replaced by a rotation system in some kind of hiring hall. The Picard report provided that each employer must rotate its own gangs so that no gang could obtain more than 44 hours of work per week unless the employer had no other gang it could utilize. Furthermore, no gang could be given more than 48 hours of work unless no other gang at the port was available. The shipping companies and stevedoring contractors first tried to establish a hiring hall run exclusively by themselves, but the union refused to play ball and "completely ransacked the premises removing even heating coils and plumbing."[46] Eventually a compromise was worked out whereby the Shipping Federation was to run the roster of employees from its own centre and the union would control the actual dispatch of employees from premises provided by the federation.

The dispatch hall was largely a telephone clearing house that used tape recordings provided by management to call out both the members of parent gangs and supernumeries needed to replace absent longshoremen. Since absenteeism for both permanent gang members and replacements was frequently as high as 30 per cent, however, the ILA had the responsibility of dispatching large numbers of additional men from the hiring hall. Thus, management once again found itself faced by a situation in which it was unable to control the work force. A man who had been "fired" by an employer would usually be redispatched, even in some cases to the same employer. The union's added control over dispatch thus gave it power that it had not formerly had. Much to management's alarm, the new system had not substantially diminished the longshoremen's ability to resist managerial control. While managerial prerogatives for disciplining the labour force had been recognized in principle, the union remained so powerful that these employer rights were for the most part mere words on paper.

The Picard decision was a shaky compromise that left employers grumbling, especially about the onerous weekly job guarantee, the still-large gang size, and the lack of control over dispatch. The resulting managerial crisis led to the formation of the Maritime Employers' Association in 1968, a unified and highly professional negotiating body (which extended into the East Coast ports in 1971), able to keep its own membership in line and to provide a unified and aggressive strategy toward labour. The abolition of "restrictive" work practices (which for management was synonymous with any form of union job control whatsoever), and the technological advances in handling general cargo, led to a reduction of the union work force by over 50 per cent in the years between 1967 and 1978, together with almost total elimination of non-union labour on the waterfront. Beginning in 1967, the work opportunities for non-union longshoremen diminished, and as the relentless "rationalization" of the industry proceeded, more and more union labour became redundant as well. The union was forced to make concessions on sling-load restrictions, gang size, rest periods, absenteeism, and the introduction of new machinery; and each new concession further undermined labour's position by creating a labour surplus on the waterfront. It was under these conditions that longshoremen seized whatever guarantees of security seemed to present themselves. Nothing could have been more consistent with the overall logic of the technological determinism that management so assiduously promoted.

During the transition period, beginning with the Picard system and culminating in total decasualization, the Montreal waterfront was the centre of almost perpetual conflict. One problem that was particularly galling to management arose out of the union's control of foremen and "walking bosses." Since these men were members of the union, they often found themselves torn between managerial responsibilities – and hence identification with management – and their union status. The union tried to ensure their allegiance by fining them up to $50 for taking the side of the employers in any dispute. Management frequently responded by reimbursing foremen and walking bosses for these fines imposed upon them by their own union. This strange situation persisted until 1969, when management succeeded in winning a provision in the collective agreement that prohibited the union from placing any penalties on walking bosses and foremen.[47]

Skirmishes of this sort, however, were mere preliminaries to a much more extensive battle. Not surprisingly, the first confrontation centred on control over the work force itself, i.e. the rules of dispatch. As long as management was unable to gain sufficient control over the work force, it could not impose what it considered to be a satisfactory level of discipline. Since the state apparatus generally shared management's view of productivity and discipline, it was merely necessary to demonstrate to an official arbitrator that labour was deliberately slowing down the pace of "progress."

The showdown finally came in 1972. Under pressure from management to eliminate the last vestiges of the "spell 'o" (which persisted despite the fact that it had been legislated out of existence by the Picard decision), and faced with increased insecurity due to technological change, the union walked out in a wildcat strike for eight weeks. The strike was ended by an act of Parliament. The union did not immediately honour the back-to-work order, however, and the union officials were fined $25,000 by the Department of Justice. Meanwhile, all longshoremen were suspended indefinitely while they were still out on strike, and even after the port had officially reopened, since it would take time before the ships could return. Judge Alan Gold was appointed arbitrator and took a stance favourable to management. Job security was revoked for two full months. Films showing the perpetuation of the "spell 'o" system were shown and served to convince Gold of the justice of management's position.

It was at this time that management gained total control over the dispatch of the work force. Under government arbitration, the right of the employer to control dispatch was considered to be a necessary part of any job-guarantee program. The old gang system was abolished altogether. In its place management instituted a computerized dispatch system which, as we saw, had been studied by the British Columbia Maritime Employer's Association, and resisted tooth and nail by the ILWU in Vancouver. This was the first computerized dispatch system utilized in North America. The computer is maintained and serviced by about thirty-five individuals and in the beginning required a yearly expense of upwards of $500,000 to operate. The expense was well worth it to management, since the ninety-six gangs were replaced by a system that allocated men entirely according to the specific needs of the employers.[48] Thus the foundations for scientific management were finally laid.

At the same time, the problem of the labour surplus had to be dealt with. The vast changes occurring at the port had enormously reduced the demand for labour. A buy-out took place in 1973-4 whereby management gave each man leaving the industry a cash payment of $12,000. A total of 500 men left the industry on this basis. Once again, the process was eased by the advanced age of the work force. Even today, after more than a 50 per cent drop in the number of union men, the average age for union members on the waterfront is said to be somewhere around 55 years. As of 1979, there were less than 1,400 men working the Montreal waterfront on a regular basis.

Even a cursory glance at recent collective agreements between the MEA and ILA Local 375 gives some idea of the incredible transformations that have taken place in the last thirteen or fourteen years. Longshoremen are now deployed from a dispatch centre tied to a large computer and controlled primarily by management. The longshoreman's right *not* to work, as well as his ability to choose *where* he works, has all but disappeared. Management has the absolute right to dispatch labour as it sees fit, with only the guarantee that eight hours of continuous work will go along with each dispatch assignment. Management also has the prerogative to recall men who have already worked eight successive hours during a day for an additional overtime shift of four hours on the same day. All cases of absenteeism must be documented and legitimate reasons provided. Rest periods are rigidly specified (thirty minutes every four hours plus a meal hour). A strict system of classification of employees exists that gives each longshoreman only one "primary" classification, along with other "secondary" and – depending on the individual – "probationary" classifications (examples of standard classifications are "hold-man" and "slingman"). Sling-load size is now open-ended and decided at "employers' discretion provided that the gear and equipment are duly checked by the Tackle Inspectors of the Department of

Transport and the Safety Officers." Safety is to be considered secondary to efficiency, which is clearly more important in the new regime. The introduction of the latest technology is a basic right of management, not to be disputed.[49]

To be sure, the new system is in many ways convenient. Longshoremen no longer have to spend time waiting for work at the hiring hall but merely need to call in to the dispatch centre at certain stipulated times. This takes a lot of the unnecessary leg work out of the job – a fact strongly emphasized by management. In the words of one employer representative, "In the Port of New York longshoremen must check in at the hiring hall twice a day. In Montreal they never have to go anywhere past the telephone."[50] Yet this is small compensation for the world that was lost, and for the changes that can be expected in the near future. The last decade has prepared the ground for the implementation of methods of scientific management through the progressive centralization of job control in the hands of the employers. It is certain that the longshoring industry in Montreal will evolve in the direction of greater subdivision of labour. In fact, the creation of a separate and highly differentiated work force at the container piers is already undermining the traditional "jack of all trades" approach that has generally characterized longshoring. Under existing conditions, it is likely that foremen and walking bosses will increasingly swap their allegiance to the union for a solid place in the managerial hierarchy (where, after all, the real power lies – i.e. short of an all-out labour revolt). Wages will become increasingly differentiated as the process of worker alienation (the managerial task) unfolds.

All this will depend, though, on the long-run stability of the industry. Somewhat paradoxically, it is the casual and unstable nature of longshoring that has, in the past, generated a strong union power structure. Insecurity was the main force in creating militancy among longshoremen, encouraging them to carve out a sphere of influence all their own. Ultimately, only a labour force with a radical perspective will be equipped to counter the offensive of the capitalist managerial program.

Whatever the future holds for the Montreal longshoremen, one thing they understood very well in 1980 was that the existing system frequently operated by means of an extension of the working day. It has become all too common for longshoremen to be forced to work a twelve-hour day under the new system. Ships need to get in and out of the port as soon as possible, since their profits are increased in direct proportion to the speed at which they deliver their goods. Yet, decasualization has so reduced the labour force that there is little latitude to provide the surge for peak activity. From a managerial standpoint, there is a certain amount of indifference about the pain that a twelve-hour day imposes on the individual worker. By forcing the men to work longer hours, management is able to circumvent any need for an enlargement of the work force or expansion of the job security plan. The longshoremen responded by making this their prime issue. In 1980, the question of the "stretch-out" overshadowed everything else.

LONGSHOREMEN AND LABOUR

From this analysis, it should be apparent that decasualization in the longshoring industry is far from being the smooth, linear process with which it has long been associated. The original motivation for decasualization came from the workers themselves and resulted in significant workers' job control. But part of the power and autonomy of longshoremen stemmed, somewhat paradoxically, from the fact that the process of decasualization was incomplete. They managed to retain some of the benefits of casual labour without its defects. Longshoremen remained in large part free to work when they chose, and had considerable discretion in choosing their specific work environment on a daily basis. Everywhere in the 1980s this system is breaking down. Where a strong hiring-hall system has evolved, as in Vancouver and the other BC ports, longshoremen have given way slowly before the force of the new cargo-handling innovations and the appearance of computerized dispatch. Where this was not the case, as in Montreal, management has been able to impose much of its own organization on the industry.

In a recent article on how the labour movement might extend its bases of power in the crisis economy of the 1980s, Jeremy Brecher has pointed to the longshoring industry, particularly the West Coast experience, as offering perhaps the single, most obvious example of an aggressive strategy through the control of hiring.[51] But longshoremen are everywhere on the defensive in relation to job control. Those ports that in many ways appear most "modern," like Montreal, have entirely bypassed "decasualization under union auspices" and are firmly in the grip of management. The task of labour on the waterfront, therefore, becomes one of avoiding this path, and of finding ways to enlarge upon the course traditionally assumed by ports like San Francisco and Vancouver. If there is to be a "born-again labour movement," the longshoremen themselves will once again have to be at the very edge of change.

NOTES

1 This essay is based upon an earlier unpublished monograph entitled, "Technology, Taylorism and 'Man Along the Shore': The Canadian Longshoring Industry and the Evolution of Job Control," written under the auspices of (and with financial support from) the University of Toronto/York University Joint Program in Transportation in July 1981. It relies heavily on interviews of various spokesmen on the Canadian longshoring industry, conducted in Ottawa, Montreal,

Vancouver, and Halifax during summer and fall 1979, fall and winter 1980, and winter 1984. In addition, several interviews were carried out in Seattle in summer 1979. Within the industry, special thanks are due to Gordon Clark, Ron Kervin, Robert Walsh, Robert Lacroix, Emil Bjarnason, Norm Cunningham, Craig Pritchett, and Don Garcia. My greatest debt is to Edgar J. Dosman of York University, who taught me the ropes in this area. Craig Heron and David Bell, also of York University, provided much needed help and encouragement. Needless to say, I claim full responsibility for the particular interpretation here, which does not necessarily reflect the views of any of the individuals listed above.

2 R.B. Oram, *Cargo Handling and the Modern Port* (Oxford 1965), 45.

3 Ibid., 48.

4 Archibald A. Evans, *Technical and Social Changes in the World's Ports* (Geneva 1969), 174.

5 Paul T. Hartman, *Collective Bargaining and Productivity: The Longshore Mechanization Agreement* (Berkeley 1969), 26.

6 Herb Mills, "The San Francisco Waterfront: The Social Consequences of Industrial Modernization," in Andrew Zimbalist, ed., *Case Studies on the Labor Process* (New York 1979), 133.

7 See Charles P. Larrowe, *The Shape-up and the Hiring Hall* (Berkeley 1955), and *Harry Bridges: The Rise and Fall of Radical Labor in the U.S.* (New York 1972); David Milton, *The Politics of U.S. Labour: From the Great Depression to the New Deal* (New York 1982), 40–52; and International Longshoremen's and Warehousemen's Union (ILWU) Local 500 Pensioners, *"Man Along the Shore"!: The Story of the Vancouver Waterfront, as Told by the Longshoremen Themselves, 1860s–1975* (Vancouver 1975).

8 Hartman, *Collective Bargaining and Productivity*, 18. In its early years, the International Longshoremen's Association (ILA) encompassed the Pacific coast as well as Eastern and Gulf coasts. The U.S. Pacific coast union merged with the ILA in 1898. In 1912, Vancouver longshoremen also joined the ILA, until the union was broken in the 1923 strike. But by the time of the 1934 strike in San Francisco, the Pacific Coast District (U.S.) was part of the ILA in name only. In 1937, the U.S. Pacific-coast locals formally broke away to join the Congress of Industrial Organizations (CIO) and formed the International Longshoremen's and Warehousemen's Union, only to be expelled from the CIO in 1949 for being "Communist dominated."

9 ILWU Pensioners, *"Man Along the Shore"!*, 34.

10 To the present day, the hiring-hall system in Vancouver is formally administered by the employers. This seems to have had little effect in the long run, however, on the degree of job control exerted by the workers themselves, which compares favourably with that of most ports.

11 ILWU Pensioners, *"Man Along the Shore"!*, 84–5.

12 Hartman, *Collective Bargaining and Productivity*, 30.

13 In the various ports, these tiers within the labour market are given different names.

In Vancouver they are known as union men, semi-casuals who work off the "numbered boards," and "disk men." In Halifax, they are union men, "card men" (semi-casuals), and "bull-pen workers" (casuals). In St John, where the shape-up still exists, there are simply union men and "highbooters" (casuals). In San Francisco, there are "A men" (union men), "B men" (semi-casuals), and "Y men" (casuals). Serious conflicts between the union and semi-casual work forces have occurred in San Francisco in the 1970s and Halifax in the 1980s.

14 Hartman, *Collective Bargaining and Productivity*, 70.

15 This is not to say that men are simply hired off the wharf, or that there is severe discrimination on a day-to-day basis. Most men who are lucky enough to be members of the union are also members of permanent gangs with fairly regular work patterns, usually tied to the demands of particular employers (shipping firms and stevedoring contractors). There is, however, no principle that evens out work opportunities among gangs, and casuals ("highbooters") are caught in the classic shape-up. See Edgar J. Dosman, *Labour/Management Relations on the Saint John Waterfront: ILA Local 273 and the Maritime Employers Association*, University of Toronto/York University Joint Program in Transportation, Transportation Paper no. 6 (April 1980).

16 Hartman, *Collective Bargaining and Productivity*, 25.

17 Stuart B. Philpott, "The Union Hiring as a Labour Market: A Sociological Analysis," *British Journal of Industrial Relations* 3, no. 1 (March 1965): 22–3ff.

18 John Dougall, et al., *Manpower on the Halifax Waterfront: Projections of Demand, Supply and Training Needs* (Halifax 1977), 23–5.

19 Frederick Winslow Taylor, *The Principles of Scientific Management* (New York 1911), 68–74.

20 Ibid., 72–3.

21 Ibid., 69.

22 Arthur I. Smith, Commissioner, *Report of Inquiry into Certain Conditions, Conduct and Matters Giving Rise to Labour Unrest at the Ports of Montreal, Trois-Rivieres and Quebec, P.Q.* (Ottawa 1969), 47–9.

23 Quoted in Hartman, *Collective Bargaining and Productivity*, 60.

24 Lawrence J. Rinaldi, *Containerization: The New Method of Intermodal Transport* (New York 1972), 55.

25 Mills, "The San Francisco Waterfront," in Zimbalist, ed., *Case Studies*, 144n.

26 Mills, "The San Francisco Waterfront: The Social Consequences of Industrial Modernization," part II, *Urban Life* 6, no. 1 (April 1977): 16.

27 Hartman, *Collective Bargaining and Productivity*, 80–2.

28 Emil Bjarnason, "Mechanization and Collective Bargaining in the British Columbia Longshore Industry" (PH D dissertation, Department of Economics, Simon Fraser University 1975), 42; Oram, *Cargo Handling and the Modern Port*, 52.

29 Bjarnason, "Mechanization and Collective Bargaining," 42–8. The share-of-the-machine concept was not actually adopted in British Columbia. Instead, what amounted to the same thing was couched in terms of a supplementary pension. The

employment guarantee was included in the BC M and M agreement but was not actually put into effect and was later dropped from the collective agreement – to be replaced by a "Supplementary Unemployment Benefit Program" – after management convinced the longshoremen that a work guarantee in terms of hours was never worth much since it did not apply where fluctuations in business conditions were concerned.

30 Hartman, *Collective Bargaining and Productivity*, 12; Gill Green, *What's Happening to Labor* (New York 1976), 98.

31 Bjarnason, "Mechanization and Collective Bargaining," 48; Donald Garcia, "Management and Labour in Waterfront Industries," in R. Gordon Hutchinson, ed., *Western Canadian Ports: Their Origins, Present, Problems and Future* (Vancouver 1977), 255.

32 The container clause was a result of the enormously complex negotiations that surrounded the consolidation of the M and M agreement in British Columbia in 1969. Management managed to win the right to employ a "regular work force" at its facilities (weakening the hiring-hall system to some extent); a smaller gang size; "flexibility and interchangeability" in the deployment of labour; and the principle of computerized dispatch. Labour's main gain, other than an increase in M and M benefits themselves, was the container clause. As it turned out, management did not win as much as it thought, since it was never able to implement computerized dispatch in the face of rank and file opposition among the longshoremen themselves.

33 See IBI Group, *Container Traffic through the Port of Vancouver and Work Opportunity for Longshoremen* (Vancouver 1976).

34 Mills, "The San Francisco Waterfront," in Zimbalist, ed., *Case Studies*, 153–4.

35 Kenneth R. Robinson, "Cargo Hooks and Computers: The ILWU and Automation," *Canadian Labour* 18, no. 1 (January 1974): 3.

36 Edgar J. Dosman, *Labour Relations on the Halifax Waterfront*, University of Toronto/York University Joint Program in Transportation, unpublished monograph (1977), III:14–15ff.

37 *MEA/ILA Local 269, Collective Agreement, 1978*, 44–5.

38 Internal BCMEA Newsletter, 15 June 1971.

39 Internal BCMEA memorandum, no date.

40 Dosman, *Labour/Management Relations on the Saint John Waterfront*, 37.

41 Ibid., 5–6.

42 In Montreal in 1983, 350,000 Twenty-Foot Equivalent Units (TEUS) moved across the docks, compared to about 114,000 in Vancouver (*Globe and Mail*, 9 January 1984).

43 Laurent A. Picard, Commissioner, *Report of the Inquiry Commission on the St. Lawrence Ports* (Ottawa 1967), 19–27ff.

44 Ibid., 91.

45 Ibid., 15–16, 68–70.

46 Smith, *Report of Inquiry into Certain Conditions*, 56.

47 Ibid., 44–6.

48 *The Province*, 6 October 1972.

49 *MEA/ILA Local 375 Collective Agreement, January 1, 1978–Dec. 31, 1980.*

50 Robert Lacroix, 3 August 1979 interview.

51 Jeremy Brecher, "Crisis Economy: Born-Again Labour Movement?" *Monthly Review* 35, no. 10 (March 1984): 13–14.

ESTER REITER

Life in a Fast-Food Factory

The growth of large multinational corporations in the service industries in the post-World War II years has transformed our lives. The needs and tastes of the public are shaped by the huge advertising budgets of a few large corporations. The development of new industries has transformed work, as well as social life. This paper focuses on the technology and the labour process in the fast-food sector of the restaurant industry. Using Marx's description of the transitions from craft to manufacture to large-scale industry, it considers the changes in the restaurant industry brought about by the development of fast-food chains. The description of life in a fast-food factory is based on my experience working in a Burger King outlet in 1980/1.

THE RISE OF THE FAST-FOOD INDUSTRY

Eating out is big business. The restaurant industry in Canada has grown from some 14,000 establishments in 1951 to nearly 30,000 in 1978.[1] Sales in 1982 were 9.6 billion dollars nationally, which, even taking into account the declining value of the dollar, is still a sixfold increase over the past thirty years.[2] Although people with higher incomes dine out more frequently, *all* Canadians are spending money on food away from home. In 1978, over 32 cents of every food dollar was spent on food outside the home.[3]

Since the late 1960s, fast-food restaurants have been growing at a much higher rate than independent restaurants, virtually colonizing the suburbs.[4] Local differences in taste and style are obliterated as each town offers the familiar array of trademarked foods: neat, clean, and orderly, the chains serve up the same goods from Nova Scotia to Vancouver Island. The casualties of this phenomenal growth are the small "mom and pop" establishments, rather than the higher-priced, full-service restaurants. Fast-food outlets all conform to a general pattern. Each has a limited menu, usually featuring hamburger, chicken, or fried fish. Most are part of a chain, and most require customers to pick up their own food at a counter.[5] The common elements are minimum delay in getting the food to the customer (hence "fast food") and prices that are relatively low compared to those at full-service restaurants.

The fast-food industry is an example of what Harry Braverman called the extension of the universal market.[6] That is, the family moves into the sphere of the market. The effect of this "extension" on the family has been varied. Often, new technology applied to some household task at first removes the activity from the home; later, still newer technologies return the activity to the home in an altered form. By the late 1930s, for example, many families had come to send a good part of their laundry to power laundries; later when washing machines were widely available, the laundry was returned to the home – to be washed most often, by women.[7] Similarly, the development of the movie industry during the first half of the twentieth century drew people out of their homes. After television was developed, however, the market at home proved more lucrative, and now virtually every Canadian family has at least one television set, while the movie industry has been declining since the 1950s.[8]

The entry of capital into the food production and consumption process has had several different effects. In the 1930s, for instance, techniques were developed for the quick freezing of foods. The perfection of these techniques made it possible to purchase increasingly diverse arrays of foods that need only be "heated and served." By the 1950s, the growth of large shopping-plaza supermarkets overwhelmed grocery stores, putting the small, independent corner grocer out of business. Shopping trips can be less frequent when large amounts of frozen and packaged foods are purchased, and the huge increase in families owning automobiles made possible visits to the more distant, large shopping plazas.

Seeking to supplement their sales to the supermarkets, large food processors like Kraft began to market their products to the restaurant industry in the late 1960s. Food production has been largely taken over by large corporations, but now different capital interests wrestle with each other to determine whether food consumption is going to take place in public businesses or in the home. Restaurant officials welcomed the new products (such as preportioned jellies, frozen entrees, canned soups) enthusiastically. In 1967, one restaurant official predicted that "custom-made food will soon be as luxurious as custom-made automobiles or shirts."[10] As these new processed, preportioned foods were introduced into public eating places, franchised restaurants began to appear in Canada. These were usually connected to larger parent companies that had started a few years earlier in the United States. "Franchising" confers the right, on payment of an agreed fee, to sell certain products under a recognized trade name; the items are backed by national advertisements and on-the-spot promotions. The products offered are limited in number and are produced in prescribed ways, using machinery specified by and purchased from the franchisor.[11]

During the early years, fast-food franchising seemed like a bottomless gold mine, and indeed a few western operators became millionaires when Colonel Sanders' Kentucky Fried Chicken was first franchised in Canada. The franchise system seemed to offer the small businessman the opportunity of a lifetime: permitting a big corporation to dictate how a business should be run promised to minimize risks in this very risky business. By 1970, *Canadian Hotel and Restaurant* magazine estimated that about 75 per cent of all fast-food outlets were controlled by franchising companies. Three companies, Kentucky Fried Chicken, A & W, and Chicken Delight – all affiliates of United States corporations – together controlled 60 per cent of the 1,457 franchised outlets in Canada. The large multinational corporations that produced grocery products extended their interest in the restaurant industry by entering it directly in the late 1960s with the purchase of restaurant chains. For example, Lever Brothers Ltd, a wholly owned subsidiary of Unilever, acquired A & W Food Services of Canada and Shopsy's Foods Ltd. General Foods acquired the White Spots restaurant chain in western Canada, as well as two other chains: Canterbury Foods (which ran the Crock 'n Block restaurants) and the "1867" restaurants. General Foods is one of the largest processors of packaged groceries, with products ranging from coffee (Maxwell House, Yuban, Sanka, Brim) to breakfast cereals and dessert foods under the "Jell-O," "Bird's Eye," and "Minute Brand" names.[12]

The largest of the fast-food restaurants – McDonald's – entered the Canadian market in 1968. Since May 1983, over 450 of its outlets were operating in Canada, posting $636.5 million in gross annual sales – part of an empire of 6,800 stores in 27 countries with more than $25 billion in sales in 1983. The second-largest fast-food chain is Burger King. Founded in 1954 by James McLamore and David Edgerton, Burger King became a wholly owned subsidiary of Pillsbury in 1967, during the first wave of mergers between packaged-food and restaurant chains. The company grew from 257 restaurants at the time of the merger to 3,022 by May 1981. About 130,000 people are employed in Burger Kings all over the world. By November 1982, there were 87 Burger King stores in Canada, 40 of them company owned.[13] The Canadian-owned company stores operated at an average gross profit of 60 per cent in 1980/81.

TRANSFORMING THE
OPERATIONS OF A KITCHEN

Until approximately twenty-five years ago, all restaurant work involved an extensive division of labour: a complex hierarchy within the kitchen required workers with varying levels of skill and training. For a restaurant to be successful, all workers' had to co-ordinate their efforts. A supervisor's function was not only to ensure that the work was done, but to see that the various parts of the operation were synchronized. William Whyte, who studied the restaurant industry in the United States, described the production process:

Timing and coordination are the keynotes of the operation. If the customer does not get his food when he wants it, he is upset. If the waitress cannot get it from the service pantry, she chafes at the delay. And so on down into the kitchen. A breakdown anywhere in the chain of production, transfer and service sends repercussions through the entire organization. No one can fail to feel its effects, for the restaurant is an organization made up of highly interdependent parts. If one part fails to function, the organization can no longer operate.

The parts are the people who handle the food and adjust their work to each other. But cooks, pantry girls, waitresses, and other workers are not the only important parts. To keep this delicately adjusted machine functioning requires supervision of a high order. At each important point there must be a supervisor helping to organize the work of the employees and to organize their relations with each other to eliminate the friction and build up the cooperation essential to efficiency.[14]

This production arrangement resembles what Marx called "manufacture." In the restaurant described by William Whyte, the skill of the worker remains central to the production process. The commodity created (the meal served to the customer) is the social product of many workers' efforts. Human beings, using tools to assist them in their work, remain the organs of the productive mechanism.

In the fast-food industry, the machines, or the instruments of labour, assume a central place. Instead of assisting workers in the production of the meal, the machines tended by workers are dominant; we now have an objective organization of machines confronting the worker. Marx described this as the transition from "manufacture" to "large-scale industry."[15] Since the motion of the factory proceeds from the machinery and not from the worker, working personnel can continually be replaced. Frequent change in workers will not disrupt the labour process – a shift in organization applauded by *Harvard Business Review* contributor, Theodore Levitt.[16] According to Levitt, this new model is intended to replace the "humanistic concept of service" with the kind of technocratic thinking that in other fields has replaced "the high cost and erratic elegance of the artisan with the low-cost munificence of the manufacturer." McDonald's is a "supreme" example of this kind of thinking.

The systematic substitution of equipment for people, combined with the carefully planned use and positioning of technology, enables McDonald's to attract and hold patronage in proportions no predecessor or imitator has managed to duplicate ... If machinery is to be viewed as a piece of equipment with the capability of producing a predictably standardized customer-satisfying output while minimizing the operating discretion of its attendant, that is what a McDonald's outlet is. It is a machine that produces with the help of totally unskilled machine tenders, a highly polished product. Through painstaking attention to total design and facilities planning, everything is built integrally into the machine itself, into the technology of the system. The only choice available to the attendant is to operate it exactly as the designers intended.

The labour process so admired by Levitt has been adopted by many of the large fast-food companies. In the case of Burger King, the adoption has been a literal one: Donald Smith, the operations executive at McDonald's who developed this system, was hired away in January 1977 to become president of Burger King. There, he initiated a number of projects under the heading "Operation Grand Slam," which changed the system of menu and food preparation in an effort to duplicate McDonald's success.[17]

MANAGING A STORE

The brain centre of all Burger King outlets, company owned or franchised, lies in Burger King headquarters in Miami, Florida. It is there that the Burger King bible, the *Manual of Operating Data*, is prepared. The procedures laid down in the manual must be followed to the letter by all Burger King stores. To ensure that procedures are indeed followed, each outlet is investigated and graded twice yearly by a team from regional headquarters. Termed a "Restaurant Operations Consultation," the assessment administered by the investigators gives each store a numerical grade according to a detailed forty-three-page list of what to look for and how many points each particular aspect is worth. When a store is being investigated, both managers and workers clean frenetically and work as hard as possible. A great deal depends on these investigations, as a manager could be transferred or demoted, or a franchisee's license withdrawn, if the showing is poor.

The criteria for grading a store give heavy weighting to those items that are crucial to a store's profitability. Profitability rests primarily on the volume of a store's sales and the cost of those sales. Therefore, cleanliness, not only in the food-production area, but also in the toilets and the surrounding parking area is stressed so that customers will be attracted to the store. In order to maximize volume and minimize labour costs, there is tremendous emphasis on what Burger King management calls sos or speed of service. The demand on an individual unit's production capacity can fluctuate as much as 1,000 per cent over an hour in the period before a lunch or dinner to the height of the meal rush. Demand is at its peak during the lunch hour, which accounts for about 20 per cent of sales for the day; the more people served during the hours of twelve to one, the higher the sales volume in the store.

Up Front, the Burger King publication for store managers, reminds them that "an aware manager understands that maintaining speed of service is like putting money in the bank."[18] Miami studies are referred to that show customers will wait patiently for only three minutes from the moment of entering the store; after that, they will walk away. Ideally, then, service time should never exceed three minutes.[19] Labour costs are also kept down by minimizing the use of full-time workers and by hiring minimum-wage part-time workers. Workers are asked to fill out an availability sheet when they are hired, indicating the hours they can work. Particularly when students are involved, management pressures them to make themselves as available as possible, though no guarantees are provided for how many hours a week work they will be given, or on which days they will be asked to work.

Burger King pushed the common restaurant industry practice of using part-time workers one step further in 1978 with the development of a new labour-scheduling method called the "people game." Under this new system, hourly sales projections are recorded, based upon the previous three weeks' sales. Hourly manning guides are then used to allot labour for each hour's projected sales. Scheduling is done each week for the coming week and workers are expected to come to the store and check the labour schedule each week to see when they are supposed to show up. The *Manual of Operating Data* recommends that as many short shifts as possible be assigned, so that few breaks will be required. This rule, the manual notes, is especially important in areas where labour laws require paid breaks.

Food and paper costs make up about 40 per cent of the cost of sales in Burger King outlets. These costs are essentially fixed, owing to company requirements that all Burger King outlets buy their stock from approved distributors. While such a policy offers the advantages of bulk purchasing, it also ties each outlet to costs set by head-office negotiations, leaving little room for purchase-cost reductions. In effect, individual stores have control over food costs in only two areas – "waste" of food and meals provided to employees. Both together make up less than 4 per cent of the cost of sales. "Waste" consists of food pre-prepared for lunch and dinner shifts that is not sold in the time limit set for each food (10 minutes for sandwiches, 5 minutes for fries). The discarded food is carefully counted and recorded after each meal rush. Employees are under pressure to have enough food ready so that customers can be served quickly, but are held responsible for any "waste" that results. A chart on the kitchen wall graphs the waste percentage each day. Employee meals are also monitored, and limits on food items available to workers are imposed. For example, while workers were formerly allowed any sandwich, fries or dessert, and a drink, they are now allowed a meal costing not more than $2.50 in menu prices. A manager must inspect all choices, and initial the meal selection listed by workers on their time cards.

Store operations are designed from head office in Miami. In 1980, this office commissioned a study to find ways of lowering labour costs, increasing workers' productivity, and maintaining the most efficient inventories. The various components of a restaurant's operations were defined: customer-arrival patterns, manning or positioning strategies, customer/cashier inter-actions, order characteristics, production-time standards, stocking rules and inventory. Time-motion reports for making the various menu items, as well as corporate standards for service were also included in the calculation, and the data were all entered into a computer. By late 1981, it was possible to provide store managers not only with a staffing chart for hourly sales – indicating how many people should be on the floor given the predicted volume of business for that hour – but also where they should be positioned, based on the type of kitchen design. Thus, although staffing had been regulated since the late 1970s, what discretion managers formerly had in assigning and utilizing workers has been eliminated. The use of labour is now calculated precisely, as is any other objectively defined component of the system, such as store design, packaging, and inventory.[20]

Having determined precisely what workers are supposed to be doing and how quickly they should be doing it, the only remaining issue is that of getting them to perform to specifications. "Burger King University," located at headquarters in Miami was set up to achieve this goal. Housed in a remodelled art gallery, the multimillion-dollar facility is staffed by a group of "professors" who have worked their way up in the Burger King system to the rank of district manager. Burger King trains its staff to do things "not well, but right," the Burger King way.[21] Tight control over Burger King restaurants throughout the world rests on standardizing operations – doing things the "right" way – so that outcomes are predictable. The manager of a Burger King outlet does not necessarily need any knowledge of restaurant operations because the company provides it. What Burger King calls "people skills" are required; thus a job description for a manager indicated that he/she

- Must have good verbal communication skills
- Must have patience, tact, fairness, and social sensitivity in dealing with customers and hourly employees
- Must be able to supervise and motivate team of youthful employees and conduct himself/herself in a professional manner
- Must present a neat, well-groomed image
- Must be willing to work nights, weekends and holidays[22]

In 1981, a new crew-training program, designed as an outcome of the computer-simulation study was developed. The training program is called

"The Basics of Our Business" and is meant to "thoroughly train crew members in all areas of operations and to educate them on how Burger King and the restaurant where they work ... fit into the American free-enterprise system." In addition, the training program involves supervised work at each station, and a new feature that requires every employee to pass a standardized test on appropriate procedures for each station in the store.

Burger King thus operates with a combination of control techniques: technology is used to simplify the work and facilitate centralization, while direct control or coercion is exercised on the floor to make sure the pace of the work remains swift. "If there's time to lean, there's time to clean," is a favourite saying among managers. In fact, workers are expected to be very busy *all* the time they are on shifts, whether or not there are customers in the store. Sitting down is never permissible; in fact, the only chair in the entire kitchen is in the manager's office in a glassed-in cubicle at the rear of the kitchen. From there, the manager can observe the workers at their jobs. The application of these techniques is supported by a legitimizing ideology that calls for "patience, fairness, and social sensitivity" in dealing with customers in order to increase sales and profits "for the betterment of Burger King corporation and its employees."[23]

WORKING AT BURGER KING

I did fieldwork on the fast-food industry by working at a Burger King outlet in suburban Toronto in 1980/1. The Burger King at which I worked was opened in 1979, and by 1981 was the highest volume store in Canada with annual sales of over one million dollars. Everything in the customers' part of the store was new, shiny, and spotlessly clean. Live plants lent a touch of class to the seating area. Muzak wafted through the air, but customers sat on chairs designed to be sufficiently uncomfortable to achieve the desired customer turnover rate of one every 20 minutes. Outside the store, customers could eat at concrete picnic tables and benches in a professionally landscaped setting, weather permitting. Lunches, particularly Thursdays, Fridays, and Saturdays, were the busiest times, and during those periods, customers were lined up at all the registers waiting to be served. During the evenings, particularly on Friday nights, families with young children were very much in evidence. Young children, kept amused by the plastic giveaway toys provided by the restaurant and sporting Burger King crowns, sat contentedly munching their fries and sipping their carbonated drinks.

Workers use the back entrance at Burger King when reporting for work. Once inside, they go to a small room (about seven by twelve feet), which is almost completely occupied by an oblong table where crew members have their meals. Built-in benches stretch along both sides of the wall, with hooks above for coats. Homemade signs, put up by management, decorate the walls. One printed, framed, sign read:

WHY CUSTOMERS QUIT

1% die
2% move away
5% develop other friendships
9% competitive reasons
14% product dissatisfactions
68% quit because of ATTITUDE OF INDIFFERENCE TOWARDS CUSTOMER BY RES-
TAURANT MANAGER OR SERVICE PERSONNEL

Another sign reminded employees that only 1/3 ounce of ketchup and 1/9 ounce of mustard is supposed to go on the hamburgers; a crew member using more is cheating the store, while one using less is not giving customers "value" for their dollar.

The crew room is usually a lively place. An AM/FM radio is tuned to a rock station while the teenage workers coming off or on shift talk about school and weekend activities or flirt with each other. Children and weddings are favourite topics of conversation for the older workers. In the evenings, the talk and horsing around among the younger workers gets quite spirited, and now and then a manager appears to quieten things down. Management initiatives are not all geared to control through discipline; social activities such as skating parties, baseball games, and dances are organized by "production leaders" with the encouragement of the managers – an indication that the potentially beneficial effects for management of channelling the informal social relationships at the workplace are understood. Each worker must punch a time card at the start of a shift. The management urges people to come upstairs five minutes before starting time. The time card, however, is not to be punched until its time for the scheduled shift to actually begin. A positioning chart, posted near the time clock, lists the crew members who are to work each meal, and indicates where in the kitchen they are to be stationed.

There are no pots and pans in the Burger King kitchen. As almost all foods enter the store ready for the final cooking process, pots and pans are not necessary. Hamburgers arrive in the form of patties; french fries are pre-cut and partially pre-cooked; so are the chicken, fish, and veal to be used in sandwiches. Buns are pre-cut and ready to be toasted, while condiments like pickles and onions arrive in the store pre-sliced. Lettuce comes pre-shredded; only the tomatoes are sliced on the premises. The major kitchen equipment consists of the broiler/toaster, the fry vats, the milkshake and coke machines, and the microwave ovens. In the near future, new drink machines will be installed in all Burger King outlets that will automatically portion the drinks; the hot-cocoa machine already operates in this way. Even when made from scratch, hamburgers do not require particularly elaborate preparation, and whatever minimal decision making might once have been necessary is now completely eliminated by machines. At Burger King, hamburgers are cooked as they pass through the broiler on a conveyor belt at a rate of 835 pattiers per hour. Furnished with a pair of tongs, the worker picks up the burgers as they drop off the conveyor belt, puts each on a toasted bun, and places the hamburgers and buns in a steamer. The jobs may be hot and boring, but they can be learned in a matter of minutes.

The more interesting part of the procedure lies in applying condiments and microwaving the hamburgers. The popularity of this task among Burger King employees rests on the fact that it is unmechanized and allows some discretion to the worker. As the instructions for preparing a "Whopper" (the Burger King name for a large hamburger) indicates, however, management is aware of this area of worker freedom and makes strenuous efforts to eliminate it by outlining exactly how this job is to be performed:

- remove preassembled sandwich from steamer
- sandwiches in the steamer are good for 10 minutes maximum
- do not take more than 2 sandwiches at one time
- the HEEL which is the lower part of the sandwich is composed of bun heel and meat patty goes in whopper carton
- on the mat we place 4 pickle slices evenly over the meat on each corner
- then we add 1/2 oz. ketchup evenly in a spiral circular motion, over the pickles, starting from the outside edges of the meat and work your way to centre
- then place 1/2 oz. of onions evenly over the ketchup in such a way that there will be a bit of onion in every bite of the sandwich ...

Despite such directives, the "Burger and Whopper Board" positions continue to hold their attraction for the workers, for this station requires two people to work side by side, and thus allows the opportunity for conversation. During busy times, as well, employees at this station also derive some work satisfaction from their ability to "keep up." At peak times, a supply of ready-made sandwiches is placed in chutes ready for the cashiers to pick up; the manager decides how many sandwiches should be in the chutes according to a formula involving sales predictions for that time period. At such times, the challenge is to keep pace with the demand and not leave the cashiers waiting for their orders. The managers will sometimes spur the "Whopper-makers" on with cries of "Come on guys, lets get with it," or "Let's go, team."

As with the production of hamburgers, the cooking of french fries involves virtually no worker discretion. The worker, following directions laid out in the *Manual of Operating Data*, empties the frozen, pre-cut, bagged fries into fry baskets about two hours before they will be needed. When cooked fries are needed, the worker takes a fry basket from the rack and places it on a raised arm above the hot oil, and presses the "on" button. The arm holding the fry basket descends into the oil, and emerges two minutes and twenty seconds later; a buzzer goes off and the worker dumps the fries into the fry station tray where they are kept warm by an overhead light. To ensure that the proper portions are placed into bags, a specially designed tool is used to scoop the fries up from the warming table. Jobs at this station are generally reserved for boys, as the work goes more quickly with a strong wrist. The job can get quite hectic when only one worker is at the station because cooked fries must be on hand when needed. The fry-tender must put new baskets down, take the cooked fries out and bag them, and all the while make certain there are enough partially cooked onion rings ready. At peak periods, the worker seems to be running constantly to keep up with the buzzers. Working near the oil makes one feel slimy; teenagers working at this station commonly complain that they tend to develop pimples.

Even at this station, though, management is concerned about limiting what little worker discretion is possible. Despite the use of a specially designed scoop to control the portions each customer is given, a sign placed in the crew room for a few weeks admonished crew about being too generous with fry portions.

FRY YIELD Fry yield is the amount of regular portions you get from the total amount of fries used. The ideal amount is 410 portions from each 100 lb. of fries used.

At the moment our fry yield is in the unacceptable range of 365–395 portions of fries for each 100 lb. of fries which is below Burger King standards.

At the cash register, the "counter hostess" takes the order and rings it up on the computerized register. The "documentor" contains eighty-eight colour coded items, ensuring that all variations of an order are automatically priced. For example, a hamburger with extra tomatoes can be punched in, and the ten-cent charge for the extra tomatoes will appear on the printout. As a menu item is punched in at the counter, it will appear on printers in the appropriate location in the kitchen. In this manner, the worker at sandwiches, for example, can look up at the printer and check what kind of sandwich is required. When the customer hands over the money, the cashier rings in "amount tendered" and the correct amount of change to be returned to the customer is rung up. Thus, cashiers need only remember to smile and ask customers to come again. Although it takes a few days working at the cash register to build up speed, the basics can be learned in a few hours.

The computerized cash register not only simplifies ordering and payment, but is used to monitor sales and thus assist in staffing. If sales are running lower than expected, some workers will be asked to leave early. It is difficult for workers to turn down the managers' request: "Wouldn't you like to go home early today?" But on more than one occasion, workers complained that the cost of bus fare ate up almost their entire earning for that shift. Output at each station is also monitored through the cash register. Finally, the computer at all company stores is linked through a modem to the head office in Miami.

Top management has access to information on the performance of each store on a daily basis, and this information is routed back to the Canadian division headquarters in Mississauga.

Unlike the tremendous variation in skills in running the restaurant of the 1940s, skill levels required in a Burger King have been reduced to a common denominator. In a traditional restaurant of the 1940s, there was a wide variation in the levels of skills needed to do each necessary job: a trained chef would have spent many years developing his or her craft, while the dishwasher would have learned the necessary skills in a few days. At Burger King, the goal is to reduce all skills to a common, easily learned level and to provide for cross-training. At the completion of the ten-hour training program, each worker is able to work at a few stations. Skills for any of the stations can be learned in a matter of hours; the simplest jobs, such as filling cups with drinks, or placing the hamburgers and buns on the conveyor belt, can be learned in minutes. As a result, although labour turnover cuts into the pace of making hamburgers, adequate functioning of the restaurant is never threatened by people leaving. However, if workers are to be as replaceable as possible, they must be taught not only to perform their jobs in the same way, but also to resemble each other in attitudes, disposition, and appearance. Thus, workers are taught not only to perform according to company rules, but also are drilled on personal hygiene, dress (shoes should be brown leather or vinyl, not suede), coiffure (hair tied up for girls and not too long for boys), and personality. Rule 17 of the handout to new employees underlines the importance of smiling: "Smile at all times, your smile is the key to our success."

While management seeks to make workers into interchangeable tools, workers themselves are expected to make a strong commitment to the store. If they wish to keep jobs at Burger King, they must abide by the labour schedule:

You must be able to close two times a week, that is be available from four o'clock till midnight on weekdays, or 1 A.M. on Friday or Saturday nights. The schedules you fill in apply for the school semester. In the summer we know everybody can work all hours. All part timers (those who work after school) must indicate availability for weekends.[24]

Workers, especially teenagers, are, then, expected to adjust their activities to the requirements of Burger King. For example, workers must apply to their manager two weeks in advance to get time off to study for exams or attend family functions. Parents are seen by management as creating problems for the store, as they do not always appreciate Burger King's demand for priority in their children's schedules. Thus, the manager warns new trainees to "remember, your parents don't work here and don't understand the situation. If you're old enough to ask for a job, you're old enough to be responsible for coming."[25]

THE WORKERS

One of the results of the transformation of the labour process from one of "manufacture" to that of "large-scale industry" is the emerging market importance of the young worker. While artisans require long training to achieve their skills, a machine-tenders' primary characteristics are swiftness and endurance. Thus, young workers become ideal commodities: they are cheap, energetic, and in plentiful supply. As well, they can be used as a marketing tool for the industry: the mass produced, smiling teenager, serving up the symbols of the good life in North America – hamburgers, cokes and fries.

Making up about 75 per cent of the Burger King work force, the youngsters who worked after school, on weekends, and on holidays were called "part-timers." The teenager workers (about half of them boys, half girls) seemed to vary considerably in background. Some were college-bound youngsters who discussed their latest physics exam while piling on the pickles. Others were marking time until they reached the age of 16 and could leave school. One brother and sister had a father who was unemployed and ill; they were helping to pay the family's rent and food. Some of the teenagers spent all the money they earned on clothes, food, and entertainment, while others saved a portion of their earnings. Given the low pay, and the erratic scheduling, none of the Burger King workers could depend on their jobs for their total financial support.

The daytime workers – the remaining 25 per cent of the workforce – were primarily married women of mixed economic backgrounds. Consistent with a recent study of part-time workers in Canada, most of these women contributed their wages to the family budget.[26] Although they were all working primarily because their families needed the money, a few women expressed their relief at getting out of the house, even to come to Burger King. One woman said: "At least when I come here, I'm appreciated. If I do a good job, a manager will say something to me. Here, I feel like a person. I'm sociable and I like being amongst people. At home, I'm always cleaning up after everybody and nobody ever notices!"[27] Many of these women would arrive at work early in order to have a coffee and talk with one another – an interaction denied them in the isolation of their homes, where they are still responsible for all of the domestic labour.

Common to both the teenagers and the housewives was the view that working at Burger King was peripheral to their major commitments and responsibilities; the part-time nature of the work contributed to this attitude. Workers saw the alternative available to them as putting up with the demands of Burger King or leaving; in fact, leaving seemed to be the dominant form of protest. During my period in the store, on average, eleven people out of ninety-four hourly employees quit at each two-week pay period. While a few workers had stayed at Burger King for periods as long as a few years, many did not last through the first two weeks. The need for workers is constant; occasionally even the paper place-mats on the customers' trays invited people to work in the "Burger King family." "If you're enthusiastic and like to learn, this is the opportunity for you. Just complete the application and return it to the counter." At other times, bounties were offered for live workers. A sign that hung in the crew room for a few weeks read:

Wanna make $10?

It's easy! All you have to do is refer a friend to me for employment. Your friend must be able to work over lunch (Monday–Friday). If your friend works here for at least one month, you get $20. (And I'm not talking Burger Bucks either.)

Burger King's ability to cope with high staff turnover means that virtually no concessions in pay or working conditions are offered to workers to entice them to remain at Burger King. In fact, more attention is paid to the maintenance of the machinery than to "maintaining" the workers; time is regularly scheduled for cleaning and servicing the equipment, but workers may not leave the kitchen to take a drink or use the bathroom during the lunch and dinner rushes.

The dominant form – in the circumstances, the only easily accessible form – of opposition to the Burger King labour process is, then, the act of quitting. Management attempts to head off any other form of protest by insisting on an appropriate "attitude" on the part of the workers. Crew members must constantly demonstrate their satisfaction with working at Burger King by smiling at all times. However, as one worker remarked, "Why should I smile? There's nothing funny around here. I do my job and that should be good enough for them." It was not, however, and this worker soon quit. Another woman who had worked in the store for over a year also left. A crew member informed me that she had been fired for having a "poor attitude." The same crew member commented: "It's a wonder she wasn't fired a long time ago. She didn't enjoy the work and everybody knew it." I myself was threatened with expulsion from the store for having a "poor attitude" when I obeyed, without sufficient enthusiasm, an order to move from the front counter station to the broiler/steamer station.

Several other incidents underlined the extent to which Burger King could impose its will on workers. One involved the new plan – developed in Miami and introduced into the Toronto outlet in February 1982 at a crew meeting – to cut down labour costs by intensifying work. The new training program made conditions especially difficult for production leaders, who were now expected to give workers tests to make sure they knew their stations (exactly how to make "Whoppers," how long to put them in the microwave oven, etc.) without taking time off from their normal duties. Workers experienced great difficulty in following through on this training scheme because under the new guidelines, fewer people were available to serve the same number of customers; however, there was no organized opposition to the scheme. Nor was there organized opposition when meal allotments were reduced to a $2.50 limit. Although workers grumbled about the change, no one challenged the decision. The one instance in which staff objections forced the outlet to back down involved the right to work: all workers had been told that they were expected to attend the Burger King picnic, and that those normally scheduled to work at that time would have to lose a day's pay. (Crews from another store were to be sent over to keep the outlet running.) Four crew members objected, stating that they could not afford to lose pay by going to the picnic, and management allowed them to work. Such instances were few and far between, however. As one manager informed me, Burger King was careful to dismiss any crew person who was dissatisfied: "One bad apple could ruin the whole barrel."

Management control and lack of worker opposition is further explained by the fact that other jobs open to teenagers are no better, and in some cases are worse, than the jobs at Burger King. The workers at Burger King all agreed that any job that paid the full rather than the student minimum wage would be preferable to a job at Burger King; but they also recognized that their real alternatives would often be worse. Work at a donut shop, for example, also paid student minimum wage, under conditions of greater social isolation; baby sitting was paid poorly; and the hours for a paper route were terrible. Work at Burger King was a first job for many of the teenagers, and they enjoyed their first experience of earning their own money. And at Burger King, these young men and women were in the position of meeting the public, even if the forms of contact were limited by a vocabulary developed in Burger King headquarters: "Hello. Welcome to Burger King. May I take your order?" Interaction with customers, who came in all shapes, sizes, and ages, had some intrinsic interest.

In sum, workers at Burger King are confronted with a labour process that puts management in complete control. Furnished with state-of-the-art restaurant technology, Burger King outlets employ vast numbers of teenagers and married women – a population with few skills and little commitment to working at Burger King. In part, this lack of commitment is understood through reference to a labour process that offers little or no room for work satisfaction. Most jobs can be learned in a very short time (a matter of minutes for some) and workers are required to learn every job, a fact that underlines the interchangeable nature of the jobs and the workers who do them. The work is most interesting when the store is busy; sweeping and mopping already clean floors, or wiping counters that do not really require wiping is not anyone's idea of necessary or interesting work. If the alternative to "leaning" is "cleaning," then it is far preferable to really be busy. Paradoxically, work intensity, Burger King's main form of assault on labour costs, remains the only aspect of the job that can provide any challenge for the worker. Workers would remark with pride how they "didn't fall behind at all," despite a busy lunch or dinner hour.

My findings in the fast-food industry are not very encouraging. In contrast to Michael Burawoy,[28] for example, who found that male workers in a unionized machine shop were able to set quotas and thereby establish some control over the labour process, I found that the women and teenagers at Burger King are under the sway of a labour process that eliminates almost completely the possibility of forming a workplace culture independent of, and in opposition to, management.

It would be reassuring to dismiss the fast-food industry as representing something of an anomaly in the workplace; teenagers will eventually finish school and become "real workers," while housewives with families are actually domestic workers, also not to be compared with adult males in more skilled jobs. Unfortunately, there are indications that the teenagers and women who work in this type of job represent not an anomalous but an increasingly typical kind of worker, in the one area of the economy that continues to grow – the service sector. The fast-food industry represents a model for other industries in which the introduction of technology will permit the employment of low-skilled, cheap, and plentiful workers. In this sense, it is easy to be pessimistic and find agreement with Andre Gorz's depressing formulation of the idea of work:

The terms "work" and "job" have become interchangeable: work is no longer something that one *does* but something that one *has*.

Workers no longer "produce" society through the mediation of the relations of production; instead the machinery of social production as a whole produces "work" and imposes it in a random way upon random, interchangeable individuals.[29]

The Burger King system represents a major triumph for capital: it has established a production unit with constant and variable components that are almost immediately replaceable. However, the reduction of the worker to a simple component of capital requires more than the introduction of a technology; workers' autonomous culture must be eliminated as well, including the relationships among workers, their skills, and their loyalties to one another. The smiling, willing, homogeneous worker must be produced and placed on the Burger King assembly line.

While working at Burger King, I saw for myself the extent to which Burger King has succeeded in reducing its work force to a set of interchangeable pieces. However, I also saw how insistently the liveliness and decency of the workers emerged in the informal interaction that occurred. Open resistance is made virtually impossible by the difficulty of identifying who is responsible for the rules that govern the workplace: the workers know that managers follow orders coming from higher up. The very high turnover of employees indicates that workers come to understand that their interests and Burger King's are not one and the same. As young people and women begin to realize that their jobs in the fast-food industry are not waystations en route to more promising and fulfilling work, they will perhaps be moved to blow the whistle on the Burger King "team." The mould for the creation of the homogeneous worker assembling the standardized meal for the homogeneous consumer is not quite perfected.

NOTES

1 Dominion Bureau of Statistics [hereafter DBS], *1951 Census* (Ottawa 1954), VII, table 6; Statistics Canada, *Restaurants, Caterers and Taverns Industry* (Ottawa 1978), cat. 65-535, table 1, 14.

2 Statistics Canada, *Market Research Handbook* (Ottawa 1983), cat. 63-224, tables 3–11, 169.

3 Statistics Canada, *Urban Family Food Expenditure* (Ottawa 1978), cat. 62-548; Dominion Bureau of Statistics, *Urban Family Food Expenditure* (Ottawa 1953), cat. 62-511.

4 Foodservice and Hospitality Magazine, *Fact File – Canada's Hospitality Business*, 4th ed. (Toronto n.d.).

5 This definition comes from the National Restaurant Association and is reprinted in Marc Leepson, "Fast Food, U.S. Growth Industry," *Editorial Research Reports* 7 (1978): 907.

6 See Harry Braverman, *Labor and Monopoly Capital* (New York 1954), 13.

7 Bonnie Fox, "Women's Domestic Labour and Their Involvement in Wage Work" (PH D dissertation, University of Alberta 1980), table 15-A, 427.

8 M.C. Urquhart and K.H.A. Buckley, *Historical Statistics of Canada*, 2nd edition (Ottawa 1983), V410-416.

9 An example of this struggle is in a Toronto *Star* article called "Fast Foods – Its Giving the Supermarkets Indigestion," 25 April 1977, 1. Both fast-food and supermarket entrepreneurs state that they are competing for the same food dollar.

10 *Foodservice and Hospitality*, 23 October 1967, 5.

11 *Foodservice and Hospitality*, February 1981, 38.

12 *Moody's Industrial Manual* (New York 1981); J.M. Stopard, *World Directory of Multinational Enterprises* (Detroit 1981–2); and *Who Owns Whom: North America* (London 1982).

13 Promotional material from Burger King Canada head office in Mississauga, Ontario.

14 William Foote Whyte, *Human Relations in the Restaurant Industry* (New York 1948), 3.

15 Karl Marx, *Capital*, vol. I ([1867]; New York 1977), ch. xv.
16 Theodore Levitt, "Production Line Approach to Service," *Harvard Business Review* 50, no. I (Sept.–Oct. 1972): 51–2.
17 Robert L. Emerson, *Fast Food, the Endless Shakeout* (New York 1979), 291.
18 *Up Front* 2, no. 6 (Miami n.d.): 2.
19 A "Shape Up" campaign instituted at the beginning of 1982 attempted to set a new goal of a 2½-minute service time.
20 "Kitchen design – the drive for efficiency," insert in *Nation's Restaurant News*, 31 August 1981.
21 Personal communication, Burger King "professor," 4 January 1982.
22 Job description handout for Burger King managers, 1981.
23 Handouts to Burger King crew members, 1981.
24 Burger King training session in local outlet, July 1981.
25 Ibid.
26 Labour Canada, *Commission of Inquiry into Part-Time Work* (Ottawa 1983) [Wallace commission].
27 Personal communication, Burger King worker, 8 August 1981.
28 Michael Burawoy, *Manufacturing Consent* (Chicago 1979).
29 Andre Gorz, *Farewell to the Working Class* (Boston 1982), 71.

DON WELLS

Autoworkers on
the Firing Line

The shift had already started. Work in the Ford plant seemed compulsive and frenetic, full of clanging and screaming and unceasing movement in a thousand directions. Sweat dripped off my face as I hurried to my new job on the assembly line, stepping over snakepits of twisting air hoses and through a tight choreography of crowded machines, workers, and steel posts. Then I came upon an area of curious calm: about a hundred workers had left the line and were standing around talking quietly. I stopped for a moment before rushing on, anxious not to be late for my first day on the job. Early the next morning, as I pulled into the Ford parking lot, I saw hundreds, perhaps thousands, of workers standing around or sitting in their cars. It was the beginning of the biggest wildcat strike in the plant's history.[1]

The wildcat grew out of a worker sit-down in one area to protest the firing of two probationary workers. The sit-downers were jubilant when management agreed to rehire the two workers and conduct an investigation into the original firings. But when management refused to guarantee that there would be no punishment for those who had taken part in the sit-down, the sit-downers decided to call for a wildcat by the entire work force. The next day, they rushed down the aisles, yelling "Hey, you scab, we need some support" and "This could happen to you." In hundreds and then thousands, workers gladly downed their tools, grabbed their street clothes, and joined the parade out of the plant. They marched through a sister plant and shut it down too, to the slack-jawed surprise of the supervisors.

Never before had these workers experienced a wildcat that was so spontaneous, so widely supported, so powerful. "It seemed like we had control," one wildcatter remembered. "We could do anything we wanted, eh?" Another worker commented that it was "quite a weird feeling" and explained: "To me it felt a little bit like, I guess, anarchism, like we were taking over the place ... that *you* actually had control over the outcome ... The boys *did* it, the labourers, the guys that do all the slugging, *we* decided what we were going to do. That's the feeling you got ... I don't know why, never experienced it before ... this sense of power." Another summed up this "good feeling" more briefly: "Power! Like I never felt it before."

Two days later, the exhilaration of collective power had given way to fear. Intimidated by management threats and advised by local union leaders to honour the no-strike provision of their contract, workers returned to their jobs. Fear turned to shock when a few hours later management announced fifteen firings and numerous other serious penalties. "It was the first time we ever got hit like that," the man who was then president of the local recalls. The worker who had felt that invigorating "little bit of anarchism" came wearily to the conclusion that "you can't win." He no longer advocates major confrontations with management because "in the end you *don't* win. Naturally we lost terribly. I think it was a mistake from the beginning," he says reflectively. He says that he is not alone in this conclusion, that most of his fellow workers judge now that they should have returned to work after the two fired probationary workers had been rehired. That would have been a victory. It was after the wildcat spread beyond their zone that defeat became inevitable, they feel. That defeat has been a lesson. "Everyone is scared now," one worker observes. Resistance has diminished. "Now they [the militants] have a heck of a time to get anybody to do anything," he says. This is especially the case in those more militant areas of the plant that took the brunt of the punishment from management.

But though resistance on a big scale is far less possible and though resistance of all kinds has been reduced considerably, it has not died. It is smaller in scale, less risky, and less significant in effect; nevertheless, it continues here and there, especially against the frontline foremen. A few workers sometimes defy minor regulations to make a point; sometimes they carry on slowdowns for a while in one area or they perform a bit of sabotage on a machine or a part. In these ways, they sometimes win little victories in one area or another area of the plant: a speedup affecting a few jobs may be delayed or a foreman may be persuaded to use more tact. Sometimes there are trade-offs: a foreman may agree not to retime a job or not to crack down on a certain amount of absenteeism if, in return, workers agree to meet or exceed certain productivity quotas or quality standards. Hard-won little victories that may help to make work a bit more tolerable and human dignity a bit more visible are still to be found; major victories or victories for large numbers of workers are, however, nowhere to be found.[2]

The presence of little victories together with periodic big defeats like the one I witnessed is part of a pattern. A major defeat is a lesson in the supremacy of management in large-scale confrontations. Workers learn to return to smaller-scale resistance at individual or work-group levels. To the extent they are able to win little victories at this lesser level, their frustrations may be partially and temporarily alleviated; the fight for small-scale victories can serve as a safety valve retarding the buildup of discontent to the level of mass action. When such major confrontation does re-emerge, however, at plant-wide levels, it has almost always been the occasion of a big defeat for workers. Either way, with little victories or big defeats, management retains the upper hand. "You don't make big gains in *any* of those illegal work stoppages," a local leader emphasizes. "Once it becomes a tool of being able to make major gains, then how do you turn it off? So they [management] are *not* going to allow you to make major gains."

This pattern of victory and defeat has come to define the frontier of resistance and control at Ford's. It leaves the lowest stratum of supervision as punching bags while militant workers shadow-box with power. It leaves the jobs that workers have to do at Ford's unchanged. And it leaves what I call "Ford Time" fundamentally unchallenged.

FORD TIME

Ford Time is the essence of the labour process as it is experienced by workers. The job of disc grinding, a job I did for almost a year in the late 1970s, illustrates it dramatically. The worker huddles inside a sheet-metal box about twenty feet long by perhaps twelve feet wide. The line lumbers steadily through the box bringing an endless procession of brown and grey metal skeletons. Each time a car skeleton comes past, the worker picks up the portable grinder that is his only tool and presses it onto bubbled welds, grinding them to flat smoothness in a shower of sparks and a screech of metal against metal. That is it. A step forward, then a shuffle backward for a couple of feet as the line pushes him along, then a couple of steps to the left and a shuffle with the line back to where it starts all over again. He does this "job" forty-eight times an hour.

There is mass anonymity. The piercing shrieks of the grinding are deafening, so it is useless to try to talk to the worker less than five feet away on the other side. The two ten-minute and two eighteen-minute breaks each shift are more for the sake of production: "If you have to take a crap or piss," the supervisor warned me on the first day on the job, "do it on your breaks." Hardly any job in the plant takes more than a day to learn, so workers are easily replaced. Workers become numbers; in fact, each has two: a punch-clock number to be paid by and a seniority number to be laid off by. Without names, workers become "the short guy" or "the guy with the cigar," or most often they become the jobs they do: "the welder on the left," "the hood sander," "the rolls tester." Of course, workers often know at least the first names of their nearest fellow workers. Some supervisors also make a point of calling workers by name, sometimes leaving the impression that they are being kind to the morons or children they have been burdened with; others use first names as a more effective way to obtain favours. But many foremen adhere to the sergeant-major school of motivating workers. They address workers as "you," "hey you," or "you over there!" These phrases are spat out loudly with a tone of disgust.

The calculated core of Ford Time is this: it is the conscious attempt to systematically reduce workers to the level of interchangeable parts of a production process by squeezing the labour of human beings – people with all their characteristically rich and individual variety of intellectual, emotional, and physical needs – into robot-like labour. Ford Time is the tyranny of clock time so compulsively detailed as to be insane; it is the mass forcing of work life into absolutely rigid, even, tiny segments, one following the other in a gruesome lock-step. Like the disc-grinder, the typical assembly-line worker is expected to perform like a puppet. But since he is not a puppet, he is encouraged to think that he has to act like one if automobiles are to be produced. The spaces, sounds, and objects of work, the pace and definition of jobs, and above all the relationships of workers to their fellow human beings are held to be the creatures of productive efficiency – as if Ford Time were the only way to make automobiles and autoworkers. Ford Time is the most audacious attempt by a powerful few to control the labour of the many in ways that leave the controllers unseen, unheard, unknown, and unnamed.

To be an autoworker was not always to be a slave to the line. Neither a product of human nature nor a simple imperative of technological efficiency, Ford Time was created as a system of social control. It remains a monument both to the supremacy of the few over the many and to the bitter defeats that autoworkers have suffered historically in the establishment of that supremacy. The first and worst defeat took away the power that the early autoworkers – skilled craftsmen – had exercised over the way they made cars. When the elder Henry Ford set up his first workshop back in 1903, he hired American and Canadian-born mechanics, draftsmen, pattern makers, and blacksmiths who used simple tools to assemble parts they either made themselves or had made by other craftsmen in outside shops.[3] Fellow craftsmen supervised them in putting cars together "in exactly the same way that one builds a house," the first Henry Ford recalled.[4]

Only ten years later, the skills and power of these craftsmen were rapidly being incorporated into the assembly-line process or being taken up into a growing hierarchy of management offices. Semi-skilled machine tenders and assemblers from eastern and southern Europe were being policed by bosses in the performance of repetitive, monotonous little tasks,[5] a "boon," Ford claimed, for the "many" workers who had "no brains." Even the "most stupid" could now learn such jobs in two days.[6] Workers fought back strenuously, using the same direct-action tactics that have retained wide popularity with their successors today. A Ford spy reported that they "neglected their work, malingered, put imperfect parts into cars, and cheated the timekeeper."[7] They also tried organizing both craft and industrial unions,[8] but their efforts were suppressed by an alliance of ruthless Detroit employers using spies, scabs, goons, judges, police, and politicians.[9] More effectively, workers quit faster than Ford could hire replacements.[10] It was to counter this high rate of turnover in particular that in 1913 Ford expanded certain welfare programs provided by the company. He increased bonus payments to some workers, rationalized the wage structure, provided a more clear-cut promotion system, created an employees savings and loan association, and curbed the powers that foremen exercised, often arbitrarily and brutally, over workers.[11] These reforms culminated in the well-known Five-Dollar Day announced in 1914.

Five dollars a day was twice the going rate for autoworkers. Together with the fact that deskilling allowed Ford to tap an enormous pool of unemployed and unskilled workers, this policy resulted in a drop of almost 90 per cent in the turnover rate and in the near abolition of absenteeism.[12] Because a major portion of the five dollars was labelled "profit-sharing," Ford was able to withhold pay as a disciplinary device.[13] Meanwhile, speedup skyrocketed[14] and, according to Henry Ford, discipline was kept "rigid."[15] At the same time, "profit-sharing" provided a pretext for Ford to send a small army of "investigators" to workers' homes to judge whether workers' home lives met American middle-class standards of thrift, sobriety, cleanliness, sexual morality, and sleep regularity. Profit sharing was tied to Ford's notion of what it meant to be an "American" worker.[16]

Though the combination of money and paternalism solved Ford's labour problems in the short run, worker resistance mounted again during World War I. Inflation and speedup strengthened the opposition to Ford Time, and militant industrial unionism was once more on the rise.[17] The Ford Motor Company, with its paternalistic strategy a failure and with its economic position made more precarious by increasing competition and financial debts, returned to the most repressive disciplinary policies after the war. Workers entered a period that business historian Allan Nevins describes as "more Prussian ... capricious and irrational,"[18] a period that was to last through the 1930s. One labour leader described how management discouraged unionism in the plants:

There are about eight hundred underworld characters in the Ford Service organization. They are the Storm Troops. They make no pretense of working, but are merely "keeping order" in the plant community through terror. Around this nucleus of eight hundred there are, however, between eight and nine thousand authentic workers in the organization, a great many of them spies and stool pigeons and a great many others who have been browbeaten into joining this industrial mafia. There are almost 90,000 workers in [the] River Rouge [plant], and because of this highly organized terror and spy system the fear in the plant is something indescribable. During the lunch hour men shout at the top of their voices about the baseball scores lest they be suspected of talking unionism. Workers seen talking together are taken off the assembly line and fired. Every man suspected of union sympathies is immediately discharged, usually under the frame-up charge of "starting a fight," in which he often gets terribly beaten up.[19]

A similar style of labour relations was practised across the river in the Ford plant in Windsor, Ontario. An industrial-relations director at Ford of Canada confirms there was "firing of workers at whim" and a regime of management "brutality."[20] According to historian Raymond Houlahan, men in the plant "were dragged from the line ... to look at the unemployed lined up at the company gates." They were warned that unless they speeded up, they would be replaced. He reports also that "fights occurred regularly between workers rushing to complete the job on time."[21] As in the American plants,[22] a foreman could exercise the kind of arbitrary power that led to the creation of "chore boys who would cut his lawn and paint his home."[23] A man who had worked in the Ford plant in Windsor in the 1930s recalls that in those days even the toilet breaks were strictly timed by foremen who could peer over specially built half-size doors on toilet stalls to identify the occupants. To limit lunch breaks, lunch buckets were placed on pallets and raised to the ceiling where they remained until the time prescribed by management.[24]

Workers' resistance failed. Attempts by the American Federation of Labor and the All Canadian Congress of Labour to organize Ford workers in Canada were defeated in the 1920s.[25] Later, in 1934 and 1937, there were major purges of union sympathizers at Ford of Canada,[26] and management crushed strike after strike in the United States,[27] giving Detroit a reputation for being a "graveyard of organizers."[28] "Ford heads knew they were safe from any work stoppage," say historians Nevins and Hill.[29] By 1939, though speedup was worse than ever and wages the lowest in the industry,[30] management remained firmly in control.

It was World War II that provided Ford workers with a favourable external situation for their struggle against Ford Time. Up to this time, the CIO, Keynesian government policies, sympathetic public opinion, and the charisma of leaders such as John L. Lewis had been insufficient.[31] Now war gave labour – the labour of the worker and of the soldier – a new, greater market value, both as cannon maker and as cannon fodder. "Feeling a new security," Ford workers became "more defiant of the plant police."[32] Autoworkers in particular gained what one worker has called a "form of sociability higher than has ever been achieved by man in industrial society."[33] Now workers could talk, smoke, eat, sleep on the job, even gamble on company time.[34] When the workers at the gigantic River Rouge plant, flagship of the Ford corporation, shut down production in a massive walkout, Ford conceded not only union recognition to his employees in the U.S., but a union-shop clause and a dues checkoff as well, together with more material improvements than the union leaders had ever hoped to achieve. Workers made formal and informal inroads into management's exclusive "rights" to discipline, set work standards, and allocate jobs.[35]

In Canada, Ford workers continued to resort to direct action to make gains in these areas, and there were major walkouts in each year of the war.[36] Like their American counterparts, they benefited from the labour shortage during World War II and from the keenness of management to meet cost-plus, war-time contracts.[37] In 1945, Ford workers in Canada went out on the long, hard strike that resulted in the well-known Rand Formula becoming a cornerstone of Canadian industrial relations.[38] Yet throughout the war, the assembly line continued to clank along. The fundamentals of automobile assembly and the control of workers had not been substantially altered. After the war, Ford management reasserted greater control over the labour process, but this time in a new, softer way. Unionism, sanctioned by law, was here to stay, and though its obvious primary function was the articulation and defence of workers' collective interests, its parallel role was to uphold the routines of conflict resolution provided in the contract, including the policing of direct action. Magnificent gains in wages and fringe benefits were attained, but at the same time there was speedup after speedup, deteriorating working conditions, and harsher, sometimes vicious supervision (though by no means comparable to the "industrial Fascist" methods used prior to the war). Worker resistance to the labour process was largely illicit and generally suppressed or deflected ·by management. Constrained by management power and by the new legal obligations, union leaders tended to become wedded to this institutionalization of conflict, though informally and especially at the lower levels of local union leadership, this coming-to-terms has not always been honoured. Direct action continued, as it continues today.

DIRECT ACTION

Neither Ford Time nor management's conception of what is good have gone wholly unchallenged. The most important day-to-day challenge to management power and the tyranny of its clock time is worker resistance. It comes in many forms, much of it small scale. Most often, workers' resistance involves a confrontation with the frontline foreman. This may involve direct action in the form of physical intimidation or threats to damage the foreman's personal car; more often, worker resistance takes the form of minor sabotage to tools or products. It is not uncommon for individual or group slowdowns to take place or for a few units to be improperly assembled. Tools may be hidden or supplies of parts allowed to run out without the foreman being told. Individual absenteeism can be another form of direct action as a protest against speedup or the treatment being meted out by a foreman. Less frequently, direct action takes the form of collective absenteeism in which several workers agree not to come to work on a particular day. This can make it difficult for the foreman to "cover" so many absent workers and to train temporary substitutes.

Sometimes there are small-scale, temporary work stoppages. This usually means a sit-down like the one that led to the big strike described earlier; sometimes it means a walkout by a work group. In nearly every case, such direct action against a foreman is petty in both scale and effect.

There is a complex relationship between direct action, on the one hand, and conflict resolution through the grievance procedure provided in the collective agreement, or through informal mediation by the union steward, on the other. Sometimes direct action is a response to the delays and inequities workers see in the grievance process; it can be either a substitute for the grievance procedure or a goad to ensure that grievances are taken more seriously by management or by the union or both. Direct action may be the culmination of a series of frustrations, not all of which may be articulated. Or it can be a response to a specific change, such as a speedup or a job reallocation or a change in a foreman's style of supervision or his degree of aggressiveness.

Another form of worker resistance to Ford Time appears as play. This includes hiding a fellow worker's clothing or tools, "bombing" fellow workers with bags of water, putting grease under car-door handles, and so on. Such resistance makes work less onerous and interrupts the rigidity of Ford Time. On the one hand, it may be regarded as a small liberation from the repressiveness of Ford Time; on the other hand, it may be regarded as a kind of (more or less sanctioned) deflected aggression, which might otherwise be directed against the labour process and management power in a more obvious and damaging way. It is a fundamental irony of worker resistance that though much of it takes the form of low-level skirmishes with foremen over what appear to be issues particular to this or that worker or workshop, the basis of worker resistance to management is far more general. This is true not only insofar as Ford Time is a common condition for workers; it is true also to the extent that management aggression against workers is conducted with regularity across much of the plant at the same time. Thus, every year, when management retools for the production of new models, it initiates changes in job structures and these are normally parts of what workers see as a speedup. Despite the broad front along which this speedup is conducted, worker resistance is normally episodic and varying from one area of the plant to another. With its near monopoly of time, expertise, and material resources, management retains most of the initiative. Worker resistance, whether sabotage or sit-down, assault or play, has been defensive. This defensive war, now more intense, now less intense, continues. It continues because Ford Time continues.

Alongside this defensive worker struggle against Ford Time, with its pattern of little victories and big defeats, lies another and directly related dynamic: adaptation. Big defeats not only reinforce a reversion to small-scale skirmishes, they also teach workers the necessity of putting up with Ford Time most of the time. This is no existential free choice. Workers often have to pay a high price for resistance that fails or even for resistance that succeeds.

Sooner or later someone is suspended or fired. They become object lessons. "Some groups start to wise up and they say 'hey, it just doesn't work,'" a veteran of many years in the plant observes. A worker in his twenties says that he, too, is a "little bit wiser now ... I seen what happened before and what actually was accomplished and you find the older guys will tell you that sitdowns and wildcats usually don't solve anything. They'll tell you that and as I get older and the longer I work there, I tend to agree with them."

Another aspect of this adaptation is a forced conditioning process I was very surprised to find in my own adaptation to Ford Time. For some while, I had been puzzled by the differences between newer workers and old-timers in their reactions to a breakdown in the line. Less experienced workers, including myself, were glad to see the line break down; it was a needed break in the monotony. But more seasoned workers said that they didn't want to see the line stop. They said that the breakdowns made them more aware of the monotony of their jobs. Their feelings became suddenly understandable when I returned to the disc-grinder's job after several days off. Seconds after starting the job I lost most of the sense of ever having been away. All along, imperceptibly, I had been adjusting to my submission to Ford Time. For some, this adaptation is about all that is redeeming in Ford Time. One worker describes his institutionalization this way:

The only good thing about working on the assembly line from the job point of view is that you do the same thing day after day. Therefore, you're so damned good at it you can do it with your eyes closed. You don't have to get up in the morning and say "well, am I going to have a bad day or a good day?" If you're up to doing the job physically, it's a snap – once you get into things. That's about the only *good* thing about working on the assembly line.

Thus Ford Time excites episodic resistance while simultaneously imposing adaptation. Yet neither resistance nor adaptation have been able to provide workers with genuine protection from the oppression of Ford Time. Given a real choice, workers prefer escape: at the end of every shift, when the line stops, when Ford Time dies for the day, workers come back to life. The listlessness and the irritation are gone. In the mad, gleeful dash to the punch clock, there are dancing eyes; in the rush to the parking lot there are exultant shouts and laughter – there is freedom from Ford Time. But the next day, almost like a minor natural catastrophe, the line starts up again.

LITTLE VICTORIES
AND BIG DEFEATS

The plant where I worked has a history of almost thirty years of direct action, helping to give it a reputation among United Automobile Workers (UAW) leaders in Canada as "the rebel local." According to a senior UAW leader in

Canada, its record for direct action has been so outstanding that it is known as "the most uncontrollable plant in the Ford chain (in North America)." Despite this level of resistance, workers in the plant have by and large carried on an ultimately ineffective retreat in the face of management aggression.

Initially, in the 1950s, when the plant was getting under way, there was little resistance activity on a day-to-day basis, despite the fact that it had taken a long winter strike to establish the local. Wages were considered excellent and most workers enjoyed far higher incomes with Ford paycheques than they had ever known. Because they were starting in a new plant that was expanding, most felt that their job security was assured. Speedup was not yet intense, these veteran workers and retirees recalled, and because the work force was small, there was less sense of either anonymity or of numerical strength that was to come later as the plant grew. In those days, it was altogether uncommon for workers to work without direct supervision, and some reported they could refuse to do undesirable jobs without being punished. However, with the harder times of the 1957 recession came speedup pressures and a somewhat harsher style of supervision. Worker resistance became more vigorous and, at least for a while, some of it was marginally effective. Thus a veteran repairman remembers that when a supervisor "got on their backs" in the late 1950s, his fellow repairmen would "go as a group right down to the end of the line ... just make that repair last twenty times longer than what we should've lasted on it, you know." Management's exercise of power was not as harsh as it would become.

In the early 1960s, management aggression grew stronger. "Foremen started pushing and it got quite rough on the line," a retiree states, echoing the recollection of others. The local union newspaper at this time was full of charges of "arrogance," "ignorance," and a "belligerent attitude" on the part of American managerial "imports" who "have come to be regarded as the typical Yankee Boss." There was a corresponding escalation in mass resistance. In 1963, a thousand workers went out on a wildcat strike, and a few months later the entire work force went out twice. There were several lesser work stoppages in between these walkouts and afterwards. Management retaliated with suspensions, and the workers responded once more with a mass wildcat. In the showdown that followed, management announced for the first time both that it would not negotiate with anyone until there was a return to work and that anyone off the job longer than three days was liable to be fired.[39] Shocked and intimidated by management recalcitrance and the magnitude of the threats, both of which were unprecedented in their experience as Ford workers, the wildcatters followed the advice of their union leadership and returned to work.[40]

At least two local union leaders contend that this showdown was a major turning point in the history of worker resistance in the plant. They argue, quite forcefully, that if there ever was a time when workers and the union had to stand fast against management, this was it. Although since that time there have been many more work stoppages, more than a few of which were plant-wide, the early 1960s appear to mark the inauguration of a more general and classic pattern in the way that Ford management deals with large-scale worker resistance in North America. Typically, when workers walk off the job in sizeable numbers, there are no official negotiations with union leaders until the work stoppage has ended. In the meantime, dire and often escalating threats are issued to workers and union leaders. As union leaders encourage the resisters to return and as other pressures on workers to return to work mount, solidarity and resolve tend to waver and then fall apart. After the workers return to work, negotiations with local union leaders are conducted. It is not unusual for management to announce a large number of firings and suspensions following which union leaders negotiate lesser and less-numerous penalties.

In this particular instance, as would happen after other such defeats, management pushed workers even harder after they returned to the "dictatorship of the job," as one worker put it, back then. Supervision generally grew harsher, speedup accelerated, and there were long hours of compulsory overtime during which workers stayed on the job ten and twelve hours a day, six and sometimes even seven days a week. Union leaders described the speed-up as "the worst in history." Once again, workers shut down the plant; they stayed out exactly three days. Their return to work was followed by a renewal of resistance, but this time resistance was conducted inside the plant on a smaller scale without shutting down production. Management was less punitive in response to this smaller-scale resistance and no disciplinary action resulted.

These were the first definite indications of the little-victories-and-big-defeats pattern of worker resistance. Combined with management's harder line toward large-scale resistance, management's softer and less-consistent line toward smaller-scale resistance has reinforced management's control of the labour process. As a safety valve for the buildup of frustrations that workers experience in their submission to Ford Time, periodic small-scale resistance can be part of a cooling-off process precluding the rise of more massive and militant resistance. Eruptions of small-scale discontent are less disruptive of production than larger-scale insurrections. They may also provide early warning devices alerting management to potential areas of resistance in the plant and to the identities of particular militants. Small-scale guerrilla warfare leaves workers battling frontline supervision, for the most part, in a buffer zone of what management generally regards as a tolerable level of conflict. Management has "always allowed little skirmishes," a veteran local leader reports, "but they've always come down very heavy-handed and hard when there's any organized resistance to their policies. And that's been pretty general," he adds. "They're pretty quick to take reprisals when they feel they're losing control of the situation."[41]

The little victories that workers sometimes achieve in these small-scale battles can be a source of improved morale to workers. Ironically, improved work-group morale can be translated into improved productivity. In the aftermath of one such little victory during the time I was in the plant, workers made various deals with the new foreman to improve productivity in return for various favours: the foreman held off the retiming of jobs by the time-study department and overlooked a certain amount of tardiness and absenteeism. At least one worker was allowed to go home as much as an hour or more early on a regular basis after exceeding his quota by a healthy margin. In return for less-obtrusive supervision, the workers' little victories gave the foreman the improved productivity that had been management's main goal all along.

As we saw, the firm repression of larger-scale resistance can act as an object lesson, periodically reminding workers of management's power. It also acts to reinforce the tendencies to resort to small-scale resistance. Finally, it functions to deter resistance of any sort, especially among those who pay the biggest price, often those with longer histories of militancy. This tends to inhibit the development of stable informal leadership. "The penalties have been so heavy," a local militant admits, "that's been the deterrent to [mass actions]." There are other elements that bolster this containment of resistance as well. One is management's policy of "progressive discipline," according to which a worker's past record of resistance is a major factor in meting out penalties, which become more and more serious with each infraction. Thus, a worker with a disciplinary record may face heavy penalties for even minor resistance. And workers complain that they can be severely punished if management decides to build up a series of petty charges against them over time. Another element containing resistance is the use of exemplary discipline against more-militant individuals involved in collective action. Both through the policy of progressive discipline and such exemplary discipline, leading militants tend to become at once sacrificial offerings and symbols of defeat. This undermines the development of an informal cadre of militant leadership and inhibits the strengthening of ties of solidarity between more-militant and less-militant workers: militants tend to tire of taking the martyr's role. The same is true of militant work groups, which end up taking more punishment than others. All of this contradicts the development of collective self-confidence, both in workers' abilities to fight management and in their capacities to stick together. Resistance tends to fragment and shatter along individual and work group lines, rather than snowballing to departmental and plant-wide levels where workers' resistance might be a more serious challenge to management control.

Similarly, the grievance procedure tends to make collective issues into individual ones since, though issues are often common to several or many workers, it is normal for grievances to be processed on an individual basis, making a legalistic "case" out of what in reality is a power struggle between workers and management. The further the grievance is processed, the more it is taken off the shop floor where workers have at least some capacity for defending their interests through collective action. Soon the grievance becomes the property of union leaders with special expertise in arguing grievances and, instead of mobilizing workers, the grievor and the union leaders often become involved in an absurdly expensive, time-consuming, delay-ridden procedure.

The grievance procedure, joined as it is to the contract's no-strike and management's-rights clauses, is designed to be a substitute for collective direct action. In addition to translating collective action into individual complaints, the grievance procedure encourages the articulation of only those issues that are held to be legitimate in the contract. The grievance procedure also performs other functions that limit labour/management conflict. As a process with legalistic rituals and procedures, it masks the inequities contained and reflected in the collective agreement. It thereby gives an air of impartiality and fair-mindedness to the enforcement of management supremacy in the workplace. Just as workers tend to legitimate a legal and political process they little understand, so they tend to legitimate the grievance procedure, especially its arbitration stage, in much the same way. Finally, the grievance procedure is advantageous to management because it tends to deflect worker resistance from direct action (through which workers are sometimes able to win little victories) to an arena where victories are normally non-existent. Local leaders report that they lose the vast majority of cases they bring to the arbitrator. Even this underestimates the loss rate, since local leaders are usually careful to cull out all but those cases they think have the best chances of winning. (Arbitration fees are almost prohibitive and some local leaders believe that strong cases give them greater credibility with the arbitrator.)

Workers who win their cases may have been defeated by the process long before the arbitrator's judgment. This results from the fact that the grievance procedure is glaringly unjust in another way: the worker suffers management's punishment unless and *until* the arbitrator rules otherwise. An arbitrator's decision can take months. For a fired or suspended worker, this delay means not only the lack of a job and the loss of income, but also means considerable anxiety. Since workers often live from paycheque to paycheque, it is not unknown for a worker who is unable to keep up payments to lose appliances, the family car, perhaps the family home, perhaps the family, while waiting for the arbitrator's ruling. To be fired or suspended is to be punished, regardless of the final result. Even the occasional victory at the arbitration hearings can be a lesson for every worker in not fighting management.

Ford management has also become more adept at the detection of resistance and the identification of resisters. For example, the physical checks embedded in the technology have been elaborated and refined over the years. A veteran union activist points out that now the assembly lines are set up so that when any one of them stops "you get whistles blowing, sirens, lights, clangers, buzzers, blue lights, red lights." Even more refined innovations have been made: "For example, the red and green lights which used to signal whether or not the car has been completed at each stage used to be easy to remove from the sockets, so the guys used to switch them around to screw things up," he says. "Now the bulbs are glued in," he laughs. The very specific nature of jobs and systematic inspection checks along the line enable management to know accurately and quickly which workers are not doing their jobs according to specifications. Management can also tell who leaves work early because there are cameras constantly scanning the parking lots. These cameras have proven invaluable as a deterrent to workers conducting walkouts because they help management to identify ringleaders. They can also provide evidence at arbitration hearings that is difficult or impossible to refute.

The company's international expansion has also been of assistance in controlling worker resistance since World War II. Over time, Ford plants have tended to become more and more specialized in the kinds of vehicles they produce. This specialization has made certain kinds of sabotage more difficult to disguise from management. Thus, a veteran worker points out that years ago there were some thirty different side panels to put on various cars assembled in the plant. If the wrong side panel were installed, it was plausible for the worker to claim that the error was inadvertent. Today, with fewer side panels to choose from, this excuse is less credible – and sabotage is a firing offence. Similarly, today it is more difficult to mix up orders for options and parts to be installed: in quite a few areas of the plant, the mix of options for each vehicle is dictated by computers.

Another benefit to managerial control that stems from international specialization is a new flexibility in co-ordinating the suppression of worker resistance and a new set of opportunities for dividing workers along lines of nationality. Ford had reduced its potential vulnerability to the shutdown of production through plant-wide work stoppages by "twinning" the same production models in different plants, so that the twin plant or plants may pick up the slack in production of the affected model. Similarly, there is a policy of "multiple sourcing" of parts and raw materials used in production. More generally, the post-war diffusion of production on an international scale has made it easier for Ford to pit workers in one country against those in other countries. Finally, the decentralization of production to smaller but more-specialized plants has permitted the Ford Motor Company to simultaneously avail itself of certain economies of production while reducing the resistance costs associated with concentrating large numbers of workers in giant plants. Mammoth complexes with histories of massive resistance, such as the River

Rouge plant in Michigan and the Dagenham plant in England, now employ but fractions of their former work forces.

At the plant where I worked, there were a host of other conditions that reinforced management control by undermining solidarity. As seems to be increasingly characteristic of the locales Ford prefers for investment, the plant I worked at was not located in a traditional blue-collar community. Instead, workers were dispersed over a fifty-mile radius in houses and apartment buildings in suburbs where there was little sense of community. Most of my fellow workers never met outside the plant and many had never met their fellow workers' families, even after ten, twenty, and more years working alongside each other in the plant. The bowling leagues, the football and baseball leagues that were popular in the early years of the local have all but died out entirely. As wave after wave of immigrants entered the plant, workers have come more and more to be divided by language, custom, ethnicity, and race. In the midst of major lay-offs, and massive technological displacement of labour in the industry, the differences between workers on the basis of seniority have also come to loom larger and larger. As workers are shifted from area to area of the plant, work groups and networks are broken up, and greater isolation and individualism are promoted by this uprooting. As work becomes more onerous and the prospects for victory less promising, workers turn ever more to what the contract is able to provide in wages and fringe benefits; they turn to individual and family consumption rather than toward meeting the collective discontents of production.

This is how Ford Time has been maintained without the earlier heavy reliance upon goon squads in the plants. Furthermore, in many respects, Ford Time has grown worse as better jobs have been lost, as work has been speeded up, and as remaining skills have been whittled away. Both direct action and collective bargaining have been ineffective in opposing a continuing rationalization of labour. An important measure of this ineffectiveness has been the decline of what workers refer to as "good jobs." These are jobs that retain a bit more skill and autonomy than other jobs in the plant. The decline in the complexity of jobs has often been associated with speedups. "It didn't speed up fast," a veteran from the plant's early days recalls. "It was more of a gradual fashion," he says, noting that it was sometimes imperceptible. "As the time study [department] would figure out a man could be cut out there and another man could do those two jobs, and things like that," good jobs were lost and bad jobs became worse. Speedup was gradual until the recession of the late 1950s and accelerated again when American management intervened as part of the buildup to the 1965 Auto Pact. It was the rationalization of production associated with the Auto Pact that "really started the erosion of all those good jobs," says a veteran worker.[42]

Though exact measures of speedup are virtually impossible because of the enormous complexities involved in comparing a host of changes in job content, every veteran worker interviewed is certain that speedup has been taking place across the plant for the last twenty years.[43] Though the rate and location of speedup varies, they report, it has been particularly strong during the introduction of new models each fall, a time when there is often considerable retooling and redesign of jobs. Speedup is also often associated with lay-offs. Thus, workers typically observe that a decrease in the work force has led to a temporary slowing down of the line and the expansion of job content only to be followed by a contraction in job content and an even greater increase in the speed of the line after the lay-off ends. After the most recent lay-offs, the speed of the line has been increased to a reported sixty-five units an hour – an increase of almost 40 per cent in the last half-dozen years.

Technological changes have also played a part in both speedup and increased job specialization. The introduction of self-tapping screws has been one source of increased job specialization; faster, more-efficient welding guns have been another. By the late 1960s, an editor of the local union newspaper was pointing out that "almost every production change, whether new machinery or work method changes, has resulted in a greater degree of monotony to the operator." By the 1970s, management was beginning to introduce even more dramatic technological changes in the form of computers and robotics, often undercutting the need for manual dexterity or mental agility or both.

Not even the remaining craft (skilled trades) workers at Ford's have been immune from such attacks on their skills. While it is apparent that the coming of more-complex machinery has led to the upgrading of skills in a few cases – such as those involving repair and maintenance of some computerized machinery – many jobs have required less skill, and old skills have atrophied from lack of use. This has been the case, for example, with the heating and ventilating technicians and with the hoisting engineers. The number of workers in these job classifications has shrunk through attrition over the years. In other instances, management has combined two or three trades classifications into one omnibus classification. Thus management created "weld to repair technicians" (dubbed "reptiles" by workers) by providing such workers with what a local leader refers to as a "smattering" of each of the skills used in three other skilled trades classifications – those of toolmaker, welder, and pipefitter. The result has been more flexibility for management, while workers have lost skilled jobs. As machinery has aged and become more obsolete, preventive maintenance has been replaced by "crisis main-tenance." This has not only contributed to a worsening of noise and fumes in parts of the plant, a union health and safety spokesperson claims, but has led to less employment for trades people who repair the machines.

The most skilled of the production workers have been subject to similar deskilling. Workers who repair defective vehicles point, for example, to noticeable declines in the variety of work they do. This is partly the result of a tendency for repairs to be done as the cars progress along the line, rather than in separate repair areas. These separate repair areas normally enjoy a certain freedom from the controls over work that are built into most line jobs. Another instance of deskilling is the gradual reduction in "lead hand" jobs across the plant. Workers in these jobs were typically required to be able to do several jobs in a work area and to perform some additional functions related to the overseeing of inventories of parts, tools, and work clothing. Perhaps the largest loss of better jobs has been the shrinkage of "subassembly jobs" that feed into the main line but are not directly paced by it. With the Auto Pact, parts production became continental in scope and in many cases the company switched to outside parts suppliers or to importation from the United States. A Canadian union leader estimates that, as a result, about five hundred subassembly and skilled trades jobs have been taken from the plant. The veteran workers have the strongest sense of the intensification of labour through deskilling and speedup, for their experience has a longer history. Looking back, a retired worker sums it up, saying he was "bloody glad to get out of there the way it was going," adding: "and I had a pretty good job." Though higher seniority permitted them to bid for preferred jobs, all the veteran workers who were interviewed reported the same basic history of the degradation of autowork, and the same basic history of resistance to this degradation.

Containment of worker resistance and the degradation and intensification of labour are the principal manifestations of management supremacy. Workers have been in a long retreat. Because worker resistance to Ford Time since the war has been largely a matter of small-scale skirmishes punctuated by occasional broader-scale resistance that has been defeated,[44] management aggression has not been paralleled by any corresponding deepening of workers' abilities to challenge it. The grievance procedure and the other state-enforced contractual obligations have been chains binding workers and their union. Management's policy of progressive discipline, management's refinement of technical controls on the assembly line, and management's international flexibility in production have been additional elements in the containment of worker resistance. Outside influences undermining the sense of community among workers, and the chastening effect of the current depression, have also contributed to this ongoing retreat by Ford workers.

OLD PROMISES, NEW PROMISES

Ford Time has not changed fundamentally since the first Model T's were driven off the line. Today there is a system of procedures protecting workers from much of the goon-squad barbarism of the past, but the line still grinds out its daily quota of submission. Even at the high point of worker power in the Ford plants during World War II, the line remained. More than once, this tenacity of Ford Time has confounded predictions of its demise at the hands of militant or revolutionary autoworkers. In the past and "in American radical folklore," says Daniel Bell, "the auto worker was considered the seedling of the indigenous class-conscious radical – if there was ever to be one in America. Uninhibited, rootless ... with his almost nihilist temper," Bell continues, "he was the raw stuff for revolutionary sentiment – once he realized (or so the Marxists thought) that he was trapped by his job."[45] As late as the 1970s, the most prominent symbol of a "new breed" of workers rising up was the conflict at the General Motors plant in Lordstown, Ohio.[46] This kind of significance attached to the struggles of autoworkers over the decades has been especially acute for Marxists and their sense of historical direction.

For Marx, the capitalist labour process was pregnant with a new society. Forced by the "anarchic" imperative of market relations to compete – to grow or die – capitalists would bring ever-larger numbers of workers under the sway of the labour process upon which continuing capital accumulation depended. According to Marx, these growing masses of workers would face ever fewer, ever more-powerful capitalists, as the capitalist economy became more centralized and concentrated, as competition bred monopoly. At the same time, the increasingly detailed division of labour, while robbing craft workers of their skills, while cheapening and intensifying labour in general, would also erode the barriers of skill and status that had kept workers from an awareness of the common basis of their alienation under capitalism.[47] "The various interests and conditions of life within the ranks of the proletariat," said Marx, "are more and more equalised, in proportion as machinery obliterates all distinctions of labour, and nearly everywhere reduces labour to the same low level."[48] The logic of the capitalist labour process, in this view, would abolish parochialism and individualism in the working class and transform scattered workers and different strata of workers into a modern proletariat, rendering solidarity out of competition, and militancy out of servility and fear.

Marx saw these tendencies in the labour process as a microcosm of the same tendencies in the capitalist society as a whole. As society, and indeed the world, became increasingly like an immense factory and hence polarized, "collisions between individual workers and individual bourgeois [would] take more and more the character of collisions between classes."[49] Worker resistance would become a "more or less veiled civil war."[50] As this civil war intensified, workers' co-operation in production would become the organizational basis of their increasing collective competence to run industry unaided by capitalist domination. Marx predicted that the profit system would lead to a growing "mass of misery, oppression, slavery, degradation, exploitation"[51] – a deepening misery leading to revolution. At the centre of this revolution, the proletariat, "disciplined and united, organised by the very mechanism of production itself,"[52] would become the "grave-diggers" of capitalism,[53] rid themselves of "all the muck of ages and become fitted to found society anew."[54]

Hence the centrality of the labour process in Marx's outline of revolutionary change. Though Ford Time dominates the work lives of but a fraction of the working class, it is the labour process that probably best epitomizes the labour process Marx foresaw developing under capitalism. In an oligopolistic industry that grew out of competitive pressures, Ford Time has come to dominate the massed labour of tens of thousands of workers. Those workers constitute a labour force that is perhaps more deskilled and more homogeneous in its composition than the labour force of any other basic industry. The wage structure under Ford Time is correspondingly unique in its flatness. Ford Time is also singular in the monotony it imposes. Such a labour process is clear evidence that Marx was not exaggerating the depths to which human beings could be alienated through the labour process – alienated not only from their own productive activity and its fruits but also from each other and from their own potential as human beings. Thus, if there is a labour process that represents a "best case" of the labour process Marx thought was pregnant with socialism, Ford Time qualifies. So if Marx's outline of revolution is valid, there should be indications that worker resistance to this labour process has been broadening and deepening over time.

As we have seen, however, worker resistance to Ford Time has not been growing. Though assembly-line production is highly interdependent and hence vulnerable to disruption by even small numbers of workers, management has been able to keep the upper hand. At the level of the work group and the zone, as well as at the level of the plant, management has improved its ability to enforce its "rights." Through the redesign of jobs, through retiming of jobs, through surveillance, through aggressive management and various forms of intimidation, management has in many ways pushed workers back along the "frontier of control" in the workplace. Though worker resistance has never been eliminated, it has largely been contained within a pattern of little victories and big defeats. This pattern has itself been a major factor in the confinement of conflict within restricted bounds. Direct action has generally been seen to contradict the institutionalization of labour/management conflict – indeed, the substitution of collective bargaining for direct action is the crux of modern unionism[55] – but this perspective overlooks the important integrative dimension of direct action as safety valve, early warning system, and provider of object lessons in the punitive reality of management power. The experience of little victories and big defeats has helped to school workers in their adaptation to Ford Time. This is not to say that the formal institutionalization of labour/management conflict has not also been productive of such adaptation. As in the instance of the Five-Dollar Day, the union contract – complete with dues checkoff, no-strike clause, and grievance procedure – has represented definite gains for workers, while leaving management even more firmly in control of the labour process.

If a broadening of workers' collective autonomy within the labour process is crucial, then Marx's revolution depends on a link that has yet to be forged. The degree of worker autonomy was at its greatest among craft workers prior to the enforcement of Ford Time. Contemporary autoworkers, however, lack the craftsman's sense of embattled righteousness in the name of hard-earned and respected skills; they lack the craftsman's sense of personal identification with his job and with the results of his labour. Add to this the deep weariness that comes with those unending eight or ten hours on the line, a weariness that is more than physical, that deadens hope and will as workers adapt to their fate. All this leads neither to an attempt to significantly broaden workers' autonomy in the work process nor to a vision of what such autonomy might mean. It leads instead to an attempt to escape Ford Time by reducing one's emotional investment in it. Workers try to forget Ford Time when they are working on the line by thinking of other things. When they leave the plant, many Ford workers will say (deceiving themselves) that they leave the experience of work behind. Dreams of a better life lie with family, not with fellow workers – with consumption, not with production. If there are dreams of a better work life, they are normally for more personal independence, for craft skills, or for a business of one's own, for some way to become a "somebody." They are dreams of becoming something other than an autoworker; they are dreams of personal escape rather than of a new co-operative society.[56]

It would appear, then, that the emphasis that Marx gave to an emerging process of class struggle at the "point of production" by members of a classical, blue-collar, deskilled, homogeneous, massed proletariat has been strongly contradicted. This is not to say, however, that there are not other elements of Marx's theory of the development of capitalism that have proved prophetic. The increasingly "boom and bust" character of capitalist development, its inherent imperialist tendencies, and the increasing rate at which workers are being displaced by machinery are all conditions Marx saw as integral to a transition to socialism. Though management power in the workplace has been abetted by the maintenance of a "reserve army of the unemployed," too large a standing army of the unemployed is itself a potential threat. And though war and the threat of war have been time-tested methods of recruiting such reserve armies into a state of mobilization and of diverting attention from domestic conflicts, war and its aftermath have also been known to promote worker resistance both in the factories and in the streets. All these contradictions are clearly of crucial relevance to the current situation.

As we enter the tenth year of the most profound structural crisis of world capitalism since the depression of the 1930s, as Pax Americana retreats before a new world division of labour, even greater constraints have been placed on the flexibility of labour/management relations in the old Western metropolitan core of world capitalism. A crux of the matter is this: the previous limits of worker resistance, both institutionalized and informal, are no longer tolerable to management in major economic sectors and institutions. The cost of this limited worker resistance has been reassessed as international competition has become sharper and as capital has been restructured on a world scale. Continued successful capital accumulation requires massive new investment to keep up with technological and other competitive requirements at the same time as profit margins have narrowed in many areas and as state fiscal resources have been strained. As a consequence, the crisis precludes the kind of buying off of discontent that workers experienced in the post-war boom. Heavier doses of consumption to cure the ills of production – the major focus of normal collective bargaining – are difficult to prescribe in this post-Keynesian era. Employers in many sectors will no longer be able to buy off workers with summer cottages and expensive cars.

In this situation, with a loosening of the golden chains that have tied workers to business unionism, attempts to devise and implement corporatist solutions to labour/management conflict are bound to appear. Indeed, some have already. Though tripartist talks between labour, management, and the Canadian government have been publicly discontinued, they continue privately and informally at the highest levels.[57] The federal minister of labour insists that tripartism be revived.[58] There is also interest in token worker representation on corporate boards and in the German model of "co-determination." Most recently, it has been reported that the federal government is seriously considering new tax incentives for companies that foster "worker ownership" through stock purchases, a plan that would "hold wages down" and give corporations a "cheap way to raise money."[59] In the federal government's speech from the throne in February 1984, there were promises to make labour "a full partner in the process of economic recovery" and to give labour "an equal voice in the resolution of issues like technological change and productivity improvement." Unions are to be given seats on government planning boards and on the boards of directors of selected crown corporations. More recently it was reported that leaders of the Canadian Labour Congress and the Business Council on National Issues have agreed to form a "think tank," the Canadian Labour Market and Productivity Centre, with a $7 million dollar annual budget, compliments of the federal government.[60]

Clearly, the corporatist pieces are falling into place. The most significant, perhaps, are a number of initiatives often referred to as Quality of Working Life (QWL) programs. Government funding of such programs at both provincial and federal levels has been increased recently. The focus of these programs is the main arena of worker struggles where little victories are sometimes achieved: the work group, zone, or departmental level under the jurisdiction of frontline supervision. The main thrust of QWL appears to be an attempt to increase management control over the labour process by providing incentives for workers to internalize management's goals. This is intended to improve productivity and reduce supervisory requirements – in short, to reduce the costs of worker resistance.[61] The Ford plant, which has been the main focus of this paper, has been the location of one such QWL program. Though the local union has since officially withdrawn from the program, various corporatist initiatives sponsored unilaterally by management have continued. The result has been a weakening of local leadership and an increase in "finking" (informing) and infighting between workers. Supervisory personnel have received training in more sophisticated, softer methods of control. In this context, there is less space than ever in which workers can achieve even the smallest of little victories.

To be sure, there are deep problems for corporations in the present crisis. If Marx was correct in stressing the contradiction between the rights enjoyed by ever fewer owners of capital on the one hand, and the needs of an increasingly interdependent and co-operative society on the other, then perhaps the politicization of industrial relations inherent in such corporatist programs will yet contribute to the creation of something like that new society he foresaw. If management becomes increasingly desperate to avoid the costs of even small-scale worker resistance, then even the smallest of little victories may take on a whole new meaning. And cumulative little victories on the shop floor, wedded to a broader sense of political objectives, may yet lead to an overcoming of the various schisms between the personal and the political, between the parochial and the general. It does seem, nevertheless, that Marx over-simplified and exaggerated the role that the labour process itself was destined to play in the emergence of that new society – though the need for a society and a world based on genuine co-operation is more imperative now than ever before. For this reason, those who subscribe to Marx's vision will need to reexamine the weight he gave to class struggle at the point of production.

Ford Time remains. The line keeps winding its way through the plant, setting the pace for the ridiculous, demanding, little jobs. While you have been reading this essay, my replacement in the grinding booth has been grinding down welds – two hundred and sixty an hour, two thousand, six hundred a day ...

NOTES

I owe a great debt to the many members of the United Automobile Workers of America (UAW) whose willingness to provide information and perspective made this essay possible. Thanks also go to Gary Lewis, Craig Heron, Robert Storey, Ed Andrew, Gerry Hunnius, and Meyer Brownstone for their detailed and insightful criticisms of a previous draft. For their crucial assistance with the research, I would like to thank Rod McNeil, Bill Pigott, Pat Clancy, and Sam

Gindin. As usual, special thanks go to Ruth Frager, my best critic and best friend, for her unstinting help – with everything.

1 This incident took place in the late 1970s at a Canadian Ford plant where I worked for nine months. In order to protect certain confidences and the identities of some informants, I have chosen not to reveal the location of the plant and the identities of those quoted.

2 Another significant factor contributing to management aggression has been the impact of the recession. In particular, plant management has been under pressure from corporate headquarters to prove its ability to control the plant's work force or risk production being moved to another plant.

3 Allan Nevins, *Ford: The Times, the Man and the Company* (New York 1954), 228.

4 Henry Ford, *My Life and Work* (Garden City, NY 1922), 80.

5 Charles Reitell, "Machinery and Its Effect upon Workers in the Automobile Industry," American Academy of Political and Social Science, *Annals* (November 1924), excerpted in A.D. Chandler, Jr, ed., *Giant Enterprise* (New York 1964), 185.

6 Henry Ford, *Today and Tomorrow* (Garden City, NY 1926), 160; Ford, *My Life and Work*, 80.

7 Nevins, *Ford*, 382.

8 J.W. Skeels, "Early Carriage and Auto Unions: The Impact of Industrialization and Rival Unionism," *Industrial and Labor Relations Review* (July 1964): 578.

9 Nevins, *Ford*, 378, 513–14; see also Jack Russell, "The Coming of the Line: The Ford Highland Park Plant, 1910–14," *Radical America* (May–June 1978), passim, concerning the repression of worker resistance at Ford in this period.

10 Keith Sward, *The Legend of Henry Ford* (New York 1948), 48–9; Agis Salpukis, "Unions: A New Role?" in J.M. Rosow, ed., *The Worker and the Job* (Englewood Cliffs, NJ 1974), 102.

11 Stephen Meyer, III, *The Five-Dollar Day* (Albany 1981), 95–108.

12 Nevins, *Ford*, 563–4.

13 Meyer, *Five-Dollar Day*, 111–14.

14 J.R. Lee, "The So-Called Profit-Sharing System in the Ford Plant," American Academy of Political and Social Science, *Annals* (May 1916), excerpted in Chandler, *Giant Enterprise*, 194.

15 Ford, *My Life and Work*, 111.

16 Meyer, *Five-Dollar Day*, 123–68.

17 Ibid., 169–72, 185–7.

18 Nevins, *Ford*, 349.

19 Allan Nevins and F.E. Hill, *Ford: Decline and Rebirth* (New York 1963), 150–1.

20 Joseph Patterson, quoted in C.W. Gonick, "Aspects of Unemployment in Canada" (PH D dissertation, University of California at Berkeley 1965), 144.

21 Raymond Houlahan, "A History of Collective Bargaining in Local 200, UAW" (MA thesis, University of Windsor 1963), 2, quoted and cited in David

Moulton, "Ford Windsor 1945," in Irving Abella, ed., *On Strike* (Toronto 1974), 154–5.

22 The arbitrary power of foremen at a Ford plant in the U.S. is described by one worker: "There was no rhyme or reason in the selection of the fortunate ones chosen to continue working. The foreman had the say; if he happened to like you, or if you sucked around him and did him favors – or if you worked like hell and turned out more production – you might be picked to work a few weeks longer than the next guy" (Clayton Fountain, *Union Guy* [New York 1949], 41).

23 Houlahan, "History of Collective Bargaining," 154–5.

24 Confidential interview.

25 Gonick, "Aspects of Unemployment," 112.

26 Moulton, "Ford Windsor 1945," 131.

27 See Victor Reuther, *The Brothers Reuther* (Boston 1976), 200–9; Huw Beynon, *Working for Ford* (East Ardsley, Wakefield, Eng. 1975), 34; Nevins and Hill, *Ford: Decline and Rebirth*, 42–3; Sidney Fine, *The Automobile under the Blue Eagle* (Ann Arbor 1963), 25, 85–93, and his "The Ford Motor Company under the N.R.A.," *Business History Review* (Winter 1958): 371–85.

28 AFL Convention Report, 1935, quoted in Fine, *Automobile under the Blue Eagle*, 21. See also Irving Bernstein, *The Turbulent Years* (Boston 1970), 509, and August Meier and Elliott Rudwick, *Black Detroit and the Rise of the UAW* (Oxford 1979), 34.

29 Nevins and Hill, *Ford: Decline and Rebirth*, 160.

30 As early as the end of World War I, Ford workers had lost most of the wage gains of the five-dollar day to inflation (Allan Nevins and F.E. Hill, *Ford: Expansion and Challenge* [New York 1957], 351). Between 1914 and 1929, real wages for Ford workers had been reduced by half (Sward, *Legend*, 347.) In the automobile industry as a whole, wages fell by another 43 per cent between 1928 and 1932 (Fine, *The Automobile under the Blue Eagle*, 20).

31 Nevertheless, these external allies to worker resistance at the point of production were not insignificant at various points during the 1930s. For example, public sympathy and tolerance contributed to the success of the famous sit-downs at General Motors in 1936 (Sidney Fine, *Sit-down* [Ann Arbor 1969], 339); James Green, *The World of the Worker* (New York 1980), 156. And the NRA codes legislated by the Roosevelt government were not negligible in their effects either (ibid., 140–1), but they appear to have had their greatest impact in industries other than auto where employers were not among the most adamant in their opposition to collective bargaining in the first place (David Brody, "The Emergence of Mass-Production Unionism," in J. Braeman et al., eds, *Change and Continuity in Twentieth Century America* [Columbus 1964], 253). Perhaps the most powerful external factor was the labour market: the mini-recovery of the mid 1930s was associated with a rise in worker militancy in auto and other basic industries (David Montgomery, *Worker's Control in America* [New York 1979], and Brody, "Emergence of Mass Production Unionism," 257.) The fact remains, however,

that it was the war that changed the balance of class forces at the point of production (and beyond).

32 Nevins and Hill, *Ford: Decline and Rebirth*, 160.

33 James Boggs, *The American Revolution: Pages from a Negro Worker's Notebook* (New York 1963), 19.

34 Martin Glaberman, *Wartime Strikes* (Detroit 1980), 37–9.

35 Richard Herding, *Job Control and Union Structure in the United States with a Comparative Perspective on West Germany* (Rotterdam 1972), 121.

36 Moulton, "Ford Windsor 1945," 132.

37 As Laurel Sefton MacDowell has noted, this was true of the Canadian labour movement as a whole. See *"Remember Kirkland Lake" : The Gold Miners' Strike of 1941–42* (Toronto 1983), 4.

38 Stephen Cako, "Labour's Struggle for Union Security: The Ford of Canada Strike, Windsor, 1945" (MA thesis, University of Guelph 1971).

39 This three-day period of grace seems to have become an informal norm. "It got to be where guys were out for three days, they'd say 'Christ, management can terminate our employment,'" a prominent local leader explains. "But management never said that. They never took the position that you had to be on work stoppage for three days before they can terminate you."

40 Apparently the local president had vowed to conduct further work stoppages after this, but these did not take place.

41 A similar policy was followed at the steel plant investigated by Maxwell Flood in his *Wildcat in Lake City*, Task Force on Labour Relations, Study no. 15 (Ottawa 1970), 33.

42 The 1965 Auto Pact also put an end to the "considerable autonomy" that management of Ford Canada enjoyed in its conduct of labour relations. See Duane Kujawa, *International Relations in the Automobile Industry* (New York 1971), 71.

43 Twenty-one retirees and veterans who had been in the plant since the founding of the local were interviewed.

44 In his study of worker ideology and resistance at the General Motors plant in Lordstown, David Moberg found a high level of what he refers to as "parochialism" in the pattern of worker resistance in the plant. Like this author, he concludes that direct action permits a "euphoric release of accumulated tensions and anger" but that "without effective organization, the mixture of rank and file discouragement and anger vacillated between individual withdrawal and sporadic rebellion bubbling forth from the simmering pot of daily conflict" (see "Rattling the Golden Chains: Conflict and Consciousness of Autoworkers" [PH D dissertation, University of Chicago 1978], 348, 363). The failure of worker resistance to succeed against speedup in the automobile industry also can be generalized; see Stan Weir, "U.S.A.: The Labor Revolt," in Maurice Zeitlin, ed., *American Society, Inc.* (Chicago 1970), 466–501.

45 Daniel Bell, *Work and Its Discontents* (Boston 1956), 32.

46 Stanley Aronowitz, *False Promises: The Shaping of American Working Class*

Consciousness (New York 1973). For a study of similar themes in Canada, see Maxwell Flood, "The Growth of the Non-Institutional Response in the Canadian Industrial Sector," *Relations industrielles/Industrial Relations* 27 (1972).

47 "Wage labour rests exclusively on competition between labourers," Marx wrote in the "Manifesto of the Communist Party," in Karl Marx and Frederick Engels, *Selected Works* (London 1970), 46.

48 Ibid., 43.

49 Ibid.

50 Ibid., 45.

51 Karl Marx, *Capital* ([1867]; London 1970), I, 763.

52 Ibid.

53 Marx and Engels, "Manifesto of the Communist Party," 46.

54 Karl Marx and Frederick Engels, *The German Ideology* ([1846–7]; New York 1970), 95.

55 "A CIO contract," affirmed John L. Lewis, founder of the CIO, "is adequate protection against sit-downs, lie-downs, or any other kind of strike." Quoted in Jeremy Brecher, *Strike!* (San Francisco 1972), 205.

56 These findings are derived from numerous informal discussions with workers in the plant and with intensive interviews with fourteen others in their homes. They fit with those of almost every major study of autoworkers' aspirations, including the massive, three-volume survey by Jonathan Goldthorpe and his colleagues, *The Affluent Worker: Industrial Attitudes and Behaviour* (Cambridge 1968); *The Affluent Worker: Political Attitudes and Behaviour* (Cambridge 1968); and *The Affluent Worker in the Class Structure* (Cambridge 1969); the excellent work of David Moberg already cited; and the pioneering study by Ely Chinoy, *Automobile Workers and the American Dream* (New York 1955).

57 See "Towards a Corporatist Canada," *Canadian Dimension*, December 1980.

58 In a presentation to the Macdonald Commission on 16 December 1983, André Oullet called for "structured consultative mechanisms to change the present adversarial system and achieve consensus," and argued that a "more desirable" industrial relations system "would be designed with the collaboration of all parties" (Information, Labour Canada, 2 January 1984).

59 "Ottawa to Promote Workers' Ownership," *Globe and Mail*, 24 November 1983, I.

60 The scheme is premised on the notion that "a worker who owns shares in the company he works for will be more likely to identify with its interests" – though, as the *Globe and Mail* notes, workers would "not necessarily have more control over their employers" (ibid., 8, 31 December 1983).

61 For two case studies on the impact of QWL processes on labour/management relations in industrial settings, see my *Soft Sell: Quality of Working Life Programmes and the Productivity Race* (Ottawa 1985).

Index